Performing Indigeneity

Performing Indigeneity

Global Histories and Contemporary Experiences

Edited by Laura R. Graham and H. Glenn Penny

University of Nebraska Press | Lincoln and London

Library of Congress Cataloging-in-Publication Data
Performing indigeneity: global histories and contemporary experiences / edited by Laura R. Graham, H. Glenn Penny.
pages   cm
Includes bibliographical references and index.
ISBN 978-0-8032-7195-1 (hardback: alk. paper)
ISBN 978-0-8032-5686-6 (paper: alk. paper)
ISBN 978-0-8032-7416-7 (epub)
ISBN 978-0-8032-7417-4 (mobi)
ISBN 978-0-8032-7415-0 (pdf)
1. Indigenous peoples—Ethnic identity. 2. Ethnicity—Social aspects. 3. Group identity. 4. Public spaces—Social aspects. I. Graham, Laura R., 1956– editor of compilation. II. Penny, H. Glenn, editor of compilation.
GN380.P474 2014
305.8—dc23
2014021535

Set in Garamond Premier Pro by Lindsey Auten.
Designed by A. Shahan.

Contents

Illustrations

Acknowledgments

The idea for this collection grew out of conversations that began at a session on the performance of Indigeneity in the Americas at the Fifty-Second Congress of Americanists in Seville, Spain. Those conversations led to a subsequent conference at the University of Iowa in 2009, which expanded the geographic scope of the discussion. It was generously supported by an International Programs' Major Projects Award and an Arts and Humanities Initiative Award from the Office of the Vice President for Research at the University of Iowa. We are grateful for that support. For their contributions toward the publication of this book we also thank the Departments of Anthropology and History, the College of Liberal Arts and Sciences, and the Office of the Vice President for Research at the University of Iowa. We would also like to thank our editor, Matthew Bokovoy, for his immediate appreciation of the project's importance, his encouragement, and his valuable insights. Heather Stauffer provided us with invaluable editorial assistance, and the anonymous readers greatly improved the collection through their comments and suggestions. Finally, we thank each other for patience, good humor, and intellectual companionship. The opportunity to share ideas and engage in this collaboration has been an invaluable experience for both of us. Our contributions are equal and our names appear in alphabetical order.

Performing Indigeneity

1

Performing Indigeneity

Emergent Identity, Self-
Determination, and Sovereignty

LAURA R. GRAHAM AND H. GLENN PENNY

Self-conscious, reflexive public performances of Indigeneity became increasingly common during the second half of the twentieth century, and they are critically important in global politics today.[1] When Indigeneity emerged as a legal and juridical category during the Cold War era, Indigenous cultural performance and display became essential to its articulation, even its substantiation.[2] Indigeneity is no one's primary identity; yet as the essays in this volume make clear, individuals and groups across the globe fashion themselves as Indigenous through performance and performative acts in intercultural spaces. Analyzing a striking variety of performers and audiences within specific historical contexts, the contributors to this collection locate individual subjects and publics interacting to shape emergent Indigenous identities in both intimate places and public spaces across wide geographic and chronological ranges. Taken together, these acts reveal rich dialogic and cumulative processes: each act has the potential to reinforce or challenge the category of Indigeneity; each can be a starting point for new conceptualizations.

Initially, some scholars (e.g., Kuper 2003) greeted with concern the trend toward codifying Indigeneity as a legal category, warning that outward acts of performance might fall back on older notions of primitivism, helping to reassert "essentialist ideologies of culture and identity," which could have "dangerous political consequences." Political and legal definitions of "Indigenous," many observed, were based too frequently on "assumptions of ties of blood and soil," rooted in Euro-American notions of culture and identity that were essentialist, even nationalist (Kuper 2003:395).

While these were valid concerns, such essentialism did not carry the day. Across the globe, people embrace Indigeneity as a process of emergence, a "bundle of generative possibilities" (Pratt 2007:402) rather than an essential category of personhood. Driven by their specific desires for recognition, self-determination, and cultural sovereignty, they perform Indigeneity, as many have long performed it, in public as well as in intimate spaces for their own particular purposes. The dialogic of these performances shaped Indigeneity as we understand it today, and it continues to shape its future.

Performance and Performativity

The concepts of performance and performativity are fundamental to understanding the emergent, processual, and contextual nature of Indigeneity. Scholars emphasize that people fashion and refashion identities through embodied speech and action. Individuals as well as groups produce identities through performances that often entail deeply contextualized and historically contingent creative acts.

While there is no single, homogeneous "performance approach" to the study of human culture and social interaction, the interdisciplinary and multidisciplinary approaches that exist consistently emphasize agency, self-conscious practice, and reflexivity. Participants' reflexivity, their accountability to themselves and their audiences, enables performers to calibrate and recalibrate, to adjust to contexts, including memories of past performances, their immediate situation, and their expectations for the future.[3]

Performances of Indigeneity are no exception. They are contextually situated embodied speech and action—as well as the products of speech and action—that are anchored in past performances, local traditions, and ideologies. At the same time, they are always creative and forward looking, infused with expected outcomes. We can in fact think of performance as analogous to the Bakhtinian utterance: each new statement is a novel creative act, but one that contains echoes of past voices and opens up the possibility for future conversation and dialogue (Bakhtin 1981).

We can locate the origins of contemporary performance analysis in ideas articulated in Aristotle's *Poetics* (1961): the notion that life is action and that the purpose of staged drama is to imitate the action of life.[4] While theater is inherently imitative and mimetic, and therefore potentially infused with deception, a concern initially expressed by Plato, performance is not restricted to the theatrical stage, nor are performances necessarily deceptive—although they may be.[5] As Shakespeare's phrase "all the world's a stage" reminds us, performance is part of everyday life and social interaction. Thus, as Clifford Geertz (1980) pointed out, conceptualizing life as drama is nothing new.

Until performance analysis began to take root in the middle of the twentieth century, however, scholarly paradigms for the interpretation of culture and human social life largely ignored the dramatic and performative nature of human interaction. Indeed, twentieth-century scholarship was linguistically inspired and text-centered (see, e.g., Geertz 1973). Attempting to counter the dominance of such paradigms, to shake off the confines of structuralism and structural-functionalism, and to undercut the prevailing metaphors of human beings as machines or animals, several midcentury scholars from distinct fields turned for inspiration to drama and theater.[6] In particular, the ideas of literary scholar and philosopher Kenneth Burke, sociologist Erving Goffman, and language philosopher John Austin provided strong foundations for the "performance turn."[7]

As Corinne Kratz (2004:399) observes, performance analysis initially stemmed from attempts in anthropology and folklore to incorporate greater attention to context and move away from text-centered approaches in dramaturgical models of social theory (see Hymes 1972; Bauman 1984[1977]; Abrahams 1972).[8] Victor Turner's work on the symbolic analysis of ritual, as well as his attention to "social dramas" and the processual unfolding of interaction, inspired scholars in multiple disciplines.[9] Turner, like the folklorist Richard Bauman, emphasized the constitutive nature of performance to counter static structural conceptions of culture and society: performance does not simply reflect culture; it acts to create and transform it.[10]

Building on Victor Turner's work, theater scholar and director Richard Schechner (1985) identified a broad array of social activity as performance. He pioneered analyses of everyday behaviors, including sports and various forms of play.[11] Literary scholar-philosopher Judith Butler pursued this constitutive nature of performance even further, and with great influence. Drawing on Turner and speech act philosophy, as well as phenomenological and psychoanalytic approaches, Butler's (1990, 1993) notion of "performativity" stresses the reiterative power of embodied action and discourse:

individuals, she argues, "make" themselves through iterative acts. The self and identity are not stable entities; rather, they shift in and through performance. Thus gender, race, class, ethnicity, and, importantly for our purposes, Indigeneit*ies* are materially constituted and embodied within specific historical constraints. People achieve, accomplish, and even improvise Indigeneity through performance and performative acts.

The geography of such acts has been not only global and national but also local and intimate.[12] As this volume demonstrates, poignant performances of Indigeneity that tie such locations together can take place in rather uncelebrated places: in law offices and courtrooms, classrooms and research sites, the halls of art galleries and museums, and the quiet corners of noisy urban centers, as well as during tourist encounters and the meetings of international political bodies, sports teams, hobby groups, and dance clubs. Their ubiquity is a marker of their importance and power, jointly produced by a broad range of actors and dialogical acts.

Even when performances of Indigeneity occur in highly marked settings, such as exhibitions, fairs, festivals, and publicized political events such as the standoffs at Alcatraz or Wounded Knee, they remain dialogic on multiple levels. "Insiders" and "outsiders," performers and audiences, publics and individual subjects continually interact to shape emergent Indigenous identities in public arenas and intimate spaces. Like museums and other heritage management venues, performances become "sites of persuasion," to borrow a phrase from Howard Morphy (2006). They are arenas in which Indigenous People engage broader publics and other interested parties (various types of intermediaries, curators, members of boards of directors, political sponsors) and attempt "to get their versions of history and regime[s] of value acknowledged and disseminated to wider audiences" (Morphy 2006:471–72; see also, e.g., Kratz and Karp 2006; Erickson and Bowechop 2002).[13] Through dialogic processes, Indigenous participants build on traditions that are much older than most scholars assume and act on stages that are increasingly intertwined.[14]

Becoming Indigenous

Indigeneity as a global identity emerged during the Cold War era.[15] Notions of scarcity and growing concerns about environmental degradation during the twentieth century together with the emergence of human rights discourses provided critical background for the successful rise of Indigenous politics in national and international arenas.[16] As historically marginalized and seemingly disparate Native Peoples across the globe have found common cause in the emergent, and often elusive, Indigenous category (see Heatherington 2010:52; see also Gupta 1998), the performance of Indigenous identity as a means of establishing membership in this community becomes increasingly important.

Whereas once the ideas about technology and progress that defined industrialized states characterized the natural world as something that was dangerous and must be tamed or regarded it as a depository of raw materials that could and should be harnessed, a new postwar consciousness increasingly recognized the natural world as valuable precisely because of its diversity. This perspective redefined the natural world. It cast nature as consisting of both known and unknown resources that, if left unprotected, could be foolishly destroyed.

At the same time, the ravages of liberal and neoliberal economic projects and the political experiments unleashed on the world during the "age of extremes" (Hobsbawm 1996) bankrupted the principles of assimilation and homogenization tied to past modernization projects. Particularly after Auschwitz and the public spectacle of the Nuremberg Trials (1945–46), human rights became ever more important in international debates and a new language of genocide and ethnocide joined, and in some cases displaced, earlier positivist discussions of acculturation, elimination, extermination, integration, and removal.[17]

Within these postwar contexts, Indigenous Peoples' arguments about the value and validity of their distinct cultures, lifeways, and knowledge gained unprecedented political traction (see Niezen 2003, 2004, 2009). Individual governments, international bodies, and nongovernmental organizations increasingly regarded Indigenous Peoples, their languages, cultures, and knowledge, and their experiences as valuable (see, e.g., United Nations 2007, 2011). Especially since the 2007 United Nations Declaration on the Rights of Indigenous Peoples (UNDRIP) affirmed the existence of general environmental rights, Indigenous Peoples—particularly those who could demonstrate their close relationships to specific environments and their need for land, water, and natural resources for the purposes of sustaining unique lifestyles, cultures, and even subsistence economies—have been well positioned to make political claims that draw together human rights and environmental issues (Inter-Commission Task Force on Indigenous Peoples 1998; Conklin 2006).

Environmental discourses that developed during the 1980s and 1990s often positioned Indigenous Peoples either as elements *of* the natural landscape or as natural guardians and stewards of threatened environments. At the same time, environmentalist concepts provided people who could make claims to being Indigenous with new forms of political argumentation and new national and international allies.

Even before discussions about Indigenous rights were developing in international forums, activists and politicians began participating in metacultural debates related to notions of culture and heritage in international arenas (see Sixth International Congress of Architects 1904; Getty Conservation Institute 2009). After World War II these discussions intensified, leading to a series of international charters, conventions, and declarations.[18]

When UNESCO began developing a set of heritage categories after World War II, specifying different types of heritage over time (see Turtinen 2000), these categories and cultural instruments became increasingly relevant to Indigenous Peoples and their interests. The UNESCO Convention for the Safeguarding of Intangible Cultural Heritage, adopted in 2003 and implemented in 2006, is the most recent such instrument and is directly related to performance as contextually situated expressive action.[19]

In the United States, the Native American Graves Protection and Repatriation Act (NAGPRA), passed by Congress in 1990, is the most prominent example of how heritage management discourses engaged Indigenous Peoples' demands in relation to cultural patrimony and human remains on a domestic front. It signaled a major shift in national policy recognizing Indigenous rights, and it has been a model for similar domestic legislation in other nations.[20]

Thus, while performances of Indigeneity were by no means new in the twentieth century (cf. Bellin and Meilke 2011; Wilmer 2009), the stakes inherent in being identified and recognized as "Indigenous" reached new levels in the systems of identity-based politics that proliferated after World War II.[21] Among other things, such recognition affords diverse peoples admission to identity-based international forums, organizations, and alliances, such as the United Nations Permanent Forum on Indigenous Issues, the International Working Group on Indigenous Peoples (IWGIA), and the World Council of Indigenous Peoples. It offers them the ability to appeal to international instruments, such as UNDRIP and International Labor Organization (ILO) Convention No. 169. It also provides them with access to a range of "transnational connections" (Hannerz 1996; Hodgson 2011).[22]

In many nation-states this recognition also entitles individuals and groups to specific benefits, such as rights to land and other resources.[23] In several Latin American nation-states, for example, such as Ecuador, Colombia, and Venezuela, new constitutions designate seats in the national congress specifically for Indigenous representatives. In other cases the language of Indigeneity may not be particularly effective, or its effectiveness may change according to historical circumstances (cf. Li 2000). Dorothy Hodgson (2011), for instance, argues that after adopting the language of Indigeneity, the Maasai of Tanzania later retreated because its utility in the national context proved to be less effective than expected. Elsewhere, as in Indonesia, as Tanya Li (2000) shows, some peoples who could legitimately claim Indigenous status have chosen to reject it.

Native Peoples may have other, even multiple motivations for displaying their difference: some may have primarily economic interests (see, e.g., Meyer and Royer 2001; Comaroff and Comaroff 2009), while others may be driven by pedagogical or humanistic objectives (see Graham 1995; Myers 2002; Morphy 2006). Their goals may be, for instance, "to become known" or to demonstrate their unique knowledge of the world and the beauty of their culture (Graham 1995, 2005; Pellegrino 2009); or they may be to protect unique knowledge of the world (see, e.g., Coombe 1998; Brown 2003) and manage cultural patrimony. Such motivations may also combine in a variety of ways.

Nevertheless, as a number of scholars have argued, these political transformations have had their share of pitfalls (see, e.g., Conklin and Graham 1995; Heatherington 2010; Tsing 2005; Warren 1998; Ball 2012). The costs of riding the coattails of romanticized Indigeneity, for example, can be quite high—especially when Indigenous Peoples do not control the means and forms of their representation to larger publics (see, e.g., Conklin and Graham 1995; Conklin 2006; Hodgson 2002b; Brosius, ed. 1999; Brosius 2003; Chernela 2005; Moore et al. 2003).[24] Gatekeepers intervene, funding bodies gain new power to designate who is and is not Indigenous, and complicated power dynamics develop between those who have achieved those designations and others who would have them.

Thus, while the territorial basis and historical primacy of Indigenous Peoples' positions offer powerful underpinnings for legal claims to economic resources and political rights, which some governments and international bodies have recognized, the ambiguities and contradictions inherent in Indigenous identity make performance and performativity especially important. In many cases performances add weight to these claims, for performance is a powerful means of expressing, asserting, and also constituting Indigenous identity. For peoples who, at first glance, may not fit with common stereotypes of the "Indigenous"—agriculturalists, pastoralists, or "urban Indians"—performance may assume even greater importance as a means of asserting claims based in difference.

Hence the concern over an emerging hegemony of essentialized notions of Indigeneity, the often-heated political and scholarly debates about who can and cannot be included within this category, and the importance of this collection of essays, which shows a striking variety of people across the globe gaining control of these processes and using them to press for greater self-determination on local, national, and global levels. This volume details, for the first time, the emergence of a global discourse on Indigeneity constituted through the dialogical interaction of a wide range of diverse, contextually situated, self-reflective performances across a broad geographic space and chronological range.

Performing Indigeneities

There is no question that self-conscious performances of Indigeneity allow some groups to embrace a shift from essential, substantial, and positivist definitions of their culture that depend on territorial precedence to constructivist, structural, and relational definitions that are based on self-identification and distinct livelihood strategies.[25] There is also little question that in many cases these are interrelated projects, with myriad groups communicating across intercultural networks to learn from each other.

Dorothy Hodgson, for instance, makes clear in her contribution to this volume that foregrounding culture and the terms of Indigeneity allowed

Maasai to champion their mobility, their access to communal lands, and their antinomial position vis-à-vis colonial, neocolonial, and neoliberal organizations of lands and peoples (see also Hodgson 2011). She also underscores that their success was made possible by new contexts, which have offered Indigenous groups new opportunities.

During their participation in meetings of the UN Working Group on Indigenous Populations and the UN Permanent Forum on Indigenous Issues, Maasai learned to understand and deploy cultural markers developed by other Indigenous Peoples to buttress their claims to Indigeneity. In many ways they "became Indigenous" by making a place for themselves in these meetings. They also learned to use these meetings as opportunities for expressing and celebrating Maasai ethnicity, identity, and culture.

Such performances, however, are often multivalent. They carry with them parameters and expectations that can be oppressive as much as liberating (cf. Levi 2003; Tsing 2007). The essays by Bernard Perley and Brendan Hokowhitu make clear that the contextually situated nature of Indigeneity, as both an analytical category and a self-conscious identity, can lead to contradictions, even clashes, between many Indigenous Peoples' multiple subject positions.

In his call for a "critical Indigeneity," Perley analyses the problem of categories, cultural codes, and the popular expectations that go with them. Most egregious is the emergence of what he calls "charismatic Indigeneity" and the "charismatic Indigene," which take shape in popular imaginations and become the ideals against which others are too often measured. No one, he notes, not even the Indigenous People who most resemble these caricatures, can live up to the concomitant popular expectations, particularly because those expectations are continually in flux (see Conklin and Graham 1995).

Each generation of Native and non-Native People seems to have been eager to create its own version of the "mythic super Indigene," or what Alcida Ramos (1994) deemed the "hyperreal Indian." In many cases, they wrap that ideal individual in the appealing trappings of a resistor who, for Perley, too often engages in a politics of identity as negation rather than emergence. Many readers will be surprised to see Perley include advocates of Indigenous decolonization among the misguided, but to his mind, many of those activists are following a long tradition of conformity rather than engaging in a process of "critical Indigeneity."

Similarly, during his analysis of the popularization of the Maori performance known as the *haka* by New Zealand's national rugby team, Hokowhitu directly engages the essentialist/nonessentialist debate that "haunts the *telos* of decolonial studies." He calls for moving past the notions of more-or less-authentic performances. For Hokowhitu, "haka is the space where the embodied anger of colonialism seeps/weeps." It is a performance that is simultaneously an example of appropriation for national patriotic agendas and the commodification of Indigenous culture, which has allowed for "the normalization of Ka Mate within 'Kiwi' masculine culture" and which is a performance of Indigeneity that is best approached, he argues, through Indigenous sovereignty. Like Perley, Hokowhitu advocates for a focus on emergence rather than negation. In this context, that requires understanding Indigenous sovereignty as tied to the ways in which Indigenous Peoples "choose to represent their worlds, whether that be through hybrid or essentialist notions of culture."

Why people engage in performing Indigeneity and what impact this has on lives, subjectivities, communities and culture itself are complex questions without unitary answers. In some instances, as Cathrine Baglo shows so well in her essay on a century of Sami performers, performances of Indigeneity develop out of previous traditions of public display in which individual performers actively harness unique cultural attributes for political pageantry as well as commercial purposes.

During the late nineteenth and early twentieth centuries, commercial ethnographic shows provided Indigenous people with opportunities to travel widely, to see the world, and to earn a decent living. At the same time, these trips also afforded many performers unique political opportunities. As Vine Deloria Jr. (1981) noted long ago, many of the North American Indians who took part in Buffalo Bill's Wild West used that opportunity to retain aspects of their cultural patrimony that were under siege. Performers also acted as cultural ambassadors and returned home to their communities in places such as the Pine Ridge Reservation in South Dakota with both personal satisfaction and significant rewards (cf. Ames 2009; Bruckner 2003; Moses 1996; Rothfels 2002).

Baglo makes clear that these sorts of activities were not limited to American Indians or even to non-Europeans. For many Indigenous groups and individuals, ethnographic performances became a crucial means for gaining political recognition and cultural authority that could be used to resist or shape economic, social, and cultural transformations. Such recognition, in turn, offered many of these people the chance to gain a voice in policy debates and political negotiations. It also enabled them to win local, national, and international allies, supporters, and sympathizers while asserting control over their identities and demonstrating their cultural sovereignty.

Baglo correctly points out that scholars often overlook these peoples' agency, and she questions the dominant trope of victimization that many continue to embrace. The types of benefits she details, which grew in part out of a global awareness among Indigenous performers of a broad commonality among peoples with similar interests and needs, are not a uniquely recent or postcolonial phenomenon, even if they continue to accrue to many Indigenous groups that purposefully present their cultures to non-Indigenous audiences in the present.

The Dialectics of Being

This volume highlights the ways in which cultural performances directed at new audiences can lead to cultural revitalization within Indigenous communities.[26] Both Hokowhitu's analysis of the haka and Fred Myers's essay on the circulation of Aboriginal art across time illustrate the dialogical processes in which performances by "insiders" for (and often with) "outsiders" generate and affirm clear articulations of cultural sovereignty.[27]

Myers argues that the performance of Indigeneity is "almost necessarily a problematic or contradictory act." It requires engaging and unsettling social, political, and cultural boundaries of regimes of value. This, he demonstrates, can be achieved through the display and exhibition of cultural objects. The Aboriginal paintings at the heart of his essay, for instance, have generated important discussions and debates about what can and cannot be shown—by artists, patrons, art galleries, and even owners who acquired such paintings decades ago. These debates, he explains, are "constitutive of Indigenous practice itself." When displayed, the paintings perform by extending local Aboriginal identities, shaping their circulation, instantiating, even "bringing into being" these identities, which are crafted and recrafted over time.

Scholars identify similar processes outside of Australia as well. Experience with the dialectic of showing while withholding, Myers reminds us, predates the colonial period in many areas of the globe, such as the northwest coast of Canada. Moreover, as Ty P. Kāwika Tengan confirms through his examination of the recuperation of masculine elements of the hula, such discussions about what to show or not to show, what to do or not do, stimulate poignant self-reflective engagements among many individuals within their respective cultural traditions.

In some cases these discussions completely recast popular perceptions of Indigenous performances among Native and non-Native Peoples alike. In Hawaii, efforts to overcome the gendered character of the hula in the popular imagination and reintegrate men into this performance tradition stimulated a rethinking of Hawaiian masculinity through performances that quite literally "embody" the possibilities and limits of decolonization. Through public performances as well as in the private clubs where Hawaiian men learn these dances, people renew identities, strengthen selves, and then, in public performances, teach others about themselves and their culture through emotive enactment, expression, signification, and explicit self-formation.

Such performances not only reconstitute precolonial gendered identities, they also, as Laura Graham explains through her analyses of Xavante performances, provide the ground for growth, development, and sometimes change within the gendered regimes of Indigenous groups today.

The Xavante have long understood the importance of managing their image in Brazil and the broader world, and they are adept at harnessing cultural performances to that end. As Graham explains, however, the dialogic is also internal. Initial, successful moves to send traditional Xavante performers into Brazilian cities to help recast their "poor" public image within the state have been followed by new discussions of performances within Xavante communities, which intersect in complex ways with performance ideologies and regimes. Coupled with understandings of Western discourses of environmentalism, those discussions have led, in the case of one community, to efforts to extend their public performances to activities and performers that are not typically deemed "spectator worthy" in local communities. And that, in turn, led to the inclusion of women and children in performances and interactions with others in traditionally male-centered domains.

In short, a critical dialogic developed between more public and "private," or local, cultural performances, which changed the ways in which people in some Xavante communities think of travel and cultural spectacle and led both men and women to accept new roles for both sexes. Such reflexive processes, however, are often overshadowed by analyses of cultural performances and traditions of managing exogenous relations that, at least for non-Indigenous audiences, tend to privilege the visually spectacular.[28]

Seeing, Feeling, Belonging

The experience of performing Indigeneity is not always spectacular. The emotive experience inherent in such performances often has the greatest impact on participants and audiences. This is particularly apparent when we shift the lens of analysis away from visually and acoustically remarkable performances to the depth of feeling evoked during the visually low-key Kamuy performed among the Ainu in Japan. As Mark Watson demonstrates in his essay, the Kamuy is so sensorially subtle as to be almost unnoticeable to many non-Ainu Tokyo residents. Yet for Ainu, its performance is constitutive of both contemporary Ainu identity and the Ainu's place in the urban context.

Such urban events are easily overlooked, but Watson reminds us that the number of Indigenous people living in urban contexts is approaching a majority. In those urban settings, discreet monuments can be performative agents of social action. They can, as he shows in his discussion of "Parkies" in urban Australia, transform urban sites in unexpected ways and, in recursive fashion, alter the people who occupy them.

Consequently, simultaneously paying attention to highly audible and visible expressions of Indigeneity, what Perley terms "charismatic Indigeneity," and to "low-key" performances and their internal dynamics can teach us much about what it means to "be" Indigenous and what matters for people who claim this identity. When Indigenous Peoples as varied as Aborigines in Australia and Ainu in Japan reveal the ways in which they engage urban landscapes, as their stories and rituals (re)cognize streets and parks, their articulations can change the face of broader, often national, and even global debates about rights. Indeed, Watson shows that such engagements can shift the focus in discussions on place and locality from notions of property to questions of *belonging*.

Such recasting of the terms of discussion is not limited to Africa, Asia, or even international forums such as the UN or the Geneva Convention. Michael Cepek demonstrates that when Randy Borman embraces an Indigenous identity and appears in public forums as the spokesman of the Cofán nation in Ecuador, when he acts as the "white face for the Cofán nation," he and his Cofán compatriots, who are staking out a position as a nation within the Ecuadorian state, call into question fundamental assumptions about the actual (essentialized and essentializing) notions of Indigeneity that are held by many politicians, scholars, and others across the world. Through these acts, they recast notions of being and belonging.

White men seldom get to claim inclusion in the Indigenous rubric. Yet Borman's Cofán identity, which is by local ideologies and metrics legitimately Cofán, patently disrupts conventional assumptions and unsettles the very category of Indigeneity. And yet Borman performs his Indigeneity frequently, through his life in Cofán settlements, by hunting and eating as Cofán, and during his participation in local ceremonies, national arguments, and international forums. He does this because he is Cofán: he *feels* Cofán; he comports and expresses himself as Cofán. And other Cofán recognize him as Cofán.

Borman's identity, like that of other Cofán, indeed his very way of living, refutes Western categories of identity that so eagerly promote the unitary, the biological, and the essential. The ambivalences of identity represented by Borman's ability to belong among the Cofán, but also among grant writers and politicians and those who live in Ecuadorian cities, stems from the dynamics of Cofán culture itself. Cofán people, Cepek teaches us, approach Indigeneity as a complicated matter of everyday interaction, overarching cultural logic, and ideals of social and political practice. With sufficient time and energy, they can transform into ethnic others.

This should surprise us only if we are committed to essential categories, not if we are cognizant of the ambivalent notions of belonging that have long permeated Indigenous cultures. This becomes clear, for example, when reading Cepek's essay on contemporary Ecuador alongside Beatriz Perrone-Moisés's essay on sixteenth-century Tupi and Norman sailors who moved between France and coastal Brazil. Perrone-Moisés reminds us that the kinds of performative notions of personhood and demonstrative belonging epitomized by Borman are historically fundamental ontologies among Indigenous groups in South America.

Drawing on recent ethnographies of Tupi and other Native Amazonian societies that underscore the ways in which their individual identities are constantly being (re)made and transformed, Perrone-Moisés offers the example of the sixteenth-century Tupi leader Itapucu, aka "Louis-Marie," who literally "became" more "French" and less Tupi when he visited France, walking on French soil, eating French food, and comporting himself in a manner similar to his French hosts. Similarly, Perrone-Moisés suggests that the Norman soldiers who were "imported" to France along with these Tupi to perform life in Tupinamba communities in royal pageants in Paris and Rouen were not "playing" Tupi. They played themselves—or perhaps more accurately, the selves that took shape during their lives in Tupi communities.

Therefore, when we consider Native Amazonian ideas of personhood and being, which emphasize process and "becoming" over presupposed essence—that is, individuals are defined not by place of birth, descent, or phenotype but by what they do, eat, speak, and relate to, as well as how, when, and where—we can better appreciate why and how Cofán embrace Borman as one of their own, how Borman can assume such identities, and how Borman's case may not, in fact, be so anomalous. Indeed, we may appreciate that in many ways "performing Indigeneity" may best be understood in terms of contextually situated processes of being and becoming.[29]

This is a critical point. Indigenous identities—such as those of Borman, "Tupi" sailors, or the participants Hodgson tracks through UN meetings—are never static. Identities may slide along a cultural scale in which multiple, intersecting subject positions take on different relationships with each other in different contexts or, depending on the given context, they may "be" and "become" more or less Indigenous (also see Jackson 1991; Maybury-Lewis 1991; Spear and Waller 1993). In some cases Indigeneity, as opposed to a distinctive and unique local identity, may increasingly offer hope for possible futures (Perley 2011).

Cepek's, Perrone-Moisés's, and also Hodgson's ostensibly unique examples remind us that Indigenous identities can never be simply local; they must always be negotiated in national, international, and, quite literally, global arenas. They are rarely, if ever, a primary identity (Pratt 2007:399).

These negotiations are also performances: they require demonstrations of Indigeneity as well as distinctive cultural characteristics, the second recognized as a subset of the first.[30]

This question of who can fit into the "Indigenous slot" (see Li 2000; also Tsing 2007), and who can participate in performances of Indigeneity is one that Perley engages directly in his essay. He argues that there are, in fact, ways in which non-Indigenous people can take part in Indigenous performances and displays. This, however, depends on certain conditions: if the requisite emotive character and affective conditions are present and if Indigenous participants consent.

What, however, if Indigenous actors are not present or no longer exist? Can Others, non-Indigenous people, people of European descent "be" or "become" Indigenous? Does the sliding scale work that way? If not, can they nevertheless "perform Indigeneity"? This remains, as Glenn Penny shows in his essay on German hobbyists, a contentious question that belies any consensus.

Diving directly in to the cultural theft versus cultural surrogacy debate, Penny, much like Baglo, takes scholars to task for embracing clichés about German hobbyists and forces us to reflect on our assumptions about the political implications of performances of Indigeneity in putatively Western settings. Here, too, there is a dialogic in play. Performative displays of Indigeneity by Germans in these settings are profoundly self-reflexive, they embrace notions of cultural time, and they have developed through interactions with various American Indians over time. Indeed, their legitimacy depends on dialogical relationships between European performers and Native Americans, in which the degree of legitimacy is directly tied to the sincerity of the Europeans' actions and their respect for Indigenous Peoples' cultural sovereignty.

Locating Cultural Sovereignty

In many ways, the question of cultural sovereignty most ties this collection of essays together. It runs like a red thread through each analysis of Indigenous performances, even in the cases in which its presence is implicit. As Myers notes while underscoring this very point, "Claims over art, a form of cultural property, are linked to the desire for what was once called 'self-determination'—combining political recognition and the pursuit of 'sovereignty.'" In the "revelatory regime" he sketches out, "structures of visibility and invisibility provide the mechanics of Indigenous visual culture, in which control over the visual—over what can be seen and by whom—is central."

Furthermore, locating and promoting cultural sovereignty can no longer be characterized as simply embracing counterhegemonic positions against dominant cultures or states. Perley makes this clear in his arguments about "emergence" and "critical Indigeneity"; Hokowhitu stresses this point in his arguments about "embodied sovereignty"; and Greg Johnson demonstrates in his work on legal battles in Hawaii that the state is not the only enemy or even the primary problem. The state can even be an ally in the quest for cultural sovereignty—if it is properly educated and, as Johnson underscores, properly maintained.

Thus the performances that most interest Johnson are also low-key performances in unheralded places, where performances of Indigenous authority have legal implications that are critical for the maintenance of cultural sovereignty and the kinds of cultural self-determination identified by the other contributors to this volume. "Mundane but intense efforts," he reminds us, can also be "significant religious and cultural happenings." Much as with the urban memorializations explored by Watson, we can easily overlook these happenings and their implications if we focus too much on the spectacular and allow "our peripheral visions to become lazy-eyed and unclear." If we combine them, however, tying together the low key and the spectacular, the networking efforts at international meetings and the intimate discussions following public events, if we take seriously the articulations of performers all across the shifting scales of identity, we will gain a sharper sense of what constitutes Indigenous practices and what cultural sovereignty must entail.

Notes

1. The same could be said for scholarship. The emergence of the Native American and Indigenous Studies Association in 2007 with its own journal, *Native American and Indigenous Studies*, and of the *International Journal of Critical Indigenous Studies* in Australia are some of the most obvious articulations.

In this chapter and throughout the book we capitalize the words "Indigenous," "Indigenous Peoples," "Indigeneity," "Native," and "Native Peoples." We adopt the editorial practice used by Cultural Survival, a leading Indigenous human rights organization, and follow the reasoning that such capitalization accords these terms dignity and recognition as collective proper nouns or derived forms. "Peoples" is capitalized only when it follows "Indigenous" and is used in the collective sense. Other nouns following "Indigenous" or "Native" are not capitalized (such as Indigenous communities, Native representatives). The term "people" is not capitalized, as in, "There are 350 million Indigenous people in the world, and perhaps a few thousand Indigenous Peoples," or, "There were 500 Indigenous people at the Permanent Forum, representing 325 Indigenous Peoples" (Cultural Survival 2010).

2. For discussions of Indigeneity as both a legal and cultural construction, see, e.g., Jackson and Warren 2005; de la Cadena and Starn 2007; Niezen 2003; Fortun et al. 2010; French 2009; Greene 2009; see also Hodgson 2002a; Levi and Maybury-Lewis 2012.

   Stuart Hall (1996[1986]) formulated the notion of articulation to describe processes of simplification, boundary making, and connection. Tanya Li (2000) productively applied this concept, as well as Hall's notion of "positioning," in her analysis of ways that some rural Indonesians, but not others, effectively position themselves as Indigenous within shifting fields of power; see also Clifford 2001 for the use of articulation.

3. For a discussion of the limits of context, see the essays in Duranti and Goodwin 1992.

4. Elizabeth Bell (2008:91) points out that "drama" is the Greek word for "action"; its roots lie in the Greek verb "dran," meaning "to do."

5. See Cohen 2011 for a discussion of Indigenous deception in early New England American colonial encounters.

6. Elizabeth Bell (2008:85) observes that performance analogies and analysis provided important correctives to metaphors that compared human beings to machines or animals, which failed to account for uniquely human creativity, critical thinking, and use of symbolic systems. Bell (2008) provides an excellent overview of the development and diversity of performance approaches.

7. Kenneth Burke's "dramatism" (1957, 1966) understood human interaction as drama and language as symbolic action. Erving Goffman (cf. 1959, 1967, 1974) applied a theatrical, or "dramaturgical" model to everyday, face-to-face interactions; his notions of framing and keying have proved productive for understanding the contextually bounded nature of communicative interactions and the ways that social actors detect cues that inform interpretation. Language philosopher John Austin (1975[1962]) identified a class of "performative" utterances that, given certain "felicity" conditions, change states of being in the world. The statements "I hereby find you guilty" and "I now pronounce you husband and wife" are examples of performative utterances that change social states when uttered by authorized persons in the proper situations. Austin as well as speech act philosophers such as John Searle viewed speech as a form of social action. Although his focus was decid-

edly cognitive, linguist Noam Chomsky (1965) also drew ideas from dramaturgical models in distinguishing between "competence," an idealized and mental language capacity, and "performance," the production of actual utterances. Scholars such as Dell Hymes (1972), who sought to draw attention to speech behavior as contextually situated social practice, critiqued Chomsky, whose focus was on idealized mental structures, for his inattention to socially situated language use. Much work in language use and verbal performance can be seen as a reaction against Chomsky's cognitive emphasis.

8. Dell Hymes (1972), Richard Bauman (1984[1977]), and Roger Abrahams (1972) were central to the move toward directing attention to speech and verbal arts as performance and to the development of performance approaches in anthropology. Milton Singer (1972) also laid some of the groundwork for the "performance turn" with his notion of "cultural performance" (Bell 2008:116).

9. Turner's approach to social drama developed from the Manchester School's emphasis on the case study method, exemplified in work such as Max Gluckman's (1958) "Analysis of a Social Situation in Modern Zululand."

10. Vásquez (2011:238) notes that in his later works Turner offers an even more radical critique of anthropological textualism and his critiques apply to Lévi-Strauss, to Derridan textualism, and also to Geertz.

11. Dwight Conquergood (1995) considers ways that performance can be transgressive; it can subvert as well as sustain culture and social norms (Conquergood 1998:32).

12. W. E. Wilmer (2009) brings together an excellent set of essays that considers how Native American and First Peoples have expressed and represented themselves, as well as how they have been presented by non-Natives in theater and dance, film, television, narratives and children's stories, and by the tourist industry. The collection highlights the diversity of traditional and contemporary Native forms of cultural expression and performance.

13. In a number of works, Howard Morphy (see, e.g., 1983, 1995, 1999, 2006) underscores that Yolngu use performances and displays of art in public spaces in Australia—such as the opening of the national museum—to educate non-Aboriginal people and set terms of engagement.

14. Essays in Bellin and Mielke 2011 bring performance perspectives to illuminate Native agency recorded in documents from the New England colonial period. Greenblatt (1992) argues that historic documents from the colonial period illuminate more about their authors and European colonial ideologies than about the subjects of these texts.

15. Minde et al. (2008:4) note that the first organized modern Indigenous movements emerged with varying forms and purposes at the beginning of the twentieth century, not only in North America and the Nordic countries but also in Australia and New Zealand. For discussion of the historical depth of Indigenous rights movements in Latin America, see Varese et al. 2008.

16. As Beth Conklin (2006:163) notes, the link with environmentalism that has developed since the 1980s greatly expanded the terrain for Indigenous advocacy, which formerly had been based on human rights arguments.

17. In some contexts today, discourses of ethnocide and genocide persist, although in most international fora human rights discourses have replaced earlier positivist discussions.

18. For a list, see Ruggles and Silverman 2009:12–13.

19. For discussions of "intangible culture," see, e.g., Ruggles and Silverman 2009; Ruggles and Silverman, eds. 2009; see also Karp and Kratz 2015. Barbara Kirshenblatt-Gimblett (2006) points to the increasing arbitrariness of the categories of tangible and intangible culture.

20. The Venezuelan Ley de Patrimonio Cultural de los Pueblos y Comunidades Indígenas, which was enacted in February 2009, is one good example. See http://www.defensoria.gob.ve/dp/index.php/leyes-pueblos-indigenas/1330, accessed January 2, 2010.

21. For example, Elizabeth Povinelli persuasively argues that liberal multicultural discourses are loaded with contradictions and embedded within power relations. Indigenous persons "struggle to inhabit the tensions and torsions of competing incitements to be and identify differentially" (2002:13).

22. For a good discussion of the legal concept of "Indigenous," see Anaya 2004; Kingsbury 1995; for discussion of Indigenous Peoples and human rights, see Anaya 1996, 2009; see also Niezen 2003.

23. It is important to keep in mind that Indigenous Peoples in general are among the earth's most oppressed peoples (cf. Hall and Patrinos 2012).

24. Alliances based on linking Indigenous Peoples to the environment often have proven to be problematic, provoking backlash and sometimes serious negative consequences. As Ranco (2007) and Langton (2003) point out for North America and Australia, respectively, alliances can undermine Indigenous self-determination. Some major environmental NGOs (ENGOs) now reject alliances founded on constructions that position Indigenous Peoples as part of the natural environment (Chapin 2004).

25. Nick Stanley (1998), who traces the public performance of cultural identities for spectators from the 1893 Columbian Exposition to the present, contends that performers' self-consciousness is the single feature that most clearly distinguishes contemporary performances from their predecessors.

26. In processes similar to this, Terence Turner (1990, 2002) discusses how new media, video specifically, is leading to cultural revitalization in Kayapó communities. Other Indigenous media projects have been noted to have similar effects and complexities. See, e.g., Michaels 1994; see also Ginsburg 1991, 1993, 1999; Wilson and Stewart, 2008; Graham 2009.

27. Karp and Kratz (2015) similarly emphasize the dialogicality of collaborations between museums and communities that takes place in the conception, development, and curation (sometimes co-curation) of museum exhibits.

28. Despite the fact that Indigenous performances are generally sensorial complex, non-Indigenous scholars have tended to privilege the visual. Graham (2002), for example, brings attention to the often-underappreciated acoustic domain of Indigenous performance in intercultural political arenas.

29. The highly contextual notion of "becoming" Indigenous, rooted in Native Amazonian ideologies (see Viveiros de Castro 1998), has been productive in discussions of lowland South American Indigeneity (see, e.g., Maybury-Lewis 1991; Jackson 1991; see also Ramos 1994, 2012) and also has recently been proving to be productive in other ethnographic contexts (see Hodgson 2009, 2011). This notion resonates with Stuart Hall's argument that identities—which "come from somewhere, have histories . . . and are subject to the continuous 'play' of history, culture, and power"—are always about becoming (Hall 1990). See Li 2000 for an excellent overview of Hall's work on this topic and its application to "being" Indigenous in Indonesia.

30. Entailed here are processes of resignification that Michael Silverstein (1996) calls "second-order indexicality," whereby the uniquely local meanings of semiotic phenomena take on new meanings to become markers of "Indigeneity" in new contexts. Graham (2002) illuminates processes of second-order indexicality in Indigenous discourses in national and international arenas. Indigeneity itself is, indeed, a "second-order identity": local—and sometimes even borrowed—behaviors and other semiotic phenomena become resignified to index Indigeneity. In a comparatively early essay, Sahlins (1992) grapples with consciousness of culture and apparently second-order cultural discourse.

Bibliography

Abrahams, Roger
   1972 Folklore and Literature as Performance. Journal of the Folklore Institute 8:75–94.
Ames, Eric
   2009 Karl Hagenbeck's Empire of Entertainments. Seattle: University of Washington Press.
Anaya, James
   1996 Indigenous Peoples in International Law. New York: Oxford University Press.
   2004 Indigenous Peoples in International Law. 2nd ed. New York: Oxford University Press.
   2009 International Human Rights and Indigenous Peoples. New York: Aspen.
Aristotle
   1961 Poetics. S. H. Butcher, trans. Introduction by Francis Fergusson. New York: Hill and Wang.

Austin, John L.

1975[1962] How to Do Things with Words. 2nd ed. J. O. Urson and M. Sbisa, eds. Cambridge MA: Harvard University Press.

Bakhtin, Mikhail M.

1981 The Dialogic Imagination: Four Essays. Austin: University of Texas Press.

Ball, Christopher

2012 Stop Loss: Developing Interethnic Relations in Brazil's Xingu Indigenous Park. Journal of Latin American and Caribbean Anthropology 17(3):413–34.

Bateson, Gregory

1972[1955] A Theory of Play and Fantasy. American Psychiatric Research Reports 2:39–51. Reprinted in Steps to an Ecology of Mind: Collected Essays in Anthropology, pp. 183–98. New York: Ballantine.

Bauman, Richard

1984[1977] Verbal Art as Performance. Prospect Heights IL: Waveland.

2004 A World of Other's Words: Cross-Cultural Perspectives on Intertextuality. Malden MA: Blackwell.

Bauman, Richard, and Charles L. Briggs

1990 Poetics and Performance as Critical Perspectives on Language and Social Life. Annual Review of Anthropology 19:59–88.

Bell, Elizabeth

2008 Theories of Performance. Thousand Oaks CA: Sage.

Bellin, Joshua David, and Laura L. Mielke, eds.

2011 Native Acts: Indian Performance, 1603–1832. Lincoln: University of Nebraska Press.

Brosius, Peter J.

2003 Voices for the Borneo Rainforest: Writing the History of an Environmental Campaign. In Nature in the Global South. Paul Greenough and Anna Tsing, eds. Pp. 319–46. Durham NC: Duke University Press.

Brosius, Peter J., ed.

1999 Environmentalism, Indigenous Rights, and Transnational Cultural Critique. Special issue, Identities 6(2–3).

Brown, Michael F.

2003 Who Owns Native Culture? Cambridge MA: Harvard University Press.

Bruckner, Sierra A.

2003 Spectacles of (Human) Nature: Commercial Ethnography between Leisure, Learning, and Schaulust. In Worldly Provincialism: German Anthropology in the Age of Empire. H. Glenn Penny and Matti Bunzl, eds. Pp. 127–55. Ann Arbor: University of Michigan Press.

Brysk, Alison

1994 Acting Globally: Indian Rights and International Politics in Latin America. In Indigenous Peoples and Politics in Latin America. Donna Lee Van Cott, ed. Pp. 29–54. New York: St. Martin's Press.

Burke, Kenneth

    1957 The Philosophy of Literary Forms: Studies in Symbolic Action. Rev. ed. New York: Vintage.

    1966 Language as Symbolic Action: Essays on Life, Literature and Method. Berkeley: University of California Press.

Butler, Judith

    1990 Gender Trouble: Feminism and the Subversion of Identity. New York: Routledge.

    1993 Bodies that Matter: On the Discursive Limits of "Sex." New York: Routledge.

Chapin, Mac

    2004 A Challenge to Conservationists. Worldwatch Magazine. November/December 17(6):17-31.

Chernela, Janet

    2005 The Politics of Mediation: Local-Global Interactions in the Central Amazon of Brazil. American Anthropologist 107(4):620-31.

Chomsky, Noam

    1965 Aspects of a Theory of Syntax. Cambridge MA: MIT Press.

Clifford, James

    2001 Indigenous Articulations. Contemporary Pacific 13(2):468–90.

Cohen, Matt

    2011 Lying Inventions: Native Dissimulation in Early Colonial New England. *In* Native Acts: Indian Performance, 1603–1832. Joshua David Bellin and Laura L. Mielke, eds. Pp. 27–52. Lincoln: University of Nebraska Press.

Comaroff, John L., and Jean Comaroff

    2009 Ethnicity Inc. Chicago: University of Chicago Press.

Conklin, Beth A.

    2006 Environmentalism, Global Community, and the New Indigenism. *In* Inclusion and Exclusion in the Global Arena. Max Kirsh, ed. Pp. 61–176. London: Routledge.

Conklin, Beth A., and Laura R. Graham

    1995 The Shifting Middle Ground: Amazonian Indians and Eco-politics. American Anthropologist 97(4):695–710.

Conquergood, Dwight

    1995 Of Caravans and Carnivals: Performance Studies in Motion. TDF: The Drama Review 39(4):137–41.

    1998 Beyond the Text: Toward a Performative Cultural Politics. *In* Future of Performance Studies. Sheron J. Daily, ed. Pp. 25–36. Annandale VA: National Communication Association.

    2007 Indigenous Experience Today. Oxford: Berg.

Coombe, Rosemary

    1998 The Cultural Life of Intellectual Properties: Authorship, Appropriation, and the Law. Durham NC: Duke University Press.

Cultural Survival

2010 Cultural Survival Style Guide, February 9. Unpublished internal document.

de la Cadena, Marisol, and Orin Starn

2007 Introduction. *In* Indigenous Experience Today. Pp. 1–30. Oxford: Berg.

Deloria, Vine, Jr.

1981 The Indians. *In* Buffalo Bill and the Wild West. Pp. 45–56. Brooklyn: Brooklyn Museum.

Duranti, Alessandro, and Charles Goodwin, eds.

1992 Rethinking Context: Language as an Interactive Phenomenon. Cambridge: Cambridge University Press.

Erickson, Patricia, and Janine Bowechop

2002 Voices of a Thousand People: The Makah Cultural Resource Center. Lincoln: University of Nebraska Press.

Fortun, Kim, Mike Fortun, and Steven Rubenstein

2010 Introduction to "Emergent Indigeneities." Cultural Anthropology 25(2):222–34.

French, Jan

2009 Legalizing Identities: Becoming Black or Indian in Brazil's Northeast. Chapel Hill: University of North Carolina Press.

Geertz, Clifford

1973 The Interpretation of Cultures: Selected Essays. New York: Basic Books.

1980 Blurred Genres: The Refiguration of Social Thought. American Scholar 29:508–13.

Gell, Alfred

1998 Art and Agency: An Anthropological Theory. Oxford: Clarendon Press; New York: Oxford University Press.

Getty Conservation Institute

2009 Cultural Heritage Policy Documents. http://www.getty.edu/conservation/publications_resources/research_resources/charters.html, accessed November 29, 2012. Last updated August 2009.

Ginsburg, Faye D.

1991 Indigenous Media: Faustian Contract or Global Village? Cultural Anthropology 6(1):92–112.

1993 Aboriginal Media and the Australian Imaginary. Public Culture: Bulletin of the Project for Transnational Cultural Studies 5:557–78.

1999 Shooting Back: From Ethnographic Film to Indigenous Production/Ethnography of Media. *In* A Companion to Film Theory. T. Miller and R. Stam, eds. Pp. 295–322. London: Blackwell.

Gluckman, Max

1958 Analysis of a Social Situation in Modern Zululand. Rhodes-Livingstone Paper no 28. Manchester: Manchester University Press for Rhodes-Livingstone Institute.

Goffman, Erving

1959 The Presentation of Self in Everyday Life. Garden City NY: Doubleday.

1967 Interaction Ritual: Essays on Face-to-Face Behavior. Garden City NY: Doubleday.

1974 Frame Analysis: An Essay on the Organization of Experience. New York: Harper.

Graham, Laura R.

1995 Performing Dreams: Discourses of Immortality among the Xavante Indians of Central Brazil. Austin: University of Texas Press.

2002 How Should an Indian Speak? Brazilian Indians and the Symbolic Politics of Language Choice in the International Public Sphere. *In* Indigenous Movements, Self-Representation, and the State in Latin America. Jean Jackson and Kay Warren, eds. Pp. 181–228. Austin: University of Texas Press.

2005 Image and Instrumentality in a Xavante Politics of Existential Recognition: The Public Outreach Work of Eténhiritipa Pimentel Barbosa. American Ethnologist 32(4):622–41.

2009 Problematizing Technologies for Documenting Intangible Culture. *In* Intangible Culture Embodied. D. Fairchild Ruggles and Helaine Silverman, eds. Pp. 185–200. New York: Springer.

Greenblatt, Stephen

1992 Marvelous Possessions: The Wonder of the New World. Chicago: University of Chicago Press.

Greene, Shane

2009 Customizing Indigeneity: Paths to a Visionary Politics in Peru. Stanford CA: Stanford University Press.

Gupta, Akhil

1998 Postcolonial Developments: Agriculture in the Making of Modern India. Durham NC: Duke University Press.

Hall, Gillette H., and Harry Anthony Patrinos

2012 Indigenous Peoples, Poverty and Development. Cambridge: Cambridge University Press.

Hall, Stuart

1990 Cultural Identity and Diaspora. *In* Identity: Community, Culture, Difference. Jonathan Rutherford, ed. Pp. 222–37. London: Lawrence and Wishart.

1996[1986] On Postmodernism and Articulation: An Interview with Stuart Hall. Lawrence Grossberg, ed. *In* Stuart Hall: Critical Dialogues in Cultural Studies. Kuan-Hsing Chen and David Morley, eds. Pp. 131–50. London: Routledge.

Hannerz, Ulf

1996 Transnational Connections: Culture, People, Places. New York: Routledge.

Heatherington, Tracey

2010 Wild Sardinia: Indigeneity and the Global Dreamtimes of Environmentalism. Seattle: University of Washington Press.

Hobsbawm, Eric

    1996 Age of Extremes: A History of the World, 1914–1991. New York: Vintage.

Hodgson, Dorothy L.

    2002a Introduction: Comparative Perspectives on the Indigenous Rights Movement in Africa and the Americas. American Anthropologist 104(4):1037–49.

    2002b Precarious Alliances: The Cultural Politics and Structural Predicaments of the Indigenous Rights Movement in Tanzania. American Anthropologist 104(4):1086–97.

    2009 Becoming Indigenous in Africa. African Studies Review 52(3):1–32.

    2011 Being Maasai, Becoming Indigenous: Postcolonial Politics in a Neoliberal World. Bloomington: Indiana University Press.

Howitt, Richard

    2001 Rethinking Resource Management: Justice, Sustainability, and Indigenous Peoples. New York: Routledge.

Hymes, Dell H.

    1972 Directions in Sociolinguistics: The Ethnography of Communication. New York: Holt, Rinehart and Winston.

Inter-Commission Task Force on Indigenous Peoples

    1998 Indigenous Peoples and Sustainability: Cases and Actions. New York: International Books.

Jackson, Jean

    1991 Being and Becoming Indian in the Vaupés. In Nation-States and Indians in Lowland South America. Greg Urban and Joel Sherzer, eds. Pp. 131–35. Austin: University of Texas Press.

Jackson, Jean E., and Kay B. Warren

    2005 Indigenous Movements in Latin America, 1992–2004: Controversies, Ironies, New Directions. Annual Reviews in Anthropology 34:549–73.

Karp, Ivan, and Corrine Kratz

    2015 The Interrogative Museum. In Museum as Process: Translating Local and Global Knowledges. Raymond Silverman, ed. New York: Routledge. Pp. 279–98.

Karp, Ivan, Corrine Kratz, Lynn Szwaja, and Tomás Ybarra-Frausto, eds., with Gustavo Buntinx, Barbara Kirshenblatt-Gimblett, and Ciraj Rassool

    2006 Museum Frictions: Public Cultures/Global Transformations. Durham NC: Duke University Press.

Kingsbury, Benedict

    1995 "Indigenous Peoples" as an International Legal Concept. In Indigenous Peoples of Asia. R. H. Barnes, Andrew Gray, and Benedict Kingsbury, eds. Pp. 13–34. Ann Arbor: Association for Asian Studies, University of Michigan.

Kirshenblatt-Gimblett, Barbara

    2006 World Heritage and Cultural Economics. In Museum Frictions: Public Cultures/Global Transformations. Ivan Karp, Corrine Kratz, Lynn Szwaja, and Tomás Ybarra-Frausto, eds. Pp. 161–204. Durham NC: Duke University Press.

Kratz, Corinne A.

2004 Ritual Performance. *In* African Folklore: An Encyclopedia. Philip Peek and Kwesi Yankah, eds. Pp. 397–400. New York: Garland Press.

Kratz, Corinne A., and Ivan Karp

2006 Introduction. *In* Museum Frictions: Public Cultures/Global Transformations. Ivan Karp, Corinne Kratz, Lynn Szwaja, and Tomás Ybarra-Frausto, eds. Pp. 1–31. Durham NC: Duke University Press.

Kuper, Adam

2003 The Return of the Native. Current Anthropology 44(3):389–402.

Langton, Marcia

2003 The "Wild," the Market and the Native: Indigenous People Face New Forms of Global Colonization. *In* Globalization, Globalism, Environments and Environmentalism. Steven Vertovec and Darrell A. Posey, eds. Pp. 141–70. Oxford: Oxford University Press.

Levi, Jerome M.

2003 Indigenous Rights and Representations in Northern Mexico: The Diverse Contexts of Rarámuri Voice. *In* At the Risk of Being Heard: Identity, Indigenous Rights, and Postcolonial States. Bartholomew Dean and Jerome M. Levi, eds. Pp. 255–91. Ann Arbor: University of Michigan Press.

Levi, Jerome M., and Biorn Maybury-Lewis

2012 Becoming Indigenous: Identity and Heterogeneity in a Global Movement. *In* Indigenous Peoples, Poverty and Development. Gillette Hall and Harry Anthony Patrinos, eds. Pp. 73–117. Cambridge: Cambridge University Press.

Li, Tanya

2000 Articulating Indigenous Identity in Indonesia: Resource Politics and the Tribal Slot. Comparative Studies in Society and History 42(1):149–79.

Maybury-Lewis, David

1991 Becoming Indian in Lowland South America. *In* Nation-States and Indians in Lowland South America. Greg Urban and Joel Sherzer, eds. Pp. 207–35. Austin: University of Texas Press.

Meyer, Carter Jones, and Diana Royer

2001 Selling the Indian: Commercializing and Appropriating American Indian Cultures. Tucson: University of Arizona Press.

Michaels, Eric

1994 Bad Aboriginal Art: Tradition, Media and Technological Horizons. Minneapolis: University of Minnesota Press.

Minde, Henry, Harald Gaski, Svein Jentoft, and Georges Midré

2008 Introduction. *In* Indigenous Peoples: Self-Determination, Knowledge, Indigeneity. Henry Minde, ed. Pp 1–26. Delft, The Netherlands: Eburon Delft.

Moore, Donald S., Jake Kosek, and Anand Pandian, eds.

2003 Race, Nature, and the Politics of Difference. Durham NC: Duke University Press.

Morphy, Howard

1983 "Now You Understand": An Analysis for the Way Yolngu Have Used Sacred Knowledge to Retain Their Autonomy. *In* Aborigines, Land, and Land Rights. Nicolas Peterson and Marcia Langton, eds. Pp. 110–33. Canberra: Australian Institute of Aboriginal Studies.

1995 Aboriginal Art in a Global Context. *In* Worlds Apart: Modernity through the Prism of the Local. Daniel Miller, ed. Pp. 221–39. London: Routledge.

1999 Manggalili Art and the Promised Land. *In* Painting the Land Story. Luke Taylor, ed. Pp. 53–74. Canberra: National Museum of Australia.

2006 Sites of Persuasion: Yingapungapu at the National Museum of Australia. *In* Museum Frictions: Public Cultures/Global Transformations. Ivan Karp, Corinne Kratz, Lynn Szwaja, and Tomás Ybarra-Frausto, eds. Pp. 469–99. Durham NC: Duke University Press.

Moses, L. G.

1996 Wild West Shows and the Images of American Indians, 1883–1933. Albuquerque: University of New Mexico Press, 1996.

Myers, Fred R.

2002 Painting Culture: The Making of an Aboriginal High Art. Durham NC: Duke University Press.

Native American Graves Protection and Repatriation Act (NAGPRA)

1990 25 U.S.C. §3001. http://www.nps.gov/nagpra/MANDATES/25USC3001etseq .htm, accessed November 29, 2012.

Niezen, Ronald

2003 The Origins of Indigenism: Human Rights and the Politics of Identity. Berkeley: University of California Press.

2004 A World beyond Difference: Cultural Identity in the Age of Globalization. Malden MA: Blackwell.

2009 Defending the Land: Sovereignty and Forest Life in James Bay Cree Society. Upper Saddle River NJ: Pearson Prentice Hall.

Pellegrino, Sílvia Pizzolante

2009 Imagens e substâncias como vínculos de pertencimento: As experiêncas Wajãpi e Yanomami. PhD thesis, Programa de Pós Graduação em Antropologia, Universidade de São Paulo (PPGAS/USP).

Perley, Bernard

2011 Defying Maliseet Language Death: Emergent Vitalities of Language, Culture and Identity in Eastern Canada. Lincoln: University of Nebraska Press.

Poignant, Roslyn

2004 Professional Savages: Captive Lives and Western Spectacle. New Haven CT: Yale University Press.

Povinelli, Elizabeth A.

2002 The Cunning of Recognition: Indigenous Alterities and the Making of Australian Multiculturalism. Durham NC: Duke University Press.

Pratt, Mary Louise

2007 Afterword. *In* Indigenous Experience Today. Marisol de la Cadena and Orin Starn, eds. Pp. 397–404. Oxford: Berg.

Ramos, Alcida

1994 The Hyperreal Indian. Critique of Anthropology 14(2):153–71.

2012 The Politics of Perspectivism. Annual Review of Anthropology 41:481–94.

Ranco, Darren J.

2007 The Ecological Indian and the Politics of Representation: Critiquing *The Ecological Indian* in the Age of Ecocide. *In* Native Americans and the Environment: Perspectives on the Ecological Indian. Michael Harkin and David Rich Lewis, eds. Pp. 32–51. Lincoln: University of Nebraska Press.

Rothfels, Nigel

2002 Savages and Beasts: The Birth of the Modern Zoo. Baltimore: Johns Hopkins University Press.

Ruggles, D. Fairchild, and Helaine Silverman

2009 From Tangible to Intangible Heritage. *In* Intangible Culture Embodied. D. Fairchild Ruggles and Helaine Silverman, eds. Pp. 1–14. New York: Springer.

Ruggles, D. Fairchild, and Helaine Silverman, eds.

2009 Intangible Culture Embodied. New York: Springer.

Sahlins, Marshall

1992 The Economics of Develop-Man in the South Pacific. Res: Anthropology and Aesthetics 21:12–25.

Schechner, Richard

1985 Between Theater and Anthropology. Philadelphia: University of Pennsylvania Press.

Searle, John

1969 Speech Acts: An Essay in the Philosophy of Language. Cambridge: Cambridge University Press.

Silverstein, Michael

1996 Indexical Order and the Dialectics of Sociolinguistic Life. *In* Proceedings of the Third Annual Symposium about Language and Society. Risako Ide, Rebecca Parker, and Yukako Sunaoshi, eds. Pp. 266–95. Austin: University of Texas Department of Linguistics.

Singer, Milton

1972 When a Great Tradition Modernizes: An Anthropological Approach to Indian Civilization. New York: Praeger.

Sixth International Congress of Architects.

1904 Recommendations of the Madrid Conference. Architectural Journal, 3rd ser., 11:343–46. Getty Conservation Institute, Cultural Heritage Policy Documents, http://www.getty.edu/conservation/publications_resources/research_resources/charters/charter01.html, accessed November 29, 2012.

Spear, Thomas, and Richard Waller

   1993 Being Maasai: Ethnicity and Identity in East Africa. London: J. Currey.

Stanley, Nick

   1998 Being Ourselves for You: The Global Display of Cultures. London: Middlesex University Press.

Tsing, Anna

   2005 Friction: An Ethnography of Global Connection. Princeton NJ: Princeton University Press.

   2007 Indigenous Voice. *In* Indigenous Experience Today. Marisol de la Cadena and Orin Starn, eds. Pp. 33–67. Oxford: Berg.

Turner, Terence

   1990 Visual Media, Cultural Politics, and Anthropological Practice: Some Implications of Recent Uses of Film and Video among the Kayapó of Brazil. Commission on Visual Anthropology Review 1:9–13.

   2002 Representation, Politics, and Cultural Imagination in Indigenous Video: General Points and Kayapó Examples. *In* Media Worlds: Anthropology on New Terrain. F. Ginsburg, L. Abu-Lughod, and B. Larkin, eds. Pp. 75–89. Berkeley: University of California Press.

Turner, Victor

   1974 Dramas, Fields, and Metaphors: Symbolic Action in Human Society. Ithaca NY: Cornell University Press.

Turtinen, Jan

   2000 Globalizing Heritage: On UNESCO and the Transnational Construction of a World Heritage. Rapportserie 12. Stockholm: SCORE [Stockholm Center for Organizational Research].

United Nations

   2007 Declaration on the Rights of Indigenous Peoples. Adopted by General Assembly Resolution 61/295, September 13. http://undesadspd.org/Indigenous Peoples/DeclarationontheRightsofIndigenousPeoples.aspx, accessed July 31, 2011.

   2011 Permanent Forum on Indigenous Issues. http://undesadspd.org/Indigenous Peoples.aspx, accessed July 31.

Varese, Stefano, Guillermo Delgado, and Rodolfo L. Meyer

   2008 Indigenous Anthropologists beyond Barbados. *In* A Companion to Latin American Anthropology. Deborah Poole, ed. Pp. 375–98. Malden MA: Blackwell.

Vásquez, Manuel A.

   2011 More than Belief: A Materialist Theory of Religion. Oxford: Oxford University Press.

Viveiros de Castro, Eduardo

   1998 Cosmological Deixis and Amerindian Perspectivism. Journal of the Royal Anthropological Institute 4:469–88.

Warren, Kay B.

1998 Indigenous Movements and Their Critics: Pan-Mayan Activism in Guatemala. Princeton NJ: Princeton University Press.

Wilmer, S. E., ed.

2009 Native American Performance and Representation. Tucson: University of Arizona Press.

Wilson, Pamela, and Michelle Stewart

2008 Introduction: Indigeneity and Indigenous Media on the Global Stage. *In* Global Indigenous Media: Cultures, Poetics, and Politics. Pamela Wilson and Michelle Stewart, eds. Pp. 1–35. Durham NC: Duke University Press.

Yeh, Emily T.

2007 Tibetan Indigeneity: Translations, Resemblances and Uptake. *In* Indigenous Experience Today. Marisol de la Cadena and Orin Starn, eds. Pp. 69–97. Oxford: Berg.

2

Living Traditions

A Manifesto for Critical Indigeneity

BERNARD PERLEY

Community members of Tobique First Nation, New Brunswick, Canada, are grappling with the realization that they may witness the extinction of their heritage language within their lifetimes.[1] Maliseet language extinction is not merely the loss of a Maliseet linguistic code. Language extinction is also the extinction of Indigenous cultural and spiritual experiences of the everyday lives of the community members. I am a member of Tobique First Nation, and I experienced and continue to experience the trauma associated with Maliseet language, cultural, and spiritual loss. I feel that trauma on a daily basis as personal alienation from Maliseet living traditions and disempowerment in contemporary regimes of colonial power. My experience is shared by members of Tobique First Nation; all Aboriginal First Nations, Métis, and Inuit in Canada; as well as Indigenous Peoples across the globe. Indigenous Peoples are not living in a postcolonial world, despite what many advocates and activists claim. In this second decade of the twenty-first century the colonial assault on Indigenous Peoples through regimes of oppression, alienation, and disempowerment continue unabated. If regimes of colonial domination continue all Indigenous living traditions will become extinct.

I will not let this happen to Maliseet living traditions. I use every creative skill I have to live Maliseet traditions, and I will use them every day to affirm and advocate Maliseet worlds and experience against colonial pressures of alienation and disempowerment. My daily practice of Indigenous experience is my manifesto for critical Indigeneity. It is a commitment to living an Indigenous Maliseet life dependent upon mutually affirming social relationships between Maliseet community members. This collective

Maliseet experience and empowerment will permit the Maliseet community to practice their living traditions on their terms, in their traditional homelands, in their belief systems, in everyday practices.

Critical Indigeneity is not just a personal or Maliseet manifesto; it is a manifesto for affirming and empowering global Indigenous living traditions. Indigenous Peoples cannot wait for the UN Declaration on the Rights of Indigenous Peoples to turn idealistic words into actionable deeds. The four colonial states to originally vote "no" to the declaration—Australia, New Zealand, Canada, and the United States—eventually accepted the declaration on the basis that it was "an aspirational document" and a non-binding resolution. Indigenous Peoples cannot count on the moral platitudes of colonial institutions and agents. They must take action by living their Indigenous traditions on their terms and in their everyday lives. My manifesto of critical Indigeneity does not promise this will be easy nor that there will be instant solutions. The various colonial practices create conditions of Indigenous complexities and contradictions that are in constant flux. Indigenous Peoples experience these conditions on a daily basis. This manifesto, then, is grounded in the contingencies of everyday life, embodied experiences over time, and the meaningful interactions of Indigenous social relationships. Each Indigenous person will have his or her own particular experiences and strategies for living his or her traditions. However, colonial power and control over Indigenous lives make it imperative that we share our experiences and strategies for survival. I share my own experiences in my daily struggle to maintain an Indigenous life in a colonial context as just one example in a shared global Indigenous struggle.

"It's Gonna Be the Coldest Winter on Record!"

In the American Indian Studies class I teach, I constantly use ethnographic vignettes to illustrate social science concepts with examples from the real world. Each year, by the fifth week of fall semester the students know that my research focuses on language endangerment and revitalization and that I come from the Maliseet community of Tobique First Nation. This is the time of the year when there is a decided chill in the air and everyone is compelled to wear coats to stay warm. It is usually on such a day that I begin the class by commenting on how cold the morning is:

Wow! It's cold this morning, isn't it? This morning I phoned my mother who lives on the reservation. We talked about how things are back home. She said they are experiencing some cold weather. She also said some of the "traditional" members of the community approached the chief, who is my uncle by marriage. The chief is not necessarily a "traditionalist," but he has great respect for traditional beliefs and practices.

"Hey Chief, is it going to be cold this winter?" the traditionalists asked.

The chief felt put on the spot. He did not want to appear clueless so he looked up at the sky. He looked at the ground. He looked all around and, with a knowing look on his face, told the traditionalists, "Yes, it's going to be a cold winter." The traditionalists responded by nodding in agreement.

"What should we do?"

"You should start collecting firewood."

"Thanks for the advice." The traditionalists went off to collect firewood.

The chief went home that evening and started to worry that he might have been wrong in telling the traditionalists that it was going to be a cold winter. To assuage his doubts he called the local television weatherman to ask him if the coming winter was going to be cold or mild. The weatherman confirmed to the chief that it was going to be a cold winter. In fact, it was going to be a very cold winter! The chief thanked the weatherman and thought that he'd better tell the traditionalists it was going to be a very cold winter.

The next day, when the chief saw the traditionalists, he went directly to them and said, "You know yesterday when I told you guys it's gonna be a cold winter?"

The traditionalists as one replied, "Yeah?"

"Well, it's going to be a very cold winter! So you better collect more firewood."

The traditionalists thanked the chief and went off to collect more firewood. Later that evening, back home, the chief feared he might have overstated how cold the winter would be so he called the weatherman again. The weatherman confirmed it was going to be cold but added that it was going to be extremely cold this winter. The chief thanked him and was relieved that he hadn't led the traditionalists astray. But "extremely cold" is colder than "very cold." He'd have to advise the traditionalists to gather more firewood.

The following day the chief saw the same traditionalists and told them that the coming winter was going to be "extremely cold" and they should gather even more firewood. The traditionalists thanked the chief and went to collect the firewood. Once again, later that evening, back home, the chief began to worry that he had overstated how cold the winter would be so he called the weatherman.

"Are you sure it's going to be an extremely cold winter?"

"Yes. In fact, it's gonna be the coldest winter on record!" replied the weatherman.

"Wow! How do you know this?" asked the chief.

"The Indians are collecting firewood like crazy!"

At this point the class erupts in laughter and they realize that I am telling them a joke. The critical questions to be asked are, Who is the object of the joke? The chief? The traditionalists? The weatherman? Or all of the above? Perhaps, more critically, was the above account really a joke? My answer is, This is critical Indigeneity in action.

No Laughing Matter? Anthropology and Indigeneity

The use of humor in the classroom is one example of my daily interventions of critical Indigeneity. It is one strategy to cope with the tensions created by my decision to obtain a PhD in anthropology and the subsequent professional practice of teaching and research in anthropology. The weatherman joke is storytelling performance, a critical interrogation of assumed values between Indigenous knowledge systems and Western science and of the perceived roles of the actors in the story—the traditionalists, the chief, and the weatherman. I also use the story to highlight the relationships between a Native anthropologist and a predominantly non-Native student audience. My objective is to make all of us laugh at the tensions that centuries of colonial domination over Indigenous Peoples of North America have bequeathed to all of us today. Those tensions include my relationship to my home community of Tobique First Nation and to the discipline of anthropology. My strategies for coping with these tensions are practiced in the colonial context of higher education and cultural expectations. These colonial cultural expectations render Indigenous experience and lives in analytical terms such as "performance" and "Indigeneity." These are the contemporary discursive descriptors used to convey the complex, conflicting, and contradictory daily practices of social relations between Indigenous Peoples and colonial/settler societies. Each generation of Indigenous critics/activists and colonial scholars/advocates has its respective descriptors; more recent examples include "postcolonial" studies and "decolonization" programs. I do not suggest that these are empty descriptors. They are abstract glosses for the kinds for everyday interventions that Indigenous Peoples practice for their survival. I highlight this temporal dimension of critical Indigeneity to emphasize the continual and contingent aspect of living Indigenous traditions.

In 2001, at the annual meeting of the American Anthropology Association in Washington DC, I presented a paper I consider my personal manifesto for my practice of Native anthropology. I stated in that manifesto that

> I envision an ethnographic practice of complexity in action; an ethnographic practice of contradiction in beginnings. I consider my ethnographic tools to include my brushes, my pencils, my voice, my vision, my keyboard, and every creative tool at my disposal. I envision an ethnographic practice that celebrates a record of cultural becoming, of cultural creativity. As Native and anthropologist, I envision such a celebration. Such a celebration embraces complexity and contradiction, but I also hope that it is a celebration of vitality *and validity*. But, I do not speak for the discipline, nor do I pretend to know what the future of the discipline will be but I hope that it could embrace, or at least validate the ethnographies I am authoring.

It was a turbulent process of self-determination that led to my public manifesto and my experience practicing critical Indigeneity as a Native and an anthropologist. The complex webs of social relationships back home at Tobique First Nation were important experiences of the complexities and contractions of Indigeneity as process.

The Perils of Native Anthropology

Sneaky Pete

The chief was going to pick me up at 9:00 a.m. He drove up in his white extended-cab, full-sized pickup. I hopped into the front passenger seat. The chief had a couple of his staff members, both of them Indians and members of the community, sitting in the backseat. Morning pleasantries were exchanged throughout the cab. The chief told me, "We have to pick up our consultant. Bernie, you'll have a lot to talk about with him. He's also an anthropologist."

We drove to the nearby town and the chief honked the horn in front of a two-story Victorian house. Out stepped a middle-aged Anglo-American. He hopped in the backseat next to the staff members. More pleasantries were exchanged, but introductions had to be made. The chief introduced the consultant to me—for the sake of this narrative let's call him "Pete" or "Sneaky Pete"—and then introduced me to him.

"Pete, Bernie is working on his PhD in anthropology at Harvard." Sneaky Pete became excited and told me he is an anthropologist.

"Where did you do your graduate work?" I asked Pete.

Pete told me he got his PhD from Columbia in the sixties. At this point the chief and his staffers were listening to the conversation.

"Where did you end up teaching?" I asked.

Sneaky Pete told me that teaching jobs were hard to find when he graduated so he ended up working for the CIA as a spy in Vietnam. There was complete silence in the cab. I remember thinking, Damn! That's all I need. Now the chief and his two staffers are going to wonder if I am working as a government spy! Nobody said anything for a few moments as we continued down the road. I was thinking that Pete was single-handedly destroying my rapport with the chief and his staffers. My project was doomed because of suspicions of collusion with the government. The tension lingered until Pete broke the silence and asked me, "Bernie, you're an anthropologist, what do you think? Do you think Indians came over on the Bering land bridge?"

I knew what the right answer was in that cab, at that moment, among fellow Indians. My response was, "We came from this earth."

At this point the two staffers said, "All right, Bern!" "Way to go, Bern!" Both of them playfully punched my shoulder.

Within a matter of minutes, I had gone from community member to nefarious intruder and back to community member; rapport turned to suspicion and back to rapport. My responses were conditioned on knowing what the chief and the staffers expected to hear so that the answer would be met with approval. I knew anthropology was regarded with suspicion by members of the community (if they have not read Vine Deloria Jr. they at least know about his criticism of anthropology), so I did not want to side with the anthropologists, especially after the CIA comment! Did (do) I actually believe "we came from the earth"? Culturally speaking, yes. Furthermore, I could not agree with the Bering land bridge theory because I knew that theory was coming under heavy criticism from archaeologists and other quaternary period specialists. I also knew that if I had made a land bridge argument my standing in the community would become as suspect as the discipline of anthropology. I suspect he did but I will never know if Sneaky Pete was aware of the long history of distrust of the government by Canada's Aboriginal First Nations. He must have been aware of the recent tensions between the government and the Indians since the Oka crisis of 1990, the failure of the Meech Lake Accord, and numerous encounters between Indians and government law enforcement agencies that resulted in conflict and sometimes the deaths of Indians.[2] Can it be that Sneaky Pete recognized the tension he created with his questions in the cab of the pickup? Can it be that Sneaky Pete found a way out for both of us when he asked the second question, about Indian origins? Did he deliberately find an opportunity for me to choose sides between the government and the Indians? Again, I will never know. I do know I was grateful for his question about Indian origins. I was relieved to be able to choose the side the Indians were on.

Yes, Kemosabi!

The Lone Ranger and Tonto had just finished their good deed for the day. They were riding out of town toward the sunset. They ride for a while before the Lone Ranger leans forward in his saddle and peers toward the distant horizon. Without taking his attention away from the horizon he says to Tonto, "Tonto."

Tonto replies, "Yes, Kemosabi?"

The Lone Ranger says, "Look! There are figures on the horizon. They look like hostile Indians to me. Perhaps we should go another direction."

Tonto says, "Yes, Kemosabi."

So they turn their horses ninety degrees to the left. They ride for another ten minutes, and again the Lone Ranger peers toward the distant horizon. Again the Lone Ranger says, "Tonto."

To which Tonto replies, "Yes, Kemosabi?"

The Lone Ranger says, "There on the horizon, it looks like more hostile Indians ahead. Maybe we should go the other direction."

Tonto says, "Yes, Kemosabi."

So they turn their horses 180 degrees and ride for a while longer. Once again, the Lone Ranger peers into the distance and says, "Tonto."

Again Tonto replies, "Yes, Kemosabi?"

Once again the Lone Ranger says, "Look! There on the horizon, more hostile Indians! We should head back to town."

Tonto says, "Yes, Kemosabi."

They ride for a while and once again he peers into the horizon and says, "Tonto."

Tonto replies, "Yes, Kemosabi?"

In an alarmed voice the Lone Ranger says, "Looks like hostile Indians ahead of us!"

The Lone Ranger looks around and says, "There are hostile Indians behind us! There are hostile Indians all around us! Tonto! We're surrounded!"

At this point Tonto says, "Waddaya mean 'we,' whiteman?"

I told this joke to the Native language teacher when I was doing my fieldwork in the Maliseet language classroom. After I told her the punch line, she just shook her head, chuckled, and said, "Kurai! Bern!" It was a simple expression of surprise and delight. However, I would later learn that the joke would be on me.

As mentioned above, there was high tension between Canadian government law enforcement agencies and the Aboriginal First Nations of Canada during the early nineties. In an attempt to relieve those tensions, the government had established a royal commission to study the sources of and solutions for those tensions. The result was a multivolume report that outlined the historical ground for contemporary tensions as well as recommended solutions to those tensions. The royal commission also issued a small booklet of recommendations for the benefit of the Aboriginal communities and the federal government as well (see Canada, Royal Commission on Aboriginal Peoples 1996). Many of Canada's Aboriginal communities were happy with the recommendations put forward by the commission, but the government was unwilling to act on the recommendations. The Aboriginal First Nations sought to put pressure on the Canadian government to take steps toward redressing past wrongs as recommended by the royal commission, so they organized a coordinated protest all across Canada. On a given day, at a particular hour, Canada's Aboriginal peoples were going to blockade the highways for one hour. Everyone on the reservation was excited about blockading the highway. It was a Friday afternoon when the protest took place. For the Maliseet at Tobique First Nation, the protest went on without much incident.[3] The drummers were there, the singers, a teepee, and men, women, and children gathered. It was an exciting event.

I have to confess I was not there to witness the excitement. I was not there to drum, chant, or experience the exhilaration of civil disobedience. I only saw what transpired on the evening news. I honestly do not recall why I didn't witness the event firsthand. But I do recall the moment when I regretted not being there. The Monday morning following that protest I arrived at the school. The Native language teacher was already in her classroom, behind her desk, preparing for the day's instructions. I greeted her as usual and the conversation drifted to the excitement of the blockade. She gave me a detailed description of what went on, who was there, and what they had accomplished. I responded by saying, "So, we accomplished everything we wanted?" She looked at me and said, "Waddaya mean, 'we,' whiteman? You weren't there!"

Ouch! I had undeservedly assumed that I was one of the Indians in that latest conflict between the Indians and the government. Because I did not protest the government's inaction on the recommendations I was immediately thrown out of the Indian side of the conflict and tossed onto the government's side. In contrast to the CIA vignette, my failure to participate in the blockade was met with disapproval. It was not what I said but what I failed to do that was evaluated and judged. But it is not as easy as that. My lack of participation in the blockade was noticed by other members of the community; the next event will reintroduce that failure, but such political activities are also weighed along with other community activities. My work at the elementary school to support the Maliseet language initiative was also being evaluated by community members who had children and grandchildren enrolled at the school. While the Kemosabi moment certainly put me in my place, I was given some measure of reinstatement when some of the Indians took me back.

I'm Mad!

I was clearly guilty of not participating in a community action that identified clear sides between the government and the Indians. However, that was one incident that was high profile yet short-lived. My work at the school was more enduring and meaningful to many members of the community. As the teacher's aide in the Maliseet language classroom, I had established a good teacher-student relationship with many of the students from first grade to sixth grade. The principal also saw me as not just a nosey anthropologist but also a member of the school staff. I was often enlisted to represent the school at various meetings and activities. At one such meeting, which took place on the reservation, officials from the New Brunswick government came to the community to promote a provincial program on arts and multiculturalism.

Community artists, tribal education officers, and traditional community leaders were gathering in the meeting room (actually, it was the Bingo Hall). We all sat in a circle. All participants had to introduce themselves and state why they were attending the meeting. One person scheduled to make a presentation was absent, so the chair of the meeting started without her. After some conversation and discussion about Aboriginal involvement in provincial arts programs the absent guest came storming into the room. She plopped herself into a vacant chair and, without greetings or pleasantries, interrupted the conversation and said, "I'm mad! I'm mad! I'm mad!"

We were all dumbstruck. She continued, "I was rereading an article I wrote about neocolonization and I'm mad!" She then proceeded to go around the room and criticize everyone there for not doing enough to assert Aboriginal rights in Canada. When her diatribe came to me, she looked at me and said, "And those academics that don't join us in the blockade are equally to blame!"

The angry woman continued until she exclaimed, "I'm exhausted." We were all still dumbstruck. Everyone was quiet while the angry woman caught her breath, still fuming from her tirade. Finally, one of our respected community elders, seated across from me in the circle, looked directly at me. She was in a wheelchair, and she wheeled herself forward to the center of the circle, locking eyes with me. I had this sinking feeling that I was about to get skewered by this traditionalist woman who had the reputation of being someone you don't mess with. She stopped and said to me, "Bernie, I just want to say that we are all very proud of what you are doing." She then turned away and left the circle.

At that point the entire circle broke up. I remember that I stayed seated and savored the moment when some of the Indians, some that I had the greatest respect for, affirmed my membership in the community. For me, at that moment, this was important.

My "perils" in the field—the surprise appearance of a former CIA anthropologist spy, the unfortunate backfiring of a joke and the subsequent inaction on my part, and the unanticipated posturing of "sides" between the angry woman and the traditionalist—are records of key experiences in my understanding of the contingent and context-dependent conditions of critical Indigeneity. Uncertainty about how the events would unfold left me feeling vulnerable to the vicissitudes of social relations. Each event was a negotiation that was codependent but not necessarily ultimately definitive. In each event, the conversations and the actions were enactments of the perceived social relations between interlocutors who were also trying to assert their own Indigenous identities. But those perceptions were then challenged and negotiated and all the social relations were consequently recalibrated. In each event, the present—as framed by the discourses and actions—was refracted by varieties of conceptualizations of how past conflicts exacerbate the tensions within Indigenous deliberations of identity. As isolated ethnographic events, they are curious for their manipulation of ontological shifts between Indigenous and non-Indigenous as well as among Indigenous Peoples themselves. These practices of being Indigenous are neither mutually exclusive nor temporally distinct because, when viewed as a sequence of embodied experiences over time, the practices of being Indigenous are not totalizing or fixed. When the stakes for Indigenous practices of everyday life determine the competence of individual enactments of Indigenous identity, when unexpected elements introduce uncertainty, then the complex interactions of subjectivities become intuitive responses based on experiences and anticipations of critical Indigeneity in action. I have suggested elsewhere that my response was based on recognizing the "contingencies of emergence" (Perley 2009). In the above ethnographic moments, my resolution of potential conflicts of Indigenous identity was based on recognizing the influences of colonial histories, Indigenous resistance, and personal experience. My perils in the field are not limited to my experiences back home in Tobique First Nation. Neither are the questions of Indigenous identity restricted to local Indigenous communities. My practice of critical Indigeneity would require different strategies of engaging a different set of social relations as I began my professional career in anthropology. Rather than managing perilous states, I had to manage trauma.

The Trauma in Colonial States

I was six years old when I experienced firsthand the trauma of Indigenous irrelevance in colonial worlds. It was my first day at school. My mother tells me that when she left me at the school I was standing there clutching my notebook and a box of crayons. I do not remember clutching a notebook or a box of crayons. I don't remember meeting lots of new friends. All I remember of that very first day of school is an impressionistic image of the school bus driver sitting in his driver's seat, twisted around so he could speak to me. His mouth was moving and sounds were coming out, but I did not understand them. I was sitting in the front seat with tears running down my cheeks. I spoke only Maliseet and the bus driver spoke only English.

I remember that day as the day my language failed me. Not only did the language fail me, all truth and certainty were rendered meaningless. I learned a hard lesson about colonial domination and Indigenous irrelevance that day. Indigenous experience and identity were irrelevant outside of the Indigenous community. Indigeneity was not a viable category of personhood. It was a null set. That single day of feeling alienated from my traditional homeland would be repeated in the decades to follow as I adjusted to colonial regimes of control and the disempowerment of Indigenous Peoples. I remember that day as the day that I began to learn how to practice critical Indigeneity. Today, every time I recall or talk about that day the visceral anguish I experienced returns. The trauma of alienation and disempowerment never goes away. It is reinforced in colonial regimes of power and control.

I've tried using English words to express my trauma on realizing the irrelevance of Indigenous experience from the perspective of a six-year-old. But those words are inadequate. Equally inadequate is my professional training in anthropology. It is important for me to recognize that that traumatic day would lead me to pursue a profession that supports Indigenous lifeways but that the academic "publish or perish" expectations fall short in helping me achieve my goal of capturing visceral emotive experiences.

Picturing Critical Indigeneity

It was cold and it was raining when I had to give my colloquium presentation. I had to transport the presentation from home to the lecture room. The audience was already in the room and I was a little late. The audience was watching as I assembled the presentation. The assembly of the unwieldy presentation was entertainment for the audience. I had to erect three panels and mount three large canvases onto them. Then I unveiled the triptych, the three paintings that presented a graphic image of Maliseet language death, Maliseet language maintenance, and Maliseet language revitalization. In the audience were anthropology students and faculty, along with a few members of the university community. The "lecture" began with the audience watching me mount the paintings onto three canvas-covered four-by-eight plywood sheets. When I finished adjusting the paintings I turned to the audience, smiled, gestured to the paintings, and said, "Tadaaaa!" (See fig. 2.1.)

The audience applauded in appreciation.

My colloquium lecture was titled "Worth a Thousand Words: Picturing Linguistic Anthropology" and was intended to provide me with the opportunity to explain that the paintings were graphic ethnographies and that they should be counted as part of my writing and publication oeuvre. I gave a detailed explanation of the symbolism and argument presented across all three paintings. I also explained why the graphic ethnography was a closer approximation of emotive aspects of language death, maintenance, and revitalization than a written presentation would be. The graphic ethnography is designed to be a proactive ethnography. It is not an ethnography that represents a snapshot of community life. It was meant to be a catalyst for action. It was intended to be engaged anthropology.[4] When I finished explaining the purpose of my graphic ethnography the lecture proceeded to the question and answer period. The question I remember was asked by one of my col-

Fig. 2.1. Triptych as "graphic" ethnography. Photo by the author (2008).

leagues: "Do you consider these Art?" That was a fair question. My answer is yes. It is Art, it is ethnography, and it is a material record of the embodiment of my Maliseet identity.[5] The triptych was an exercise in putting the fragments of experience into a purposeful configuration of my Maliseet identity.

To adequately experience my representation of childhood trauma it is imperative to see the big picture. As a six-year-old I experienced the trauma and could not see the big picture. I've constructed the big picture today. As a wordsmith I can arrange a string of words to limit the slippage of floating signifiers. I am relegated to writing sentences to build a textual representation of trauma. However, words are inadequate. How, then, can I convey the visceral emotive force of trauma? I needed to use broad gestures and multiple genres. I needed to "translate" the visceral force by ripping, painting, sewing, and assembling all the pieces. First I had to re-experience the fragmentation of Maliseet worlds. I had to embody the experience of Maliseet dissolution. Second, I had to embody the reconstruction of the pieces left over from fragmentation and dissolution. I had to use my mind, my body, and my spirit to overcome the double consciousness of being Maliseet in non-Maliseet worlds. Third, I had to organize the experiences into three vignettes that represented three personal dispositions toward language and identity. The first tells the story of trauma and language extinction. The second tells the story of determination and language maintenance. The third tells the story of optimism and language revitalization.

Together they present a bigger picture—a multigenre, personal engagement with my Maliseet identity. Together they tell my story as I embodied the trauma of language loss, the determination for language maintenance, and finally the optimism of language revitalization. This project brings the past, the present, and the future into codependent intersections of my personal experiences of time and place. Just as words are inadequate to represent trauma, so too the graphic representation is also inadequate. The triptych must be experienced together with the accompanying text so that the emotive force of trauma is more accurately expressed.

The multigenre representations of Maliseet identity may be read independent of my presence or performance. Those instances when I can present these representations are opportunities to share such experiences with others. The unveiling was the first public sharing of my experiences. The second public sharing was at the 2007 American Anthropological Association annual meeting. The major differences between the two public presentations were, the first had the paintings present and the second did not; the second had "poetic" texts that were read along with the details of the paintings whereas the first performance did not; and finally, the audience for the first public presentation was largely colleagues, students, and other members of the university community whereas the AAA audience was composed of individuals with whom I was less familiar. Both public presentations were well received. This is not to say that the presentations were received with the same kind of appreciation. Rather, the presentations generated responses that prompted audience members to express their appreciation of my representation of emotive expressions—trauma, determination, and optimism. This would seem to be a positive outcome, but it raises some critical questions: Were these merely public presentations or were they embodiments of Indigeneity? Were the representations intended for Indigenous empowerment or general appreciation? Were the positive receptions I received from the various non-Indigenous audiences indicative of acceptable and expected expressions of Indigenous identity? Or were they examples of critical Indigeneity?

The simple answer to these questions is that through the decades since first grade I have found ways to manage the alienation and disempowerment that the suppression of Indigenous experience in colonial North America continues to perpetuate. My daily acts of living Indigenous traditions allow me to conceive of Maliseet identity embodiment as the ability to take fragments of Maliseet embodied experiences and assemble them in new configurations that move beyond personal Indigeneity and toward community self-determination. This strategy allows me to create the conditions by which members of the Maliseet community of Tobique First Nation can experience Maliseet lives in Maliseet terms. It also invites non-Indigenous interlocutors to participate in Maliseet world-making. My work as an anthropologist is directed toward Indigenous language and cultural revitalization. It is my attempt to promote the future of Indigenous living traditions. For the Maliseet I call the project Wəlastəkwi (Maliseet) Cosmogenesis.

Imagining Self-Determination

Wəlastəkwi Cosmogenesis is my deliberate attempt to initiate a new Maliseet cosmogony that incorporates the Maliseet language, Maliseet oral traditions, Maliseet prayer, and the Maliseet landscape. Wəlastəkwi means "Maliseet" and cosmogenesis is a general term referring to the origin of the universe. Together, Wəlastəkwi Cosmogenesis is the origin of the Maliseet universe. Key to my usage of this term is its application as critical Indigeneity—the everyday embodiment of Maliseet worlds by Maliseet people in and on their own terms, thereby constantly re-creating Maliseet worlds. The importance of this strategy lies in creating possibilities for Maliseet futures as variously conceived by members of the community. My intended audience is the Maliseet community and I am happy to share the project with other observers. The project serves multiple needs. I intend the project to serve as a catalyst for the Maliseet community to maintain and revitalize the Maliseet language. It serves as a personal commitment to reintegrate many cultural attributes with the Maliseet language. I hope the project can inspire other communities to develop culturally integrated and semiotically rich language revitalization projects. On a personal level, the project is important for reintegration. It is a personal repatriation of culture, language, landscape, and religion. It allows me to offer this model of reintegration and repatriation to the community. The potential for the project to change my status in the community cannot be predicted, as all members of the community are partial members in both senses of the word—part members and biased members. Again, I cannot predict the reception of this project on the part of community members, as I do not know many of the seventeen hundred individuals who belong (or who live in the community, or who call the community "home"). However, I anticipate that those whom I have worked with on language, culture, and education respect my skills and experience as well as appreciate my intentions. They will be very receptive to this project.

It is a project of many pieces. The most important piece is the legendary Tobique Rock, the primordial axis mundi, the center of my imagined and configured (Maliseet) cosmogenesis.[6] The rock is located at the confluence of the Tobique and Saint John Rivers. The second significant piece of the project is a reconstructed 360-degree primordial landscape as seen from the Tobique Rock. This landscape serves as the background for twelve panels that are thirty-six inches by seventy inches and are aligned to twelve compass points as arrayed about the axis mundi. Four of the twelve panels are oriented to the four cardinal directions, where east represents the first light of dawn, the first line of prayer, and the direction for new beginnings.

These are just the pieces in the first draft of the cosmogenesis project. Just as the triptych was an exercise in the embodiment of the conceptualization, the production, and the assembly of my multigenre construction of Maliseet language endangerment, maintenance, and revitalization, this cosmogenesis project is the embodied imaginings of being the first peoples of Maliseet traditional homelands. It represents the continuity of Maliseet worlds from time immemorial to the present so that Maliseet worlds will survive well into the future. How, then, do the pieces fit together? What implications do the pieces have for Maliseet self-determination? This question brings me to my discussion on imagining self-determination.

I designed the twelve panels to be arranged in a thirty-foot-diameter circle (see fig. 2.2). Within the circle, the enclosed space is designated for prayer and meditation. I designed, constructed, and experienced (and continue to experience) Wəlastəkwi Cosmogenesis as an act of prayer. Cosmogenesis is the direct result of my earlier work on the Maliseet prayer project in the tribal elementary school.

Fig. 2.2. "Cosmogenesis" as Maliseet experiential space. Photo by the author (2008).

The Native language teacher and I designed the prayer to serve multiple functions. It is a Maliseet prayer of thanksgiving, a lesson in Maliseet language, and a critical link to the Maliseet language, Maliseet prayer, and Maliseet landscape (Perley 2009). I coordinated the text of the language, the text of the prayer, and the text of landscape as interdependent modes of Indigenous experience. Each line of the prayer illustrates explicit connections to Maliseet lived experiences by locating the illustrations in particular places. I showed my drawings for the prayer to members of the community and they made comments such as, "I know exactly where you stood when you drew this." Together, the teacher and I designed the prayer to promote Maliseet spiritual and social relations across generations in the Maliseet language. Some of those relations that cross generational experiences include the students reciting the prayer to their parents, to their grandparents at home, and to general audiences at public events. The prayer project achieved our intended goals. My cosmogenesis project would develop a few years later.

I completed my research and my PhD and found myself removed from the Maliseet homeland. This allowed me time and space to reflect on the efficacy of the prayer project. I perceived the prayer project's greatest limitation was its textual form. Beyond the occasional performance, the prayer remained textually inert. My goal for language revitalization prompted me to look critically at much of the language revitalization literature. Much of the "best practices" focused on language nests, immersion programs, and technological panaceas. Language nests (multigenerational family gatherings in living rooms or kitchens in order to speak Maliseet to one another) were tried on the reservation, but they failed. Immersion programs were initiated but met with little interest from the community. Fantasies of technological cure-alls are always promoted but never realized. What, then, should the community do? Too often, the solution has been to dissolve the language from all the social and cultural experiences of everyday lives and focus on language practice per se. My solution is to resolve the social and cultural experiences with language practice. This is not an academic exercise; rather, it establishes the conditions by which members of the Maliseet community are immersed in Maliseet experiences. Cosmogenesis is a space and a place where Maliseet deep history in their traditional landscape is relevant to the Maliseet present and the foundation for Maliseet futures. I configured the rich variety of Maliseet cultural symbols and personal experiences to initiate emergent Maliseet identities. These emergent identities are not merely conceptual abstractions. When a person stands in the center of the arrangement, facing east, and voices each line of the prayer in sequence the individual embodies Maliseet self-determination and in doing so creates Maliseet worlds. My intention for the project was to immerse the participant in Maliseet sacred space and evoke the experience of the Maliseet sacred world. Despite my intentions, I cannot control how any participant will interpret his or her experience. Will non-Maliseet participants experience a Maliseet experiential world?

In September 2008 I organized an exhibit of my creative work titled *Journeys in Spirited Landscapes*, which included the cosmogenesis project.[7] The exhibit was both a retrospective of creative work and statement of directions for future work. It was not only an "art" exhibit and a presentation of alternative forms of ethnographic representation but also an invitation to experience Maliseet cosmogenesis. The goal was to present the exhibit as part of my academic research and writing. The audience included university students and faculty, American Indian students and faculty, and community members from outside the university. The responses from gallery visitors indicated that there was something for everyone. A physicist was captivated by a series of four drawings depicting the quality of light at four times of day at four times of the year (rainbow, starlight, dawn, sundogs).[8] An American Indian student was entranced by a nine-foot canvas that graphically represented the power of storytelling. Archaeologists were intrigued by the preparatory drawings for the "prayer" because they showed the organizational structure for the cycle of paintings. A geologist found "joy" in the twenty-eight-foot-diameter cosmogenesis paintings. A couple of weeks after the opening, a gallery assistant told me that an American Indian student visited the cycle of paintings daily to meditate. I share this to indicate that the mixed audience found within the multigenre and multimedia environment something that various individuals, or a variety of individuals with different backgrounds, could understand and enjoy. The exhibit was not about mutually exclusive experiential worlds. Rather, it was a coordination of familiar and unfamiliar experiences within constructed spaces where all could experience the Maliseet prayer of thanksgiving. On opening night I was there to guide the guests on a journey into Maliseet sacred space and assist them in experiencing the prayer. Afterward, gallery guests were left to experience the prayer according to their own predispositions. Do those various predispositions and the subsequent experience of the sacred space and recitation/reading of the prayer constitute experiences of Indigeneity? Critical Indigeneity offers an approach to answer that question. Critical Indigeneity is not an Indigenous-only experience. The exhibit, conceived as an act of critical Indigeneity, allows any visitor (Indigenous and non-Indigenous) to experience Maliseet worlds. In this ongoing colonial context (an art exhibit in an art gallery), colonial peoples cannot help but participate and experience critical Indigeneity.

Manifesto: Toward a Critical Indigeneity

I have to be honest. I was pleased to be one of three applicants selected for the short list that was drawn from over two hundred applications for an academic position. I was more delighted when I received a job offer. My skills as an anthropologist who can teach linguistic anthropology and American Indian Studies were being recognized. Those were my thoughts as my first year of university teaching was drawing to a close. My self-congratulation would come to a cruel end. My successful first year as a professional anthropologist came to a close when a senior colleague informed me that I was hired because they needed "an Indian" to teach the "Indian class." I was disappointed because I thought they hired me for my capabilities as a skilled anthropologist. It was not the first time I was disappointed by such expressions of dismissal and denigration. While working as an architect in Washington DC I decided to apply to the PhD program in anthropology at Harvard. The news that I had been accepted spread through the office, prompting one senior architect to remark, "They just needed to fill a quota." These disparaging personal attacks remind me that my experience as an American Indian will always be the experience of colonized peoples. It does not matter what I accomplish in the professions (art, architecture, and anthropology in my case), in various locations (galleries, business, and academia), and working among non-Indigenous personnel (employers and colleagues). I know from my experience I could never be equal. I will be judged through the lens of centuries of colonial subjugation of Indigenous Peoples. The trauma of alienation and disempowerment continues to be the daily condition of Indigeneity in the twenty-first century. These are harsh lessons and I learned them the hard way. What can be done?

My school bus experience was the personal trauma that stands out as the most alienating and disempowering experience I endured as an American Indian. It is a reminder that the oppressive power of colonial states and their institutions wielded against Indigenous populations on a constant and daily basis is a key condition of Indigeneity. Conversely, another key condition of Indigeneity is the everyday actions taken by Indigenous Peoples to assert their right to self-determination. Despite the rhetoric of postcolonial activists, many calls for decolonizing methodologies, and the UN Declaration on the Rights of Indigenous Peoples, it is hard to discern where those words have been turned into deeds. Words are not enough. Indigenous Peoples worldwide continue to struggle against oppressive state regimes, neoliberal interests, and the readily identifiable imagined mythic super Indigene that I call charismatic Indigeneity in their efforts to maintain their living traditions. That is why I shared my personal manifesto for Native anthropology from the 2001 American Anthropological Association annual meeting. That is why I organized the *Journeys* exhibit, despite the dismissal by my senior colleague. That is why I use humor, storytelling, and art in my anthropology teaching, writing, and research. All of these everyday practices of critical Indigeneity are engaged practices of self-determination against the daily traumas of colonial domination of Indigenous Peoples in the twenty-first century.

Manifesto

If we are to survive as Indigenous Peoples:

> We must continue to practice living our traditions on our terms, in our homelands, in our belief systems.
> We must resist colonial and settler society's unrelenting domination and oppression of Indigenous Peoples and their worlds by living our respective Indigenous traditions.
> We must practice acts of self-determination every single day.
> We must practice critical Indigeneity.

Acknowledgments

I would like to thank the University of Alabama Press for their permission to reprint figures 2.1 and 2.2.

Notes

1. I have been given permission from the chief of Tobique First Nation to use the name in my scholarly publications.
2. In 1990, in the municipality of Oka, Québec, the municipal government decided to expand a nine-hole golf course into an eighteen-hole course. The problem was, they were expanding into parkland and a sacred Mohawk burial ground. The Mohawk erected blockades and armed themselves as bulldozers approached to clear the land. The Québec security police force was called in. Tensions escalated and shots were fired. One Québec officer was killed. The Mohawk, the Québec, and Canadian armed forces were engaged in a two-month standoff.

   The Meech Lake Accord was an agreement between Canada's prime minister Brian Mulroney and the provincial premiers to recognize Québec as a distinct society (among other provisions) in order to ratify a new constitution for Canada. The accord was to be presented to all the provincial legislatures for approval. Canada's First Nations argued that they should have been consulted in the process.

Elijah Harper, MLA of the Manitoba Legislative Assembly, blocked the vote on the accord and thereby contributed to its defeat.

3. There were some complaints from members of the community that a white waitress working at the truck stop where the blockade was organized made racist comments about some of the children participating in the blockade.

4. By using the term "engaged anthropology" I am indicating that I am making a personal commitment to provide any assistance my professional training can offer to language revitalization advocates at Tobique First Nation as well as communities working on language revitalization projects. My position is more a personal need to be "part of the solution" rather than "part of the problem." There are contentious debates within anthropology regarding the theory, merit, and practice of "engaged anthropology." For example, engaged anthropology can be called "public anthropology," "applied anthropology," "advocacy anthropology," etc. Unfortunately, I do not have the space for a more detailed discussion.

5. I capitalize "Art" in this context with some ambivalence. I do not have the space to discuss the historical disintegration of American Indian sacred objects as "framed" by Western aesthetic principles of formal analysis and appreciation and displayed as "art objects" in museums and galleries. Similarly, "exhibiting" my work in a gallery "reframes" the work as "Art" as well as "framing" its "appreciation."

6. For one version of the story as told by Gwen Bear, please see "Koluskap and the Giant Beaver," at Virtual Museum of Canada, *Koluskap: Wolastoquewi-atkuhkakonol—Stories from Wolastoqiyik* (virtual exhibit), http://website.nbm -mnb.ca/Koluskap/English/Stories/story2.php.

7. Please visit my personal webpage, https://pantherfile.uwm.edu/bcperley/trickster cosmos/Welcome.html.

8. A sundog (parhelion) is a sky phenomenon whereby ice crystals refract sunlight to create bright spots at either side of the sun.

Bibliography

Canada, Royal Commission on Aboriginal Peoples
    1996 People to People, Nation to Nation/À l'aube d'un rapprochement: Highlights from the Report of the Royal Commission on Aboriginal Peoples. Ottawa: Minister of Supply and Services.
Perley, Bernard C.
    2009 Contingencies of Emergence: Planning Maliseet Language Ideologies. *In* Native American Language Ideologies: Language Beliefs, Practices, and Struggles in Indian Country. Paul V. Kroskrity and Margaret Field, eds. Pp. 255–70. Tucson: University of Arizona Press.

3

Culture Claims

Being Maasai at the United Nations

DOROTHY L. HODGSON

In contrast to other rubrics (such as women's rights) for demanding recognition and rights under international human rights protocols, claims of Indigeneity foreground questions of culture as a critical arena of political struggle and entitlement. In the face of long histories of condemnation and disparagement of their cultural practices and beliefs (especially their dress and adornment) as vestiges of "primitiveness" and relics of the past by colonial invaders, missionaries, postcolonial elites, and fellow citizens, Indigenous activists demanded that the recently ratified United Nations Declaration on the Rights of Indigenous Peoples include the rights to practice, protect, promote, and control their "cultural traditions and customs" and all "past, present and future manifestations of their cultures" (United Nations 2007, esp. articles 11, 31). Moreover, in addition to being a right to be protected, culture is also a means for certain groups to claim recognition and acceptance as "Indigenous" peoples by states, donors, the media, and other Indigenous peoples (e.g., Conklin and Graham 1995). As a result, Indigenous activists from across the globe have, over the years, developed a repertoire of visual signifiers of Indigeneity, many of which are (or draw from) the very same elements and objects that were the target of colonial and postcolonial derision and hostility, including feathers, beads, bright cloth, and body paint (Conklin 2007).

The United Nations (UN) is a key institutional site where Indigenous activists from across the globe gather to debate, discuss, and voice their claims to donors, state representatives, and others. But it is also an institution in which culture is often depoliticized and expressed through art exhibitions, performances, gift shop artifacts, cafeteria food, and "multi-cultural" gatherings. As such, the UN, especially the annual meetings of the UN Working Group on Indigenous Populations and UN Permanent Forum on Indigenous Issues, provides a fascinating space through which to explore how Indigenous Peoples deploy, perform, practice, negotiate, and challenge "culture" both in formal sessions and in informal interactions in the hallways, caucuses, restaurants, and streets of Geneva and New York.

In this chapter I probe the tension between culture as performance and culture as practice, between culture as display and culture as the basis for claims for rights and historical restitution, by exploring deployments of culture and displays of Indigeneity by Maasai activists from Tanzania and Kenya at the United Nations. Drawing on insights from recent work by anthropologists, historians, and others on the politics of dress and "embodied identities" in Africa (Hendrickson 1996; Allman 2004) and the cultural politics of "body arts" by Indigenous Peoples (Ewart and O'Hanlon 2007), I focus primarily on the visual aspects of the multiple and sometimes contradictory deployments of culture by Indigenous activists, UN officials, and others participating in UN meetings for Indigenous Peoples.[1] Specifically, I explore how Maasai, who, like other African groups, are relatively recent participants in the Indigenous rights movement, have learned and deployed the cultural codes developed by other Indigenous Peoples in the UN in order to buttress their claims to Indigeneity. I examine the relationship between Indigenous codes and ethnic codes and how individuals reflect and produce distinctions of class and cosmopolitanism through their complex sartorial displays and consider the political gains and costs of staking their claims for recognition, rights, and resources on culture instead of history.

Being Maasai, Becoming Indigenous: A Brief History

I begin with a brief overview of the history of Maasai struggles for representation, rights, and resources in Tanzania in order to highlight the centrality of representations of their culture to their political oppression and economic marginalization during the colonial and postcolonial periods, to outline the historical basis for their claims to Indigeneity, and to convey their long history of cultural fashioning and self-fashioning through the creative incorporation of new materials, images, and patterns.

For almost a century, Maasai have been perceived by Euro-Americans and increasing numbers of Africans as icons of "primitive" Africa, an image produced and sustained by their prolific representations in colonial travelogues and journals, tourist brochures, "coffee-table" picture books, postcards, movies, commercials, newspapers, billboards, fashion magazines, and other venues. As always, these static visual images—of men perched on one leg with cattle grazing in the background and women dressed in elaborate beadwork and colorful cloths milking cows—and stereotyped narratives—of savage warriors stealing cattle from defenseless farmers or brutal patriarchs controlling docile women—mask a complicated historical and contemporary reality (Hodgson 2001, 2005). Given the focus of this chapter on Maasai claims to Indigeneity, key aspects of their history include the following: Maa-speaking peoples migrated from the north into what is now known as Kenya and Tanzania at least several hundred years ago. Although they were originally agro-pastoralists, in time certain changes in technology (mastery of iron forging), climate (decades of relatively high rainfall), and social organization (the emergence of male age grades) enabled a group of Maa speakers to specialize almost solely in livestock herding and develop a heightened sense of themselves as pastoralists.

By the late 1870s the ethnonym "Maasai" was used by early Euro-American travelers and others to refer to these Maa speakers who specialized in pastoralism, in contrast to other Maa speakers who were agro-pastoralists or hunter-gatherers. The conflation of ethnonym with livelihood and the reification of Maasai identity as "pure pastoralists" were further reinforced during the colonial period with the division of Maasai social networks by colonial boundaries between present-day Kenya and Tanzania; the creation of Maasai "reserves" in both colonies to contain and control the seemingly chaotic movements of these seminomadic herders and take possession of their most fertile rangelands and permanent water supplies; and ambivalent colonial policies that sought either to protect and "preserve" Maasai "culture" by limiting their access to education, health care, and other "detribalizing" influences or to demand immediate, radical changes to their lives and livelihoods in the name of "progress," "productivity," and "prosperity" (Hodgson 2001; Börjeson et al. 2008).

At independence, the African elites who took power in both Kenya and Tanzania mocked Maasai as remnants of primitive Africa better to be ignored or forced to "modernize." As a result, Tanzanian government officials alienated and redistributed the most fertile areas of Maasai territory to more economically "productive" people and enterprises, launched a multimillion-dollar project to rapidly increase the "productivity" of Maasai livestock, promoted Maasai as icons of "traditional," "primitive" Africa in order to expand the increasingly lucrative tourist industry, and conducted national campaigns such as "Operation Dress-up" to force Maasai men to wear trousers in towns and forbid the application of ochre on Maasai bodies (Hodgson 2001; see also Schneider 2006).

As the reference to "Operation Dress-up" suggests, a central feature of colonial and postcolonial interventions into Maasai life were attacks on Maasai cultural signifiers—especially their apparel and adornment.[2] In the early 1900s, in the interest of "hygiene" (and commerce), colonial administrators encouraged Maasai to replace their ochre-dyed leather clothing with brightly colored cotton cloth and, for old men, plaid woolen blankets. In time, Maasai men and women eagerly adopted the new materials, which were lighter and required no labor to produce—although they did need to be purchased with currency or trade goods. Different clans and sections adopted distinct colors and patterns to distinguish themselves, used certain colors (such as black) to mark ritual statuses and occasions, and wore the cloth differently according to age and gender.[3] Women (who controlled and processed hides) continued to produce beaded and stained leather skirts and shawls for ceremonies and rituals such as marriage and circumcision, but these leather items were rarely worn for daily use. During this period Maasai women also incorporated new materials and designs in their beaded jewelry, switching from glass and ceramic beads to cheap plastic beads imported from Czechoslovakia (now the Czech Republic) and creating new patterns based on airplanes, watches, and other novel items they began to encounter in their lives (Klumpp 1987; Kratz and Pido 2000). Maasai men and women continued to apply ochre (usually mixed with cow fat) to their skins, and young men applied it to their long hair and often elaborate hairstyles.

Over the years the dress and appearance of rural Maasai have continued to change. Some younger men wear jeans and T-shirts at home, and most have a shirt and pair of pants to wear to town (Hodgson 1999). Similarly, younger women may own a dress or shirt-and-skirt outfit for church or travel to town. Those who have attended secondary school, have worked in offices, or live in towns rarely wear Maasai dress, even at home. But most rural men and women still prefer the comfort of draped loose cloth instead of tight clothes, zippers, and buttons. Ironically, while contemporary Maasai face ridicule of their dress by the government, media, and everyday Tanzanians, growing numbers of elite non-Maasai Tanzanian couples now incorporate a time when they wear "traditional Maasai dress" as part of their wedding ceremony and celebration.

The criticisms of Maasai dress and appearance reflect and inform larger attacks on their livelihoods by the state and fellow citizens. Under pressure from the World Bank, the International Monetary Fund, and northern countries to meet global demands for increased competition, the Tanzanian government has privatized key industries, revised land regulations to encourage the sale and alienation of land, promoted large-scale commercial agriculture, expanded the highly profitable wildlife tourism and big-game hunting sectors, instituted service fees for health care, withdrawn support for education and other social services, and encouraged pastoralists to replace transhumant pastoralism with more "productive" and less "environmentally harmful" modes of livestock "farming" (as opposed to "herding"), such as ranches. As a result, there has been increased alienation of pastoralist lands (especially drought and dry-season grazing land), competition for water sources and other livestock-related resources, decline in the use of health facilities, and increased impoverishment. As pastoralism becomes less economically viable, growing numbers of pastoralist men are leaving their homesteads to seek work as miners or guards and laborers in towns (May 2002; May and McCabe 2004; May and Ikayo 2007; Hodgson 2011, 2001; Sikar and Hodgson 2006).

About twenty years ago, in response to these challenges, Maasai and other pastoralists formed several nongovernmental organizations (NGOs) to advocate for their political rights and seek donor support for health delivery, education, water, and other development needs in the wake of state withdrawal. For various reasons that I explore in great detail elsewhere, many of these NGOs (by 2000 they numbered over one hundred in northern Tanzania) decided to join the international Indigenous rights movement as a way to circumvent the state and seek international support for their political and economic struggles (Hodgson 2002b, 2008, 2009, 2011). Briefly, their motivations included frustration with the failure of the

Tanzanian state to respond to their demands; concern over their escalating economic impoverishment and political disenfranchisement in the wake of state-implemented neoliberal "reforms"; a growing realization that they shared in common with long-recognized "first peoples" from the Americas, Australia, New Zealand, and elsewhere a history of discrimination by the state because of their distinct livelihoods and cultural practices; a desire to learn from the experiences and practices of other groups; and a strategic hope that by reframing their demands in the language of "Indigenous rights" they could leverage international support for their claims against the state (Hodgson 2008, 2009, 2011). Their involvement in the transnational Indigenous Peoples' movement was supported and encouraged by several international advocacy organizations and by a general shift in the interest of donors during this time from supporting state-sponsored development to financing the proliferation of NGOs that (supposedly) represented and worked with the "grassroots."

By reframing their long-standing demands and grievances against the Tanzanian state in the language of Indigenous rights, Maasai NGOs turned the cultural politics of their treatment by the colonial and postcolonial states on its head. Rather than continuing to challenge enduring stereotypes of Maasai as culturally (and even, at times, racially) distinct, inferior, backward, and primitive, these NGOs appropriated and reconfigured these fixed, ahistorical images in order to appeal to global Indigenous rights advocates and initiatives. As I discuss below, their decision to "become Indigenous" by "making place" (Muehlebach 2001) for themselves at the UN has provided opportunities for the expression and celebration of Maasai ethnicity, identity, and "culture," in marked contrast to their continuing experiences of disdain and disparagement outside of their communities in Tanzania. Yet their deployments of Maasai culture at the UN, especially through their dress and appearance, raise important questions about the possible political gains and limitations of foregrounding culture instead of history as a platform for political struggle.

Culture as Collage

The UN offices, events, and publicity associated with Indigenous Peoples are suffused with "culture"—in terms of images, performances, art, and artifacts. The UN website for the Permanent Forum and, while it existed, the UN Working Group, as well as assorted informational and publicity materials, often featured a collage of *National Geographic*–style photos of Indigenous people, stylized geometric shapes and icons (birds, hands shaking, spirals, animals, headdresses), and bright colors.[4] Similarly, the idea of culture as collage was replicated on the web page of the Secretariat of the UN Permanent Forum, where a rotating series of untitled images appeared in a photo box on the home page in March 2009. The images included a group of men in feather headdresses pointing into the air, surrounded by skyscrapers; a child playing a mouthpipe; an older Maasai man wearing a hat, plaid blanket, and beaded necklace; and a child dancing with musicians in the background. The men in feather headdresses looking and pointing up in the air (to other skyscrapers?) with the tall skyscrapers of New York in the background reflected the familiar (and tired) tropes of juxtaposing Indigeneity against modernity. The reflective older (Maasai) man looking into the camera suggested the wisdom of Indigenous experience. And the children playing instruments and dancing supported the idea of culture as something to be performed, displayed, and consumed. The lack of titles or descriptions for the photos emphasized their shared identity as "Indigenous," rather than their distinct ethnic affiliations or individuality as persons.

The "cultural events" for the 2004 Working Group were also representative—an opening reception featuring brief "welcome addresses" from key United Nations officials followed by cultural performances by Indigenous artists, usually accompanied by an exhibition of Indigenous art and/or artifacts. For example, the 2004 Working Group exhibit *Mamaa: The Untouchable Ones* featured "Wanjina works from the Ngarinyin of the North West Kimberley" in Australia, and the reception included "the official Ngarinyin smoking ceremony <<bedjagun>> performed by the Ngarinyin artists and lawpeople from North West Kimberley." Similarly, the 2004 Permanent Forum "cultural exhibit" included the following: color photos of Aborigines, two color photos of Maasai, several paintings from a Maasai artist in Kenya, weavings, Native American beadwork, headdresses from Ecuador, and a picture of Kayapon, an internationally renowned Kayapo leader from Brazil. The welcoming remarks from various UN officials were followed by a series of cultural performances, including an Aborigine playing the long pipe, a "native women's a cappella group" named Ulali, a

Fig. 3.1. Maasai artifacts in exhibition case at the 2007 UN Permanent Forum. The sheet in the upper right-hand corner of the case explains the meaning and function of each item. Photo by the author.

dance group from Ecuador, and more. In addition, most meetings of the Permanent Forum and Working Group included displays like the one of Maasai artifacts pictured in figure 3.1—enclosed in a protective plastic display case, with detailed descriptions of the use and "meaning" of each item.

Like the stereotypical images of Maasai that have long circulated in colonial and postcolonial travelogues, photo displays, media, postcards, and "coffee-table" picture books, the photos, websites, posters, cultural exhibits, and performances at the UN condense (and obscure?) long histories of marginalization, oppression, and struggle into a pastiche of photos and performances.[5] The UN presentations draw on and reproduce familiar tropes and images of Indigenous people as colorful, spiritual, "authentic," and artistic. The Indigenous performers are clearly complicit in these representations, and UN organizers try to attend to every detail (like the program descriptions) in as culturally "sensitive" a manner as possible. Yet the hierarchies of power at these formal gatherings are clear; the UN officials speak, the Indigenous delegates, with few exceptions, perform. As Beth Conklin, among others, has argued, however rewarding and inspiring these cultural productions may be for Indigenous activists, they respond "not only to indigenous values and internal societal dynamics, but also to foreign ideas, aesthetics, and expectations" (1997:712) about Indigenous Peoples (in her case, Amazonian Indians). According to Conklin (1997:712), Indigenous activists must draw on and appeal to "Western visual codes to position themselves politically." In 2004 I had a conversation with a woman whose organization had sponsored a Maasai man from Tanzania for the UN's Indigenous fellowship program. She complained about many things, including how he claimed outrageous and ever-changing travel expenses, requested that she buy him a computer, and failed to participate fully in his UN training. But perhaps most egregiously, she grumbled, "he didn't even bring a Maasai outfit!" Or, as Kyung-wha Kang, chairperson of the UN Commission on the Status of Women (COSWA), noted when addressing the 2004 Permanent Forum, "I used to think that when COSWA met for two weeks, we were the most colorful, but I must concede that this gathering is more colorful in clothing, culture, and traditions." Nonetheless, as discussed below, in the context of the United Nations, Indigenous activists must learn, understand, and respond to not only Western visual codes, but Indigenous visual codes as well.

Reading Signs at the UN

The opening session of the second annual meeting of the UN Permanent Forum in 2003 in New York was a lively, noisy, vibrant occasion. Indigenous representatives, most wearing some rendition of their customary dress, wandered around the huge meeting room greeting one another with hugs, handshakes, bows, and kisses. Many of the delegates seemed to know each other well, presumably from prior meetings of the UN Working Group in Geneva and other international gatherings and networks. I sat in the balcony, trying to make sense of the dizzying kaleidoscope of clothing, jewelry, ornamentation, hairstyles, and other cultural signs—Maori? Yanomami? Saami? I was certainly not alone in my inability to decode the dense cultural iconography displayed in the attire and adornment of Indigenous delegates, since many of the outfits drew on common tropes of feathers, cowries, beads, hides, and bright cloth. Soon I realized that my ethnographic zeal to distinguish and identify distinct groups was probably beside the point. Rather, much as with the photos featured on the UN website, posters, and publicity materials, while their dress and appearance was predicated on their ethnic identities, the overriding purpose of their apparel in the context of the United Nations was to signify "Indigeneity" to each other, government representatives, UN officers, and others in order to mark their connections to one another and difference from the rest of us, the "non-Indigenous." The boundaries of belonging (or not) were visually marked by cultural symbols that at once drew on Indigenous sartorial repertoires and were recognized as "Indigenous" by Indigenous and non-Indigenous alike.

Despite my confusion, I quickly identified several Maasai: a young man draped in a short, plain red-plaid cloth, wearing tire sandals and a beaded bracelet, carrying a beaded *rungu* (a short stick marking him as a junior elder in the Maasai age-grade system), with partially extended earlobes and teased-out hair; two middle-aged men wearing long, bright-red cotton cloths with circular aluminum dangles sewn along the edges, socks and loafers, and close-cropped hair; a wizened old man wrapped in a well-worn long cloth and red blanket, with extended earlobes, tire sandals, short hair, and an old khaki safari hat, accompanied by a young girl in printed cloth (commonly called a *kitenge*), beaded necklaces, socks, and tennis shoes; and a heavyset middle-aged woman with shoulder-length, straightened red hair in a dark skirt, a beaded red shirt and red shawl, pantyhose, and pumps. While certain key signs, such as the beaded jewelry and red cloths, signaled that they were Maasai, the differences (tire sandals versus loafers and pumps, plain cloth versus cloth with dangles, natural versus straightened and dyed hair) suggested distinctions of age, gender, class, education, and rural versus urban backgrounds. My ability to "read" the claims of similarity (being Maasai) and difference (class) indicated by their apparel was informed by my years of research and work with Maasai in Tanzania.

But other Indigenous delegates, donors, and government representatives clearly recognized them as Maasai and accepted them as "Indigenous" in 2003, based in part on their distinct attire and prominent presence at the Permanent Forum and other sites of transnational Indigenous advocacy as leaders, speakers, and performers. The acceptance of Maasai (and other African peoples) as Indigenous at the UN was the product of almost fifteen years of struggle for recognition (Hodgson 2001, 2002a, 2002b,

2008, 2009, 2011). Since 1989, when Moringe Parkipuny, a Maasai who was a member of the Tanzanian Parliament at the time, was the first African to address the UN Working Group in Geneva, Maasai and other African groups had, with the help of certain advocacy groups, pressed their case to UN experts, officials, administrators, fellow Indigenous delegates, and donors that, although they were not "first peoples" (recall the migration of Maasai into Tanzania and Kenya), they shared similar structural positions with Native Americans, Maoris, and other Indigenous Peoples in terms of their long-standing historical marginalization and oppression by colonial and postcolonial state actors based, in part, on their efforts to maintain their cultural and linguistic differences. In Africa, as suggested by the brief history of the Maasai situation, "the main groups that could be considered indigenous were pastoralists and hunter-gatherers, whose 'cultural distinctiveness' was in great part produced and predicated on their distinct livelihood strategies (especially their reliance on mobility and access to communal lands), which contrasted and often conflicted with the dominant, state-endorsed livelihoods of settled farmers, resulting in their economic, political and social marginalization as 'second-class-citizens'" (Hodgson 2009:8–9). Scholars and advocates have termed these arguments a "constructivist," "structural," or "relational" definition of Indigenous, in contrast to more "essential," "substantial," or "positivist" definitions that depend on evidence of territorial precedence.[6]

The success of African groups in achieving international recognition as "Indigenous Peoples" was facilitated by the emerging principle of "self-identification" among movement activists, whereby they welcomed (most) groups that claimed to be Indigenous, rather than subscribing to a strict definition or set of criteria.[7] Despite the political space provided by the principle of self-identification, however, Maasai, like other African groups, had to buttress their claims to Indigeneity by appearing Indigenous—not just to donors and UN officials but especially to other Indigenous activists. Without recognition and acceptance as Indigenous by other Indigenous delegates, these activists would have little influence and voice at Indigenous caucus meetings, in informal deliberations and discussions with other delegates about policies and strategies, and in the formal sessions of UN meetings. In addition, for those activists like Maasai who faced tremendous hostility from African state representatives about their claims of Indigeneity (since most African states claimed that all Africans were Indigenous), recognition and acceptance as Indigenous by recognized Indigenous activists provided them some protection, legitimacy, and leverage against state challenges.

While, given the accepted principle of self-identification, no activists who claimed to be Indigenous were barred from the UN proceedings, long-standing Indigenous activists and leaders communicated a lack of recognition in subtle and not-so-subtle ways. These included remaining silent or responding with a faint smattering of polite applause after the suspect delegates presented formal statements, ignoring them at caucus meetings, and not inviting them to the informal discussions, strategy sessions, and social events that were crucial for successful networking and the production of political coalitions and consensus. Almost every year that I attended the annual UN meetings, I witnessed the polite but chilly dismissal by recognized Indigenous activists of new groups whose claims to Indigeneity they suspected as mere political opportunism. For example, at the 2008 Permanent Forum I sat next to a delegation of self-proclaimed "indigenous Irish" representing three NGOs (Retrieve Foundation Indigenous Irish Council, Indigenous Irish Youth, and The Grandmothers of Mother Earth) who presented several statements calling for recognition of their sacred grandmother. Fellow activists responded with polite applause but little interest, and I did not see the delegation the following year.

As such, more recent activists, especially those from Africa and Asia, had to learn the accepted cultural codes produced over time by long-recognized Indigenous groups from the Americas, Australia, and New Zealand who started and dominated the international Indigenous rights movement. They had to develop a certain cultural competence in the deployment and performance of a dynamic repertoire of Indigenous cultural codes at the same time that they developed their political competence about the protocols and processes of effective advocacy at the UN. Most activists signaled their belonging in the Indigenous Peoples' movement in part through adopting their ethnic cultural codes to the dominant visual repertoires of Indigeneity. Since, as discussed earlier in this chapter, rural Maasai had retained their distinctive attire and adornment despite (and sometimes because of) repeated efforts by state representatives, missionaries, and others to force them to "modernize" their appearance, Maasai activists from all backgrounds were able to draw on these developed, dynamic ethnic cultural codes to present themselves at the UN as Maasai, and therefore Indigenous. In other words, since the meanings of cultural symbols depend in part on their context, the same attire and adornment that would be interpreted as "Maasai" in Tanzania (or Kenya) was read as "Indigenous" at the UN. Moreover, the intentional (and, presumably, sometimes unintentional) incorporation of seemingly "non-Indigenous" elements—likes pumps, pantyhose, and pants—did not undermine the power of the ethnic/Indigenous elements, at least for other Indigenous activists. Instead, these sophisticated sartorial combinations signaled what we might call an "Indigenous cosmopolitanism," a class-based cultural repertoire acquired and deployed by longtime, successful activists, including those who would rarely, if ever, wear ethnic/Indigenous dress in public spaces in their home countries.

I also quickly learned how certain informal and formal conventions of the Permanent Forum shaped the appearance and participation of Indigenous delegates. For example, most of them wore their "Indigenous" dress to the ceremonial opening meeting of the forum, which included extended Indigenous performances and welcoming remarks by high-level UN officials. On subsequent days, however, they might wear culturally unmarked dress, like blue jeans, pantsuits, and dresses, but usually with some cultural accent such as a beaded bangle, embroidered shawl, or head covering. There are at least two possible explanations for the pattern, both of which could be operating simultaneously. First, the opening meeting of the UN Permanent Forum was recognized by everyone as an important ceremonial occasion—full of prayers, greetings, and addresses by high-level UN officials (usually the UN secretary general, if he was available) and thus attended by all the Indigenous, state, and donor delegates. In contrast, subsequent meetings were focused on discussing different agenda items, so delegates came and went according to their interest in the topic and other demands on their time. Second, having established their Indigenous credentials the first day, they could choose whether they wanted to blend in or draw attention to themselves in subsequent days. Figures 3.2a and 3.2b show me with Ndinini Kimesera Sikar, a Maasai activist from Tanzania, at the 2004 and 2007 Permanent Forums, respectively.

In the 2004 photo Ndinini is wearing the elite rendition of Maasai customary dress—a brown cotton cloth (to look like leather) with a beaded border (a similar cloth is wrapped around her waist as a skirt) and a bead-

ed collar, headdress and bangle. The day after this photo was taken Ndinini wore a stunning silk dress, a black jacket, and pumps—a "businesslike" outfit similar to the one she is wearing in the 2007 photo.

The appearance of Maasai men reflected a similar range of social backgrounds and sartorial choices. The few uneducated men who attended (like the older man pictured on the UN website) wore their everyday Maasai attire of well-worn plaid cloth, beaded accessories, and tire sandals or tennis shoes. In contrast, elite Maasai men, like the lawyers and NGO leaders pictured in figure 3.3, wore brightly colored red or blue shirts decorated with aluminum dangles and colorful beads.[8] While chatting with one of them at the 2005 Permanent Forum (he was wearing a red tunic with beaded designs and aluminum dangles, black pants, and a hat), I asked him about his outfit. "Half Maasai?" I joked. "And half modern!" (*Nusu kisasa!*) he replied, chuckling. His response is telling, and it reflects the aesthetic dilemmas of elite Maasai, who seek ways to signal both their ethnicity and their class—thus the recent creation of beaded cloth shirts for men and "leatherlike" brown cloth drapes for women. For many elites, this was more than a performed identity like those found in many tourist venues (e.g., Bruner and Kirshenblatt-Gimblett 1994; Bruner 2001, 2004); it was a nostalgic reassertion and claiming of a still often fiercely held ethnic pride that took advantage of the elision or slippage between "ethnic" and "Indigenous" dress at the UN. Moreover, the adoption of these modern, neutral forms of Maasai dress asserted a shared ethnic identity in their public appearances that obscured the differences of nationality, clan, and section that shaped more private interactions among the Maasai delegates as they maneuvered for media and donor attention (Hodgson 2009, 2011). (And of course, the representatives of state governments, UN agencies, and other participants, including anthropologists, all dressed according to certain understood aesthetic codes—business suits for most men and jackets, skirts, pants, or other "business casual" outfits for women.)

Figs. 3.2a and 3.2b (*opposite*). Ndinini Kimesera Sikar, director of Maasai Women and Development Organization (MWEDO) in Tanzania, with author at the 2004 UN Permanent Forum (in UN cafeteria) and 2007 UN Permanent Forum (on UN patio in front of globe). Photos by the author.

Fig. 3.3. Maasai activists from Kenya, wearing red and blue beaded cotton shirts, speaking at a side event about mining issues in Kenya. 2004 UN Permanent Forum on Indigenous Issues. Photo by the author.

In addition to daily patterns of dress, every morning the formal plenary session was opened by a performance and/or prayer from a different Indigenous group. Often the words of these performances were not translated, so people continued to talk and move around while they occurred. So, for example, at the UN Permanent Forum on May 10, 2004 (the annual theme was "Indigenous Women"), four women from different Indigenous groups took the front stage to request "blessing from the four corners of the universe." They asked everyone to stand and hold hands as they prayed together. The next day a group Maasai delegates, two men and four women, opened the morning session by singing a praise song in Maa to their divinity, Eng'ai, onstage. Adorned in their ethnic finery, they stood proudly on the stage praising their god, savoring the admiration and applause of their fellow delegates at the end.

For Maasai activists, like other Indigenous activists, these and other opportunities to display their ethnic dress, sing in their primary language, and publicly praise their divinity provided rare opportunities to proudly celebrate their cultural heritage and language. Given the decades of attacks by the Tanzanian state, media, Christian missionaries, and dominant populations on Maasai dress, culture, and language, these moments of pride contrasted dramatically with the ongoing prejudice and disdain they experienced at home (Hodgson 2001, 2011) or the commodified performances produced for tourists (Bruner and Kirshenblatt-Gimblett 1994; Bruner 2001, 2004).

Although Indigenous activists actively embraced these opportunities to proudly display and perform their ethnicity, they also enjoyed challenging the assumptions and expectations associated with such cultural stereotypes. For example, an outdoor dinner hosted by the Swiss NGO doCip at the 2004 Working Group included performances by several Indigenous activists.[9] Toward the end, an Indigenous activist in full regalia (I have no idea where he was from) first played several "traditional" instruments and then, to the immense pleasure of the crowd, broke into a rowdy rock-and-roll song. Everyone danced together, beers and sodas in hand, cheering for an encore when he was done.

Moreover, as the topic of cultural rights became more central to Indigenous debates at the UN, the irony of the juxtapositions between culture as performed and exhibited at the UN and debates about Western exploitations and expropriations of Indigenous culture intensified. The 2004 Working Group meeting, which marked the conclusion of the first International Decade of the World's Indigenous People, also included several special events to commemorate the occasion. Indigenous people studying at the UN as part of its fellows program organized an outdoor celebration on July 22. After a long series of speeches and cultural performances, everyone in attendance was invited to join hands in several huge extended circles and dance to the steady drumbeat produced by about eight male Indigenous representatives from different groups (fig. 3.4). As I (reluctantly) joined hands, I felt like I was in some kind of eerie rendition of the Disney ride "It's a Small World," which has long served as the butt of anthropological jokes. Ironically, the key issue for discussion in the regular sessions of the Working Group that immediately preceded and followed the celebration was the "exploitation of cultural heritage." As Les Malezer, an Aborigine from Australia, asked, "Who gets to display our culture?" He criticized the Australian government for using Aboriginal art in its campaigns to

Fig. 3.4. Louise Arbour, then UN high commissioner for human rights, dancing in a circle with Indigenous delegates and others as part of a celebration of the decade of the world's Indigenous Peoples at the 2004 Working Group meeting. Photo by the author.

increase tourism and "brand" Australia as unique while simultaneously refusing to support the rights and claims of Indigenous Peoples. Other Indigenous delegates raised questions about access to and control of cultural heritage, possible modes of benefit sharing, and the protection of the "collective creativity of Indigenous Peoples" from the predations of nation-states and unauthorized use and exploitation by non-Indigenous people and institutions. No one, however, commented on the possible complicity of the United Nations in such cultural appropriations.

Visual Cultures

Given the centrality of visual culture to Indigenous activism at the UN, photography was a key site of claims making and controversy. Photography (still and video) was implicitly accepted at formal sessions, cultural performances, and other public, collective events. Figure 3.5, for example, shows spectators, many with cameras, enjoying a cultural performance as part of the celebration of the world's Indigenous people held during the 2004 UN Working Group meeting in Geneva. Despite this tacit understanding, I was stunned by how photographers mobbed certain Indigenous delegates as they presented formal statements at the 2002 Permanent Forum, closely surrounding them with cameras, video cameras, and occasionally, tape recorders. These "video vultures" (as I nicknamed them) were ever-present at the formal sessions, although their numbers seemed to dissipate in later years. Some videographers working for doCip and other advocacy organizations were recording the statements for posterity and dissemination, but others just seemed attracted to the novelty of capturing Indigenous delegates in full regalia addressing the UN. They were clearly more interested in the visual spectacle than the political statements being made.

The response to these "video vultures" was mixed. Some Indigenous delegates were willing, even eager, to have their photographs taken, while others ignored requests or just rolled their eyes. At the 2004 Working Group meeting I witnessed the annoyance of an Indigenous delegate from Ecuador, wearing a feather headdress and face paint, as someone took repeated photos of him without ever asking permission. In contrast, I sat in the hallway outside the UN conference room watching Simon, a young Maasai man, as he was surrounded by people (students? scholars? anthropologists?) asking to have their picture taken with him. He happily complied but requested everyone's email address to "keep in touch."

A few delegates cleverly took advantage of the "photo pariahs" to stage political protests during formal sessions that were clearly designed to attract media attention. For example, at the 2004 Working Group meeting, two members of the Free Papua Movement (Organisasi Papua Merdeka, or OPM), a separatist movement from Irian Jaya in Indonesia that has protested forced "Javanization," or assimilation by the Indonesian government (but has been accused of human rights violations itself), marched down the aisle in full "Indigenous" dress during the middle of a session, followed by a man carrying the movement's flag (often called the Morning Star flag). They then sat, stone-faced, while fellow delegates (and others, like me) rushed to take their picture (fig. 3.6).

The white sign held by the man with a camera case hanging off of his

Fig. 3.5. Audience members with cameras watching a cultural performance at the 2004 Working Group meeting. Photo by the author.

Fig. 3.6. Protest at the 2004 Working Group meeting by members of the Free Papua Movement. Photo by the author.

shoulder in the foreground of figure 3.6 reads, "Do we look INDONE-SIANS to you? Papua Merdeka!" The yellow sign held by the man clutching his UN Working Group ID card in the background reads, "Just Leave Us Alone! Papua Merdeka!" (I, of course, like others unable to decode the cultural markers and flag, had to ask other, more knowledgeable delegates who the protesters were and what they were protesting.) When the chair of the session chided the protesters for displaying the flag and setting a bad precedent, they rolled up the flag and sat quietly through the rest of the session.

And of course, as figure 3.6 also shows, many Indigenous delegates carried cameras and video cameras themselves—to record their own statements and activities for donors and supporters, to document the statements of other Indigenous delegates, and to capture memories of their experiences. (I was often asked by Indigenous delegates to use their camera to take a picture of them with some of their friends and acquaintances.) As Terrence Turner (1991, 2002), among others, has documented, the adoption and use of photographic and video technology by Indigenous Peoples to represent themselves, record political actions, and communicate their activism to the communities they represent has become a powerful tool of Indigenous advocacy.

Protagonists or Photo Ops?

As Kofi Annan proclaimed in his welcoming remarks to the 2004 Permanent Forum, the creation of the forum "marks a dramatic shift in attitudes. As I told you at the first session of [the] Forum, you have a home here." While Indigenous activists certainly do not consider the Permanent Forum as their home, they do recognize that the UN has provided them with a critical and rare political space in which to voice their claims, vent their struggles, and seek justice and restitution. Only at the UN are Indigenous activists now welcome to directly address state representatives, donors, UN officers, and each other in a regular, internationally recognized, state-sanctioned forum. Yet, as the various examples included in this chapter suggest, this unique political space is deeply infused with culture in its various manifestations. Through its website, publicity materials, exhibits, and formal programs, the United Nations celebrates culture, especially

Indigenous culture, as performance and display. Indigenous delegates like Maasai signal their access to the space and belonging to the emergent collectivity of "Indigenous Peoples" through a careful crafting of their own images and visibility that simultaneously appeals to prevailing Indigenous and Western visual codes of Indigeneity.

As a result, "culture" rather than "history" has become the central strategy for making political claims for recognition, resources, and rights at the UN (Hodgson 2002a, 2009, 2011). Complicated stories of historical injustice are condensed in cultural signifiers that, merely by their association with Indigeneity, imply a shared past of oppression and marginalization. Such strategic positionings have been fundamental to the success of Indigenous Peoples in building an effective transnational social movement, especially given the tremendous importance of "the visual" to their ability to make political claims and build support through media coverage, websites, and other visually based information and communication technologies. Moreover, for activists from Africa (and Asia) who have only recently become involved with the international Indigenous Peoples movement, the need to stress and symbolically mark their cultural connections with recognized Indigenous Peoples has been heightened, given the still-evolving definitions of Indigeneity.

Some scholars have argued that the reliance of Indigenous activists on this kind of symbolic politics is precarious precisely because it masks the complexities of history, social change, and power that have produced their contemporary struggles and situations (Conklin and Graham 1995; Conklin 1997; Sylvain 2002). By reproducing and responding to Western imaginaries of Indigenous culture as a reified representation of some kind of fixed, ahistorical essence, to be encountered through performance and display, these strategies, they argue, obscure the dynamic and complicated realities of cultural meanings and practices for Indigenous Peoples in their everyday lives as parents, workers, spouses, and citizens.

Although these are important concerns, they fail to capture the complex motivations and agency of Indigenous Peoples as they position themselves symbolically as well as politically to make claims on states and international institutions. As described in this chapter, for Maasai and other Indigenous activists, the opportunities provided by the UN to proudly and publically wear their ethnic dress, praise their deities, and speak their primary languages without fear of disparagement and denigration are rare, significant, and sometimes emotional experiences; the capacity to present these forms of expression in an honored forum makes the emotional experience especially powerful. Moreover, Maasai, like other African and Indigenous Peoples, have long adopted their clothing and adornment in response to the availability of new materials, shifting social codes, the protocols of different places and contexts, and individual tastes, desires, and creativity (cf. Allman 2004; Ewart and O'Hanlon 2007). These changes in aesthetic preferences mirror changes in cultural practices and beliefs as well, a vibrant, contested process that is hard to capture in the temporally fixed representations of UN websites, photo ops, video vultures, and cultural performances.

Finally, these activists are choosing to represent themselves in ways that respond to structures of power—both Western and Indigenous—that shape what is possible, appropriate, and politically pragmatic but also in ways that are a visible expression of their claims to self-identification and self-determination, the central principles advocated by the Indigenous rights movement. The participation of Maasai and other Indigenous activists in these cultural performances and representations of Indigeneity at the UN does not, therefore, diminish their political agency or discredit their motives. Instead, they suggest, perhaps, ways of bridging the binaries of "photo op" versus "protagonist," of culture as "display" versus "practice," in novel if complicated ways.

Acknowledgments

This chapter is based on ethnographic research at meetings of the UN Permanent Forum in New York (2003–5, 2007–9) and the UN Working Group in Geneva (2004), as well as over twenty-five years of historical and ethnographic research with Maasai in Tanzania on the cultural politics of gender, ethnicity, class, and, more recently, Indigeneity. Sections of it are drawn from Hodgson 2011 and 2009. Support for research and writing for the project were provided by the John Simon Guggenheim Foundation, American Council of Learned Societies, Fulbright-Hays, National Endowment for the Humanities, Center for Advanced Study in the Behavioral Sciences, and Rutgers University Competitive Fellowship Leave Program.

I am grateful to the many people in Tanzania who have shared their lives and words with me, to Laurie Graham and Glenn Penny for encouraging me to reflect further on the UN as a space for performing Indigeneity, and to the participants of the "Performing Indigeneity" workshop for their critical comments and suggestions.

Notes

1. Although Graham (2002), among others, has analyzed the symbolic and political significance of the acoustic realm, especially language choice, to claims of Indigeneity, the visual realm is widely acknowledged as the dominant site for cultural representations, circulations, contestations, and claims in the contemporary world (Jay 1992).
2. Certain rituals, such as male age-grade ceremonies, were also attacked, especially in Kenya, but with little success (Hodgson 2001). For thoughtful reflections on the origins and consequences of the persistence of pastoralist stereotypes, see Kratz and Gordon 2002; Galaty 2002.
3. See Hodgson 2005 for the meanings and associations of different colors; Klumpp 1987 and Kratz and Pido 2000 for a discussion of different styles and of women's use of beadwork and color to signal ethnicity, clan, section, and other affiliations.
4. The UN Working Group on Indigenous Populations was disbanded in 2007, after the establishment and institutionalization of the UN Permanent Forum on Indigenous Issues. It was replaced, in part, by a more powerfully situated Expert Mechanism on the Rights of Indigenous Peoples.
5. Lutz and Collins (1993) make similar arguments in their analysis of photos from *National Geographic*.
6. For a discussion of these debates and use of these terms, see Berge 1993; Kingsbury 1998; Murumbi 1994; Saugestad 2001a, 2001b; Wæhle 1990; Hodgson 2002a, 2009, 2011.
7. For more about the principle of self-identification in facilitating the involvement of Africans, see Hodgson 2009, 2011.
8. The aluminum dangles are a recent adaptation that distinguishes Maasai visually as well as aurally—the dangles produced a noticeable rhythmic jangle as Maasai men and women walked down the hallway and into the UN chamber.
9. doCip is the Indigenous People's Center for Documentation, Research and Information. Its activities include documenting Indigenous activism and supporting and serving Indigenous activists at UN meetings and other fora by providing access to computers, photocopiers, and translation services. See www.docip.org for more information.

Bibliography

Allman, Jean, ed.

2004 Fashioning Africa: Power and the Politics of Dress. Bloomington: Indiana University Press.

Berge, Gunnvor

1993 Reflections on the Concept of Indigenous Peoples in Africa: The Case of the Tuareg. In ". . . Never Drink from the Same Cup": Proceedings of the Conference on Indigenous Peoples in Africa (Tune, Denmark, 1993). Hanne Veber, Jens Dahl, Fiona Wilson, and Espen Wæhle, eds. Pp. 235–46. IWGIA Document No. 74. Copenhagen: IWGIA.

Börjeson, Lowe, Dorothy L. Hodgson, and Pius Z. Yanda

2008 Northeast Tanzania's Disappearing Rangelands: Historical Perspectives on Recent Regional Land Use/Cover Change. International Journal of African Historical Studies 41(3):523–56.

Bruner, Edward M.

2001 The Maasai and the Lion King: Authenticity, Nationalism, and Globalization in African Tourism. American Ethnologist 28(4):881–908.

2004 Culture on Tour: Ethnographies of Travel. Chicago: University of Chicago Press.

Bruner, Edward M., and Barbara Kirshenblatt-Gimblett

1994 Maasai on the Lawn: Tourist Realism in East Africa. Cultural Anthropology 9(4):435–70.

Conklin, Beth A.

1997 Body Paint, Feathers and VCRs: Aesthetics and Authenticity in Amazonian Activism. American Ethnologist 24(4):711–37.

2007 Ski Masks, Veils, Nose-Rings and Feathers: Identity on the Frontlines of Modernity. In Body Arts and Modernity. Elizabeth Ewart and Michael O'Hanlon, eds. Pp.18–35. Wantage, UK: Sean Kingston Publishing.

Conklin, Beth A., and Laura Graham

1995 The Shifting Middle Ground: Amazonian Indians and Eco-Politics. American Anthropologist 97(4):695–710.

Corbey, Raymond

1993 Ethnographic Showcases, 1870–1930. Cultural Anthropology 8(3):338–69.

Ewart, Elizabeth, and Michael O'Hanlon, eds.

2007 Body Arts and Modernity. Wantage, UK: Sean Kingston Publishing.

Galaty, John

2002 How Visual Figures Speak: Narrative Inventions of "The Pastoralist" in East Africa. Visual Anthropology 15:347–67.

Graham, Laura R.

2002 How Should an Indian Speak? Amazonian Indians and the Symbolic Politics of Language in the Global Public Sphere. In Indigenous Movements, Self-

Representation and the State in Latin America. Kay B. Warren and Jean E. Jackson, eds. Pp. 181–228. Austin: University of Texas Press.

Hendrickson, Hildi, ed.

1996 Clothing and Difference: Embodied Identities in Colonial and Post-Colonial Africa. Durham NC: Duke University Press.

Hodgson, Dorothy L.

1999 "Once Intrepid Warriors": Modernity and the Production of Maasai Masculinities. Ethnology 38(2):121–50.

2001 Once Intrepid Warriors: Gender, Ethnicity and the Cultural Politics of Maasai Development. Bloomington: Indiana University Press.

2002a Introduction: Comparative Perspectives on the Indigenous Rights Movement in Africa and the Americas. American Anthropologist 104(4):1037–49.

2002b Precarious Alliances: The Cultural Politics and Structural Predicaments of the Indigenous Rights Movement in Tanzania. American Anthropologist 104(4):1086–97.

2005 The Church of Women: Gendered Encounters between Maasai and Missionaries. Bloomington: Indiana University Press.

2008 Cosmopolitics, Neoliberalism, and the State: The Indigenous Rights Movement in Africa. *In* Anthropology and the New Cosmopolitanism: Rooted, Feminist and Vernacular Perspectives. Pnina Werbner, ed. Pp. 215–30. Oxford: Berg.

2009 Becoming Indigenous in Africa. African Studies Review 52(3):1–32.

2011 Being Maasai, Becoming Indigenous: Postcolonial Politics in a Neoliberal World. Bloomington: Indiana University Press.

Jay, Martin

1992 Scopic Regimes of Modernity. *In* Modernity and Identity. Scott Lash and Jonathan Friedman, eds. Pp. 178–195. Oxford: Blackwell.

Kingsbury, Benedict

1998 "Indigenous Peoples" in International Law: A Constructivist Approach to the Asian Controversy. American Journal of International Law 92(3):414–57.

Klumpp, Donna

1987 Maasai Art and Society: Age and Sex, Time and Space, Cash and Cattle. PhD dissertation, Teachers College, Columbia University.

Kratz, Corinne A., and Donna Pido

2000 Gender, Ethnicity and Social Aesthetics in Maasai and Okiek Beadwork. *In* Rethinking Pastoralism in Africa: Gender, Culture and the Myth of the Patriarchal Pastoralist. Dorothy L. Hodgson, ed. Pp. 43–71. Oxford: James Currey.

Kratz, Corinne A., and Robert J. Gordon

2002 Persistent Popular Images of Pastoralists. Visual Anthropology 15:247–65.

Lutz, Catherine A., and Jane L. Collins

1993 Reading *National Geographic*. Chicago: University of Chicago Press.

MacCannell, Dean

1976 The Tourist: A New View of the Leisure Class. New York: Schocken Books.

May, Ann

    2002 Unexpected Migrations: Urban Labor Migration of Rural Youth and Maasai Pastoralists in Tanzania. PhD dissertation, Department of Anthropology, University of Colorado.

May, Ann, and Frances Ndipapa Ole Ikayo

    2007 Wearing *Ilkarash*: Narratives of Image, Identity and Change among Maasai Labour Migrants in Tanzania. Development and Change 38(2):275–98.

May, Ann, and J. Terrence McCabe

    2004 City Work in a Time of AIDS: Maasai Labor Migration in Tanzania. Africa Today 51(2):3–32.

Muehlebach, Andrea

    2001 "Making Place" at the United Nations: Indigenous Cultural Politics at the U.N. Working Group on Indigenous Populations. Cultural Anthropology 16(3):415–48.

Murumbi, Daniel

    1994 The Concept of Indigenous. Indigenous Affairs 1:52–57.

O'Hanlon, Michael

    2007 Body Arts and Modernity: An Introduction. *In* Body Arts and Modernity. Elizabeth Ewart and Michael O'Hanlon, eds. Pp. 1–17. Wantage, UK: Sean Kingston Publishing.

Saugestad, Sidsel

    2001a Contested Images: "First Peoples" or "Marginalized Minorities" in Africa? *In* Africa's Indigenous Peoples: "First Peoples" or "Marginalized Minorities"? Alan Barnard and Justin Kenrick, eds. Pp. 299–322. Edinburgh: Centre for African Studies, University of Edinburgh.

    2001b The Inconvenient Indigenous: Remote Area Development in Botswana, Donor Assistance, and the First People of the Kalahari. Uppsala: Nordic Africa Institute.

Schneider, Leander

    2006 The Maasai's New Clothes: A Developmentalist Modernity and Its Exclusions. Africa Today 53(1):100–131.

Sikar, Ndinini Kimesera, and Dorothy L. Hodgson

    2006 In the Shadows of the MDGs: The Situation of Pastoralist Women and Children in Tanzania. Indigenous Affairs 1:30–37.

Sylvain, Renee

    2002 "Land, Water and Truth": San Identity and Global Indigenism. American Anthropologist 104(4):1074–85.

Turner, Terence

    1991 Representing, Resisting, Rethinking: Historical Transformations of Kayapo Culture and Anthropological Consciousness. *In* Colonial Situations: Essays on the Contextualization of Ethnographic Knowledge. George Stocking, ed. Pp. 285–313. Madison: University of Wisconsin Press.

2002 Representation, Politics and Cultural Imagination in Indigenous Video: General Points and Kayapo Examples. *In* Media Worlds: Anthropology on New Terrain. Faye Ginsburg, Lila Abu-Lughod, and Brian Larkin, eds. Pp. 75–89. Berkeley: University of California Press.

United Nations

2007 Declaration on the Rights of Indigenous Peoples. United Nations General Assembly Resolution 61/295. September 13.

Wæhle, Espen

1990 Africa and the Concept of Indigenous Peoples. IWGIA Yearbook 1990:144–48.

4

A White Face for the Cofán Nation?

Randy Borman and the
Ambivalence of Indigeneity

MICHAEL L. CEPEK

According to commonly accepted criteria, the Cofán people of Amazonian Ecuador are an undeniably "Indigenous" ethnic group. Numbering approximately 1,200, they are the earliest recorded inhabitants of the region, and their myths contain innumerable references to the cultural and natural features of the lands on which they live.[1] They reside in scattered settlements along the rivers of western Amazonia's forests, on which they depend for the majority of their necessities. Although they are increasingly bilingual in Spanish, their main means of communication continues to be A'ingae, an unclassified language (Fischer 2007). In addition, the Cofán maintain a rich shamanic practice, and their knowledge of plant-based medicines is renowned throughout the area. As a marginal and oppressed people, they face serious threats from the transnational petroleum industry, the Colombian civil war and drug trade, and an expanding colonization front.[2] While in some cases an ethnic group's Indigeneity is in dispute because of uncertainties regarding historical depth, sociocultural continuity, or distinctness from settler populations, the Cofán would appear to be immune to any such questioning.

There is, however, one striking fact that complicates perceptions of Cofán people's Indigeneity: their most important political representative is Randy Borman, a man whose blue eyes, pale skin, and flawless English point directly to his Euro-American descent. Borman was born in the region to a couple affiliated with the Summer Institute of Linguistics, and he spent most of his early childhood in the Cofán community of Dureno. After attending missionary schools and urban universities, he married a Cofán woman, founded the village of Zábalo, and became a central player in Cofán political activism. Although trilingual in English, Spanish, and A'ingae, he identifies primarily as Cofán—a claim that his Cofán family members, coresidents, and political allies acknowledge and accept.

Over the past decade and a half, Borman has emerged as a popular, if peculiar, icon of Amazonian Indigeneity. His story has been told in episodes on CBS's *America Tonight* (1994), Australian *60 Minutes* (1998), *A&E Investigative Reports* (2001), and *National Geographic Today* (2003). He has appeared in *Life* magazine (1993), *Earth Island Journal* (1994), *Condé Nast Traveler* (1998), and *Cultural Survival Quarterly* (1999). He is a supporting figure in Joe Kane's *Savages* (1995) and the central character in *Amazon Stranger* (1996), a book about Zábalo's fight against the oil industry by the journalist Mike Tidwell. Alison Brysk suggests that, alongside Rigoberta Menchú and Subcomandante Marcos, Borman is one of the most important faces of Latin America's transnational Indigenous movement. In her words, "Randy Borman personifies the collisions brought about by globalization" (Brysk 2000:4).

In this chapter I explore Borman's position in order to reflect on the contextual nature and cultural dynamics of claims to Indigeneity. For ethical, political, and intellectual reasons, I privilege the perspectives of Borman and the wider Ecuadorian Cofán community. My central stance is that if Cofán people deem Borman to be Cofán—and if Borman thinks of himself as Cofán—then he is, in fact, Cofán. By extension, he is also Indigenous, given the Cofán nation's unquestionable status as an Indigenous People. I suggest that Borman's cultural and political persona represents one of the most provocative performances of Indigeneity in the global era. His case affords a unique perspective from which to reflect on three important questions regarding relations between ethnoracial difference, Indigenous identity, and contemporary political practice: First, what kinds of individuals can claim to be Indigenous? Second, who gets to decide on the validity of their assertions? And third, what is the relationship between the ambivalence of their identities and their ability to speak and to act on behalf of the people with whom they identify?

Borman's ethnoracial ambiguity suggests connections with a wide variety of topics in history and anthropology, including European and North American discourses of "going native" (Deloria 1999; Huhndorf 2001),

Indigenous Amazonians' supposedly "messianic" devotion to the leadership of ethnoracial others (Brown 1991; Brown and Fernández 1995; Cepek 2009; Veber 2003), and the complex relationship between the effectiveness and the "authenticity" of global Indigenous activists (Brown 1993; Conklin 1997; Conklin and Graham 1995; Graham 2002; Jackson 1995; Jackson and Warren 2005; Lauer 2006; Ramos 1994, 1998; Rappaport 2005; Viatori 2007; Warren 1998; Warren and Jackson 2002). One could emphasize Borman's commonality with the cases explored in each of these literatures. Instead, I choose to highlight his specificity. His genealogical origin points to the racial difference shared by other ambivalent figures in Indigenous histories, but Borman grew up with Cofán people, and he has identified with them throughout his life. Moreover, his central role in the impressive successes of Cofán politics makes him a unique international phenomenon. He is, without doubt, the most visible face and the most effective weapon of the Cofán nation.

I begin by sketching Borman's biography. I explore the development of his self-interpretation as a Cofán person and the steps by which he emerged as the Cofán nation's most important representative. I then investigate Cofán understandings of his identity. In my analysis of the logic by which Cofán people include Borman in their *ethnie*, I describe situations in which his identity becomes an issue, whether in interactions between Cofán people or in encounters between Cofán and ethnic others. I conclude by examining Borman's leadership within the context of Cofán social structure and value discourse, which demand ethnic and moral ambiguity of the individuals who mediate community-internal life and external sociocosmological domains. In this way, I argue that the ambivalence of Borman's Indigeneity is not simply the result of a juxtaposition of North American whiteness with an Amazonian lifeway—it is also a reflection of the dynamics of Cofán culture itself.[3]

Randy Borman: Biographical and Political Sketch

More than any other Cofán person, Borman has lived within a myriad of cultural contexts: Cofán communities, missionary bases, urban high schools, American workplaces, cosmopolitan centers, and universities in Ecuador and the United States. Although he identifies primarily as Cofán, he con-

Fig. 4.1. Randy Borman (*second from right*) and other Cofán leaders marching in Quito, Ecuador. Photo by Federico Borman.

tinues to operate across such locations. His constant movement supports the intercultural competence that enables his political activism in local, national, and international arenas.

Borman was born in 1955 at a lowland missionary hospital in Shell-Mera, Ecuador. He spent the first five years of his life in the Cofán community of Dureno. He simultaneously learned A'ingae and English, the language of his parents, who were assigned by the Summer Institute of Linguistics (SIL) to create a writing system for the Cofán. At the age of five, Borman began elementary school at Limoncocha, an SIL base camp near the Napo River. During vacations he returned to his parents, his younger siblings, and his Cofán friends at Dureno.

While growing up, Borman lived for a year and a half in Pasadena, California, during his parents' two furloughs. The majority of his high school education took place at Quito's Alliance Academy, a school populated largely by North American missionary children. He used weekends and vacations to visit Dureno and Limoncocha and to hunt in the highland valleys surrounding the capital. From his earliest years, Borman loved the forest-based lifestyle that Cofán people taught him. He took every opportunity to head into the jungle with a blowgun or shotgun on his shoulder.

Borman graduated from the Alliance Academy in 1973. After a summer in Dureno, he moved to Geneva, Illinois, to work in a furniture factory and earn money for his education at Michigan State University, which began the following January. After less than a year of difficult studies, Borman left the university and returned to the familiar locations of Limoncocha and Dureno. In December 1974 he went back to Illinois to take classes at Waubonsee Community College, where he studied for a year. After Waubonsee, Borman returned to Ecuador. Following a brief respite in the Amazonian region, he moved to Quito to attend the Universidad Católica, but he never earned a degree. Following college, Borman wandered between Limoncocha, Dureno, and other parts of Cofán territory. In 1977 he took a job in Guatemala to help rebuild after the major earthquake. After four months, he returned to Ecuador. With his saved money, he bought a canoe motor and worked with Cofán people to guide tourists who wanted to see western Amazonia's ecosystems, which were made increasingly accessible by an expanding network of oil roads.

In 1978, at the age of twenty-two, Borman committed himself permanently to a Cofán-centered life. At Dureno, he became an elected community officer and helped secure a land title. From the late 1970s to the early 1980s, he worked to form the settlement of Zábalo, which was distant from the colonization front. More than any other Cofán person, Borman recognized the need to establish Cofán claims in areas far from petroleum-based development, which was destroying the land surrounding Dureno. In 1987 he married Amelia Quenamá, a Cofán woman, and settled into life at Zábalo. In the mid-1990s he began to shift his residence to Quito after his three children entered school at the Alliance Academy. Although all of them identify as Cofán, Borman wanted to make sure that they would be proficient in English and Spanish. He knew that they would need significant educational resources to confront the uncertain prospects of the Cofán nation.

During the past decade and a half, Borman has resided mainly in Quito, where he lives with his family and manages two Cofán-affiliated NGOs: the Foundation for the Survival of the Cofán People (FSC) and the Institute for Environmental Conservation and Training (ICCA). He also works as an elected officer of the Indigenous Federation of the Cofán Nationality of Ecuador (FEINCE). During my main fieldwork years, he spent less than half of his time in Cofán communities. He told me that his ideal life would consist of equal time in Zábalo, other Cofán communities, and Quito. Borman begrudgingly accepts the fact that the future of the Cofán nation depends to a large degree on his cosmopolitan activism. He laments the great irony of his existence: he has dedicated himself to protecting a place and a way of life that his political responsibilities prevent him from enjoying. Although outsiders suspect that he manipulates his position to live a commodity-rich life in urban Ecuador, anyone who knows him well is convinced that he would rather spend his days hunting tapir and tending plantain fields in Zábalo.

Apart from their acceptance of his identity, Cofán people embrace Borman's leadership for a number of reasons. Many Cofán do not feel comfortable speaking Spanish, let alone English. Few are proficient in the skills typically demanded by NGO politics: writing grants and reports, planning projects and meetings, and forming alliances with pro-Indigenous and pro-environment outsiders, whether in Ecuador or abroad. In the last of these abilities, Borman truly excels. He has built solid partnerships with such institutions as the MacArthur Foundation, the Moore Foundation, the Nature Conservancy, and the Field Museum of Natural History. In conservationist circles he enjoys a reputation for innovation and reliability. His ability to appear both "familiar" (i.e., North American) and "different" (i.e., Indigenous/Cofán) inspires fascination and trust among representatives of powerful agencies.

At a deeper and more individual level, Borman is a very intelligent man with an encyclopedic frame of mind and a talent for strategic presentation, whether in English, Spanish, or A'ingae. He is a master at delivering pleas and proposals to any number of differently situated actors. In addition, he possesses supreme confidence in the face of political crisis and physical danger. Although his religious beliefs are too complex to describe in this chapter, I can state confidently that they give him a generalized sense of certainty and determination, even when the odds are squarely against him and the people he represents.

Borman identifies as Cofán. The question, however, is complicated. Borman talks about his embodiment of Cofán and national-Ecuadorian "cultures" and "worlds," and he often uses the terms "American" or "North

American" to describe the third element of his identity. Usually he says that he thinks of himself first as Cofán, second as Ecuadorian, and third as American. More often than not, though, he speaks of his "biculturality." Although his Ecuadorian citizenship is central to his self-understanding, he focuses mainly on his Cofán and American "sides." He asserts that his participation in both the "Christian" and the "Western scientific" aspects of American culture is compatible with his immersion in the Cofán way of life.

In the mid-1980s, after his move to Zábalo and his marriage to Quenamá, Borman's identity appeared to be set. Nevertheless, he had yet to emerge as the central Cofán spokesperson. In the early 1990s he led the people of Zábalo on their campaign against the oil industry (Cepek 1996; Tidwell 1996). From 1994 to 1997 he served as the elected president of the Cofán ethnic federation, which represents all Ecuadorian Cofán and acts as the official mediator between Cofán people, the national Indigenous movement, and the government. Both positions put him into regular contact with ethnic others as well as the national and international media.

Borman indicated in conversations I had with him that he has always felt somewhat strange about his reception by various sectors of Ecuador's Indigenous and non-Indigenous population. Most North Americans and Europeans view him as a unique yet supportable cultural phenomenon. Highland Indigenous leaders are skeptical of his gringo appearance and heritage, but lowland leaders are more open to his political representation. Non-Indigenous Ecuadorians rarely question him. Borman suggests that he invites conflicting responses from many Ecuadorians: to denigrate the *indio* and to accept the cultural capital of the gringo. In his own words,

Among the [Ecuadorian] government people there's . . . a confusion, because here's a gringo who's automatically of a status equal to—you know, it doesn't really matter whether your parents were blue blood or not—you're automatically accepted into that upper level of society just because you're a gringo. . . . But then to find out that this gringo, whom you have to accept as a social equal, is also an Indian—BOOM!—it twists their world thoroughly. And makes it very, very difficult to know how to relate. Because an Indian is something that you kick in the butt and offer him $1 for his potatoes. That's what an Indian is. Automatically dirty, automatically socially unacceptable, automatically very . . . you know, a nonentity. And to have that combined in one person throws government people. (personal communication)

The backing of Cofán people is the most important element of Borman's political confidence. After Cofán individuals elected him as a community leader in Dureno and Zábalo, as well as president of their ethnic federation, he became certain of his support. A recent FEINCE booklet—*Ingita gi A'indeccu'fa* (We are Cofán)—features a full-page picture of Borman directing a meeting. There is no explanation for why a man who appears "white" is a Cofán representative. The message is clear: as a Cofán leader, Borman is not to be set off from the others. (Borman had no role in writing or designing the publication.)

During the oil struggles of the early 1990s, Borman became aware of Cofán people's desire to declare him their public representative. He and three other Zábalo men traveled to Quito to gather support for their campaign. Before the trip Borman was uncomfortable wearing ceremonial dress in community-external political contexts, although he asserts that his discomfort in no way reflected his community-internal acceptance. At an essential moment, his Cofán compatriots "forced" him to assume the bodily appearance of a Cofán leader by demanding that he don traditional clothing and ornamentation in meetings with non-Cofán people. As he recalls,

> When we were getting ready to go over to the Fundación Natura [a Quito NGO], Lorenzo, Atanasio, and Mauricio [Zábalo elders, all monolingual in A'ingae, and all regular wearers of the Cofán *ondiccu'je*, or tunic] say, "You're not going in this suit, guy. You're going dressed up as Cofán. And we're not going like this if you're not." And that's when I told them, I said, "Well, I feel kind of funny going in like this." And they say, "We're the ones who can say whether you have that right or not, not them. Don't worry about them. We're the ones who have the right of decision." And, "O.K." But that, I felt, was the point where I really took on my role, my identity in the outside world, as a Cofán leader. (personal communication)

The Zábalo elders' choice was a wise one. Borman's leadership has been a boon for the Cofán nation. In the 1920s a measles epidemic decimated a population that had already suffered hundreds of years of demographic disaster. Only four hundred Cofán people survived. With the early vaccination efforts and medical care supplied by Borman's parents in the 1950s, the population started to rebound. When the oil boom began in the 1960s, however, many observers predicted the "extinction" of the Cofán. After Borman helped the people of Dureno get the first Cofán land title, the luck of the Cofán nation began to turn.

More than thirty years after Borman's initial steps toward political mobilization, Ecuador's Cofán population continues to grow. Currently the Cofán maintain legal control of more than one million acres of Andean and Amazonian forests, the great majority of which overlap with protected natural areas. Each territorial agreement came after a long battle, and Borman was central in nearly all of them. In addition, Borman has negotiated a set of mutually beneficial partnerships with Ecuador's Ministry of Environment, conservationist NGOs, and academic institutions. Many Cofán people now earn a living as park guards, research assistants, and tour guides.

The Cofán continue to face tremendous threats from the oil industry, a steady influx of colonists, and the spillover of Colombian violence, but their future looks increasingly bright. Few observers who witnessed the Cofán at the time of Borman's birth and childhood would have predicted their survival into the twenty-first century. None, I wager, would have imagined their remarkable accomplishments—nor, of course, would they have foreseen the central role of a "gringo chief."

Cofán Understandings of Borman's Cofán-ness

Although the Cofán have repeatedly elected Borman as their representative, he is not without critics. Gustavo Noteno is one of them.[4] As the eldest son of a former FEINCE officer, Gustavo, not surprisingly, took an early interest in Indigenous politics. Unlike his calm and nonconfrontational father, Gustavo is rather aggressive. His questioning of Borman, which typically occurs behind Borman's back, is more pointed than that of other Cofán I know. It is tempting to equate Gustavo's attitude with resentment and scapegoating. As a past community president, a liaison with unfamiliar European NGOs, and the owner of a tiny hut-cum-bar in a Cofán community, Gustavo has suffered accusations of corruption and unfair enrichment.

Any chance he gets, he works to shift attention to the uncertainties surrounding other political figures. As a powerful Cofán leader with a gringo appearance, Borman fits the bill all too well.

Although Gustavo's questioning of Borman's position and identity is not representative of the majority of Cofán people, its extremity is telling. His perspective appears to be influenced by his frequent interactions with other aspiring Indigenous leaders, especially those of the neighboring Napo Runa and Shuar people, whom most Cofán view as deceptive invaders of their territory. Gustavo has told me that these ethnic others ask him about Borman. He responds by telling them that he "hates" to be "commanded" by a gringo. On one occasion, conducting a community census for an Indigenous NGO, Gustavo refused to classify Borman as Cofán. He listed him as an *extranjero* (foreigner, in Spanish) instead. In another incident Gustavo arrived at an intercommunity feast with a canoe-load of drunken young men. His first words to me were that if I "wanted to be Cofán," I had to walk on the *camino de los a'i* (path of the Cofán, in Spanish) by getting drunk on cheap rum. He then proclaimed that Borman is not Cofán because he, too, refuses to inebriate himself with purchased liquor, the sale of which the people of Zábalo have chosen to prohibit in their community. Most Cofán laugh at Gustavo's notions of Cofán-ness. But they hope that one day he might apply his familiarity with the Spanish language and other cultures to more useful political ends.

Gustavo's criticisms are interesting because of their unique content and their direct delivery. Although their love of gossip and speculation makes the Cofán similar to many people in the world, they rarely voice hostile criticisms of one another, especially in face-to-face situations. When Cofán individuals question Borman's identity, it typically occurs in specific contexts and for specific reasons. In routine circumstances, neither the identity of Borman nor those of other people are objects of debate. Instead, a generalized assumption of shared Cofán-ness forms the background to community life.

The absence of a critical ethnic discourse betrays an important fact: in Zábalo and most other Cofán settlements, there is not a single genealogically "pure" Cofán person. For example, Gustavo's last name marks his connection to Quichua-speaking peoples, even though both he and his parents speak A'ingae and identify as Cofán. Even more extreme is the case of a past president of FEINCE who has absolutely no Cofán ancestors. By descent he is completely mestizo, although he married a Cofán woman, lives in a Cofán community, and has children who identify as Cofán. In comparison, Borman's ethnoracial ambiguity is not as extraordinary as it first appears.

Similar to many Indigenous Amazonians, the Cofán participate in an interethnic interface (Whitten 1981) with a long history and a dynamic structure. Priests, soldiers, rubber tappers, oil workers, and colonists have moved into and out of Cofán territory for centuries. Many of them had forced or consensual relations with Cofán people that produced children who were raised as Cofán. Most of them were *cocama* (mestizo), but some were *singo* (Afro-Ecuadorian) or gringo (Euro-American). In addition, the Cofán have intermarried with other Indigenous peoples for generations: Siona, Secoya, Napo Runa, Canelos Quichua, Shuar, and Witoto, among others. Some Cofán speak three or four languages, and there is a particularly high degree of bilingualism in A'ingae and Siona-Secoya (a Western Tukanoan language). Reflecting on their history, most Cofán laughingly admit that they are *echhoen'cho* (mixed). They constantly joke about the wide variation in skin tone, eye color, hair type, and physical size and shape in their communities. Their interethnic heritage, however, does not preclude their Cofán-ness, which is much more than a genealogical or racial fact.

Cofán identity is not a simple affair. People disagree—most often jokingly—about which of their coresidents are or are not Cofán. In different situations, a person may admit or deny the Cofán-ness of herself or someone else. One Zábalo resident with a Siona-identifying father and a Cofán-identifying mother told me that he is Siona when he is in a Siona community and Cofán when he is in a Cofán community. Usually he claims that he is "both." The same individual typically describes Borman as Cofán. But sometimes he labels Borman an "*a'i* gringo." (*A'i* is the A'ingae lexeme for "human being," and it also functions as a synonym for "Cofán" [Cepek 2012:57–58], which is how I use it in this chapter.) One day the young man asked me what Borman calls himself. "Cofán," I replied. He then concluded that Borman is clearly Cofán.

As a total social fact, Cofán identity involves both instrumental and essential dynamics (see discussions in Calhoun 1991; Hutchinson and Smith 1996; Sokefeld 1999; Spivak 1985). Although it makes a claim about what is most "basic" (Barth 1969:13) to an individual, Cofán-ness involves the recognition of a constructed fact: a person's practical enculturation as he or she labors to learn how to participate in what Cofán individuals recognize as their way of life, which they define in terms of forest-based subsistence, community-based conviviality, and use of A'ingae. In other words, one is not born into Cofán-ness, nor is it the product of an autonomous and instantaneous act of ascription. Rather, it is the product of labor-intensive development, which is itself socially mediated by the individual desire and the collective permission to accomplish that work in the context of a Cofán community.

The notion of a socially articulated and practically produced identity is a common concept among Amazonian peoples, many of whom view the person as a being under constant construction through forms of bodily, discursive, and ritual practice (Conklin 2001; Gow 1991; McCallum 2001; Rival 2005; Turner 1995; Vilaça 2010; Viveiros de Castro 1992). From the Cofán perspective, if identities are processual and substantive, they are also open. In other words, Cofán people suggest that, with sufficient time and energy, they can transform into ethnic others. In turn, they believe that once-different people can become Cofán. Moreover, they hold that individuals can reverse the movements as long as they have access to the appropriate social contexts and are willing to do the work.

At the most basic level, a person proves their Cofán-ness by residing in a Cofán community in a satisfactory manner. Typically numbering between twenty-five and two hundred inhabitants, Cofán villages are not large. Daily interactions create solidarity through laughter and mutual aid, but they also demand similarity. Cofán sociality can be disrupted by atypical individuals, whose psychological states, linguistic capacities, practical customs, and social norms can lead to identification as *fuesu* (other)—especially if they provoke violence, conflict, or tension or generate inequality.

The social and pragmatic logic of Cofán-ness underpins the position of such ambiguous figures as Borman. In private conversations, most Zábalo residents are willing to entertain the complexities of Borman's identity, although they typically conclude by claiming him as an ethnic compatriot. In everyday interactions, I have never heard a Cofán person question Borman about his Cofán-ness. Given Cofán culture's suppression of conflict and confrontation, unwillingness to engage Borman on a potentially sensitive topic should not come as a surprise. At a deeper level, though, Borman's Cofán-ness is like that of all Zábalo residents: it is presupposed as the basic identity of anyone who participates willingly and felicitously in the peaceful flow of community life.

Given the mixed ethnoracial heritage of the Cofán, anyone's identity can be called into question if circumstances merit. Typically, ethnic exclusion occurs when individuals display behavior that contrasts with the expected comportment of a successfully socialized Cofán person, for example, when they are violent, stingy, or boastful or when they attempt to command others. For example, Cofán people denied a Zábalo man's Cofán-ness after he committed a violent act. His primary language was A'ingae, he spent most of his childhood in the community, and he married a Cofán woman, with whom he produced a house full of Cofán-identifying children. By all accepted criteria—and by the man's own assertions—he was Cofán. Nevertheless, the incident made people recall his father's descent from Siona people, whom Cofán associate with hostility and anger. Suddenly, villagers declared him "other." They labeled him an *a'ive dambi'choa* (literally, "one who has not become Cofán").

Borman, too, is susceptible to ethnic exclusion. During an interview about exchange and reciprocity in Zábalo, one community resident questioned Borman's generosity, stating that he sometimes refuses to lend his purchased tools to others. When I asked for an explanation, the man shrugged his shoulders, smiled, and said that Borman is a *sepipa* (prohibitor) and thus "other people." On a different occasion, an act of ethnic exclusion occurred as I was helping a team of journalists film an interview with Borman. They asked me to tell a group of young men to turn down their stereo, as the noise bled into the scene. When I explained to the Cofán that Borman wanted them to be quiet, one man called him a "gringo." He cited the request as an unacceptable act of "commanding." (Incidentally, the man refused to comply.)[5] In another incident I expressed my concern to a Zábalo woman about Borman's delayed arrival in the community after an extended absence. Although normally on friendly terms with Borman, she pointed to his failure to arrive on the promised date and laughingly proclaimed him a gringo *afopa'cho* (gringo liar).

Questioning Borman's identity involves calling attention to conventional understandings of "un-Cofán-like" qualities, which revolve around notions of reciprocity, inequality, and disruptive sociality. Nearly every person in

Zábalo, including Borman, is susceptible to accusations of ethnic other-ness. Typically, however, the Cofán-ness of Borman and other Zábalo residents is not in doubt because they happily and successfully perform the sociopractical norms that define life as a Cofán person.

I do not mean to exaggerate Borman's normality. He is clearly a unique figure, no matter how well he meets expectations of appropriate behavior. The ambiguity of his identity does not reflect Cofán perspectives on "whiteness" as an exceptional kind of ethnoracial difference. Rather, Borman's Cofán-ness is a particularly complex issue because he is an extremely prominent leader. His status as a political representative complicates his identity for two reasons: it exposes him to the questioning of non-Cofán people, and it places him in a position that expresses the paradoxes of Cofán social structure and value discourse.

As reflected in Borman's account of the Zábalo elders who urged him to wear ceremonial dress in a meeting with cocama officials, Cofán people realize that outsiders are suspicious of a gringo chief. In 2014, however, Borman is a familiar figure in both Quito and northeastern Ecuador, and most outsiders have learned to accept him as an Indigenous spokesperson. In a few special cases, non-Cofán people continue to question Borman's Indigeneity. For example, Borman and other Cofán leaders are aware that officials of the Revolutionary Armed Forces of Colombia (FARC), a left-ist guerilla group with a heavy presence along the Ecuadorian border, are hesitant to cooperate with any man who has a Euro-American heritage. In contrast, the FARC gives other Cofán people free passage through lands that it controls, as the guerillas claim an anti-imperialist alliance with the region's Indigenous Peoples. When I explained to the same Zábalo woman who called Borman a "gringo liar" that he could not travel to certain border communities because he risked kidnapping or murder, she expressed shock, dismay, and concern. In a strident tone, she said that Borman should explain to the FARC that he is an *A'ingae afa'je'cho* (a Cofán-speaker), that he was *a'i coen'cho* (raised as Cofán), and that he has an *a'i injama'cho* (a Cofán heart). In other words, he should tell them that he is, despite appearances, Cofán.

One of the Zábalo elders who encouraged Borman to don his tunic and feather crown for the Quito meetings told me about the early days of Borman's leadership. He explained that the Cofán accepted Borman but that they had to express their reasons for doing so to critical others. In his words,

[When in Dureno] Randy was just a small child. He grew up and he spoke all of our language. He understood well. And he would say, "I'm a'i." That's what he would say. The cocama didn't like that. They would say that he's a gringo, that he's not really a'i. That's what the cocama would say. That he's a gringo, that he's a liar. They used to speak like that. But then we said, "No, he's not a gringo. He's a'i. We raised him from when he was a little child, really small like this [raising his hand a couple feet off the floor]. That's why he's helping us." We'd say that, and the cocama would stop and think and not know what to say [laughs]!

Perhaps the most defining Cofán defense of Borman's identity occurred during an important political act: the people of Zábalo's 1993 "takeover" of the Paujil exploratory well, which Petroecuador illegally constructed near their territory. The Cofán invited a pair of gringo allies on their long hike to the drilling site because they wanted their act to be videotaped and publicized for the international media. At least two television documentaries featured the episode, which eventually led to the expulsion of oil companies from Zábalo territory. After the Cofán contingent reached the site, confronted the workers with palm-wood spears, and halted the operation, a military unit arrived in a helicopter. An enraged Ecuadorian colonel refused to speak with Borman, who wore a tunic, face paint, and a reed headband. Bolivar Lucitante, a longtime resident of Zábalo, confronted the colonel with an argument for Borman's rightful status as a Cofán representative. As reported in the documentaries, whose versions I have confirmed with Zábalo residents, the dialogue occurred in the following terms, as translated from Spanish by the producers:

> [NARRATOR:] When the delegation arrived, the chief negotiator was an indignant army colonel with armed soldiers ready for a fight, but not prepared for a gringo chief.
> [COLONEL, SPEAKING TO BORMAN:] Listen, you are an American. And I'm asking you, Do Americans allow us to come to your country and decide your fate? I will only talk to someone who is a native, with the authority to decide matters that affect the Cofán people.
> [NARRATOR:] What happened next was a defining moment for Randy and the tribe.

[BOLIVAR LUCITANTE:] Hey listen. He is a native. He was born here in Ecuador. You don't even speak our language. He speaks it fluently. He is a Cofán, and he speaks for all of us.

[NARRATOR:] Suddenly the army and oil company were facing Cofáns armed with a new weapon: Randy Borman. . . . When Randy spelled out, point for point, the details of Ecuadorian environmental law, it was all but over. You could see it on the colonel's face.[6]

Negative Identity, Value, and Political Representation

Employing long-held criteria, Cofán people accept Borman's claim to Cofán-ness. They defend him as their representative to doubting outsiders, who sometimes question his combination of Euro-American whiteness and Amazonian Indigeneity. Nevertheless, Cofán people recognize Borman as a special kind of Cofán person. Unlike most community members, he is a master at negotiating the dangers and promises of external sociopolitical domains. From their perspective, he possesses a level of agency that is beyond their reach. The ambivalence of his identity reflects most Cofán people's realization that he can do what they can do, but that he also can do more.

Observing a different situation, David Harvey (1996) offers a pertinent insight: many identity-based movements aim to transform or transcend the very conditions that unite their members. His main example is the collective struggle of homeless people. In a somewhat paradoxical dynamic, homeless activists fight to leave behind the basic characteristic—homelessness—that gives them an identity and makes them a collectivity. Ultimately, their movement is about overcoming, rather than representing, an identity that is largely "negative" in nature. In a similar sense, Cofán-ness has a negative component that is the object of a self-critiquing politics. The dynamic revolves around central Cofán values that orient Cofán people's social relations and guiding aspirations, and the important roles that individuals such as Borman play in their political projects.

In a very real sense, Cofán people conceptualize Cofán-ness as a set of incapacities. Many of their self-defining foibles and inabilities are objects of joking commentary. They typically involve difficulties in reference to which individuals can articulate their identity with self-effacing humor.

During my time in Zábalo and Quito, I witnessed Cofán people's admitted consternation in relation to a number of objects, questions, and actions, including their "inability" to eat or cook certain kinds of foods, their difficulties navigating Quito without getting lost, and their basic confusion with the instruments that compose urban environments.

For example, a group of Cofán people from a remote lowland community traveled to Quito for political and medical reasons. They stayed at the complex in which Borman's family and Cofán students reside. Unfamiliar with the "modern" setting, they washed their clothes in the toilet. The event led to hours of joking by the resident Cofán, who laughed with the visitors for being *ña'me a'i* (truly Cofán). Self-deprecation is an important form of Cofán sociality. It evidences confidence in a forest-based way of life and awareness of the broader geohistorical moment. Cofán appreciate their lifeway enough to find self-mockery a benign form of humor, even if they realize that many Ecuadorians see them as nothing more than country bumpkins and savage indios.

Other aspects of Cofán-ness, such as not being able to speak Spanish or earn money, are more serious concerns. The most negative elements arise in commentary surrounding atypical individuals, such as Borman. Reflecting on Borman's unique capacities, one Zábalo resident said,

> Is Randy really a'i? Has he really become a'i? He knows a'i customs. He lives, like an a'i he lives. Yes, he can live an a'i lifestyle. If he comes to Zábalo he can live here forever. But he also lives in Quito. Because of that, I think he really isn't a'i. If you're like an a'i person, you wouldn't be able to live in Quito. Let's say that I'm like Randy, and that I leave here to live in Quito. So I go to Randy's house in Quito, and how do I know where to look for money? How to buy things to eat? How to help the kids going to school there? I can't—that's what it means to be a'i.

As reflected in this passage, many Cofán ask themselves and each other, How could Borman be Cofán, given his mastery of formal schooling, NGO politics, economic opportunity, and urban living? Clearly Cofán people would like to share Borman's powers, even if they do not want to lose their forest- and community-centered capacities. In a statement that elegantly inverts typical narratives of Borman's transformation, one Zábalo man reflected, "Randy is a'i. He's knowledgeable about a'i customs. He knows the a'i life. But yes, he's gringo—but now. He went away to do political work in Quito, and now he's in the process of becoming a gringo. Before, he resided here." The paradox is undeniable: cosmopolitan activism and political-economic empowerment entail complicating one's Cofán-ness.

Whereas they feel comfortable, secure, and capable in community contexts, most Cofán people define themselves negatively in relation to the knowledge, skills, and equipment that would allow them to be effective actors in other spaces. From their perspective, to be Cofán is to lack material resources; it is to be illiterate and innumerate; it is to be monolingual; it is to be ill at ease outside of rainforest villages; it is to be shy, embarrassed, and timid in the presence of non-Cofán people; and, most importantly, it is to be more or less incapable of dealing effectively with the great challenges that threaten their continued survival as an Indigenous Amazonian people. Although it might be a truism to say that everyone would like to change something about him- or herself, the Cofán truly do articulate a large part of their identity according to their possession of one set of powers and their lack of another.

The negative quality of Cofán identity, however, is more complicated than it first appears. Many of Cofán people's self-critical commentaries are reflections of their key conception of the desirable—or their paradigmatic "value," as I define and operationalize the term in another article (Cepek 2008). The great majority of Cofán people structure their everyday actions and long-term projects according to an ideal that they identify by the term *opatssi*. The word refers to a socioexistential state of freedom from fear, conflict, need, and sickness as well as more positive notions of health, strength, satiation, equality, and good-natured hedonism. The key metaphor that Cofán people use to explicate the value is the *opa con'sin*, a phrase that refers to woolly monkeys who live in remote, unhunted areas. These game animals are so unaware of potentials for violence that they approach human beings with enthusiastic, fearless curiosity, which typically leads to their demise.

As a paradigmatic value, the concept of opatssi describes an essential part of what Cofán people want from life: a calm, symmetrical, and fulfilling form of community-internal sociality. They oppose this collective state of conviviality to encompassing forms of ethnoracial otherness, which they associate with violence, aggression, and exploitation. An opatssi life is one

Fig. 4.2. Randy Borman speaking at the TED^x Amazon conference in Manaus, Brazil. Photo by Bruno Fernandes.

in which an individual is isolated from and unaware of enemies and therefore happy, healthy, and satisfied. To a large degree, to be opatssi is to live in a Cofán community populated by successfully socialized Cofán people. As Cofán explain, *A'inaccu'ta qui opatssiya* (Living together as a group of Cofán, you will be opatssi). In the most basic terms, to be Cofán is to be desirous and capable of an opatssi existence.

Nonetheless, the opatssi ideal is impossible to realize. Ethnoracial otherness pervades Cofán communities in their centers (in the mixed genealogies, unstable identities, and socially disruptive practices of their members) and at their margins (in the constantly encroaching forces of oil, colonization, and political violence). To increase the opatssi quality of their lives, Cofán people hope to maximize their separation from violent difference, even if they are interethnically enmeshed and in desperate need of non-Cofán resources. Unfortunately, distance from others implies ignorance of the means by which antagonistic difference can be known, combated, and utilized. As one Zábalo resident explained in a statement that connects the opatssi ideal to the negative aspects of Cofán identity, "We a'i are *opa a'i*. We don't know. We don't understand."

The opa con'sin is not the only life-metaphor in the Cofán cultural and political imaginary. In opposition to the notion of the ingenuous, unsuspecting, and content game animal is the *ttesi* (jaguar)—a key metaphor for prowess, aggression, and strength, three characteristics that define the overlapping positions of shamans and *na'su* (chiefs or leaders). Unlike opa a'i, shamans and leaders are experts at mediating exterior realms, which they must understand, master, and combat. They define themselves through a contrasting form of fearlessness: an eagerness to identify, confront, and overcome enemies. In their pursuits, they abandon the value of opatssi and partially acquire the substance of ethnoracial others and supernatural agents, who often appear in ethnoracial guises (Cepek 2008; also see Kohn 2002). By learning the language and manners of hostile others, shamans and leaders oppose themselves to the affective core of Cofán society. Cofán people consequently distrust and question the identity of these powerful figures, who form the center and the periphery of their sociocosmological world.

Currently, leaders "represent" Cofán society in a multiplicity of spaces, including government offices, international conferences, and urban protest events. In what might appear as a paradox, Cofán people define themselves in opposition to their representatives, who engage and embody the threats and promises of encompassing otherness. As the most visible and far-ranging Cofán spokesperson, Borman is the most extreme example of this dynamic. By Cofán standards, it is only logical that he is one of the most peculiar Cofán people. In order to fight for the Cofán nation, he has thrown himself into the heart of a hostile world. Consequently, he appears as an ambivalent, powerful, and "proper" advocate for Cofán survival.

Although it might seem contradictory to Western observers with simplistic notions of Indigenous values and identities, Borman is an "authentic" representative of Cofán culture and politics precisely because he is so atypically Cofán. His peculiar identity is a product of his simultaneous participation in Cofán and non-Cofán contexts. As a super-agentive being, he is not simply different from Cofán people—he is something *more* than a Cofán person. As a successful leader in the age of global politics, Borman meets and exceeds Cofán standards of appropriate and acceptable Cofán-ness.

I began this chapter with a set of questions concerning relations between ethnoracial difference, Indigeneity, and political representation. On the basis of self-ascription and community acceptance, I argued that Randy Borman is Cofán, and thus Indigenous, no matter how much his Euro-American origin troubles skeptical outsiders, whether Colombian guerrillas, Ecuadorian army officers, or North American academics. Although no scholars have published critical accounts of Borman's activist involvements, many colleagues have responded to my descriptions of Cofán politics with concerns about "great white father" mythology and colonialist images of Kurtz and Crusoe.

No matter what resonance Borman has for academic observers, I am more interested in Cofán perspectives. I base my position on the principle that Cofán people are the rightful arbiters of claims to Cofán-ness. When contemplating actual assertions of Borman's identity, it becomes clear that Cofán people approach Indigeneity as a complicated matter of everyday interaction, overarching cultural logic, and ideals of social and political practice. Needless to say, the conditions of Borman's Indigeneity are contextually, culturally, and historically defined. From the perspective of a different ethnic group, and even in the eyes of some Cofán people, Borman's status as an Indigenous person is questionable, at best. For most

Cofán, though, the matter is settled: although undeniably unique, Borman is one of them.

Borman's case suggests that effective representation need not depend upon an "iconic" relationship between leader and led. Rather, Indigenous representatives can exhibit a complex combination of characteristics, from the threatening specter of violent difference to the envied capacity for political-economic mediation. Most Cofán do not desire or strive to become a gringo chief. Nonetheless, they realize that Borman's work is essential for their future. For this reason, they hope to make at least some of their children into Borman-esque figures, even if their Cofán-ness is complicated in the process. Many families from Zábalo and other Cofán communities sacrifice time, labor, and resources to send their children to Quito schools as part of the FSC's "Education Project." This effort takes Borman as a prototype of the ideal future leader, who will need to match Borman's ability to negotiate local, regional, national, and international political-economic realities. Reflecting on the project, one Zábalo resident explained, "Truly, we only have one knowledgeable, capable person like Randy here. Because of that, we really want a lot of people, my own children or other people's children, to learn and then to become the supporters, the helpers, of this community, as well as all of Cofán land and the other Cofán communities. With this, we will exist securely."

As Cofán individuals repeatedly state, Borman is and is not Cofán. He can do all that they can do, but he also can do more. He is therefore a reflection of their culture as well as their position in a world that poses their way of life as a problem and a deficit. He represents who they are and who they want to become in order to survive the challenges that face them, no matter how much they define a desirable life in opposition to the necessary moments and ultimate product of that political and cultural movement.

Acknowledgments

For their essential commentary on earlier drafts of this chapter, I wish to thank Laura Graham, Glenn Penny, Bernard Perley, Stuart Kirsch, and Fred Myers. In addition, I would like to acknowledge the financial support provided by the National Science Foundation, the Mellon Foundation, the Fulbright Program, the Woodrow Wilson Foundation, and the

University of Chicago. Finally, all of my work has been made possible by the continuing support of my Cofán collaborators in the eastern lowlands and national capital of Ecuador.

Notes

1. Cofán people live on both sides of border between Colombia and Ecuador, but the difficult political situation in Colombia allowed me to work only with Ecuadorian Cofán. The population estimate comes from the Indigenous Federation of the Cofán Nationality of Ecuador (FEINCE) (personal communication, Roberto Aguinda, FEINCE vice president, July 2009). In Colombia there are at least one thousand Cofán people (Fundación Zio-A'i 2001).

2. Many sources attest to the social, political, and ecological transformation of Ecuador's northeastern border with Colombia over the past four decades (e.g., Fundación Zio-A'i 2001; Kimerling 1991; Ramírez 2002; Vickers 2003). See also ChevronToxico: The Campaign for Justice in Ecuador, www.chevrontoxico.org.

3. I base my analysis on approximately three years of ethnographic research with Cofán people, beginning in 1994 and continuing through the present. I conducted participant-observation fieldwork and directed interviewing with Borman, other Cofán people, and Cofán contacts and allies. My investigation included a year of residence in Zábalo and a year in Quito (2001–2), where I lived with Borman, his family, and a group of Cofán students and activists who came to the capital to pursue political and educational objectives. Although his cultural and political position is complicated, I found Borman to be an open, ethical man. As Zábalo's elected president, he set one condition on my research: that I learn A'ingae and live in Cofán communities long enough to understand the broader perspectives behind Cofán politics. I complied with his request. In return, he gave me near-total access to his life, his writings, and his social circle. I conducted the majority of my research in A'ingae, but I resorted to Spanish and English with certain individuals, in certain situations.

4. I have used a pseudonym to protect this man's privacy.

5. Interestingly, a few weeks earlier a different person had called the man who questioned Borman a "gringo," citing his new canoe motor and relative wealth—even though he has absolutely no Euro-American heritage.

6. This version comes from the episode "American Son," which aired on CBS's *America Tonight* on June 8, 1994.

Bibliography

Barth, Frederik
   1969 Introduction. *In* Ethnic Groups and Boundaries: The Organization of Cultural Difference. Frederik Barth, ed. Pp. 9–38. Boston: Little, Brown.

Brown, Michael

1991 Beyond Resistance: A Comparative Study of Utopian Renewal in Amazonia. Ethnohistory 38(4):388–413.

1993 Facing the State, Facing the World: Amazonia's Native Leaders and the New Politics of Identity. L'Homme 126:307–26.

Brown, Michael, and Eduardo Fernández

1995 War of Shadows: The Struggle for Utopia in the Peruvian Amazon. Berkeley: University of California Press.

Brysk, Alison

2000 From Tribal Village to Global Village: Indian Rights and International Relations in Latin America. Stanford CA: Stanford University Press.

Calhoun, Craig

1991 Nationalism. Minneapolis: University of Minnesota Press.

Cepek, Michael L.

1996 Reorganization and Resistance: Petroleum, Conservation, and Cofán Transformations. BA thesis, Department of Anthropology, University of Illinois at Urbana-Champaign.

2008 Bold Jaguars and Unsuspecting Monkeys: The Value of Fearlessness in Cofán Politics. Journal of the Royal Anthropological Institute 14:331–49.

2009 The Myth of the *Gringo* Chief: Amazonian Messiahs and the Power of Immediacy. Identities: Global Studies in Culture and Power 16(2):227–48.

2012 A Future for Amazonia: Randy Borman and Cofán Environmental Politics. Austin: University of Texas Press.

Conklin, Beth A.

1997 Body Paint, Feathers, and VCRs: Aesthetics and Authenticity in Amazonian Activism. American Ethnologist 24(4):711–37.

2001 Consuming Grief: Compassionate Cannibalism in an Amazonian Society. Austin: University of Texas Press.

Conklin, Beth A., and Laura R. Graham

1995 The Shifting Middle Ground: Amazonian Indians and Eco-politics. American Anthropologist 97:695–710.

Deloria, Philip J.

1999 Playing Indian. New Haven CT: Yale University Press.

Fischer, Rafael

2007 Clause Linkage in Cofán (A'ingae), a Language of the Ecuadorian-Colombian Border Region. *In* Language Endangerment and Endangered Languages: Linguistic and Anthropological Studies with Special Emphasis on the Languages and Cultures of the Andean-Amazonian Border Area. L. Wetzels, ed. Pp. 381–400. Leiden: CNWS Publications.

Fundación Zio-A'i

2001 Plan de vida del Pueblo Cofán y cabildos indígenas del Valle del Guamuéz y San Miguel. Bogotá: Fundación Zio-A'i, Unión de Sabiduría.

Gow, Peter

    1991 Of Mixed Blood: Kinship and History in Peruvian Amazonia. Oxford: Clarendon Press.

Graham, Laura R.

    2002 How Should an Indian Speak? Brazilian Indians and the Symbolic Politics of Language Choice in the International Public Sphere. *In* Indigenous Movements, Self-Representation, and the State in Latin America. Jean Jackson and Kay Warren, eds. Pp. 181–228. Austin: University of Texas Press.

Harvey, David

    1996 Justice, Nature, and the Geography of Difference. Oxford: Blackwell.

Huhndorf, Shari M.

    2001 Going Native: Indians in the American Cultural Imagination. Ithaca NY: Cornell University Press.

Hutchinson, John, and Anthony A. Smith

    1996 Introduction. *In* Ethnicity. John Hutchinson and Anthony A. Smith, eds. Pp. 3–16. Oxford: Oxford University Press.

Jackson, Jean

    1995 Culture, Genuine and Spurious: The Politics of Indianness in the Vaupes, Colombia. American Ethnologist 22(1):3–27.

Jackson, Jean E., and Kay B. Warren

    2005 Indigenous Movements in Latin America, 1994–2004: Controversies, Ironies, New Directions. Annual Reviews in Anthropology 35:549–73.

Kane, Joe

    1995 Savages. New York: Knopf.

Kimerling, Judith S., with S. Jacob Scherr, J. Eugene Gibson, Glenn Prickett, Jennifer Gale, and Lynn Fischer

    1991 Amazon Crude. New York: Natural Resources Defense Council.

Kohn, Eduardo

    2002 Infidels, Virgins, and the Black-Robed Priest: A Backwoods History of Ecuador's Montaña Region. Ethnohistory 49(3):545–82.

Lauer, Matthew

    2006 State-Led Democratic Politics and Emerging Forms of Indigenous Leadership among the Ye'kwana of the Upper Orinoco. Journal of Latin American Anthropology 11:51–108.

McCallum, Cecilia

    2001 Gender and Sociality in Amazonia: How Real People Are Made. Oxford: Berg.

Ramírez, María

    2002 The Politics of Identity and Cultural Difference in the Colombian Amazon: Claiming Indigenous Rights in the Putumayo Region. *In* The Politics of Ethnicity: Indigenous Peoples in Latin American States. D. Maybury-Lewis, ed. Pp. 135–68. Cambridge MA: David Rockefeller Center for Latin American Studies, Harvard University.

Ramos, Alcida Rita

  1994 The Hyperreal Indian. Critique of Anthropology 14:153–71.

  1998 Indigenism: Ethnic Politics in Brazil. Madison: University of Wisconsin Press.

Rappaport, Joanna

  2005 Intercultural Utopias: Public Intellectuals, Cultural Experimentation, and Ethnic Pluralism in Colombia. Durham NC: Duke University Press.

Rival, Laura

  2005 Introduction: What Constitutes a Human Body in Amazonia? Tipití 3(2):105–10.

Sokefeld, Martin

  1999 Debating Self, Culture, and Identity in Anthropology. Current Anthropology 40(4):417–47.

Spivak, Gayatri C.

  1985 Strategies of Vigilance: An Interview with Gayatri Chakravorti Spivak. Block 10:5–9.

Tidwell, Mike

  1996 Amazon Stranger. New York: Lyons & Buford.

Turner, Terence

  1995 Social Body and Embodied Subject: Bodiliness, Subjectivity, and Sociality among the Kayapó. Cultural Anthropology 10(2):143–70.

Veber, Hanne

  2003 Asháninka Messianism: The Production of a "Black Hole" in Western Amazonian Ethnography. Current Anthropology 44(2):183–211.

Viatori, Maximilian

  2007 Zápara Leaders and Identity Construction in Ecuador: The Complexities of Indigenous Self-Representation. Journal of Latin American and Caribbean Anthropology 12(1):104–33.

Vickers, William

  2003 The Modern Political Transformation of the Secoya. In Millennial Ecuador: Critical Essays on Cultural Transformations and Social Dynamics. Norman E. Whitten Jr., ed. Pp. 46–74. Iowa City: University of Iowa Press.

Vilaça, Aparecida

  2010 Strange Enemies: Indigenous Agency and Scenes of Encounters in Amazonia. David Rogers, trans. Durham NC: Duke University Press.

Viveiros de Castro, Eduardo.

  1992 From the Enemy's Point of View: Humanity and Divinity in an Amazonian Society. Catherine Howard, trans. Chicago: University of Chicago Press.

Warren, Kay

  1998 Indigenous Movements and Their Critics. Princeton NJ: Princeton University Press.

Warren, Kay, and Jean Jackson, eds.

2002 Indigenous Movements, Self-Representation, and the State in Latin America. Austin: University of Texas Press.

Whitten, Norman E., Jr.

1981 Amazonia Today at the Base of the Andes: An Ethnic Interface in Ecological, Social, and Ideological Perspectives. *In* Cultural Transformations and Ethnicity in Modern Ecuador. Norman E. Whitten Jr., ed. Pp. 1–41. Urbana: University of Illinois Press.

5

Performed Alliances and Performative Identities

Tupinamba in the Kingdom of France

BEATRIZ PERRONE-MOISÉS

This paper explores two performances staged by Native inhabitants of coastal Brazil before kings of France. One took place in the city of Rouen, Normandy, in 1550, the other in Paris in 1613. Events such as these tend to be cast as performances of exoticism for the Europeans' amusement or, in the all-encompassing "colonial encounters" frame, as symbolic expressions of Europe's colonial power over Native Americans. Although an aspect of "colonialism" can always be located in each performance by Native Americans before European audiences, analysis that is shaped by the general opposition of European to Native American fails to offer means for interpreting the particular contextual significance of individual performances. Such performances were (and are) always staged by specific Native Americans, for specific Europeans, and in very particular relational contexts.

To move beyond a "colonial" situation, I underscore the importance of acknowledging that these two performances were staged by members of Tupi groups (not generic Native Americans), with and for specific subjects of the French king (not undistinguished Europeans), within the context of very particular—and particularly close—relations between the two groups.[1] This framework adds new information to and also explains problems with existing interpretations that I elaborate below. Ultimately, I submit that these performances are best understood as diplomatic rituals between specific coastal Tupi groups and subjects of the kings of France in the context of full-fledged alliances sealed between them in Brazil during the sixteenth and the first quarter of the seventeenth centuries. I see them not as expressions of "colonial domination" but as performances of alliance, of which Amerindian agency is as constitutive as European intentions or interpretations.[2]

Another set of questions arises from the consideration of Amerindian philosophies. Drawing on a growing body of scholarship on Amerindian peoples in lowland South America concerning Native conceptions of personhood and being, and on a number of ethnographies from other parts of the continent, I propose to set aside the firm, Eurocentric belief in essential, unchanging beings (Selves), in relation to which any performance is judged. This enables us to appreciate the meanings of these performances from a different point of view, and ultimately to challenge current definitions of "performance" as applied to contexts involving Native Americans. In Amerindian ontologies and practices, no essence (individual or otherwise) is given and stable. "Identity" (the Self) is a performance. Transformation (into some Other) is a central theme of mythologies, a constant risk for every person, and, in the particular case of the coastal Tupi, great men's destiny.

Context: Coastal Brazil and France in the Sixteenth and Seventeenth Centuries

"Tupinamba" is the ethnonym generally used to denote a number of groups that spoke languages of the Tupi stock and inhabited the coast of Brazil in the sixteenth and seventeenth centuries.[3] Coastal Tupi groups were among the first Amerindians to be described in detail by travelers and missionaries, and their accounts produced a strong and lasting effect on Europeans' imaginaries. These peoples immediately became the exemplary cannibals, the paradigm of savagery (Acosta's [1577]1999 "third-class barbarians") and also the *bon sauvage*.[4] Jesuit missionaries in Brazil described them as "fierce warriors" who devoted their lives to war and whose only purpose was to capture enemies and eat them at great festivities with amazing quantities of manioc beer, where they were joined by all members of allied groups (see Leite 1956). French and Portuguese chroniclers observed that, for the Tupi, war appeared to be more important than anything else. Gabriel Soares de Souza, a member of the Portuguese colonial administration in Brazil, formulated what is probably the best-known and most condensed statement concerning the importance of war among coastal Tupi: "Since the Tupinamba are very bellicose, all their fundaments rest on how they shall wage war against their enemies" (Souza [1587]1971:ch. 167). These accounts circulated widely, so much so that it is possible to speak of a "tupinambization" of European imagery throughout the continent (Sturtevant 1988). Indeed, as Lestringant (2006) notes, the formation of Europeans' vision of the New World and its inhabitants began largely with Brazil and the Tupinamba.

At the outset of the sixteenth century, some subjects of the king of France began to make frequent trips to what is now the Brazilian coastline. They focused their interests on the portion of the New World "granted" to the Portuguese by the papal bull (*Inter coetera*) of 1493 and confirmed in 1494 by the Treaty of Tordesilhas—documents that divided the South American "New World" between Portugal and Spain. In response to them, the French king Francis I launched diplomatic complaints about his exclusion from the partitioning of the newfound continent.[5] Meanwhile, Francis I's vassals haunted the Brazilian coast, befriending the coastal Tupi and establishing trade outposts close to Tupi villages. The Tupi helped the French traders gather some of the "land's riches": primarily brazilwood, but also parrots, monkeys, dyes, and spices. The French reciprocated with European goods and supported the Tupi in their wars against their enemies. Their supplies provided their Native allies with significant advantages.

The Portuguese crown remained deeply concerned about French ventures into territory it regarded as its own during this period. It acted to secure its interests and, just as the French supplied the Tupinamba with armaments and direct support against their enemies, the Portuguese fought them with their own Brazilian Native allies, enemies of the Tupinamba. Thus a system of double oppositions and alliances was formed along the coastline of colonial Brazil: French and Tupinamba on one side, Portuguese and their Tupi allies on the other. This context is critical to understanding the character of the performances in Rouen. By the mid-sixteenth century, when Rouen included a "Tupi presentation" in its reception for the French king, the bonds between the Normans and the Tupinamba were especially strong.

Indeed, by then the "French threat," as it was called in Portuguese sources, had become Portugal's major problem in its South American colony. Under the command of Brazil's third governor general, Mem de Sá, in 1558 the Portuguese undertook a massive offensive along the coast against the French and their Tupinamba allies. Their chief target was "Antarctic

France," a French colony founded in 1555 in the region of Guanabara Bay (now Rio de Janeiro). In what is considered Mem de Sá's greatest achievement, the Portuguese destroyed Antarctic France in 1560 and expelled the French "invaders" from most of their outposts.

Despite that loss, Tupi-French alliances persisted, especially along the northern coast. In 1612 a second French colony in Brazil, named "Equinoxial France," was founded not far from the mouth of the Amazon River in Maragnan, in the region that is now the Brazilian state of Maranhão. Another Portuguese offensive against the French in Brazil was launched; it eliminated the equally short-lived colony at Maragnan (1612–15) and ended the period of the so-called French invasions.

Fête brésilienne

The first Tupi performance for a king of France under analysis here took place during the first era of French ventures in Brazil, on October 1, 1550, during Henry II's "royal entry" (*joyeuse entrée*) into Rouen, Normandy.[6] Following a medieval tradition that grew in importance during the Renaissance (see Wintroub 1998), French kings regularly toured the most important cities of the kingdom, making their "entries" in the midst of great festivities.[7] At the time of Henry II's arrival, Rouen was a hub of what was then called "Brazilian trade." Strong commercial ties linked sixteenth-century Normandy to the Tupinamba homeland.

These festive royal visits were composed of a series of highly codified elements, themes, and sequences, including pageants, music, and theater performances. They were meant to reinforce the relationship between the city and the king. The royal entry of 1550, however, stands out in this history of festivities by virtue of its central element: the theatrical representation of the lives of the Tupinamba from coastal Brazil. This unique performance was "rescued" from long-forgotten archives by historian Ferdinand Denis (1850) and, *following Denis,* became known as *fête brésilienne (Brazilian festival).* Some historians consider this event to be a "turning point" in the tradition of royal entries (Massa 1975:111).

The Brazilian festival was staged on an open field located between the outskirts of the city of Rouen and the Seine River, which had been carefully prepared to look "like Brazil."[8] The local vegetation was "completed" with trees and bushes of various species to convey the impression of a thick tropical rainforest. Parrots and other exotic birds flew over the trees, and monkeys, also imported from Brazil, swayed between branches. At the edge of the terrain stood a Tupi village, with its large thatched communal houses and its central square, surrounded by palisades. One witness and anonymous chronicler of the event observed that three hundred Tupi, some of them women, all painted and ornamented "as they usually do," wandered about in the "jungle" and the village. In their performance of Tupinamba daily life, these three hundred "actors" conducted various activities. They shot arrows with their long bows, chased monkeys, lounged in their cotton hammocks under the trees, cut and transported brazilwood to a small French fortress, and there traded the wood for iron objects. When their bartering was done, the logs of brazilwood were embarked on a ship anchored in the bay (see fig. 5.1). Among these 300 performers, 50 were "natural savages freshly brought" from Brazil. The other 250 were Norman sailors, all of whom, according to witnesses, spoke "the language [Tupi] as well and [expressed] the savages' gestures and manners as naturally as if they were Natives."

The peaceful rhythm of activities was then interrupted by the sudden appearance of a group of "Tabajara" enemies who, after listening to a speech by their *morubixaba* (leader), attacked the Tupinamba.[9] A "furious" battle followed, with arrows flying swiftly from all directions and warriors engaged in hand-to-hand combat with their clubs. The Tupinamba beat the Tabajara, who retreated as their village burned to the ground (note the flames bursting in the upper right side of fig. 5.1).

The chronicler (Anonymous 1550) commented that the simulated battle was so faithfully represented that it "looked real." He attributed this "effect of reality," to borrow Barthes's (1984) expression, to the presence of fifty "real savages" as much as to the long Brazilian experience of the Norman sailors, which enabled them to perform as Tupinamba. The chronicler added as well that spectators "who had regularly visited the land of Brazil and of Cannibals for many years attested in good faith that the effect [of this] figuration was a perfect simulation of the truth."

Another sequence of scenes that constituted the "Brazilian performance" simulated sea combat, consisting of a French vessel opposing a caravel that was clearly identified as Portuguese by Portugal's coat of arms.

Fig. 5.1. Engraving illustrating the "Brazilian performance" in Rouen, 1550. From Anonymous 1551.

The French won. Historians such as Jean-Marie Massa (1975), have long been intrigued by one particular detail concerning this battle. One of the documents describing the festivities, apparently a program, states that the combat takes place between *sauvages* and the Portuguese. Another document, clearly written by a witness, describes a combat between French and Portuguese. We can easily understand Massa's confusion over the apparently "odd" use of "le terme *sauvage*" (Massa 1975:110) to denote the French. But when we consider this naval combat in its broader context, it ceases to appear "odd." Those particular *savages*, the Tupinamba, were the close allies of those particular French, the Rouennais. The two simulated combats in Rouen—the first on land, between Tupinamba and Tabajara, the second on the sea, between French and Portuguese—were in fact one and the same battle, or rather enactments of the same war, fought on the Brazilian coast. In the double system of alliances prevailing there, those "*sauvages*" and the French subjects were united in their opposition to their respective and shared *tabajara* (enemies): the Portuguese and their Native allies. The performed naval combat resumed and redoubled the terrestrial battle, even in formal aspects: much like the "Tabajerre" village, the Portuguese caravel was consumed by fire (see flames on the upper left side of fig. 5.1).

Spectacular battles, on earth or sea, were expected in such well-prepared royal entries. Usually they depicted a classical setting, featuring tritons and mermaids. During the Rouen royal entry, however, the protocol changed. Tupi lives and the wars they waged with their French allies occupied a space that was usually devoted to religious scenes, such as the Passion of Christ and the lives of saints. Scholars such as Massa (1975) have generally overlooked that departure in protocol and missed its significance while focusing instead on the oddity of the event. In most of their analyses, specialists have regarded the "Brazilian festival" more as a typical European display of non-European Others, a kind of proto-*Völkerschau*, rather than a testimony to Tupi-Norman relations and to the nature of the Brazilian trade.

Royal entries were an occasion for host cities to present (both in the sense of show and gift) themselves to the king, a celebration of each city's riches and uniqueness. The *Brazilian festival* displayed both; it reflected the importance of the Brazilian trade in Rouen and celebrated the unique relationship the city and its inhabitants had with coastal Brazil and its Tupinamba inhabitants. The thoroughness and ethnographic accuracy of this impressive spectacle were consistent with the fact that so many of the city's inhabitants were deeply familiar with Tupi life. At this moment in its history, Rouen distinguished itself as a flourishing harbor with critical connections. Most of the city's riches stemmed from the highly lucrative trade with Brazil, which was based on a solid network of alliances established with the Tupinamba.

The city's most prominent bourgeoisie and the vast majority of its inhabitants were directly connected to that trade. Like the fifty "freshly brought" individuals, Tupi allies came regularly to Normandy. In 1550, after at least thirty years of intense relations with the Brazilians, the Rouennais were quite used to the constant presence of some of their Tupinamba allies in their streets and in their houses, since many visitors came in every returning ship.[10] Twelve years later, in 1562, Michel de Montaigne spoke to one of these Tupi visitors in Rouen, who would attend to another "royal entry," that of Charles IX (Montaigne 1967:103).

Consequently, in mid-sixteenth-century Rouen, Brazil and its Native inhabitants were not exotic curiosities. They were, in fact, part of everyday life. Thus, when Steven Mullaney argues that "the occasion [Henry II's royal entry into Rouen] can hardly explain the genesis of one of the most thorough performances of an *alien* culture staged by the Renaissance" (1983:45, emphasis added), he misses essential features of the historical context depicted and performed in Rouen's royal entry, since both the occasion and its setting do explain the genesis and the quality of this particular performance. For the people of Rouen, the Tupinamba, different as they might be, would be envisioned as *allies* and *partners* rather than as mere "aliens." In this sense, another point made by Mullaney (1983:52), namely that the royal entry at Rouen was an "exhibition of what is to be effaced, repressed, or subjected," would also call for reconsideration. Far from displaying what was to be repressed, subjected, or effaced, the city of Rouen was proudly exhibiting itself to the king; and the Tupinamba were an integral part of Rouen itself, not as subjected "savages" but as partners and allies.

The Maragnan Ambassadors

In 1613, when the leaders of Equinoxial France decided that one of their members should return to France to seek financial support for the colony, Tupi allies from different villages chose six men to accompany the delegation in order to see the Frenchmen's country and meet their king (Abbeville 1614).[11] On April 12, 1613, Louis XIII received three Maragnan ambassadors in the Louvre.[12] One of them, Chief Itapucu, spoke before the king and the assembled courtiers. David Migan, one of the most important interpreters (*truchements*) in Equinoxial France, translated Itapucu's harangue. Itapucu was later solemnly baptized "Louis-Marie." The description that accompanies the engraving shown in figure 5.2 informs us that Itapucu/Louis-Marie came from the village named Ipiacaba and that "Itapucu" was only one among ten different war names he possessed. The caption also states that Itapucu/Louis-Marie "liked discourses and war stories" (Abbeville 1614:392).

Migan, a Norman, was even more knowledgeable about Tupinamba ways and culture than the Norman sailors who had performed in Rouen. Having been sent from France to Maragnan as a teenager to become a truchement, Migan grew up in the Tupinamba village of Juniparã, and before his 1613 return trip to France, and until his death in the last battle fought for Equinoxial France, he served the chief of his home village as his interpreter.[13] Migan started his translation of Itapucu's speech with greetings to the "great monarch." He then portrayed Tupi lives in Maragnan before the arrival of French as "miserable," "without law or faith, eating each other" (Abbeville 1614:342). He indicated that the French had brought them pleasant transformations and, in name of his nation, he pledged allegiance and obedience to the king of France. This is a strange translation, for it seems highly unlikely that Itapucu would speak of "law," "faith," "monarchs," and "pledges of allegiance" or that he would characterize Tupi lives as "miserable" when they "ate each other." Migan's translation, as recorded by Claude d'Abbeville, appears to have transformed Itapucu's speech into yet another performance of "formal submission" (Dickason 1984).

However, I submit that the translation may be viewed as accurate in its intentions and effects, if not in its phrasing. The speech certainly conveyed both sides' desire to remain allies in war and partners in trade. Similarly, Migan's Tupi translation of Louis XIII's reply may well have put into Tupi "terms" what the French declared to their allies. The French king spoke of "royal protection," and his "willingness to convert" (Abbeville 1614:341–42) his Tupi subjects, and those intentions materialized into what the Tupinamba chief may have described as reasons why his group was interested in renewing their alliance. The Tupi desired French warriors and weapons to assist them in their wars as well as missionaries (paí), whose knowledge (i.e., powers) would also be of great help in the "invisible wars" waged by shamans. Thus, while some of Migan's translations may have been "unfaithful" to the actors' words, they helped to solidify an enduring alliance between Tupi groups and the French. Here once more, Tupinamba, Normans, and the king of France were joined in a performance of alliance, of which Migan himself was living proof.[14]

Louis-Marie, as well as two of his fellow Maragnan ambassadors, was piously married to a French woman. These marriages constitute an exception in the history of European-Amerindian relations, and they provide us with further evidence of the peculiar character of the alliances between the French and the Tupi.[15] In 1614 these ambassadors and their respective French wives returned to Maragnan in the last French boat to reach Equinoxial France.[16] Beginning in November 1615, Portuguese attacks led to the expulsion of the French from that last stronghold in Brazil and ended the era of Franco-Tupi alliances.

The point is, of course, that neither the Rouen fête brésilienne nor the performances by Tupinamba ambassadors in the Louvre can be reduced to displays of exotic cultures. For the French who saw them in Normandy, and particularly for those who participated in them, the Tupi representatives were not indistinct or generic sauvages. The situation was somewhat different in Paris, whose inhabitants were not so close to the Tupinamba. Nevertheless, Parisians were "used to the marvelous and exotic," having seen "people from all corners of the earth," as the Capuchin missionary Claude d'Abbeville (1614:339–40) notes. Mere curiosity might account for the Parisian crowds that, according to the missionary, packed the streets to witness the passage of the Tupi visitors.

But the king's reception, their baptisms (with the king and queen mother as godparents), and their marriages to French women do not fit the standard models of "ceremonies of possession" (Seed 1995) or "spectacles of conversion" (Daher 1996). Accepting such interpretations would ignore the specificity of the actors and the specific contexts in which these performances took place, as well as Amerindian agency. It is, however, possible to understand them as performances of alliance rather than displays of European colonial domination.[17]

What more can we draw from these performances? How can we make further sense of their character, which seems unique in the historical traces of encounters between Europeans and numerous Others? By reading the historical descriptions through the prism of contemporary ethnological studies among Tupi peoples, we may infer that, like present-day Indigenous travelers, those Tupinamba who traveled across the sea were curious to see the land of their powerful allies. They were also, for their own reasons, as interested as the French in diplomatic rituals of alliance renewal. It is thus reasonable to infer that these Tupinamba of the sixteenth and early seventeenth centuries were eager to show off their looks and manners and to perform battles for the visiting king and the population of Rouen, to dance for them with their maracas (hand rattles) while wearing their feather ornaments, and to display their honorable scarifications and their body painting in Paris.

Contemporary Indigenous groups in Brazil help us imagine the moti-

Fig. 5.2. Louis-Marie (Itapucu), dressed *à la française* after his baptism in Paris in 1613. From Abbeville 1614.

vations of the Tupinamba; modern Indigenous leaders and spokespersons declare that they perform in theaters and festivals because they want people to know them, to see what they look like, to appreciate the beauty of their songs and dances, and to learn what they know. For the same reason, the Wajãpi, a Tupi group that resides in northeastern Amazonia, recently agreed to let pictures of them circulate on the Internet—despite the threat of having parts of their persons possessed by the photos—because they want to be "better known by others, as they are" (see Pellegrino 2009). Similarly, Paulo Xavante stated to Laura Graham, "I want to show my culture" (Graham 2005), and the elder Warodi declared that he "wanted to reach an audience beyond the sea" (Graham 1995). Those sixteenth- and seventeenth-century Tupinamba literally did reach such audiences.

Performing Identities

The antinomian concepts of "genuine" versus "fake" performances, or "being" versus "acting," were already present in the Rouen audiences' comments: as the chronicler noted, the representation was considered "so faithful" to reality that "it *seemed* true" (cf. Anonymous 1550, quoted above).[18] In spite of the fact that the anonymous chronicler of the event himself credited the accuracy of the representation to the presence of *both* the Tupinamba and the Norman actors, these latter tend to be dismissed by more recent appreciations of the "Brazilian festival" as the "false" aspect of the performance. Massa, for instance, qualifies the Norman performers as actors perpetrating an "illusion," people "dressed, so to speak, as Indians" (1975:111). Similarly, Mullaney makes a point of distinguishing between "natives real and counterfeit" (1983:46) in his analysis of the event.

In fact, the Norman actors were just as "real" as their fellow Tupi. I submit that in the Rouen performance, the sailors were authentically (re)presenting their own lives in Tupi villages, on the Brazilian coast. They were able to "undress" as Tupi, speak the Tupi language, handle Tupi weapons in war, and move around naturally in a "counterfeit" Tupi village; in sum, they performed Tupi life so well that it appeared "true" because these and other Norman sailors spent many months each year in Brazil living among the Tupinamba while they waited for their ships to be loaded. In performing Tupi life, they were in fact performing their own lives on the other side of the Atlantic, just as the "genuine" Tupi actors did. The critical point is that, insofar as identities are "constantly constructed and staged" (Schechner 2003[1977]: x), we can regard "Tupi" as but one of these men's "multiple identities." Thus, to accept the "authenticity" of those performers and discuss interpretations of events such as those mentioned above, we do not even have to depart from "Western" notions of identity.

Amerindian conceptions of personhood dislocate the discussion even further. To shift to a perspective inspired by Native American philosophies, we must move away from reliance on notions of inherent essences and changing, staged performances. We must think instead of being, indeed of identity itself, as constituted through (continuous) performance. Decades of research among lowland South American groups have shown that in Tupi (and much Amerindian) thought, a person is given not an essence but rather a process. "For the Araweté," Viveiros de Castro argues, "the person is inherently in transition, human destiny is a process of 'Other-becoming'" (1992:1). With the Araweté, as with other Tupi groups (including the historical coastal Tupi), "we move into a universe where Becoming is prior to Being and unsubmissive to it" (Viveiros de Castro 1992:4). From this point of view, discussions of "Tupi" identity that are framed in terms of "selves" that are given rather than "selves" that are constantly made in performance, so to speak, miss the point.

Ethnographies dedicated to various Native groups all over lowland South America reveal philosophies in which persons are constantly, even daily (see Overing 1991), being remade to ensure their "human" identity, which is always at risk. The human "body"—far from being something given, as in "biological nature"—is central to ideas of personhood and becoming (Seeger, DaMatta, and Viveiros de Castro 1979); its appearance and transformations define, in each given context and always temporarily, one's identity.[19] One *is* what or how others perceive one. Identity is an "appearance," like a "dress" or "clothing," as illustrated in dozens of examples in Lévi-Strauss's *Mythologiques* (1964–71). It is important to note that no "real unchanging self" is "hidden" beneath different appearances, as in dominant Western ontologies, and that "appearances" are also made of *habitus* (see Viveiros de Castro 2002:394 passim): competences, modes of action.

Since the late 1970s scholars of lowland South America have underscored "the performed rather than given character of the body" in Amerindian philosophies (Viveiros de Castro 2002:390). Within the context of these cultures, one's "body" is constantly in the process of being fabricated and transformed through the performance of a series of appropriate gestures and relations, ornaments, paintings, haircuts, foods, ways of speaking, moving, and relating to others. Sets of practices literally fabricate bodies, and these consequently make up a "real human" or a perspective. Native Amazonians, Yudja in this case, "might say to us: what you consider as human characteristics (defined both naturally and metaphysically) do not belong by right to human beings. We have to produce them in ourselves, in the body" (Lima 1996:27).

Native Amazonian bodies, as Vilaça stresses, "are not a genetic given" (2000:60). A series of differentiating devices, both visible (bodily appearance, ornamentation) and invisible (language, diet, and relationships), that are able to transform bodies also transform one's identity. Anne-Christine Taylor (1998) aptly labels Native Amazonian conceptions of bodies as "chronically unstable." The definition of the human self vis-à-vis other beings necessarily involves bodily discipline as well as constant performance of behaviors that are "appropriate for humans." All persons are constantly at risk of losing their contextually situated, constantly transforming identity, the "I." A person *is* what she or he does, eats, speaks, and relates to in specific contexts. The self is not defined by place of birth, descent, or phenotype, although these may be contextually relevant.

Numerous ethnographic examples illustrate this conception of identity. For example, during my field research in the 1980s among the Krahô, a Gê-speaking people who now live in the Brazilian state of Tocantins, people constantly declared that individuals and groups who were Krahô by birth were becoming *kupē* (non-Krahô, literally non-us) because they did not cut their hair properly, ate chicken, did not know how to perform rituals anymore, or hardly spoke Krahô, having switched to Portuguese. Among Krahô and other Gê groups, it is consequently possible to "lose" one's "ethnic identity" within a relatively short time, by eating chicken, speaking another language, or using a different hairstyle, for instance. This ontology goes further: an individual can become *more* or *less* human, and even *more* or *less* kin (Coelho de Souza 2004:27). Throughout lowland South America, ethnographies show that distance from one's relatives has the effect of weakening kinship bonds. In many cases this distance is literally expressed as a bodily transformation that results from not sharing food, failure to participate in daily activities and rituals, and so on. Living far from one's kin changes one's body components. It makes a person *less* kin in a substantial, not metaphoric, sense. Thus Aparecida Vilaça (2002) speaks of "performative aspects of kinship" that hold even for peoples in regions such as the Upper Rio Negro, where, unlike among Tupi and Gê groups, descent is a fundamental element of personhood. An individual cannot *cease* to be *índio* but can certainly *become* less índio by living among non-índios, eating like them, speaking their language, listening to their music, and so on (Lasmar 2005). As Gow (2003:66) observed among the Cocama, an Arawakan people of eastern Peru, Native girls' daily contacts with non-Natives—in cities, for example—are thought to produce bodily and identity transformations in them. The Yanomami speak of *napëprou* as an ongoing and always reversible process of becoming non-Indian (Other, *napë*). Transformative process "consists in a body/habitus transformation and in the acquisition of knowledge, [a transformation that is] intentionally produced" (Kelly 2005:218).

Vilaça, who explores and analyzes the complexities of Native conceptions of personhood in lowland South America in a number of works (2000, 2005, 2007), calls attention to the centrality of a food regime in a person's identity. Among the Wari, "commensality plays a central role, not simply because the same food makes similar bodies but because being able to share food is an important sign of perspectival identity. Those who eat together are above all confirming that they share like points of view, which is the opposite of what happens with those who eat each other" (Vilaça 2005:454).

Similarly, Oakdale concludes that from the point of view of the Kayabi, the food one eats may indeed "impact . . . the eaters' ethnic/racial identity. . . . One man who had a fondness for coffee, for example, was spoken about as 'having transformed himself into a white' as a result. Another person explained to me that even though he had lived away from his relatives to such an extent that he had forgotten the Kayabi language, he had never forgotten and stopped eating Kayabi foods and therefore never ceased being a Kayabi" (2008:798).[20]

Any "identity" is a performance, though not exactly in the sense posited by Erving Goffman, for whom identity was an essential aspect of persons.[21] *Being* human depends on a set of appropriate performances, a correct behavior, that both constitutes and displays identities as processes of becoming, and these transformations continue throughout the life cycle. As Viveiros de Castro put it, "body changes should not be taken as indexes or even symbols of changes in [social] identity. Transformations of the body and of social position are one and the same thing" (1977:40–41).

On the opposite side of the Americas, we find another example of the principle, which seems to be common to all Native Americans, that no identity is given and stable and that a to *be* someone, one has to *behave* accordingly. John Swanton, ethnologist of the Tlingit, reported that one of his "informants insisted that a person of high-birth would also be considered low caste if he did not conform to [standards of action; etiquette]" (Swanton 1908:427). In the Americas, where one can become non-kin, one can even become of low birth—an apparent oxymoron.

Within this ontological framework, individuals such as Migan, who spent most of his life as a Tupi, might be considered more Tupi than Norman. Certainly this would at least have been the case when he was "at home" in the village of Junipará. Similarly, during the trip to Paris, Migan, as well as the other Maragnans he accompanied, would have become "less Tupi" and "more French," since they ate like Frenchmen, dressed like them, spoke like them, and so on. When identity is constantly (re)defined in performance, the whole idea of performance is dislocated.[22]

Considering the assimilation of "being" to "clothing"—another aspect of Native Amazonian conceptions of person and identity—we can look at the iconography of Amerindians in Europe with fresh eyes. The engraved portrait of Louis-Marie shown in figure 5.2 offers an illustrative example. Dressed in French taffeta, carrying a royal lily and a hat, and "wearing" a new French royal and Christian name, Louis-Marie, who came to France as Itapucu, could be interpreted as a perfect example of cultural (identity) loss. For some his outfit might signify imposed acculturation. But this interpretation rests on the presupposition that the existence of a "real" and immutable Tupi body and an essential Tupi being is somehow covered up by the European appearances that have been imposed upon it and that suppress or repress the bearer's Tupi essence.

The disjunctures between these essentializing assumptions and Native American conceptions of self, person, and identity should now be clear. Clothing is one among several "differentiating resources" (Vilaça 2000) that can make or change bodies and, therefore, identities. Since, for Tupi, there is no no given immutable "biology" that exists beneath "superficial," changing appearances, Itapucu's body would not have been, indeed could not have been, "hidden" under French taffeta. Instead, informed by Tupi ideologies of person and being, we can see that Louis-Marie and Itapucu were, in fact, different bodies. They were not the same person. Like the Wari that Vilaça (2000) describes, Itapucu/Louis-Marie may have considered those Frenchman's clothes and adornments (as much as his French name) as constitutive of a "double body," in fact another self, or identity. The essential point here is that none of these identities, and none of these bodies, can be qualified in terms of "authenticity," at least not in Native American terms. Becoming "other" and acquiring new names is a fitting Tupi destiny.

The "ouverture à l'autre" characteristic of Amerindian philosophy (Lévi-Strauss 1991) provides a framework for understanding that the Other is, however, not the opposite of the Self. The Other is, in fact, what makes the Self. Difference is not understood as a problem. It is the condition of all being. This philosophy allows us to understand how, in many cases throughout the Americas, identity can be authentically performed through elements taken from alterity (see, e.g., Graham, this volume). Viewing Louis-Marie, alias Itapucu, and his "conversion" from this vantage point opens up a whole new set of interpretive possibilities.

Ultimately there is no way for us to know what the European performances I have discussed here really meant for the Tupinamba who took part in them. However, given the complexity of Tupi conceptions of Self and Other and their multifaceted relationships with the Europeans (both French and Portuguese), I have suggested revisiting our interpretations of historic events using the insight we have gained of Native American philosophies in recent years. In their performances in Rouen and in Paris, Norman and Tupi were confirming their alliance. Their identities were being made and came into being through those performances.

Acknowledgments

I would like to thank Laura Graham and Glenn Penny for inviting me to the seminar "Performing Indigeneity: Historic and Contemporary Displays of Indigeneity in Public Spaces," held at the University of Iowa, May

21–24, 2009, where a first version of this paper was presented. I would also like to thank the participants in this seminar for their comments and suggestions. The present version—whose flaws, needless to say, are my sole responsibility—would not exist without Laura Graham's generosity and patience, and I cannot thank her enough for that. I also thank Andre Drago and Renato Martelli Soares for their suggestions. I'd finally like to quote Devon Mihesuah's rendering of what seems to be a general trait of Amerindians' conception of the "vantage point" of any speaker: "The opinions expressed here are my own, and I'm not talking for anyone or any group. . . . These are my views and I'm not saying you have to agree with me" (2006:127).

Notes

1. Although they are usually referred to as "French," the Normans, Britons, and others involved in these events were not (yet) French but subjects of the king of France. I follow the convention of calling them French throughout this chapter.
2. As Carneiro da Cunha (1992:17) points out, appraisals of colonial history in the Americas have long tended to dismiss Amerindian agency, albeit with the best intentions. European-Indian relations cannot be understood if one of the sides is simply forgotten.
3. Tupi is one of the major lowland South American language groups, along with Gê, Carib, and Arawak. Our knowledge of the coastal Tupi rests on contemporary accounts by Europeans who, in different contexts, shared their lives. The main sources are Léry (1994[1578]) and Thevet, both of whom were engaged at the French colony in Rio de Janeiro; the capuchin missionaries in Equinoxial France, Abbeville (1614) and Évreux (1864[1615]); and the mercenary Staden (1941[1557]), made captive by a coastal Tupi group allied with the French, as well as the copious documentation produced by Jesuit missionaries working in the Portuguese colonies and compiled by Leite (1938–50, 1956). For a list of primary sources concerning the coastal Tupi, see Fernandes 1970:402–6; for a condensed description of Tupi social life in the sixteenth century, based on those sources, see Perrone-Moisés 2000.
4. In Acosta's classification, all "barbarian nations" (i.e., non-Europeans) were reduced to three broad categories: (1) those "who do not depart considerably from right reason" and have a "stable republic," laws, cities, and above all, writing and books (e.g., Chinese and Japanese); (2) those who lack writing but possess civil organization, laws, and "some solemn form of religious cult" and are sedentary (e.g., Incas); (3) the "beastlike savages," those "without law, without king, without pacts," who are either nomadic or live like animals (e.g., Carib and "the majority of those from Brazil" and Florida) (Acosta [1577]1999:prologue). Among the latter,

the coastal Tupi represent, along with other cannibals, the most "inhuman" of all and, consequently, the most difficult to evangelize. Methods of evangelization are the main subject of Acosta's work, a sort of manual for Jesuit missionaries.

5. These diplomatic discussions between the Portuguese and French Crowns regarding the partition of the New World gave rise to a famous *boutade* by Francis I, in which he said he would like to see "the clause in Adam's testament by which [he was] excluded from the partitioning of the Globe." Whatever his intention, the challenge to the papal bull of 1493 was certainly reinforced by growing theological debates concerning the temporal power of the popes.

6. The fête brésilienne was the central subject of my previous article (Perrone-Moisés 2008); the following paragraphs resume its basic arguments, introducing new elements and considerations suggested by the comparison made here between this festival and the "Louvre performance," and the central theme of this chapter.

7. Henry II visited Lyon and Paris in 1548 and 1549; Nantes would follow Rouen.

8. This description of the event draws on the three primary sources available concerning it, listed under "Anonymous" in the bibliography. All the quotes included in this paragraph were taken from the 1550 document, written by a witness to the festivities in Rouen.

9. In contemporary descriptions, "Tabagerre" is the name used to refer to the group opposing the Toupinaboux (Tupinamba). Neither is the name of any particular group. As Carneiro da Cunha and Viveiros de Castro (1985) have pointed out, "Tabajara" is an adjective-noun denoting a relational class, the position of "enemy." Hans Staden's assertion on the subject leaves no doubt: "Diese [Tupinamba] werden von ihre Feinden auch Tabayaras gennant, was einfach Feinde bedeutet" (1941[1557]:54; These [Tupinamba] are also known by their enemies as Tabayaras, which simply means enemy).

10. For an overview of different contexts of the presence of Amerindians in France, see Dickason 1984, chapter 10.

11. The main sources of accounts of the activities of the Maragnan—as those local Tupi groups are referred to—during their stay in France are the descriptions provided by Claude d'Abbeville (1614), the Capuchin missionary who accompanied them, and the newspaper *Le Mercure François*.

12. Claude d'Abbeville informs us that the other three "Maragnan" died, either at sea or shortly after their arrival in France.

13. The importance of mediators such as Migan in colonial Brazil is shown and analyzed by Metcalf (2005). However, these Norman interpreters, or truchements, cannot be classified as "transactional go-betweens," as Metcalf (2005:64) proposes, which would put them in the same group as Pocahontas and the Portuguese *degredados*, for example. Briefly, Migan and the other "French" interpreters who lived and died among their Amerindian allies did not come to America against their will, were not clearly on the Europeans' side, and can hardly be said to have

had "shifting loyalties" (Metcalf 2005:10). For further analysis of the central role of truchements in French-Amerindian relations and explanation of the fundamental differences between them and other interpreters and cultural mediators in colonial America, see Perrone-Moisés 2008, 2012, and forthcoming.

14. As proof of this alliance, Migan would also die leading his Tupi relatives and companions in the last battle fought for Equinoxial France. He died among the Maragnan with whom he had spent most of his life.

15. For an analysis of the specificity of Amerindian-French alliances, see Perrone-Moisés, forthcoming.

16. Not much is known about these French women. Most of the documents pertaining to Equinoxial France were destroyed following its conquest by the Portuguese, and subsequent diplomatic arrangements between the two kings, also meant to "erase" the very existence of the colony, account for the relative paucity of sources relating to it. Unless new records are found—unlikely, but not impossible—nothing can be added to the simple information found in Abbeville's account of this rare and extremely intriguing fact.

17. The differences between these two diplomatic rituals of alliance might be analyzed as an expression of the differences between the sorts of Tupi-French alliances they express, like transformations of each other. From a French point of view the events in Rouen might be characterized as a performance of war and trade, while those in Paris would instead consist of vows of allegiance and conversion (but war and trade were also present there). The first was a trade theater reinforcing subject-king relations, the other a political ritual reinforcing a trade company (the administrator of Equinoxial France). War was performed at Rouen and promised at the Louvre. The "key" of these performances changed from festive to solemn between the era of Norman trade with Brazil, under a king who let his vassals challenge Portuguese rights in the New World, and the rule of Louis XIII, which established the foundation of absolutism, accompanied by royal control over its subjects' activities and a religious "unification."

Tupi-French alliances shaped the history of colonial Brazil and are also responsible for Tupinamba's immortality in Western imagery, thanks to the accounts made by French authors such as Montaigne, Léry, Thevet, Abbeville, and Évreux. The coastal Tupi disappeared from the records shortly after the French left Brazil once and for all. This "extinction" of the Tupinamba has been attributed to many factors, including war against the Portuguese, ensuing enslavement of the survivors, epidemics, missionization, and the exodus of many groups to the Amazonian hinterland. Nowadays, after a 250-year absence, Tupinamba communities—which trace their descent from those older groups—can be found in northeastern Brazil (see Viegas 2010).

18. In recent years a considerable number of works have discussed the problem of real vs. fake, genuine/spurious, authentic/inauthentic, or folklore/fakelore. For further

discussion, see, e.g., Bendix 1997; Handler and Gable 1997; Hobsbawm and Ranger 1983.

19. The term "body" appears here in quotation marks because these Amerindian ideas suppose a wholly different conception of what a body is. That discussion cannot be developed here.

20. For references on commensality, identity, and the production of kinship in lowland South America, see Fausto 2002, 2007; Gow 1991, 2000; Lagrou 2000; Rival 1998; Vilaça 2005.

21. A comparison of Native Americans' and Goffman's views on performance would be illuminating.

22. This might shed new light on the declaration by Mohawk delegates to German hobbyists that "re-enactment is the highest form of admiration." Indeed, since "playing Indian" in this context is not the (false) impersonation of Indians by whites but a mechanism of transforming oneself, this can be understood as really "going Native." See Penny, this volume.

Bibliography

Abbeville, Claude d'
    1614 Histoire de la mission des Pères Capucins en l'Isle de Maragnan et terres circonvoysines. Paris: François Huby.
Acosta, José de
    [1577]1999 Predicación del evangelio en las Indias. Alicante: Biblioteca Virtual Miguel de Cervantes.
Anonymous
    1550 L'entrée du Roy nostre Sire faicte en sa ville de Rouen le mercredy premier de ce mois d'Octobre, pareillement celle de la Royne, qui fut le jour ensuivant. Paris: Robert Masselin.
    1551 C'est la deduction du sumptueux ordre plaisantz spectacles et magnifiques tréatres dressés, ... Rouen: Robert Le Hoy.
    1557 Les pourtres et figures du sumptueux ordre, plaisantz spectacles, & magnifiques theatres, dressés & exhibés par les citoiens de Rouen, ... faictz à l'entrée de la sacrée majesté du treschretien roy de France, Henry second, ... qui fut es jours de mercredi &jeudi, premier & second jour d'octobre mil cinq cens cinquante. Rouen: Jean Dugort.
Barthes, Roland
    1984 Le bruissement de la langue. Paris: Seuil.
Bendix, Regina
    1997 In Search of Authenticity: The Formation of Folklore Studies. Madison: University of Wisconsin Press.
Carneiro da Cunha, Manuela
    1978 Os mortos e os outros. Campinas: Hucitec.

1992 Introdução a uma história indígena. *In* História dos Indios no Brasil. Pp. 9–24. São Paulo: FAPESP/SMC/Cia das Letras.

Carneiro da Cunha, Manuela, and Eduardo Viveiros de Castro

1985 Vingança e temporalidade: Os Tupinambá. Journal de la Société des Américanistes 71:191–208.

Coelho de Souza, Marcela

2004 Parentes de sangue: Incesto, substância e relação no pensamento Timbira. Mana 10(1):25–60.

Daher, Andréa

1996 L'image de la conversion: Le baptême spectaculaire des Tupinamba à Paris (1613–1614). Revista do IFAC (Universidade de Ouro Preto) 3:26–36.

Denis, Ferdinand

1850 Une fête brésilienne célébrée à Rouen en 1550. Paris: J. Techener.

Dickason, Olive Patricia

1984 The Myth of the Savage and the Beginnings of French Colonialism in the Americas. Edmonton: University of Alberta Press.

Documentos sobre a expedição de Jerônimo de Albuquerque ao Maranhão

1970[1615] Anais da Biblioteca Nacional (Rio de Janeiro) 26:261–304.

Évreux, Yves d'

1864[1615] Voyage dans le nord du Brésil fait en 1613 et 1614, avec introduction et notes de Ferdinand Denis. Bibliotheca Americana. Leipzig: A. Franck.

Fausto, Carlos

2002 Banquete de gente: Comensalidade e canibalismo no Amazonia. Mana 8(2):7–44.

2007 Feasting on People: Eating Animals and Humans in Amazonia. Current Anthropology 48:497–530.

Fernandes, Florestan

1970 A função social da guerra na sociedade tupinambá. São Paulo: Pioneira/EDUSP.

Gow, Peter

1991 Of Mixed Blood: Kinship and History in Peruvian Amazonia. Oxford: Clarendon Press.

2000 Helpless: The Affective Preconditions of Piro Social Life. *In* The Anthropology of Love and Anger: The Aesthetics of Conviviality in Native Amazonia. Joanna Overing and A. Passes, eds. Pp. 46–63. London: Routledge.

2003 "Ex-Cocama": Identidades em transformação na amazônia peruana. Mana 9(1):57–79.

Graham, Laura R.

1995 Performing Dreams: Discourses of Immortality among the Xavante of Central Brazil. Austin: University of Texas Press.

2002 How Should an Indian Speak? Amazonian Indians and the Symbolic Politics of Language in the Global Public Sphere. *In* Indigenous Movements and the

State in Latin America. Kay Warren and Jean Jackson, eds. Pp. 181–228. Austin: University of Texas Press.

Handler, Richard, and Eric Gable
1997 The New History in an Old Museum: Creating the Past at Colonial Williamsburg. Durham NC: Duke University Press.

Hobsbawm, Eric, and Terence Ranger
1983 The Invention of Tradition. Cambridge: Cambridge University Press.

Kelly, José Antonio
2005 Notas para uma teoria do "virar branco." Mana 11(1):201–34.

Lagrou, E.
2000 Homesickness and the Cashinahua Self: A Reflection on the Embodied Condition of Relatedness. In The Anthropology of Love and Anger: The Aesthetics of Conviviality in Native Amazonia. Joanna Overing and A. Passes, eds. Pp. 152–69. London: Routledge.

Lasmar, Cristiane
2005 De volta ao Lago de Leite: Gênero e transformação no Alto Rio Negro. São Paulo: UNESP/ISA; Rio de Janeiro: NUTI.

Leite, Serafim, S. J. (ed.)
1938–50 História da Companhia de Jesus no Brasil. 10 vols. Lisboa: EDITORA.
1956 Cartas dos primeiros jesuítas do Brasil. 3 vols. Coimbra: Comissão do IV Centenário da Cidade de São Paulo.

Léry, Jean de
1994[1578] Histoire d'un voyage en la terre de Brésil. Frank Lestringant, ed. Paris: Le Livre de Poche.

Lestringant, Frank
1990 Le huguenot et le sauvage. Paris: Aux Amateurs de Livres.
1994 Le cannibale: Grandeur et décadence. Paris: Perrin.
2006 O Brasil de Montaigne. Revista de Antropologia 49(2):515–56.

Lévi-Strauss, Claude
1964–71 Mythologiques. 4 vols. Paris: Plon.
1991 Histoire de Lynx. Paris: Plon.

Lima, Tania Stolze
1996 O dois e seu múltiplo: Reflexões sobre o perspectivismo em uma cosmologia tupi. Mana 2(2):21–47.

Massa, Jean-Marie
1975 Le monde luso-brésilien dans la joyeuse entrée of Rouen. In Les fêtes de la Renaissance. Jean Jacquot and Elie Konigson, eds. Pp. 3:105–16. XVe Colloque International d'Études Humanistes Paris: CNRS.

Metcalf, Alida
2005 Go-Betweens and the Colonization of Brazil, 1500–1600. Austin: University of Texas Press.

Mihesuah, Devon A.

2006 Indigenizing the Academy: Keynote Talk at the Sixth Annual American Indian Studies Consortium Conference, Arizona State University, February 10–11, 2005. Wicazo Sa Review 21(1):127–38.

Montaigne, Michel de

1967 Oeuvres completes. Paris: Seuil.

Mullaney, Steven

1983 Strange Things, Gross Terms, Curious Customs: The Rehearsal of Cultures in the Late Renaissance. Representations 3:40–67.

Oakdale, Suzanne

2008 The Commensality of "Contact," "Pacification," and Inter-ethnic Relations in the Amazon: Kayabi Autobiographical Perspectives. Journal of the Royal Anthropological Institute, n.s., 14:791–807.

Overing, Joana

1991 A estética da produção: O senso de comunidade entre os Cubeo e os Piaroa. Revista de Antropologia (São Paulo) 34:7–33.

Pellegrino, Silvia

2009 Imagens e substâncias como vínculos de pertencimento: As experiências Wajãpi e Yanomami. PhD thesis, FFLCH, Universidade de São Paulo.

Perrone-Moisés, Beatriz

2000 A vida nas aldeias dos Tupi da Costa. Oceanos (Lisbon) 42:8–20.

2008 L'alliance normando-tupi au XVIe siècle: La célébration de Rouen. Journal de la Société des Américanistes 94(1):45–64.

2012 Franceses no Maranhão: Histórias de dois intérpretes. *In* Invasões, missões, irrupções: 500 anos de presença francesa no Brasil. L. Perrone-Moisés, ed. Pp. 37–53. São Paulo: EDUSP.

Forthcoming Un étroit commerce: Français et Amérindiens au XVIe siècle. Paris: Champion.

Pezieu, Louis de

1613 Bref recueil des particularitez contenues aux lettres envoyées, par Monsieur de Pezieu, à Messieurs ses parents & amis de France: De l'Isle de Marignan au Brézil, oú il est encore à présent. Lyon: Jean Poyet.

Rival, Laura

1998 Androgynous Parents and Guest Children: The Hoaurani Couvade. Journal of the Royal Anthropological Institute 4:619–42.

Schechner, Richard

2003[1977] Performance Theory. London: Routledge.

Seed, Patricia

1995 Ceremonies of Possession in Europe's Conquest of the New World, 1492–1640. Cambridge: Cambridge University Press.

Seeger, Anthony, Roberto DaMatta, and Eduardo Viveiros de Castro
  1979 A construção da pessoa nas sociedades indígenas brasileiras. Boletim do Museu Nacional 32:2–19.
Souza, Gabriel Soares de
  [1587]1971 Tratado descritivo do Brasil em 1587. São Paulo: Cia. Editora Nacional/EDUSP.
Staden, Hans
  1941[1557] Zwei Reisen nach Brasilien. São Paulo: Sociedade Hans Staden.
Sturtevant, William C.
  1988 La "tupinambisation" des Indiens d'Amérique du Nord. In Les figures de l'indien. G. Thérrien, ed. Pp. 293–303. Montréal: UQAM.
Swanton, John H.
  1908 Social Conditions, Beliefs and Linguistic Relationship of the Tlingit Indians. In U.S. Bureau of American Ethnology, Twenty-Sixth Annual Report. Pp. 391–486. Washington DC: Government Printing Office.
Taylor, Anne-Christine
  1996 The Soul's Body and Its States: An Amazonian Perspective on the Nature of Being Human. Journal of the Royal Anthropological Institute, n.s., 2:201–15.
  1998 Corps immortels, devoir d'oubli: Formes humaines et trajectoires de vie chez les Achuar. In La production du corps: Approches anthropologiques e thistoriques. M. Godelier and M. Panoff, eds. Pp. 317–38. Amsterdam: Éditions des Archives Contemporaines.
Viegas, Suzana de Matos
  2010 Tupinambá. Povos Indígenas no Brasil. Instituto Socioambiental, São Paulo. http://pib.socioambiental.org/pt/povo/tupinamba.
Vilaça, Aparecida
  2000 O que significa tornar-se outro? Xamanismo e contato interétnico na Amazônia. Revista Brasileira de Ciências Sociais 15(44):56–72.
  2002 Making Kin Out of Others in Amazonia. Journal of the Royal Anthropological Institute 8:347–65.
  2005 Chronically Unstable Bodies: Reflections on Amazonian Corporalities. Journal of the Royal Anthropological Institute, n.s., 11:445–64.
  2007 Cultural Change as Body Metamorphosis. In When Time Matters: History, Memory and Identity in Amazonia. Carlos Fausto and Michael Heckenberger, eds. Pp. 169–93. Gainesville: University of Florida Press.
Viveiros de Castro, Eduardo
  1977 A fabricação do corpo na sociedade xinguana. Boletim 32. Rio de Janeiro: Museu Nacional.
  1992 From the Enemy's Point of View: Humanity and Divinity in an Amazonian Society. Catherine Howard, trans. Chicago: University of Chicago Press.

1993 Le marbre et le myrte: De l'inconstance de l'âme sauvage. *In* Mémoires de la tradition. A. Becquelin and A. Molinié, eds. Pp. 365–431. Nanterre: Société d'Ethnologie.

1998 Cosmological Deixis and Amerindian Perspectivism. Journal of the Royal Anthropological Institute 4:469–88.

2002 A inconstância da alma selvagem e outros ensaios de antropologia. São Paulo: Cosac Naify.

2007 The Crystal Forest: Notes on the Ontology of Amazonian Spirits. InnerAsia 9(2):153–72.

2009 Métaphysiques cannibales. Paris: Presses Universitaires de France.

Wintroub, Michael

1998 Civilizing the Savage and Making a King: The Royal Entry Festival of Henri II (Rouen, 1550). Sixteenth Century Journal 29(2):465–94.

6

Rethinking Sami Agency during Living Exhibitions

From the Age of Empire to the Postwar World

CATHRINE BAGLO

In the fall of 2008 the state-owned Norwegian Broadcasting Company (NRK), a noncommercial and highly regarded channel, presented its new Saturday-night show, *The Great Travel*. The premise was simple. Three Norwegian families were sent into the "bush" to live for three weeks with three different Indigenous groups from around the world. The show was an immediate success. Almost a fourth of the country's inhabitants, including myself, followed the first episodes. But it also immediately caused an uproar, especially among anthropologists. Members of one of the groups, the Waorani in the Ecuadorian Amazon, appeared more or less naked on the screen. Many alleged that NRK had paid the Waorani, who normally wear Western clothes, to appear naked. These critics asserted that the Waorani's authenticity had been "staged." Even the former president of the Sami parliament, Ole Henrik Magga, made a public statement claiming that the show degraded and toyed with Indigenous Peoples. Others explicitly called the show racist and claimed that it represented an attitude toward Native Peoples that belonged to colonial times (Nordlys 2008).

NRK, somewhat astounded by the criticism since anthropologists had been part of the research team, rejected the accusations and asserted that it had paid the Waorani to host a family for three weeks but not to appear naked. According to an NRK spokesperson no stipulations had been made regarding the Waorani's appearance or performance (Dagbladet 2008). Apparently the Waorani had voluntarily taken their clothes off as part of performing their "ethnic life," to stage their own "primitivity," so to speak.

However, none of the critics seemed inclined to attribute the Waorani's decision to their own agency.

Similar things had occurred in Germany and Sweden a few years earlier. In Germany, plans to open an "African village" in the Augsberg Zoo from July 9 to July 12, 2005, sparked scholars to issue an immediate appeal calling for public protest against the event; they considered the exhibit to be exploitative and humiliating, particularly because it was situated next to exotic animals in the zoo (H-Afro-Am 2005). In Sweden the following summer, Kolmården Wildlife Park, working in collaboration with a Kenyan safari park, hired a group of Maasai to entertain visitors. This display caused massive protests as well. The spokesperson of a Swedish anti-racism organization was furious, claiming that it reinforced prejudices and discriminating structures within society and that performing among wild animals painted "a primitive picture of Africans." The perspective of the performers themselves, however, was again conspicuously absent from the debate. In fact, the performers were surprised by the spokesperson's statement, and one of them, Daniel Ole Leuka, made the group's task clear in a recording on Swedish Television: "We are doing a good PR for our own country, we earn good money. We do not feel that we are being compared to animals. We are doing PR for our park and for Kenya in general" (Local 2006).

The neglect of Indigenous performers' agency when staging ethnographic displays, or at least an unwillingness to acknowledge it, seems to be common, including among scholars. The performers are often perceived as victims who lack the ability to influence or benefit from their circumstances. Moreover, when their agency is considered, it tends to be dismissed as unfortunate. Similar attitudes are evident in scholarship on Indigenous performances in the nineteenth and early twentieth centuries. As pointed out by L. G. Moses (1996), cautioned again by James Clifford (1997), and repeated again by Eric Ames (2008), much of the scholarship on historic Indigenous display contains assumptions about the exploitation of Indigenous Peoples and their lack of agency as participants in these performances. It is striking, for example, to see how such stereotypic expectations have shaped the analysis of Sami participation in ethnographical exhibitions in Europe and America during this period. This is true of scholarship concerning not only the performers but also the go-betweens (exhibitors, agents, and others).

To a certain extent, Indigenous people have accepted this position, which has strengthened the view that they are victims.

There are, of course, historical precedents for adopting the position that Indigenous performers are victims, and scholars have provided us with important insights into the machinations of colonial discourse and the sociopolitical context of the display of Indigenous Peoples. The lens of their observations, however, has become skewed, and despite the important insights gained, many have unintentionally contributed to the reproduction of the structures of asymmetry they criticize by representing "the Other" as exclusively a client or a victim.[1] Or, as the historian Gunnar Broberg (1981–82:36) concluded in his work on Sami participation in these exhibitions, "It goes without saying that these [the Sami's] travels were convoys of prisoners more than anything else."[2]

In this chapter I challenge the dominant trope of victimization in the study of Sami exhibitions by sketching out a more complex history of these tremendously popular displays as they developed across the nineteenth and into the twentieth centuries. In doing so, I demonstrate that rather than being hapless victims, the Sami exploited these exhibitions for their own ends during a time when their way of life became increasingly difficult. I suggest that the circumstances and historical context of Sami participation in these exhibitions have much in common with North American Indian participation in Wild West shows (see, e.g., V. Deloria 1981; Moses 1996; Kasson 2000). Here, too, the nomadic lifestyle of herders, hunters, and gatherers was relegated to the past, even as these people continued to exist in the present. This made reindeer-herding groups of Sami, much like the North American Indians from the Great Plains, attractive to entrepreneurs engaged in commercial ethnography. I show that a comprehensive and persistent network of performers and entrepreneurs emerged, and I demonstrate that a culture of Sami performance took shape, one that continued through the postwar period and has resurfaced more recently.

The Sami as Subjects in Living Displays

The Sami, an Indigenous people inhabiting areas of northern Norway, Sweden, Finland, and Russia, hold a unique position in European cultural history. While their nomadic lifestyle, based mainly on reindeer herding, hunting, and fishing, represented something fundamentally different from the sedentary farming and developing industrial societies in other areas of Europe, that lifestyle was sustained on the European continent well into the twentieth century and, in fact, never ceased to exist. During the first half of the nineteenth century, this radical otherness made some Sami, notably Sami who practiced or engaged in nomadic reindeer husbandry, attractive to entrepreneurs, who sought them out as subjects of their "living displays." This was an exhibition practice in which representatives of so-called savage peoples from all over the globe were brought to various urban stages in the West, where they performed their everyday life in reconstructed "authentic" settings.[3] During the nineteenth and early twentieth centuries, close to four hundred reindeer-herding Sami—or approximately thirty troupes, most of them families—traveled with their tents, dogs, sleds, and reindeer from their homes to European and North American cities, where they stayed for shorter or longer periods, some for more than two years, traveling from city to city.

The first important display took place in London in 1822, when traveler, naturalist, and antiquarian William Bullock brought Sami herdsman Jens Thomassen-Holm, his wife, Karen, and their little child to his London Museum, along with many of their belongings and several reindeer. Thousands of visitors turned out to see the Native performers drive their sledge round the "spacious plains" of one of the museum halls (Altick 1978:273–74). Their canvas tent was assembled against a painted snowy backdrop, with artifacts mounted on the surrounding walls. Although primarily known for his showmanship, Bullock was also an important museologist and one of the first to introduce "habitat displays," or dioramas, to Europe. Specifically, he developed an innovative design that exhibited figures (more specifically, animals preserved by taxidermy, while other exhibitors would also include wax mannequins) surrounded by appropriate vegetation, arranged in representative scenes, and set against a background evoking the special locality in which the specimens were typically found. Bullock had come across the Sami couple in Stavanger, a city on the southwest coast of Norway, far from traditional Sami settlement areas. This was, as Phillip Deloria (2004) would put it, a rather "unexpected place" for Sami to be. The Thomassen-Holms, originally from the Røros area farther north, were involved in a project initiated by a local entrepreneur of establishing reindeer husbandry

Fig. 6.1. "Laplanders, Reindeer & C. as Exhibited at the Egyptian Hall Piccadilly, 1822."
Thomas Rowlandson. Aquatint: I. R. Cruikshank. Source: National Library of Norway.

in mountain areas not far from Stavanger, and Bullock was intrigued by these efforts (*Literary Gazette*, February 9, 1822, p. 87). In fact, Bullock's original plan was to introduce reindeer herding in England, and this may very well have appealed to the Thomassen-Holms and have coincided with their own interests. Although the reindeer herding did not occur, it was not necessarily a bad experience for the family. Several sources indicate that as a result of this endeavor, Thomassen-Holm became a prestigious person in his local community. More than fifty years after his death, he was still remembered as "English Jens" by his townsmen (Løøv 2001).

After this early and singular display, Sami were not exhibited again until the 1870s, when numerous groups began to travel, entering new arenas of performance that were emerging across Europe parallel to the popularization of commercial ethnography. Central among these performance venues were the world's fairs and large international expositions that spread across Europe and North America. Sami were displayed in connection with the world's fair in Vienna in 1873 as well as the ones in Paris in 1878 and 1889, although not as a part of the official program. They gained their most prominent position at the World's Columbian Exhibition in Chicago in 1893, where a "Lapland Village" constituted one of the attractions on the Midway Palisades. More frequently, however, Sami exhibitions were to be found in zoological gardens, amusement parks, and circuses. The animal trader and zoo owner Carl Hagenbeck was critical in this regard. His Hamburg-based firm was enormously successful at organizing traveling "anthropological-zoological" exhibitions, which toured most European cities for more than half a century. In fact, his very first showing of exotic people in 1875, a date that can be seen as a watershed in the development of ethnographic performances, consisted of a group of six Sami from Karesuando in Sweden accompanied by thirty reindeer and three herding dogs. As Eric Ames (2008:63) has recently noted, despite many scholars' assumptions about such displays, the *anthropologisch-zoologische Austellungen* did not assert the idea of a biological continuum between humans and animals. Rather, Hagenbeck and other impresarios followed a model similar to Bullock's, which grouped foreign peoples together with their exotic animals within the same display space. Through Hagenbeck, such methods became widespread. Although Hagenbeck's human displays were never featured at world's fairs or international expositions and his relationship to them was indirect and largely unacknowledged, he became a highly influential entrepreneur in this context as he exported a series of shows from Hamburg to the Jardin d'Acclimatation in Paris between 1877 and 1887. These displays set the stage for the Exposition Universelle of 1889, which some scholars (e.g., Greenhalgh 1991:85) see as a defining moment in the exhibition of exotic peoples.

The living displays of Sami reached their height with the 1911 Northland Exhibition held in Berlin and sponsored by Hagenbeck. More than fifty Sami from northern Sweden performed along with other "Polar inhabitants" (Inuit, Nenets, and Swedish folk dancers) and various "polar animals." One of the last times Sami seem to have been displayed in this particular manner was in 1933–34, when a group of Southern Sami were hired by the Danish circus director Povl Neve to travel Central Europe and demonstrate the Sami way of living. The history of the living exhibitions, however, does not seem to end with this tour. Information is available about at least one additional tour, organized in the early 1950s, in which Sami from Finland performed (Baglo 2011).

Fig. 6.2. The Lapland Village at the World's Columbian Exposition, Chicago, 1893. Source: Chicago History Museum.

Fig. 6.3. Twelve-year-old Trygve Danielsen from Røros, Norway, at an exhibition in Denmark in 1933 or 1934, with draft reindeer. Source: Private collection.

The Development of the "Living Displays"

The pattern of displaying Sami conforms to displays of other Indigenous Peoples in the same time period. Before the 1870s the pattern was still taking shape. Sporadic shows took place on both sides of the Atlantic, but London was the indisputable capital (Altick 1978; Durbach 2008). In addition to Sami, various African groups, American Indians, Inuit, South Sea Islanders, and others made appearances in Europe before the mid-nineteenth century (see, e.g., Debrunner 1979; Feest 1989; Sturtevant 1989). Although the idea of hierarchical differences between peoples certainly constituted a condition for these displays, we should also bear in mind that these differences, even though increasingly perceived as "racial," were not yet understood in biological terms. The shows preceded and persisted through the emergence of popular and scientific evolutionary and racial frameworks. Such frameworks became dominant only later in the story.

Hierarchical patterns began to emerge during the 1870s, when an exhibition model took shape in which race became one constitutive element. This was particularly true for performances organized by the nation-states, such as the universal and colonial exhibitions, which to a much larger extent reflected the comparative method of anthropology based on the social Darwinian ideas that dominated public discourse in the last part of the nineteenth century. Some independent performances evidenced this pattern as well. Indeed, toward the end of the nineteenth century, exhibitions of exotic people became integral to colonial displays through the emergence of the so-called native village (*village indigènes*) model (Paris 1889; see Greenhalgh 1991). Race typology and evolutionary principles often grounded the spatial organization of the villages at the universal exhibitions, particularly the ones organized by France and the United States (Baglo 2011:243).

According to the historian Sierra Bruckner (1999), the use of typologies and other scientific classifications was less articulated and more random in commercial shows such as those organized by Hagenbeck, which initially merged with scholarly interests and sometimes facilitated anthropological research by providing "objects" for (physical) anthropological examinations. That partnership worked in multiple directions; the involvement of anthropologists provided the shows with "scientific validation" even as the shows became regarded as sites of research and "instructive education."

Most displays took place in continental Europe, and they were mainly based in Germany, France, Switzerland, the Austro-Hungarian Empire, and Britain. Outside Europe, the United States and Japan experienced similar shows, while other countries (such as Argentina, Australia, Russia, and South Africa) and even Hanoi and present-day Burkina Faso were also involved. During the 1880s and 1890s, commercial ethnography developed into a full-fledged "industry" with its own codes and professionals. The business rose steadily until the beginning of World War I, and the growing number of troupes and international exhibitions generated a tremendous increase in the opportunities for Western spectators to see exotic Native Peoples. Indeed, there appear to have been as many as two to three thousand individuals employed every year as "Native performers" in the dozen or so countries that hosted such displays by the turn of the twentieth century (Blanchard et al. 2008). After World War I exhibitions of Native Peoples became less frequent—only four traveling Sami troupes can be identified after the war.[4]

By that time the interface with anthropology—the study of authentic Natives—and the associated scholarly interest had gradually evaporated.[5] As anthropology started to reorient toward social and cultural fields, the display of human bodies increasingly became insignificant and even threatening toward its new identity as a discipline concerned with *social* relations. Moreover, as fieldwork became established as a disciplinary imperative and anthropologists went *to* the Natives in their homes, rather than the other way around, such displays lost their scientific allure and became relegated to the realm of popular entertainment and education (see Baglo 2011). Nevertheless, a more "plebeian" version of these exhibitions, to use Anne Maxwell's (1999:17) wording, continued in a rather unaltered state in zoological gardens, circuses, and amusement parks well beyond this time. Relegated largely to the realm of mass entertainment by the 1930s, ethnographic displays became part of a cultural industry unfolding in opposition, and even as a possible threat, to high arts, science, and scholarly interest.

The Notion of the Sami as "Authentic"

A central feature of the living exhibitions was the reconstruction of the peoples' "natural habitat." Although exhibitions were affected by the expectations of local audiences, by the type of peoples who were displayed, and by the spaces in which they were presented, they invariably featured a domestic scene set with a dwelling containing implements that were deemed ethnographically appropriate. Living Natives represented themselves, but their "authenticity" was confirmed through the accompanying dwellings, costumes, equipment, animals, and sometimes even plants. A statement in a contract between Hagenbeck's Norwegian agent, Adrian Jacobsen, and a South Sami performer in 1926 makes this abundantly clear: "The person concerned is committed to carry the costume and things Hagenbeck's representative imposes her to, and which shall mirror the Sami costume in earlier days and places" (Skal gjengive Samernes dragt i tidligere tider og steder) (contract, Hagenbeck Zoo archive). Moreover, the fact that most of the living displays took place in the open air was regarded by many organizers as adding authenticity to them—the huts and tents set up by the performers were deemed "natural" extensions of the troupe and its way of life. Performances were highly standardized, featuring regular attractions and entertainments. As such, certain elements and activities were incessantly repeated in Sami exhibits—the pitching and disassembling of the camp (most often the *lavvu*, the conical tent used by herders while staying out with the herd or on the move across the tundra), the *komse* (the cradle made out of a hollow tree trunk), catching the reindeer with lassos, driving the sledge, and skiing—and were paramount means of authenticating their display.

First and foremost, the exhibitions staged the lifestyle of nomadic reindeer herding, and with few exceptions the performers were exclusively recruited from reindeer-herding communities.[6] The majority of Sami were sedentary, with their subsistence based on mixed economies (including sheep, goat, and small-scale cattle herding), and were not considered "authentic" enough for English, Americans, and Germans, nor were they represented in the early ethnographic museums. The sedentary, fishing and agricultural Sea Sami, Village Sami, Forest Sami, River Sami, and others were seen as deteriorations or "hybridizations." They had lost the "nearness to nature" and their "natural" animals. The reindeer-herding Mountain Sami, on the other hand, were widely regarded as representing the "authentic" Sami lifestyle, a view that was frequently asserted by Sami too.[7] As stated in a booklet published in relation to Bullock's exhibition in 1822, "The proper Laplanders . . . are constantly wanderers" (Lapland Sketches 1822).

Another important feature of the Sami displays, as well as the ethnographic displays in general, was the family unit, which, since Bullock's display in 1822, was central to the organization of the exhibitions. As an element of display, the family provided an inviting framework that had the advantage of being understood by all potential audiences; it constituted the familiar within the strange. Indeed, despite the fact that collective cultural difference was the primary concern in these exhibitions—lifestyles that deviated from the most prominent modes of existence in Western societies—they also retained elements of sameness and a concern for the authentic and the original in a rapidly modernizing world. The Lapland Village at the Chicago world's fair exemplifies these notions of Sami authenticity. The village, advertised as "a miniature reproduction of a Lapland settlement and a source of knowledge of people whom few care to visit," was open daily from 8:00 a.m. to 9:00 p.m. While it was open, visitors could experience musical performances, dancing, and traditional singing (*joik*). Performers also demonstrated their skills at making handicrafts, which they offered for sale to the public for their own profit. Perhaps most importantly, as one journalist noted, the village also served as an illustration of the "mutual dependency" between the Sami and the reindeer, and as a result a calf that was born during the exhibition and consequently given the name "Columbia" became a central attraction (Chicago Daily Tribune 1893).

The harshness of the climate in which the Sami lived was another feature that was typically emphasized by the organizers. This frequently caused performers to dress in inappropriate ways—with fur boots and mittens—for the midsummer heat. Often the organizers would make fake snow, and many a Sami performer had a good laugh from entrepreneurs' more-or-less successful attempts at staging the contexts for the expression of their Indigeneity. A Sami from Malå in Sweden who had been working for the impresarios (Emma) Willardt and Böhle during a two-year period in the early 1870s recalled an impresario's ingenious invention:

Well, it was in 1876, and I was 12 years old. A German came along, and since we could not understand a word he was saying he was accompanied by an interpreter. He [Böhle] promised a lot of money. Nor was it going to be difficult; we were only to walk around and look nice at an exhibition. . . . Two sledges were also brought along, but geez, I say, there were no snow down there, only summer. But Bö[h]le knew what to do: he attached little wheels underneath the sledges. Then we drove across the pavement stone so that it clattered between the houses. People looked at us in astonishment. And then they swarmed to the exhibition. (Manker 1939:211)

Spectators sometimes expressed disappointment when performers did not conform to their expectations. A visitor to the Lapland Village reported in the *New York Times* (1893), "There is a painful incongruity in discovering that one whom you are entitled to take for a native of Lapland speaks English with an accent blended of Stockholm and Chicago." Signs of cultural adaptation, especially modern technology, could be similarly disturbing. The same journalist complained about the reindeer being "washed with a garden hose." Performances typically conformed to the spectators' expectations, however, catering to the wishes of scientific and popular audiences alike. According to the young performer from Malå, the impresario thought the troupe "did not look sufficiently wild so we were told to paint our faces and dress like Eskimos" (Manker 1939:211). And indeed they did. Several advertisements show the same illustration: four individuals dressed in anoraks while in the background we see igloos and a kayak lying in a lane through the ice in front of them (Illustrirtes Wiener Extrablatt 1875).[8] Other times the performers, who of course were cognizant of, or soon noticed, these expectations, consciously staged the very cultural fantasies that they were supposed to (naïvely) embody.

These sorts of adaptations were not unique to the Sami. As Eric Ames has demonstrated, the records of the Berlin Phonogram Archive offer compelling evidence that the "Death Song" sung by a group of Hopi Indians recorded during a special performance at Cirkus Schumann in Berlin in 1906, where Kaiser Wilhelm II and three hundred members of the Berlin Society for Anthropology were among the audience, proved to be fake. Although the song itself was authentic, funeral chants were not part of Hopi culture. The title had been invented for the sake of the audience. The performing Hopi had probably been advised by their manager to offer the emperor, who had expressed the desire to obtain war songs for his private collection, the types of songs he expected. Consequently the informant, a member of the troupe who understood German, wrote the following annotation to the recording (under which label it was later archived): "Death Song, very old" (Ames 2000:142–45).

However, although performances undoubtedly were contrived to meet audience expectations, and some more than others, they were not fake simulations. They were cultural enactments, self-representations in new situations. The performers brought their own biographies, material expressions, practices, and voices to the performance even as they were engaging in popular displays and conforming to observers' expectations. The outcomes of these encounters were never a given. Outcomes were negotiated. To borrow a distinction from Bruno Latour (2005:39–40), the performers were not transparent *intermediaries* who obediently transported meaning without translation. They were instead *mediators*, agents who transformed, translated, distorted, and modified.

Professionalization and Agency

The establishment of the Lapland Exhibit Company, the organizer of the Sami Village on the Midway Palisades in Chicago in 1893, offers an example of the professionalization of the living exhibitions that took place in the late nineteenth century. This Kansas-based company resulted from a collaboration between a group of local businessmen and two Swedish immigrants. Captain Patrick Henry Coney of Topeka—a lawyer, writer, publisher, and Civil War veteran—managed the company with his wife, Emma, and Emil Arner ("Amer" in American sources), a Swede from Salina, was the vice president. Arner had signed contracts with the performers in Sweden and Norway, and he traveled with them to Chicago.

Contracts dating from the late nineteenth century onward suggest a new perception of shared interests and a relative leveling of the relationship between the organizers and participants. It seems to be a well-kept secret that, from the very beginning of their operations, both Carl Hagenbeck and William F. Cody, or Buffalo Bill, formally contracted with the participants for their performances. Several examples exist that demonstrate how Sami negotiated—even dictated—the terms of their contracts. They required, for example, that salaries be paid to substitute herdsmen for the period of their absence, that a guide chaperone them to the town or church whenever they wanted, and that they should stay in first-class hotels dur-

Fig. 6.4. "Group from Far-Away Lapland." Chicago, 1893. In the middle is manager P. H. Coney. Source: Chicago History Museum.

ing the journey. In one case a group of Sami went on strike in Budapest in order to get their money after the impresario left them (Svenska Dagbladet 1913). It may sound surprising, but some of the performers even preferred to be displayed in zoological gardens rather than at other venues because their reindeer received proper care at the zoos, where a veterinarian could look after them. Others have emphasized the tranquility of a zoological garden, which made it a more attractive place to lodge than other venues (Baglo 2011:291–92).

The performers in the Lapland Village at the Chicago fair exemplify the Sami's skill as contract negotiators. Nils Thomassen Bull, or "King Bull," as the American press referred to him, is a good example. Like many of the Sami in Chicago, Thomassen Bull was an experienced traveler and performer who had been a part of a group that was contracted by the Jardin d'Acclimatation in Paris in 1889; a contemporary source describes him as a lively person who "knew his business well" (Chicago Daily Mail 1893). Bull was one of the most popular personalities of the village, if not on the whole midway. He was billed as being 112 years old (he was actually in his late forties), and the troupe's advertisements played up his personality. Thomassen Bull had brought his family to Chicago on his own choosing, accompanied not by "eight generations," as one book claimed, but by his wife and "two rebellious children" (Scott 1991:331), and he demanded and received good treatment. While the other performers in the group were paid by the week, he and his wife negotiated a contract that specified a salary of twelve *kroner* a day. In comparison, the second-highest salary in the troupe seems to have been twenty-eight kroner a week (Coney Collection n.d.). To put this in perspective, the average payment a widow would receive from the Poor Relief Fund in Norway (which would have been the alternative source of income for some) was five kroner a month! The Lapland Exhibit Company also had its own physician to care for the performers' health.

Advertising even created imaginary links to another, by then deceased, Native celebrity, Sitting Bull, the famous Hunkpapa chief whose log cabin was displayed opposite the Lapland Village. Sitting Bull, the most prominent North American Indian leader to appear in Buffalo Bill's Wild West shows, had also been well aware of his commercial value and effect on an audience. Not only did he demand a salary of $50 a week, with two week's pay in advance and a bonus of $125 for participation in his first show in 1885, he was also to be accompanied by no less than nine other people, including his own chosen interpreter—and all were to be included on the payroll (*Middle Border Bulletin* 1943, cited in Kasson 2000). In addition to salary and terms related to transportation, health care, and lodging, other special "exhibition conditions" could be demanded by performers, such as refusing to perform in hot or bad weather or calling for supervisory care for animals on rest days. Performers such as Sitting Bull and Thomassen Bull, in other words, evidenced a significant amount of agency in negotiating their contracts and showed that they were savvy participants in these exhibitions who put themselves on display for a host of reasons.

Motives: Crisis, Pleasures, and Desires

In order to understand the motives for the Sami's participation in the living displays it is crucial to investigate the economic, political, and spiritual premises that made commercial performance an attractive option for them. These premises were to a great extent shared with other Native Peoples and minority groups, and they changed radically from the time of

Bullock's exhibition in 1822 to a tour organized by Povl Neve in the 1930s. The motives of the first Sami performers, the Thomassen-Holms, were less affected by processes of colonization and state-imposed regulations, although agriculture and other industries had long been promoted in place of reindeer husbandry, hunting, and fishing, a policy that had contributed to increased poverty among the Sami. From the middle of the nineteenth century on, however, the Sami communities in the Nordic countries were under constant pressure. Processes of colonization, increasing state control, and forced assimilation were rampant. By the beginning of the twentieth century their social and cultural positions had been radically weakened. Sami language was prohibited in most schools, freedom of movement was restricted through the establishment of guardian "Lap officials," and traditional pastures were gradually lost as national borders were closed to the Sami's traditional migratory patterns. Many reindeer-herding Sami were forced to move, change their citizenship, or give up their nomadic lifestyles. In Sweden those who became "sedentary" (subsisting, for example, on farming, fishing, hunting, mining, or construction) lost their legal protection and were no longer considered Sami by the state while a strict distinction policy ("Lapps should be Lapps") barred the reindeer-herding Sami entry into the growing industrial society. The situation was especially severe in the southern Sami area, where the majority of the performers were recruited from the end of the 1880s onward. This suggests that the crisis in reindeer husbandry—a situation that only worsened in the 1920s and 1930s—made participation in living exhibitions a viable economic alternative for some. It was also a natural alternative; reliance on mixed or alternating economies in times of crisis was by no means new to these communities.

Although economic gain was an important motivation for most of the Sami participants during this period, it was not necessarily the decisive factor. Nils Nilsson Skum, for example, was a wealthy man with nearly two thousand reindeer in his herd. According to a local Norwegian newspaper the members of a Sami troupe that performed at the Alexandra Palace in London in 1885 were all "relatively well off and seem motivated as much by travelling excitement as profit" (Tromsøposten 1885). In fact, one of the performers, Ole Nilsen Ravna, embarked on a new journey three years later, this time as the "Native advisor" on Norwegian polar hero Fridtjof Nansen's expedition to Greenland, and then again with the Danish explorer Knud

Rasmussen to the same place in 1905. Three of the five adults in the group performing at Alexandra Palace stated that they were sedentary (Keane 1886). Recognition that their traditional way of life was threatened may also have motivated some Sami to perform their culture. Members of other Indigenous groups performed culture for this reason, and their reasons, like the Sami's, were quite compatible with salvage anthropology and the exhibitors' motives (see, e.g., V. Deloria 1981; Moses 1996; Raibmon 2005).

In addition to offering financial compensation, travel opportunities, and the demonstration of cultural distinctiveness, participation in these exhibitions may—paradoxically—have meant a greater chance for freedom and the possibility of being treated as equal human beings than participants experienced in their respective home countries, a motive that is also apparent in Glenn Penny's investigation of the Indian performers in Wild West shows (this volume). In fact, quite a number of Sami participants returned repeatedly—at times across generations.

This was the case with Daniel Mortensson, who performed at the Lapland Village in Chicago in 1893 along with his wife, Brita, the daughter of a rich reindeer herder, and their children. Mortensson was a teacher, catechist, reindeer herder, and later a well-known Sami rights advocate. He was also the founder of the Sami newspaper *Waren Sardne* (News from the mountains), which was characterized by its strong social commitment. He often used the newspaper to report on exhibitions of Sami, and in 1910, he published a poem, "The Sami People," that illustrated the precariousness of their situation.

The poem tells about Norway, his beautiful mother country that deserted him and the Sami people: "You are my mother and I belong to you. But tell me, then, why don't you love, embrace and protect me? Am I not like the others?" Then he recalls times when the Sami were free-roaming "reindeer-owning people":

I know you once loved me—and loved me a lot
with pure love from above.
Yes, I do remember—if only this could satisfy my soul!
But is this any comfort at all?
Oh, I wish I could make you love me before
my days of sorrow are gone.

Oh, I wish I could only own that part of the land which—as is
    known—
was meant for me.
(Waren Sardne 1910)[9]

That would prove difficult. Performance, however, remained as a possible means of employment and economic gain, and two of Mortensson's
children continued to participate in exhibitions with their own families in
the 1920s and 1930s (Baglo 2011). When Mortensson died in 1924 a monument was raised in his honor with the inscription "The fearless leader of
the Sami" (fig. 6.5; see also fig. 6.4, the man holding the boy in the cradle).
His story is a poignant reminder of how inadequate the all-too-common
client image of the victimized Other may be.

One of the reasons that Mortensson and other Sami were able to take
advantage of these performing opportunities was the mobile and flexible
technology that these groups lived with and their long experience with
travel, trade, and intercultural contact. Their willingness to adapt to and
embrace new ways had also prepared them for the experiences they encountered as performing travelers. Indeed, this knowledge smoothed their negotiations with entrepreneurs and allowed them to translate these putatively
colonial situations into hybrid constellations—something that also served
their interests and made their situation livable. As James Clifford (2001:471)
reminds us, tribal peoples have never been faced with simply choosing one
or the other, tribe or city, tradition or modernity, but have the option of
sustaining a livable interaction as part of an ongoing struggle for power.

Historians of Native American performers, such as Vine Deloria Jr. (1981)
and L. G. Moses (1996), have argued that performing Indians had much
to gain from participating in shows such as Buffalo Bill's Wild West. They
could display skills that reflected positively on their culture and give the
audiences a more nuanced sense of Indian life; they also received good pay,
secured leadership, and were given the chance to travel and interact with
others. For some, such as Sitting Bull, work in the Wild West shows was
literally an alternative to imprisonment. Moses, in fact, argues that the performances actually helped to preserve elements of traditional Native culture. Despite being shaped to meet the expectations of non-Native audiences, Native American performances also became an arena for Native

Fig. 6.5. Daniel Mortensson (1860–1924), "the fearless leader of the Sami." Artist: Ludvik Marius Eggen. Source: Røros Museum, Norway. Photo courtesy of the author.

people to communicate information about their cultures to foreign audiences, to express pride in their heritage and traditions, to make a living, and to survive emotionally and culturally within a colonial context. Like Native American interpreters working at living history sites today, they often actively challenged the very same stereotypes they were expected to meet in the process (Peers 2007).

As a result, during a meeting at the U.S. Department of the Interior when a commissioner expressed his displeasure with the Buffalo Bill's Wild West show and charged Cody and his partners with maltreating and compromising Indians, the Lakota performer Black Heart gave an impassioned defense of his employers and argued for the right of Indians to work for Wild West shows. "We were raised on horseback," Black Heart argued, "that is the way we had to work. These men furnished us the same kind of work we were raised to; that is the reason we want to work for these kinds of men" (quoted in Moses 1996:103). Playing Indian (P. Deloria 1998) allowed many of them to continue some aspects of their former lives, demonstrate their considerable skills, and prosper.

Another Lakota performer, Luther Standing Bear, who later wrote *My People the Sioux* (1928), was explicitly proud of his career. He had decided to travel to England with the Wild West show in 1902 after new Indian Bureau policies made it impossible to support his family as a cattle rancher. Trained at the Carlisle Indian School in Pennsylvania, he worked as an interpreter and manager for the show Indians. Like several other Native performers, Standing Bear and his wife agreed to have their newborn child exhibited on the show grounds, and they named her Alexandra Birmingham Cody Standing Bear, after Princess Alexandra of Wales, who visited the show before the grand opening in London, the city where she was born, and their employer (William F. Cody). This was not unique. In a similar manner, the son of the Sami performers Signe and Elias Danielsen was baptized Samuel Paul Christian, after the Christian prophet Samuel, the Danish employer Povl Neve, and the Danish king (Christian X of Denmark), during an exhibition in Copenhagen in the 1930s. It both cases, such acts proved fortuitous. "It was a great drawing card for the show," Standing Bear wrote, pleased that the exhibition benefited both the Wild West and his family, since visitors gave them gifts and money for the baby. "The work was very light for my wife, and as for the baby, before she was twenty-four hours old she was making more money than my wife and I together" (Standing Bear 1928:266). The Sami performers on a tour organized by Hagenbeck in 1926 were equally enthusiastic about their experiences, "and who would not bestow them, considering the fact that they have visited no less than 37 German cities—and seen all their beauty and splendors and all kinds of strange things of which most narrow-minded wilderness residents could ever dream" *Waren Sardne* (1926) reported, with an obvious knock toward local people's prejudice against such shows.

Without doubt, the participants' travels and encounters had a great impact on them as well as their Native communities. They often returned with both financial and cultural capital. It is important to recognize, however, that their encounters were not limited to those between the people on display and their foreign audiences. Encounters also took place, and interfaces were created, among the Indigenous Peoples themselves. This was particularly true at the various world's fairs, where the people on display typically lived side by side "under normal conditions in their natural habitations" during the six months the fairs lasted.

Recognizing the existence of such contacts is crucial, because it reminds us that the global awareness among Indigenous people of a broader commonality with similar interests and needs is not a uniquely recent or postcolonial phenomenon. There were significant precedents. Thus, although Sami historian Henry Minde (1996:228) has argued that there are no examples from the period before World War I of the Sami comparing their situation with that of other Indigenous Peoples, there were clearly many moments in which that could and surely did take place. While there may be a dearth of written records of such comparison and bonding, it is likely that the exhibitions constituted a new and globalized context that allowed the performers to realize that they were not isolated "instances" in a broader march of progress. Rather, in many ways these encounters afforded opportunities for participants to recognize that they shared histories with other Indigenous people they met at exhibitions.

Surely the Sami's participation in the Lapland Village at the Midway Palisades in Chicago in 1893 was crucial, and in at least one case it led to activism. At the beginning of the twentieth century, Daniel Mortensson both became central in the establishment of a South Sami organization (Nordre Trondhjems Amts Lappeforening, 1908) that advocated for the interests of reindeer herders and modernization of the herding industry and played a leading role in organizing the first national meeting of Sami in Norway, in 1917.

Of course, many of the people on display recognized the implications of their cultural performances. Some also acted on that knowledge and sought to control representations of themselves. For example, in her innovative study *Authentic Indians*, Paige Raibmon notes that Standing Bear, dissatisfied with the plans for live displays of Indians at the Chicago world's fair, wrote to the Indian commissioner asking him to arrange government funding for old chiefs who wanted to attend the fair. Standing Bear explained that he and his people would like to come to the fair but they wanted "to come as men and not like cattle driving to a show" (Raibmon 2005:47–48). Similarly, sixty-four leaders from the Brulé and Crow Creek Agencies wrote a petition to the World's Columbian Commission and the U.S. president asking to organize their own exhibit of Native American life and history since Columbus's arrival. Their people, they explained, were discouraged by the destruction of their herds and the failure of their agricultural attempts. And they knew the origin of their difficulties: "We are almost in despair," they wrote, and "our people trace the cause of that despairing to the very event which, with such large expending [*sic*] of wealth you are about to celebrate." The group was anxious to demonstrate that their progress over the last four hundred years had been "much greater than usually supposed." Nor did they perceive it as "fitting" or "wise" to celebrate Columbus's arrival in America without considering what that event had meant for their people, who were "once great in numbers, power and empire." The petition and the letter to the president, however, went no further than the organizers' file.

Modern Performances

After a period in which the living exhibitions seem to have persisted but on a smaller scale and in more random contexts, live performances of Sami culture have again emerged. Performances organized by both non-Sami and Sami entrepreneurs have become common. In these performances, the joik singing, the lavvu, reindeer racing (in which racers stand on skis behind a specially trained reindeer), and in particular the often very elaborate Sami frieze costume, called *gákti* by Northern Sami (or elements from this), on which cut, color, pattern, decoration, and headdress vary from district to district, have gained an ever-increasing importance. During the last thirty years, wearing the gákti in public has become an important assertion of Sami identity. Old costumes are reconstructed, new variants are designed, and the gákti is used in an increasing variety of arenas, such as the Sami People's Day, February 6, which is celebrated in Norway, Sweden, Finland, and Russia. It is also common at the music and cultural festival Riddu Riđđu, which takes place in Kåfjord, Northern Norway.

The Riddu Riđđu festival began as part of a movement by a group of Sami youth to revive their culture and language, and since its start in 1991 has become one of the largest international festivals for Indigenous Peoples. In addition to musical performances, the festival encompasses an Indigenous youth camp, a children's festival, film screenings, plays, workshops, seminars, exhibitions, dance performances, and outdoor activities (Riddu Riđđu 2010).

These are not isolated developments; during the last two decades Scandinavia has witnessed a boom in experience-based representations and enactments of history and culture. Reconstructions of Iron Age houses and boats, performances of historical plays, and the establishment of "Viking Lands" and "Laplands" are all expressions of this phenomenon. Another example is Sápmi in the Sami center of Karasjok, Northern Norway—a theme park that the municipality's English-language web page claims presents "Sami culture and history in an enthralling, informative and entertaining way" (Sápmi Park 2010). The performances and activities offered are adapted to today's traveling audience, with a particular emphasis on Sami cuisine.

A third, non-Sami example, which has caused some stir within the tourist industry and communities in Finnmark, Northern Norway, is the newly established Lapland UK, located an hour's drive south of London. Under the slogan "Christmas Magic for everyone," elves and young Brits in lookalike Sami costumes will show you around the park and escort you to Santa's lodge. This tourist attraction follows a display tradition of its own. As early as 1893, Nils Thomassen Bull and the Lapland Village in Chicago were associated with Santa Claus; the "Sami" are also conspicuously present at the internationally visited Santa Claus's Village outside Rovaniemi in northern Finland as well as on numerous Finnish-produced postcards.

The Sami's presence in Santa Claus's Village caused a sensation, but less because of the presentation than the presenters. In 2006 hundreds of Sami

Fig. 6.6. Finnish postcard from the 1990s showing Northern Sami in gákti. On the lavvu (tent) in the background is the common trademark of the Nordic Sami artisans, which guarantees the authenticity of Sami handicraft. Photo by Kalevi Asplund. Source: Tromsø University Museum.

youth protested against the park's employment of non-Sami in fake gáktis. They denounced the Finnish tourist industry's exploitation of Sami culture in general (Gáldu—Resource Centre for the Rights of Indigenous Peoples 2010). Other nation-states have taken notice. At the Skansen theme park in Stockholm, for example, where a Sami encampment has been a part of the outdoor display since 1891, management started collaborating with the Swedish Sami Association in 2002. Among other things, the collaboration resulted in the inauguration of a new camp consisting of reconstructed dwellings made by Sami craftsmen as well as the re-creation of a representational "mountain flora" around the site (Nylund 2008). Since 2003 Sami People's Day has been celebrated in this location on February 6, the date when the first Sami congress was held in Trondheim, Norway, in 1917, at which Daniel Mortenson was one of the central figures. That celebration, however, also caused controversy within Sami communities because of the setting and, as expressed by Lillian Mikaelsson, the leader of the Stockholm Sami Association, because of Skansen's association with wild animals, extinct traditions, and tourism (Mikaelsson 2003).

The commercialized Sami camp has continued to be a popular—as well as portable—attraction both within and outside Fennoscandinavia. Indeed, the lavvu has become an important ethnopolitical symbol and is considered to be *the* real Sami dwelling by both Sami and non-Sami alike (this in many ways presents a paradox, as less than 10 percent of the contemporary Sami population is involved in reindeer herding). According to Ivar Bjørklund (2013), the starting point of this was Sami demonstrations against the hydroelectric development of the Alta-Kautokeino River around 1980, when Sami hunger strikers put up a lavvu in front of the Norwegian Parliament building. Since then the figure of the lavvu has been adopted as a logo by (or has inspired the form of logos for) all kinds of Sami institutions and organizations, including the Norwegian Sami Parliament (Sámediggi), the Swedish Sami Parliament (Sametinget), Ájtte Swedish Mountain and the Sami Museum (Ájtte), and the Árran Lulesami Center (Árran).

Meanwhile, through a set of actions that can be understood as "branding" (Comaroff and Comaroff 2009), the architectural form of the lavvu has been adopted in a wide range of buildings, from parliaments (Sámediggi) to hotels, cafés, and restaurants (Hotel Lapland, Lycksele).

Indeed, the lavvu itself has been turned into an industrial product. A

Fig. 6.7. The architectural form of the lavvu has been adopted in a wide range of buildings. Lappkåtan, Hotel Lapland, Lycksele, Sweden. Photo by Gösta Ericsson. Source: Tromsø University Museum.

growing number of companies began manufacturing a high-tech version, which in a few years became the standard tent for herders on the move as well as among the Sami population in general.

Today the lavvu is standard inventory in Norwegian schools, kindergartens, and last but not least, different tourist enterprises. Most tourists in northern Fennoscandinavia will at one point pass a Sami camp along the highway where they can stop and buy handicrafts, souvenirs, local products, and foods. The family firm Heia Adventures has managed its camp in the uplands of Tromsø in Northern Norway for more than a decade, and it has also sold its project internationally.

In 1994 Heia Adventures arranged a camp during the Winter Olympic Games in Lillehammer where the internationally recognized Sami artist and performer Ailohaš (Nils-Aslak Valkeapää) joiked at the opening ceremony. It was also his joik singing that, less than two decades earlier, had convinced the Latin American delegates at the WGIA (World Council of Indigenous Peoples) meeting in Port Alberni, Canada, that the Sami were in fact genuine Indigenous Peoples (Minde 2003:85).

In Lillehammer the employees of Heia Adventures befriended Prince Albert of Monaco, and since then they have visited the city-state several times; they even arranged to set up a lavvu camp outside one of the city's casinos. In addition, during the Winter Olympics in Turin in 2006, the same firm arranged a camp in partnership with entrepreneurs within the Northern Norwegian tourist industry, including Lofoten Stock Fish Company and Norwegian Traditional Food. More than seven thousand people visited the camp and approximately two and a half tons of reindeer meat were roasted and consumed during the event. Indeed, despite the fact that the country received twenty-one gold, fourteen silver, and seven bronze medals, *Dagbladet*, the biggest newspaper in Norway, exclaimed that "Sami culture was our greatest winner during the Olympics in Turin" (Dagbladet 2006).

Similar trends of performing ethnic or traditional life can be identified in the rest of the world—a tendency that has resulted in the rise of the disparaging term "heritage industry." This industry unfolds independent of and in partial competition with institutionalized, public representations of culture, and many in the professional establishment look down on it. There is no question that sometimes these performances shift into bizarre, at times impolitic events. It is imperative, however, to be circumspect in making judgments and with our moral contempt and to bear in mind that such living displays have a long history, one that was never limited to a history of victimization. As Christopher Tilley (1997) has pointed out, such cultural performances are often seen as modern forms of alienation, as a "loss of soul" and authenticity, but as many Sami performers have shown for generations, that is not always the case. Indeed, that is a rather myopic reading of history.

Acknowledgments

I thank Laura Graham and Glenn Penny for inviting me to their workshop in Iowa and for their invaluable comments on this chapter. I am also very grateful to the Centre for Sami Studies at the University of Tromsø, Norway, for making it possible to make the trip with a newborn.

Notes

1. As pointed out by Clifford (1997) and Ames (2008), the focus of the historiography of ethnographic displays has been on structural and impersonal power rela-

tions. As a result, dimensions of agency have been closed off and the experiences of the Native performers at shows and their roles as partners have been largely overlooked or reduced to footnotes and tables at the end of books. Such approaches are partly maintained in the work of Hilke Thode-Arora (1989), Werner Michael Schwarz (2001), Anne Dreesbach (2005), and Pascal Blanchard et al. (2008). I too emphasize a scientific perspective in Baglo 2006.

2. In all fairness, the exact Swedish wording in Broberg's otherwise excellent article is, "Givet är ändå att dessa resor snarare var transporter i bur [transportation in cages] än något annat."

3. Several scholars have described other groups being toured, including Africans (Lindfors 1996), North Queensland Aborigines (Poignant 2004), North American Indians (Moses 1996), and South American Indians (Eissenberger 1996). For a more general description of this exhibition practice, see, e.g., Blanchard et al. 2008.

4. Ludwig Ruhe's "Lappenschau" (1924–25), Hagenbeck's Cirkus (1926), Carl Gabriel and Ludwig Ruhe's "Riesenpolarschau" (1930), and a tour organized by the Dane Povl Neve (1933–34) (Baglo 2011). See also *Min far har råkjørt med reinsdyr og slede—i Paris* (My dad has raced with reindeer and sledge—in Paris) (Waage Danielsen 2007) and *Samer på utstilling i Tyskland* (Sami on display in Germany) (Hætta 2007).

5. The support and interest of anthropologists seem to have lasted until 1885–90 in France and Britain, and sometime later in Germany. In the reports in the *Verhandlungen* (transactions) of the Berliner Gesellschaft für Anthropologie, Ethnologie und Urgeschichte only two troupes are mentioned in the early nineteenth century: a Chinese group in 1905 and a "Tscherkessen-Troupe" that was examined in the Berlin Zoological Garden in the spring of 1900.

6. Around 1910 a couple of Sami troupes from the Lake Inari area in Finland participated in exhibitions in Germany, including one organized by Hagenbeck. The majority of these groups are identified as "fiskarlappar"—that is, as groups that subsist mainly by fishing (Hufvudstadsbladet 1910).

7. Or as Sami rights advocate and educator Torkel Tomasson wrote in a Swedish newspaper in 1911 regarding the Sami camp at Skansen, Stockholm, "There is something degrading in the display." He continued, "A real Sami family would never lend itself to an exhibition of this kind, that is why Skansen has to content itself with non–reindeer owning Sami who are not in possession of the virtues, cleanliness and house-pride of the Mountain Sami" (En ordentlig lappfamilj lånar sig ej häller åt en förevisning af denne art, hvarför Skansen fått nöja sig med ikcerenägande lappar som ofta ej äro i besittning af fjälllapparnas framträdande dygder, renlighet och huslighet) (Uppsala Nya Tidning 1911).

8. The troupe, Herr Böhle and Frau Willardt's Laplanders, is also mentioned in an article by anthropologist Alexander Ecker, in which he testifies to their authenticity (Ecker 1878).

9. "Jeg vet du har elsket—og elsket mig høit-, med kjærlighet ren i fra høid. Ja, dette jeg mindes—ak var jeg blot nøid!-Men gavner dog dette en døit? O, kunde jeg faa

dig at elske førend, mine dage av smerte er endt. O, fik jeg blot eie den del—som bekjendt—av landet, som mig jo var tænkt."

Bibliography

Ájtte, Swedish Mountain and Sami Museum

  2011 http://www.ajtte.com, accessed July 12.

Altick, Richard Daniel

  1978 The Shows of London. Cambridge MA: Belknap Press of Harvard University Press.

Ames, Eric

  2000 Where the Wild Things Are: Locating the Exotic in German Modernity. PhD dissertation, Department of German, University of California, Berkeley.

  2008 Carl Hagenbeck's Empire of Entertainments. Seattle: University of Washington Press.

Árran, Lulesami Center

  2011 http://www.arran.no, accessed July 12.

Baglo, Cathrine

  2001a From Universal Homogeneity to Essential Heterogeneity: On the Visual Construction of "The Lappish Race." Acta Borealia 2:23–38.

  2001b Vitenskapelige stereotypier: Om konstruksjonen av samene som kulturhistorisk enhet i tida fram mot 1910 [Scientific stereotypes: On the construction of the Sámi as a cultural historical category before 1910]. MA thesis, Department of Archaeology, University of Tromsø, Norway.

  2006 Samer på ville veger? Om "levende utstillinger," antropologi og vitenskapelige praksiser. Nordisk Museologi 1:3–20.

  2011 På ville veger? Levende utstillinger av samer i Europa og Amerika [Agents Abroad: Living Exhibitions of Sami in Europe and America]. PhD thesis, Department of Anthropology and Archaeology, University of Tromsø, Norway.

Bjørklund, I.

  2013 The Mobile Sámi Dwelling: From Pastoral Necessity to Ethno-political Master Paradigm. *In* About the Hearth: Perspectives on the Home, Hearth, and Household in the Circumpolar North. David G. Anderson, Robert P. Wishart, and Virginie Vaté, eds. Pp. 69–79. New York: Berghahn.

Blanchard, Pascal, Nicolas Bancel, Gilles Boëtsch, Eric Deroo, Sandrine Lemaire, and Charles Forsdick, eds.

  2008 Human Zoos: Science and Spectacle in the Age of Colonial Empires. Liverpool: Liverpool University Press.

Broberg, Gunnar

  1981–82 Lappkaravaner på villovägar: Antropologin och synen på samerna fram mot sekelskiftet 1900. Lychnos (Stockholm):25–86.

Bruckner, Sierra

 1999 The Tingle-Tangle of Modernity: Popular Anthropology and the Cultural Policy of Identity in Imperial Germany. PhD dissertation, Department of History, University of Iowa.

Chicago Daily Mail

 1893 Like a Kaleidoscope. May 29:2.

Chicago Daily Tribune

 1893 Born at the Fair. May 22:3.

Clifford, James

 1997 Routes: Travel and Translation in the Late Twentieth Century. Cambridge MA: Harvard University Press.

 2001 Indigenous Articulations. Contemporary Pacific 13(2):468–90.

Comaroff, Jean, and John Comaroff

 2009 Ethnicity Inc. Chicago: University of Chicago Press.

Coney Collection

 n.d. Contract entered between Emil Arner and Nils Bull, his wife Margareta Bull, and their six-year-old son, Morten Bull. Box C38/39197. Kansas Historical Society, Topeka.

Dagbladet

 2006 Samisk kultur vår største OL-vinner i Torino. February 26.

 2008 NRK avviser nakenbløff. October 2:60.

Debrunner, Hans Werner

 1979 Presence and Prestige: Africans in Europe. Basel: Basler Afrika Bibliographien.

Deloria, Philip J.

 1998 Playing Indian. New Haven CT: Yale University Press.

 2004 Indians in Unexpected Places. Lawrence: University Press of Kansas.

Deloria, Vine, Jr.

 1981 The Indians. In Buffalo Bill and the Wild West. Pp. 45–56. New York: Brooklyn Museum.

Dreesbach, Anne

 2005 Gezähmte Wilde: Die Zurschaustellung "exotischer" Menschen in Deutschland, 1870–1949. Frankfurt: Campus.

Durbach, Nadja

 2008 London, Capital of Exotic Exhibitions from 1830–1860. In Human Zoos: Science and Spectacle in the Age of Colonial Empires. Pascal Blanchard et al., eds. Pp. 81–88. Liverpool: Liverpool University Press.

Ecker, Alexander

 1878 Lappland und die Lappländer: Oeffentlicher Votrag auf Veranlassung der Naturforschenden Gesellschaft und des Antropologischen Vereins. Freiburg: Verlag Stroll und Bader.

Eissenberger, Gabi

1996 Entführt, verspottet und gestorben: Latinamerikanische Völkerschauen in deutschen Zoos. Frankfurt am Main: IKO-Verlag für Interkulturelle Kommunikation.

Feest, Christian F.

1989 Indians and Europe: An Interdisciplinary Collection of Essays. Aachen: Alano.

Gáldu, Resource Centre for the Rights of Indigenous Peoples

2010 No Fake Samis: Stop the Misuse of Our Culture. http://www.galdu.org/web /index.php?odas=3374&giella1=eng, accessed December.

Greenhalgh, Paul

1991 Ephemeral Vistas: The Expositions Universelles, Great Exhibitions and World's Fairs, 1851–1939. Manchester: Manchester University Press.

Hætta, Odd Mathis

2007 Samer på utstilling i Tyskland i 1930. Ottar 4:33–41.

Hagenbeck Archive

1926 Contract entered between Karin Fjellner for Anna Fjellner and Adrian Jacobsen, Røros, February 2. Tierpark Carl Hagenbeck, Stellingen, Hamburg, Germany.

H-Afro-Am

2005 STOP the exhibition of AFRICANS in the Augsberg ZOO. June 8. H-Net: Humanities and Social Sciences Online. http://h-net.msu.edu/.

Hotell Lappland

2011 http://www.hotelllappland.se, accessed July 12.

Hufvudstadsbladet

1910 Lappar på fård söderut. February 4.

Illustrirtes Wiener Extrablatt

1875 Lappländer in Wien. November 26:1.

Kasson, Joy S.

2000 Buffalo Bill's Wild West: Celebrity, Memory and Popular History. New York: Hill and Wang.

Keane, A. H.

1886 The Lapps: Their Origin, Ethical Affinities, Physical and Mental Characteristics, Usages, Present Status, and Future Prospects. Journal of the Anthropological Institute of Great Britain and Ireland, no. 15:213–35.

Lapland Sketches

1822 Lapland Sketches; or, Delineations of the Costume, Habits, and Peculiarities of Jens Holm and his Wife Karina Christian, with accurate Representations of the Deer, Sledges, Huts, &c. as exhibited at Bullock's Museum London. London: S&R Bentley.

Latour, Bruno

2005 Reassembling the Social. Oxford: Oxford University Press.

Lindfors, Bernth, ed.

1996 Africans on Stage: Studies in Ethnological Show Business. Bloomington: Indiana University Press.

Local

2006 Masai Performances under Fire. August 2.

Løøv, Anders, ed.

2001 Lappefogd I. B. Herstads Årsberetninger, 1894–1904. Snåsa: Saemien Sijte.

Manker, Ernst

1939 Under samma himmel. Stockholm: Lars Hökerbergs bokförlag.

Maxwell, Anne

1999 Colonial Photography and Exhibitions: Representations of the "Native" and the Making of European Identities. London: Leicester University Press.

Mikaelsson, Lilian

2003 Aporna och Skansen. Replik till Skansen. Samefolket. http://info.samefolket .se/, accessed March 19, 2010.

Minde, Henry

1996 The Making of an International Movement of Indigenous Peoples. Scandinavian Journal of History 2:221–46.

2003 The Challenge of Indigenism: The Struggle for Sami Land Rights and Self-Government in Norway, 1960–1990. *In* Indigenous Peoples: Resource Management and Global Rights. Svein Jentoft, Henry Minde, and Ragnar Nilsen, eds. Pp. 75–103. Delft: Eburon Academic Publishers.

Moses, L. G.

1996 Wild West Shows and the Images of American Indians, 1883–1938. Albuquerque: University of New Mexico Press.

Neue Preußische (Kreuz-)Zeitung

1875 Die Lappländer Polar-Menschen. January 15:3.

New York Times

1893 Wonderful Place for Fun. June 19:9.

Nordlys

2008 Editorial. September 25:2.

Nylund, Anna-Vera

2008 Sameliv på Skansen. *In* För Sápmi i tiden: Nordiska Museets och Skansens Årsbok. Christina Westergren and Eva Silvén, eds. Pp. 138–57. Stockholm: Nordiska museets förlag.

Peers, L.

2007 Playing Ourselves: Interpreting Native Histories at Historic Reconstructions. Lanham MD: Alta Mira Press.

Poignant, Roslyn

2004 Professional Savages: Captive Lives and Western Spectacle. New Haven CT: Yale University Press.

Raibmon, Paige

2005 Authentic Indians: Episodes of Encounter from the Late-Nineteenth-Century Northwest Coast. Durham NC: Duke University Press.

Riddu Riđđu
2010 http://www.riddu.no/hjem.21023.no.html, accessed March 20.
Sámediggi—Sametinget
2011 http://www.samediggi.no, accessed July 12.
Sametinget
2011 http://www.sametinget.se, accessed July 12.
Sápmi Park
2010 www.visitsapmi.no, accessed March 19.
n.d. Welcome to Sápmi Park in Kárášjohka/Karasjok 70°N.
Scheffy, Zoë-hateehc D.
1995 Running to the Wind: Sami Participation in "Indigenous Peoples' Wisdom from the Earth" at Expo 2000. Paper presented at the Annual Meeting of the Society for the Advancement of Scandinavian Studies, Portland, Oregon, May 7.
Schwarz, Michael Werner
2001 Anthropologische Spektakel: Zur Schaustellung "exotischer" Menschen, Wien 1870–1910. Wien: Turia and Kant.
Scott, Gertrude M.
1991 Village Performance: Villages at the Chicago World's Columbian Exposition, 1893. PhD dissertation, Department of Performance Studies, New York University.
Standing Bear, Luther
1928 My People the Sioux. Cambridge: Riverside Press.
Sturtevant, William C., and David B. Quinn
1989 This New Prey: Eskimos in Europe in 1567, 1576, and 1577. *In* Indians in Europe. Christian Feest, ed. Pp. 61–92. Aachen: Alano.
Svenska Dagbladet
1913 Lappar i Budapest zoologiska Trädgård. January 24.
Thode-Arora, Hilke
1989 Für fünfzig Pfennig um die Welt. Frankfurt: Campus.
Tilley, Christopher
1997 Performing Culture in the Global Village. Critique of Anthropology 17(1):67–89.
Tromsøposten
1885 Fra Karasjok. April 15:2.
Uppsala Nya Tidning
1911 Nomaderna på Skansen. August 18.
Waren Sardne
1910 Lappeslegten. January 29.
1926 Samerne ved Hagenbecks Cirkus er kommet hjem igjen. December 1.

7

Not Playing Indian

Surrogate Indigeneity and the German Hobbyist Scene

H. GLENN PENNY

The truth is that Indians have been dressing like Europeans since first contact.... So why do we think it is so unusual for Europeans to dress Indian?

JOLENE RICKARD, 1998

In the fall of 2000, shortly after I arrived at the University of Missouri–
Kansas City, one of my new colleagues handed me a story from the *Kansas
City Star* headlined "Germans Emulate American Indians." I was amused;
but not because the reporter, Daniel Rubin, had discovered over a thousand German hobbyists living like various nineteenth-century American
Indians in a large encampment near Stolpe, Germany. I already knew about
that. It also was not because the essay had appeared in such a provincial
paper; in one form or another, it has been in most papers. Indeed, what
amused me, and has since begun to irritate me, was how much Rubin's article resembled the scores of other essays written about German hobbyists
over the last fifty years. They essentialize these people and their actions in
the most superficial way.[1]

Such gatherings of German hobbyists—people devoted to what they
call "practical ethnology": the effort to study, simulate, and emulate various
aspects of American Indian lifeways—are not isolated events. They are one
accentuated manifestation of the pervasive fascination with North American Indians among Germans. Shared by men and women alike, this fascination cuts across political, confessional, social, and generational boundaries. It is also much more than a current, postmodern enchantment with
"the primitive."

During the early nineteenth century, stories set among American Indians became popular in German-speaking Central Europe. Literature about them became ubiquitous. The fantastic success of James Fennimore Cooper's *Leatherstocking Tales* is perhaps the most poignant example: the first volume was quickly translated into German in 1826, and it was ultimately condensed with the four following volumes into a single tome, released in abbreviated versions for children, and put through countless new editions during the next decades. It became, in fact, a classic of German literature, familiar to the literate classes in all German states across the nineteenth and twentieth centuries (Rossbacher 1972).

The Leatherstocking Tales were followed by a host of other, similar translations from English, French, and Spanish, which appeared in German periodicals and as swiftly consumed monographs. A series of German travel writers and novelists built on the success of those stories. By writing about American Indians, they became best-selling authors over the rest of the nineteenth century and well into the twentieth. The most prominent of these was Karl May, whose books sold over seventy million copies by the 1980s, about twenty million more than the most well-known American author of Westerns, Louis L'Amour. The enthusiasm continued during the postwar period and moved rapidly into other media. May's books, for example, inspired West Germany's most popular set of movies; a similar set was fantastically successful in East Germany; and in 2003, after the fall of the Berlin wall and German unification, *The Manitou's Shoe*, a spoof on those popular films, broke all records in the German film industry.

Such successes seem astonishing until we recognize that by the end of the nineteenth century thinking about American Indians had become integral to German culture. They were not only a popular subject among novelists and other writers; they were incorporated into the production of toys, theater, circus, high and low art, and the new cinema. Across Imperial, Weimar, and Nazi Germany, children of all ages and both genders "played Indian," emulating the characters from Cooper and May and the people they encountered in Buffalo Bill's Wild West and German circuses, as well as those performing with other impresarios who sought to capitalize on Germans' fascination with Native America. Adults "played Indian" as well, and not simply those individuals who joined the first hobby clubs in the early twentieth century. Artists such as Georg Grosz, Otto Dix, and Rudolf

Schlichter, for example, turned to their childhood engagement with American Indians while dealing with their personal crises and the crises of modernity (Sell Tower 1990). Art historian Aby Warburg traveled to the Hopi and Zuni pueblos for the same reason (Warburg 1995); the artist Max Ernst, the psychiatrist Carl Jung, and the ethnologists Karl von den Steinen and Paul Ehrenreich followed. Adolf Hitler remained in Germany; but he continued to read Karl May's *Winnetou* for insights into crisis situations, recommending it to his General Staff during the battles of World War II (Haible 1998).

"American Indians," in short, became deeply ingrained in German culture during the nineteenth century, their stories became ciphers for modern struggles during the twentieth century, and that long cultural history continued unabated through the postwar era, resurfacing during Cold War clashes, at peace protests, and in environmental movements, esoteric musings, and the persistent settings of backyard play and hobbyists' camps. The unrelenting breadth and depth of this preoccupation is remarkable.

It is also well documented. Journalists have been writing about it for decades. Indeed, they have repeatedly discovered it with elation. The spectacle of Germans emulating American Indians is particularly titillating and evidently hard to resist. Writing about this obsession, especially the hobbyist meetings, is guaranteed to generate smirks and laughter among readers, even righteous anger from some, and that is a recipe for publishing success: those reactions have allowed reporters, as well as a number of scholars, to reap attention from the sensation and then position themselves to disclose astute revelations.

Rubin, for example, attempted to do this by focusing on one man, Jörg Diecke, forty-four, whom he found "dressed in the handcrafted clothing a Hidatsa warrior might have worn on the Great Plains 150 years ago." As Rubin showed, however, Diecke was neither a social misfit nor insane. His wife was a dentist, and his compatriots included "doctors, engineers, cooks, and scholars." He was, if we were to believe the reporter, the product of an odd national politics. Diecke and other East German hobbyists had been weaned on state-sanctioned history books that endorsed viewing American Indians as freedom-loving heroes struggling against oppression; they watched movies in which "Indians were the good guys"; and they were quite adamant on one issue. As Diecke put it, "We do not 'play' at being Indians" (Rubin 2000; cf. Turski 1994; Kalshoven 2005, 2012).

Diecke was not offering a witty retort to Phillip Deloria's 1998 book *Playing Indian*. Rather, he was restating what German hobbyists had been saying about their endeavor for decades. In 1972, for instance, an East German newspaper ran an essay on the club Manitou in the town of Radebeul, one of the oldest German clubs. It included a photograph from a 1928 meeting of the association and an interview with Johannes Hüttner, one of the early members who survived World War II and refounded the group afterward. Hüttner, a pharmacist, together with Fred Metasch, a forester, stressed that their activities were "more than a hobby." Members of the club gained impressive handworking skills, and they engaged in outreach: they had recently finished a successful exhibit of American Indian crafts (made by them) in the Dresden Museum of Folk Art. Moreover, they were activists of sorts: since 1954 they had been making themselves into living displays in Dresden's Zoological Gardens, raising over seven thousand East German marks for the zoo's expansion and educating Germans about different American Indian tribes. They studied ethnological texts and museum exhibits, and they consulted leading authors such as Liselotte Welskopf-Henrich, who had written a dozen novels and stories about Plains Indians, and the ethnologist Eva Lips at Leipzig's Institute of Ethnology. In 1975 they set up a solidarity bazaar in an effort to raise awareness of North American Indians' plight. Acknowledging that most of their members had become enamored with American Indians during childhood, they nevertheless argued adamantly that they had long since moved beyond childish things (E. U. n.d.; KKN 1964).

Journalists highlighted the same attitudes in West Germany. In 1966, for instance, a Cologne paper ran a story headlined "When Papa becomes a Sioux," in which one of the participants in the yearly gathering of West German hobby clubs was quoted as saying that while some people might think that he and his friends were trying to live out a kind of "second childhood, in reality we only want to practice what we have learned from Indians. No, we are not a kindergarten," he argued, "rather we are an ethnological association," focused on practical ethnology instead of theoretical anthropology and consisting of "handworkers, clerical workers, and business people." Even "a genuine professor is here in actual Indian clothing" (Oliv 1988:185; cf. Oliv 1997).

While covering these meetings in Dresden in 1964, Cologne in 1966, and Stople in 2000, journalists consistently reveled in the sensation of hobbyists' activities, connecting them to clichés inherent in popular texts about American Indians, especially the books written by the famous Karl May. At the same time, the various hobbyists, during each of these separate interviews, attempted to redirect the discourse about themselves by explaining that the point of their meetings was not to live out childhood fantasies and reinforce old clichés. Rather, during all of these gatherings, the goal was to undercut the clichés by showing what they knew about "actual American Indians." In that sense the hobbyists often saw themselves as engaged in damage control. Theirs was an effort to correct Germans' misconceptions of North America's Indigenous Peoples by placing themselves and the knowledge they had acquired through "practical ethnology" on display. Hüttner's group did this at the Dresden Zoo and also in places as diverse as "vacation campgrounds, schools, International Children's Day celebrations, the Children's Clinic in Johannstadt, a meeting of journalists in Magdeburg," and veterans' clubs. Moreover, through these efforts and during their private meetings, they also sought to learn more about their subjects through lived experience, through praxis, as well as through an exchange of knowledge among themselves, all of which they insisted was "serious and necessarily scientific" work (KKN 1964).

Thus by the time Rubin wrote his report, the only real news in his column was that East German hobbyists could now leave the territory of the former German Democratic Republic. Some did, traveling to events such as the UN Working Group on Indigenous Populations in Geneva, where they lent their support to activists attending the meetings and where representatives of the Mohawk delegation were able to confirm the legitimacy of the hobbyists' endeavors by telling them that "re-enactment is the highest form of admiration." Few of the journalists, however, were interested in that.

Rather, it was and is the spectacle that drives journalists to hobbyist camps and their annual meetings in order to posit the same puzzled questions again and again until many hobbyists, much like some of the American Indians they emulate, have grown accustomed to the attention and irritated by the visits. They have learned to receive their inquisitors with well-rehearsed answers, if they agree to receive them at all (e.g., in 1996 alone: Aeppel 1996; Kinzer 1996; Neuffer 1996; cf. Gilders 2003).

One characteristic of these reports is typical of even the most scholarly analyses of Germans' interests in American Indians: they harness multiple enticing clichés. As Susanne Zantop has noted, such analyses are not only replete with a focus on clichéd and stereotypical depictions of American Indians by hobbyists and others "but also stereotypical accounts of Germans and their national character or alleged (sinister) motivations" (Calloway et al. 2002:5; cf. Bolz 1999).

Literary scholar Katrin Sieg's essay on West German hobbyists, written about the same time as Rubin's column, is exemplary (Sieg 2002). Although the essay is theoretically sophisticated and analytically incisive, Sieg nevertheless assumes that some sinister notion of "Germanness" was being worked out through hobbyist actions. Based on a small number of interviews, and eschewing the kinds of ambivalences at the heart of Eric Lott's masterful work on ethnic transvestitism in antebellum American minstrelsy (Lott 1993), Sieg attempts to argue that Germans' "impersonations" of American Indians were essentially masked "attempts to cope with the guilt of the Holocaust as well as the widespread shame and resentment provoked by the accusations brought against Germans in the international war crimes tribunals and the denazification procedures." Embodying Zantop's lament, Sieg argues that donning American Indian garb from the nineteenth century somehow "allowed Germans to align themselves with the victims and avengers of genocide, rather than its perpetrators and accomplices" (Sieg 2002:13). That is an unfortunate conclusion. For Sieg's assertions not only lack a historical understanding of the many motivations that drove German hobbyists, before, during, and after the period of National Socialism, it also fails to recognize the long history of German condemnation of the United States' efforts to eradicate American Indians, which predated the 1950s by a century. She has hardly been alone (e.g., Grewling 2007; Guettel 2007).[2]

Friedrich von Borries and Jens-Uwe Fischer's book (2008) on hobbyists in former East Germany is framed in a similar manner. It is driven by the assumption that the German Democratic Republic's ominous character best explains East German hobbyists' actions and behaviors. Dependent on a small number of extreme statements by a few participants (they interviewed Diecke as well) and spurred by their fascination with the secret police (Stasi) and its interest in these groups, the book's conclusions that East German hobbyists were drawn to the study of American Indians because the German Democratic Republic was its own kind of reservation are foregone in the first pages. These authors also leave no room for either historical continuities or social and cultural explanations unhinged from the parameters of nation-states and national identities. They seem blithely unaware that the hobbyist scene is a phenomenon that has persisted across many chronological and geographic borders, including the so-called iron curtain.

It is hardly surprising to learn that few hobbyists are satisfied with such "scholarly" portraits of their passions and endeavors or that even fewer are eager to see more such studies pursued. Nevertheless, hobbyists' efforts are worthy of earnest scholarly consideration. Christian F. Feest, perhaps the leading authority on the subject of Europeans' interests in North American Indians, has noted in several essays that he has been "as puzzled and intrigued" by the "subcultural practices" of hobbyists as he is "puzzled and intrigued by other cultures" and "regrets that so little serious attention has been devoted to understanding and explaining them beyond the assertion that they are a form of cultural escapism" (Feest 2002:31; cf. Bolz 1999a; González 1989; Kalshoven 2007, 2012).

One goal of this chapter is to respond to Feest's regret by taking hobbyists' actions seriously and decoupling them from both the sensational aspects of their performances and an overdetermined link to the nation-state and national identity. The more central purpose of the chapter, however, is to use the history of German hobbyists' associations and actions to explore the notion of surrogate Indigeneity. We know that German hobbyists emerged in the wake of performances by North American Indians who traveled to Germany in the late nineteenth and early twentieth centuries. Some came with Buffalo Bill or other Wild West shows from North America, while others were hired directly by German entrepreneurs, especially the directors of German circuses. All these performers inspired imitators. German hobbyists dedicated themselves to reproducing the material culture of specific Native American tribes and emulating their rituals, their social organizations, and on occasion, some aspects of their religions. Among themselves, and occasionally in front of other Germans, they acted as surrogates for those performers, imitating and enhancing the Indigenous displays.

Through those actions, these surrogate groups developed an intricate, multigenerational subculture of their own, one that has drawn a range of responses from Native America, many more positive than most academics would assume. My goal here is to detail the development of this subculture and use it as a means to engage, in a rather idiosyncratic way, the questions of what constitutes Indigeneity, who gets to be Indigenous, and how categories of Indigeneity relate to and interact with categories such as race. My hope is that this will broaden our understanding of the political ramifications of the public production of Indigeneity in local, national, and global contexts.

Play and Displays of Indigeneity

Despite adamant statements by Jörg Diecke and other hobbyists at the end of the twentieth century, the hobby scene they embraced emerged from an interest in play. More than two decades ago, Rayna Green (1988:38) argued, "Wild West Shows are the places where Indians join whites in playing Indian." In Germany these shows were also the place where white Europeans were inspired to play Indian en mass. Buffalo Bill appeared for the first time in Imperial Germany in 1890, moving through that country with even more success than in other European nations (Moses 1996). His tour inspired people across German-speaking Central Europe to engage in acts of mimesis. Marcus Kreis has studied this moment in detail, revealing that directly after Buffalo Bill's first visit to Berlin, boys set up a village that one reporter called "the Wild West on a reduced scale." Similar reactions occurred in Leipzig, Vienna, and many other Central European cities, leading Kreis to conclude that "the main effect of Buffalo Bill's Wild West Show and all the shows that imitated his schema was to make Indians, like cowboys, a role one could play and which was fun to play." Part of the appeal was the verisimilitude; Buffalo Bill's Wild West claimed to offer its visitors the real thing. At the same time, however, it was also a performance, a moment of play as well as display, and the "live action, simple plot, and utopian setting" all contributed to its "attractiveness to children, adolescents, and many adults, by making the Indian someone or something you can play" (Calloway et al. 2002:202). German hobbyist clubs emerged as a direct result, focused initially on imitation and emulation of what could be seen in these performances (Bolz 1999a).

Overwhelmingly, what Germans saw were Plains Indians. As a result, Plains Indians, and in particular Lakotas from the Pine Ridge Reservation in South Dakota, came to dominate the image of American Indians in

Fig. 7.1. Postcard showing participants in Hagenbeck's famous 1910 exhibition of Sioux. Karl Markus Kreis Postcard Collection.

Germany for most of the twentieth century (R. Green 1988). They came as part of various attractions: groups of Omahas and Oglalas toured Germany in the 1880s, Lakotas followed with Buffalo Bill and Doc Carver in 1889 and 1890, and many smaller Wild West shows continued to try to capitalize on the other shows' astounding success.[3] German entrepreneurs such as Carl Hagenbeck, who had long organized exhibitions of non-Europeans, or *Völkerschauen*, in Germany, recognized the appeal Plains Indians had for the public and began bringing their own groups to Germany. Indeed, Hagenbeck's 1910 troupe of Lakotas was by far the most successful display of non-Europeans during the course of his career (Ames 2009; Rothfels 2002; Thode-Arora 1989). So impressive were the crowds turning out for these exhibitions that in 1907 the circus impresario Hans Stosch-Sarrasani began incorporating Lakotas and other American Indians into his shows. Indeed, only a few years later he negotiated to get precisely those Lakotas who had been such a success for Hagenbeck. His competitors followed suit, looking for their own performers, and after Germany recovered from World War I, the demand for these performers led to the regular transportation of American Indians from places such as Pine Ridge to Dresden and other German cities until the outbreak of

World War II.[4] In fact, these performers became so common that by the mid-1920s the Miller Brothers 101 Ranch in Oklahoma, which developed into a kind of clearinghouse for American Indian performers, began to worry about overtaxing the German enthusiasm for these kinds of exhibitions and reducing the size of the crowds that each impresario could command. As a result, the 101 Ranch made a concerted effort to try and control the flow of performers across the Atlantic in order to preserve the market's integrity.[5]

The older hobby clubs around Dresden, Munich, and Freiberg were indebted to the contacts they had with these performers. In Dresden in particular, enthusiasts were able to have direct and fairly regular interactions with the American Indians that worked for Sarrasani, and in some cases they took part in their performances. Those lucky few were able to join American Indians in playing Indian, as Green put it, and after the troupes of American Indians left, the Germans went on with the show (Conrad 1999; Rietschel 2012).[6] Other groups outside of Dresden, such as the Munich Cowboy Club, had contact as well. They not only traveled to performances in other cities, visited those troupes that came to Munich, and met the performers who came to work for Circus Krone, they also purchased clothing and artifacts directly from Sarrasani's performers, using them to create their own costumes, to fill their showrooms, and as models for their own craft production.[7]

Some of these members developed strong relationships with performers. Artist Elk Eber, for example, who gained some notoriety for his unique painting of the Battle of Little Big Horn, which has long been used to

Fig. 7.2. (*opposite top*) Albert Richter, *The Albert-Fest in Central Park* [Großen Garten] *in Dresden: The Indians of the Art Association 'Mappe'*, in imitation of Buffalo Bill's performers. *Leipziger Illustrirte Zeitung* 101, no. 2618 (1893): 272.

Fig. 7.3. (*opposite bottom*) Front page of an article titled "The flight from the everyday into an Indian romantic: Cowboy-club Munich-south. Adults who play Wild West." The article describes the thirty-year history of such play, beginning with the Velo Club, which often substituted bicycles for horses, and then turning to the Munich Cowboy Club, founded in 1914. Its members, the article stresses, now ride horses. *Münchener Illustrirte Presse* no. 16 (1930): 543.

Münchner Illustrierte Presse

DIE FLUCHT AUS DEM ALLTAG IN DIE ROMANTIK:

COWBOY-CLUB

MÜNCHEN-SÜD

ERWACHSENE, DIE WILDWEST SPIELEN

illustrate pamphlets at the Little Bighorn Battlefield National Monument, maintained a correspondence from November 1933 to December 1938 with White Buffalo Man (also known as Thomas Stabber) and Sam Lone Bear.[8] Eber befriended Stabber in 1929, while Stabber was working for Sarrasani. After a performance in Munich, Eber and the other members of the Munich Cowboy Club invited Stabber and his wife to spend an evening with them, and during the following days Eber made paintings of different members of the Lakota troupe, including several of Stabber.[9] After Stabber returned to the Pine Ridge Reservation, Eber sent Stabber and Lone Bear money, medicine, eagle feathers, satin, calico, dye, trade beads, and other objects in exchange for older artifacts (e.g., a rawhide shield, bows and arrows, a scalp), finished clothing (e.g., moccasins, a dance bustle, leggings, bead and quill work), and in one case, drawings. Unable to travel to the United States but eager to ground his images in authentic details, Eber turned to Stabber for information about Lakota culture. He sent Stabber outlines of warriors' faces and asked him to color in the drawings in ways appropriate to dances, celebrations, and warfare. Once Stabber returned those drawings, Eber used them as templates for his paintings (cf. Rietschel 2012).[10]

Like many other performers, Stabber began working in Germany with troupes organized by the Miller Brothers 101 Ranch. When J. C. Miller passed away in 1927, however, Stabber turned directly to the Germans for contracts. He wrote to Sarrasani looking for work for himself and others, and Sarrasani, in turn, contacted the U.S. commissioner of Indian affairs in March 1931 and explained that "Mr. Thomas Stabber, (aka White Buffalo Man) the chief of the party, and Sam Lone Bear, the interpreter, have writte[n] and cabled me intimating their desire to re-new their engagements with me. These Indians have been employed in my Circus periodically since 1915, having last returned to USA in December 1930."[11] As a result of these negotiations, Stabber was able to work with Sarrasani for another season in the 1930s, and afterward he continued to negotiate for further opportunities to return to Germany, if not to work with Sarrasani, than to work with other companies, like Circus Krone in Munich, an opportunity that his friend Elk Eber helped him and Lone Bear secure. In several of his letters to Eber, Stabber made his desire to return explicit, writing, for example, in 1936, "My country is no good. No work and no money. . . . I don't want to go to American show, no good, I like to go to Deutschland show."[12] Both he and Lone Bear preferred to work in Germany.

Stabber and other American Indians had good reasons for seeking work in these shows. Vine Deloria Jr. made this clear in the early 1980s when he argued that working with Buffalo Bill gave performers "confidence in themselves by emphasizing the nobility of their most cherished exploits and memories." In many cases it also placed them on a more equal footing with the whites around them, something Stabber and Lone Bear articulated as well. "Unlike the government programs," Deloria noted, Buffalo Bill "treated the Indians as mature adults capable of making intelligent decisions and of contributing to an important enterprise," which had an obvious appeal. Moreover, for many, the Wild West shows "provided a platform for displaying natural ability that transcended racial and political antagonisms and, when contrasted with other contemporary attitudes toward Indians, represented one that was amazingly sophisticated and liberal" (V. Deloria 1981:53).

There were other reasons as well. As Philip Deloria reminds us, most of the performers joined up for the money, which was scarce on Pine Ridge and other reservations. For many, however, these performances also offered the opportunity to find out more about the white world, to demonstrate bravery by leaving home, or to recapture remembered lives. Some also thought they could use these shows as an opportunity to "educate their audiences to the virtues of Indian cultures," "to craft new visions of themselves," and to act as "visiting dignitaries involved in cultural and political exchange" (P. Deloria 2004:70). To wit: self-conscious Indigenous display.

The point, then, is that the tours and the shows were sites in which Indigenous Americans engaged in both playing Indian and fashioning themselves (cf. Baglo, Perrone-Moisés, this volume). And as the nascent hobbyist groups took shape, emulating these show Indians, interacting with them on occasion, seeking to learn what the dignitaries offered to teach, they became surrogates for these performers once they were gone. The hobbyist groups continued their performances for themselves and others long after World War II made it impossible for Stabber, Lone Bear, and others to return. This is evidenced in part by the fact that what began as play and emulation of show Indians gradually transformed into focused studies of American Indian tribes, their histories, their ethnological details, the production of their material culture, and as much as possible, their ways of life, all of which were performed in public places as forms of education as well as play.

Surrogate Indigeneity

Current definitions of Indigeneity could logically be extended to many Europeans, especially since, as Ronald Niezen (2003:70) has pointed out, "ambiguity of the term is its most significant feature." Many representatives at the UN Working Group meetings in Geneva have balked at developing a more precise definition of the term for fear that it could become too confining. There is, however, consensus on some points. One of "the most commonly recognized features of indigenous peoples," Niezen writes, is "descent from original inhabitants of a region prior to the arrival of settlers who have since become the dominant population." Another is connections to "a primordial identity" and references "to people with primary attachments to land and culture, 'traditional' people with lasting connections to ways of life that have survived 'from time immemorial'" (Niezen 2003:3, 19, 23). These are people who suffer or have suffered from the transformations wrought by external forces but "have survived on their lands through the upheavals of colonialism and corporate exploitation." He notes as well that the "unbroken ancestry" of these people "is not seen as protecting them from the deleterious impacts of industrial and state ambitions." Rather, "their territories are imposed upon by extractive industries; their beliefs and rituals are imposed upon by those who would convert them (or selfishly acquire their knowledge); and their independence is imposed upon by states striving for political and territorial control. They are those people whose position in the modern world is least tenable. They are especially vulnerable to warfare, genocide, dispossession, disease, and famine" (Niezen 2003:5).

I do not wish to make an argument in favor of Germans' identity as Indigenous Europeans "with primary attachment to land and culture" who "have survived on their lands through the upheavals of colonialism and corporate exploitation." I would like to point out, however, that the idea has circulated widely in German culture for as long as Germans have shown a fascination with American Indians. Indeed, in German literature, putative commonalities in German and American Indian histories have long been regarded as a foundation for affinity. The central source for that comparison stemmed from the Roman senator Cornelius Tacitus. In *Germania*, Tacitus portrayed Germans at the end of the first century CE as a noble tribal people with a clear connection to the forests and lands of Central Europe, who suffered at the hands of an expansive, colonial civilization. Indeed, he wrote about Germans much in the same way German authors would later write about American Indians, as noble savages and formidable, violent warriors whose most honorable qualities exposed the decadence and failings of the civilized world.

Already in the seventeenth century, Germans conflated the ancient Teutons with contemporary American Indians, and by the middle of the nineteenth century such comparisons circulated widely, coupled in many cases with the sufferings of the German populations during the Thirty Years War (Egmond and Mason 1997). While visiting the Standing Rock Reservation in 1881, for example, the artist and author Rudolf Cronau wrote extensively in his notebooks about the similarities and differences between the Roman onslaught faced by German tribes and the European invasion faced by American Indians (Penny 2010, 2013). And in a lecture titled "The Decimated Race," which he presented to German audiences in the United States in 1882 and across Imperial Germany from 1884 to 1887, he discussed the similarities and differences between German resistance to Roman invasion and the American Indians' efforts to resist European encroachment. Then he described the devastation wreaked on American Indians during the 1870s and 1880s in a manner analogous to Dee Brown's work almost a century later (1971).[13] Similarly, in the 1960s Liselotte Welskopf-Henrich, who was a professor of ancient history, a prolific author of novels about American Indians, and a staunch supporter of the American Indian Movement, described at length the similarities between German tribes and American Indians in her correspondence with Lakota artist Arthur Amiotte—stressing the comparable connections to landscapes, victimization by Christian missionaries, and the loss of culture through conquest.[14] These are neither isolated nor dated examples. Indeed, while I was doing interviews for this project in 2003–4, one Berlin hobbyist told me with conviction, "If you really want to understand the German fascination with American Indians you have to read Tacitus."[15]

That is a useful assignment, especially if coupled with analyses of the ways in which Germans have read Tacitus over the last two centuries. For behind the sensational national history of Germany that dominates the discourse on German character and identity is a less thrilling but perhaps more poignant history, one that is fragmented and more aware of the degree to which Germans have been focused on local spaces, towns, regions, dialects, and landscapes across the modern age (e.g., Blackbourn and Retallack 2007). Even during the Imperial period (1871–1918), during the height of nation making, it was common for Germans to envision their state as first and foremost an aggregate of tribes (*Stämme*). The German tribes (defined in a variety of ways, e.g., as regional, ethnic, linguistic, or cultural groups) were often evoked during political debates at the national and regional level (e.g., A. Green 2003; Smith 2008). This rhetoric persisted through the period of National Socialism as well, even if it was turned to new, more exclusionary, and racial arguments, which made the terminology fall out of favor, if not out of mind, in the postwar period.

The point that the Berlin hobbyist was making to me in 2003, however, is that the challenges American Indians faced as Indigenous Peoples, especially their self-reflective connections to land, culture, and space and their resistance to overwhelming external forces, have long evoked a sense of empathy among many Germans who felt that they share some of those connections to the land and have faced, and in some ways continue to face, many of those same challenges. The multiple ways in which Germans have been able to map those identifying markers of Indigeneity onto their cultural identities helps to explain the origins of the sense of affinity many Germans felt toward American Indians and their plight during the last two centuries. Moreover, the emotional connection that many felt toward the challenges Indigenous North Americans faced helps to explain hobbyists' transformation during the postwar period, as they moved away from emulation of circus Indians and toward the protracted and concerted study of historically and ethnically specific groups.[16] This search for knowledge about specific groups of American Indians was always already a search for self. It was, in essence, a quest for a lifestyle lost, now corrupted; for an organic sense of self, grounded in nature, freedom, and holistic community; and for the possibility of resistance, even spiritual redemption, in an increasingly materialist world.

Recently Colin Calloway commented that "Indian scholars from Canasatego to Charles Eastman to Vine Deloria have pointed out that Indian America has a lot to teach Europe if Europeans are willing to look and listen." He also noted that "Germans, perhaps more than any other nation, have demonstrated the willingness to do so" (Calloway et al. 2002:69; cf. LaDuke 1984). I would add that many German hobbyists were particularly eager to learn and eager to teach what they had learned to broader audiences. Indeed, by the 1950s many hobbyists saw themselves engaged in an effort at preservation, an attempt to locate the traces of specific American Indian cultures both for their own edification and, ultimately, for the use of the survivors of ethnocide in North America.

That desire was captured succinctly in a letter from Willy Linder, "Chief" of the Oglala Indianerclub in Mannheim, to Ethel Merrival and the Oglala Sioux Tribal Council in Pine Ridge. In the 1950s the U. S. military, recognizing Germans' fascination with all things Indian and having learned about the hobbyist clubs, took the initiative to encourage American Indian servicemen to participate in the West German clubs' activities as part of a broader effort to promote German-American relations.[17] In Munich the U.S. military helped the Munich Cowboy Club build a new clubhouse, and Major General J. F. R. Seitz, head of the Southern Area Command, attended the ceremony for the emplacement of the building's cornerstone and allowed one of his soldiers, Sergeant Silkirtis Nichols, to dance at the ceremony in regalia.[18] In Mannheim the U. S. military encouraged some of its soldiers and officers to take part in the Oglala Indianerclub's activities as well and recorded the presentation of a peace pipe, made by one of these soldiers, to Linder and the club. The military also facilitated contact with Pine Ridge and the Tribal Council, which sent Linder a gift.

Linder thanked the Tribal Council for that gesture, noting that it was "of greatest importance" to him "in a moral sense," because it had given him "courage to further pursue the aims of our club." Those aims included "the preservation of Indian culture and the study of Indian lore," which, he noted, "is by no means an easy job for me as a German." Complaining that many Germans did not understand his group's efforts, he also lamented that many American Indian servicemen seemed to have little interest in its aims. He stressed that "it would mean much for me if they would find their way to me and my people. Only from them we would [sic] be able to learn Indian customs and habits." Linder was dismayed that he was forced

Fig. 7.4. Chief Willy Linder and Captain Mattingly engaged in "promoting German-American relations." The caption on the back of this U.S. Army photograph states, "Indian Jamboree, Mannheim, Germany. July 1956. Chief Willi Linder, of the Heidelberg Ogalala Tribe, places the honorary headdress on Capt. Mattingly, and smokes the peace pipe to further German American relations." PFC Lester Ermis made the pipe and presented it to Linder. Courtesy of the National Archives at Kansas City, 75-PR-2799.

to rely on books to expand his knowledge. He was also disappointed by the lack of knowledge and interest in so many of the American Indian servicemen he met. These young men "look only for pleasure and thus bury the pride of their old tradition." Thus he had written to the Tribal Council in an effort to initiate contact with people who still held on to their traditions. In particular, he hoped to connect with their "Chief": "I ask him to help us in our efforts—to preserve the Indian culture for our German youth."[19]

One can image the eyebrows Linder's letter raised in Pine Ridge as Merrival and the Tribal Council wondered at his desire to "preserve Indian culture for [the] German youth." But the message was clear. Convinced that American Indians, who had yet to submit completely to the homogenizing forces of modern civilization, could help hobbyists locate the elements of tribal life that had been erased from German society and culture, Linder and his group reached out to the people they thought most able to teach them: traditionalists.

It is uncertain whether the Tribal Council ever answered these hobbyists' requests. But we know that many other American Indians did. Indeed, in Munich, for example, Major General Lloyd Moses, a Rosebud Sioux and former commander of the Southern Area Command, endorsed the organization of a powwow in 1959 that included hobbyists and American Indian servicemen. One of those men was Silkirtis Nichols, who adopted the name Buffalo Child Long Lance; another was Charles Trimble, who was born on Pine Ridge and later became (among many other things) the principal founder of the American Indian Press Association in 1969 and the executive director of the National Congress of American Indians from 1972 to 1978. He, in fact, supplied some of the artwork used in the advertisements for the powwow and happily spent time with the Munich hobbyists in their club.[20]

As they sought knowledge from books, scholars, and American Indians, the more dedicated hobbyists began a campaign that continues to this day: to seek out the truth about specific American Indian cultures, customs, and histories and then to disseminate that knowledge through exhibitions, performances, and lectures. As they set out to educate, they also began policing the German discourse on Indianness.

On occasion that policing has been extreme. On September 7, 1959, for example, a Munich newspaper reported with glee the public burning of three thousand "bad books about Indians" at an event hosted by the Munich Cowboy Club and attended by some one thousand people, including U.S. military personnel, public school officials, and Sergeant Nichols, who danced again. It described how children who brought the greatest number of "bad books" to the conflagration received in exchange books that portrayed "the real wild west" as well as free entry to the Indian exhibition set up in the botanical garden, which had attracted some twenty thousand visitors.[21]

The mind reels at the spectacle of Nichols, a black man who claimed a Choctaw/Cherokee heritage, dancing near an area where Germans publicly burned "bad books" while U.S. military personnel and school officials looked on. Nevertheless, this event captured in vivid colors the hobbyists' quest to gain and promote the most accurate information available. It also demonstrated their recognition that one of their chief challenges, as Linder

Fig. 7.5. A hand-drawn advertisement for a German-American powwow, created by Charles Trimble. Buffalo Bill Historical Center, Cody, Wyoming, MS3.2.1.A.07.1.

too had noted, was to combat the great amount of misinformation about American Indians in the public domain. That action remained a critical mission of hobbyist groups in both East and West Germany through the end of the Cold War and even after German unification in 1990.

The challenges faced by East German hobbyists in gaining and disseminating information about American Indians were even greater than those lamented by Linder, especially after the erection of the Berlin Wall and the strengthening of the borders between the two Germanys. With no American Indian servicemen to invite to the encampments (although Nichols did visit East Germany in the 1960s) (Heermann 1995), radically reduced access to American books, and only limited contact with their counterparts in the west, East German hobbyists worked at times in extreme isolation. That isolation, however, promoted conviction, the paucity of new information enhanced the value of what they could obtain, and these conditions led at times to ingenious efforts to locate and disseminate newly released books, periodicals, and newspapers on the American West and even more ingenious means of pursuing American Indian crafts.

Despite the purposeful isolation of East Germany from Western Europe and the United States, however, East German hobbyists were, much like Linder, still able to gain information about the lives and the struggles of contemporary American Indians and they were also able to engage in the kinds of exchanges that Elk Eber had with people living on different reservations. Indeed, during the era of peace movements, student unrest, and the rise of the American Indian Movement (AIM), East Germans became particularly active in their efforts to support AIM's endeavors, welcoming a number of AIM activists and later other American Indian spokesmen in East Germany (Penny 2008).

It was perhaps in East Germany, because of its state-imposed isolation, that hobbyists engaged most explicitly, even effectively, in surrogate Indigeneity. For decades the clubs, which consistently increased in number and diversified, offered the other Germans around them a point of access to non-European cultures that they could no longer contemplate visiting personally and with which they had contact only through literature and films. Karl May's books were not allowed to be printed or distributed in East Germany until the 1980s, and the incredibly successful West German films based on his books were not allowed to be publicly shown; yet East Germans still read those books, James Fenimore Cooper's *Leatherstocking Tales*, and a host of others. Moreover, the East German film industry produced a series of *Indianer* films that were incredibly successful as well, and the hobbyists fed off the popular enthusiasm for the films and novels to act out their roles as surrogates (Penny 2008).

At the same time, much as in West Germany, East German hobbyists began to expand their studies and interests beyond the various Plains Indians. The citizens of Leipzig and nearby Taucha, for example, had long shown an interest in Woodlands Indians because of an ostensible visit by a group of Iroquois to the area in 1887. Large folk festivals had taken place in the interwar era, which at times incorporated thousands of Germans playing Indian.[22] In 1983 Siegfried Jahn founded a group focused initially on the Ojibwas and then on the Mohawks. Much like the Manitou club in the 1950s, Jahn's group too engaged in significant public outreach, setting up exhibitions in the longhouse the members built in town and working toward solidarity with the Mohawk nation. The group organized fund drives, purchased and collected materials for Mohawk schools, and like many other East German groups, sent care packages across the Atlantic to contemporary American Indians. Before unification (1990), Jahn's group was quite popular, a frequent presence in schools. Invited to a variety of public events, the members set up exhibits and offered slide shows to promote Germans' knowledge of and interest in the Mohawks, their history, culture, and political situation. In 1991 the group set up an exhibition in Leipzig's internationally recognized ethnographic museum, and in 1987 it received a visit from Bob Smith, the director of the Oneida National Museum, whose enthusiasm for its efforts earned it a mention in volume 4 of the *Handbook of North American Indians*, under Indian-white relations (Jahn 1994).

The Non-Western Gaze

Given the number and variety of American Indians who have encountered German hobbyists it is not surprising that their reactions have been mixed. Moreover, considering that in 1990 the number of German hobbyists ran into the tens of thousands, "enough to stock a mid-sized reservation," as Christian Feest once put it, there have been a wide variety of encounters (Feest 1990:327). Indeed, one of the amazing things about this movement is how quickly Germans returned to it after the devastation of World War II. Older clubs, such as the Munich Cowboy Club, were almost immediately reconstituted, while new ones were created. The Western Club Dakota Karlsruhe, for example, was officially registered in 1948. In 1951 the annual national meeting of these clubs under an umbrella organization, the Westernbund, began taking place across West Germany. Each year it moved from one host location to the next, until the late 1980s, when members secured a permanent spot for the annual meeting in the Westerwald forest next to Hundsdorf, a small town near Koblenz. The first meeting boasted only three tipis and some forty participants, but the numbers more than doubled the next year, and by the mid-1970s literally thousands of participants and hundreds of tipis appeared every year: the organizers counted 170 tipis in 1979, 209 in 1981, 306 in 1986, and 439 in 1993, after which they became increasingly concerned with finding parking for the over one thousand cars and trucks needed to transport all these tipis and the people who occupied them to the annual event (Oliv 1988, 1997).

In 1982 the number of clubs that participated in the meeting surpassed one hundred. By 1998 there were 156 clubs associated with the Westernbund and 53 former East German clubs connected to its eastern counterpart, the Indianist Union, which organized an event called The Week. In southwestern Germany, the city of Freiberg alone boasted ten such associations in 2004. Dresden, in former East Germany, claimed twelve. Those numbers, however, are only part of the story. There have always been clubs that were not registered and clubs and individuals that did not participate in the annual mass meetings, and while everyone involved in these movements recognized a steady growth through the postwar era, no one has ever been in a position to accumulate exact figures. Thus, during the last decade of the twentieth century, estimates of active hobbyists in Germany ranged widely, from forty thousand to upwards of one hundred thousand (Bolz and Sanner 1999; Hagengruber 2002).

Members of hobby clubs have always ranged from part-time participants interested mostly in socialization and play to dedicated enthusiasts focused on the minutiae of material culture, the intricacies of microhistory, and the political plight of contemporary tribes. Some enthusiasts have refused to become involved in contemporary politics, while others have abandoned the past to focus on the political actions of the present, forsaking as well their interest in dressing like nineteenth-century Indians in favor of the jeans and T-shirts worn by so many today. Individuals who have participated in the hobby for long periods of time have also generally seen their interests and actions shift and change over the years. Consequently, it is impossible

Fig. 7.6. The Week near Cottbus in 2006. Photo by the author.

to make more than the most simplistic general statements about what one might encounter during a "typical" hobbyist meeting or how such a meeting might be received.

One consistency, however, is that American Indians have always been honored guests. They offer the possibility of critical reflection, of authoritative confirmation or equally imposing condemnation of the hobbyists' goals. Throughout the Cold War era, the hobbyist journals produced in West Germany—most notably *Dakota Scout*, *Fährte*, and *Der Indianerfreund*— and the three-volume chronicle of their yearly meetings compiled by Max Oliv delighted in discussing the various American Indians who attended their local or national meetings. In the east as well, visits by people such as the Lakota Archie Fire Lame Deer in 1983 were sensations that have since become a critical part of hobbyist lore. In 1999 Rudolf Conrad produced a short essay on these meetings with Lame Deer, and during my own 2006 visit to The Week I heard a number of accounts of his impact on the associations. What became clear during these discussions was the degree to which the hobbyists bowed to their visitor's authority as an actual American Indian, sought his approval, listened with great attention to his suggestions, and tried to incorporate them into their activities. In Conrad's words, he helped fulfill their "deep wish" to "become acquainted more thoroughly with Indian mentality and religion in order to better understand the Indians' way of life, their culture, history, and present political efforts." He provided them with his own instructional performances, including singing, sweat lodge, and pipe ceremonies, and ingratiated himself with the hobbyists who sought to learn from him. At the same time, Conrad argued that the feeling was mutual: "Archie expressed his pleasure to be here and to see tipis and excellent bead and quill work. This he regarded as a stimulus for his own people to resume some of their old traditions." In short, Lame Deer assured them that they had done their part as surrogates well (Conrad 1999:455–74).[23]

That point is critical. As Michael Brown has remarked, not everyone takes emulation as a compliment. "Indigenous peoples," he stressed, "now perceive themselves as more threatened by outsiders who claim to love their religion than by missionaries dedicated to its overthrow," and "at present" the "critical literature is dominated by the idea that the use of musical and artistic genres by non-natives is theft, the final assault after colonialism has taken away everything else" (Brown 2003:23, 63) That position was certainly embraced by Katrin Sieg, who drew liberally on Ward Churchill's condemnations of hobbyists in Europe, and some American Indian scholars who have visited German hobbyists also embraced the notion that they are engaged in theft. American Indians, once victims of colonialism, they wrote, are now victims of impersonators (e.g., Carlson 2002; Mayo 1991).

That critical literature, however, has not carried the day, even if it has made many hobbyists more circumspect. There are too many tales similar to Conrad's, and too many positive reports from American Indians such as the Choctaw film director Phil Lucas. Lucas learned about German hobbyists from his friend the Blackfeet director George Burdeau, who had seen hobbyists' teepees during the mid-1970s when he was stationed in Germany. While Lucas was working on the five-part TV series *Images of Indians* with the well-known Creek actor Will Sampson he traveled with his crew to Germany in the hopes of locating some hobbyists and including some European clichés about American Indians into the series. After locating a group of German Yakimas in Cologne, he learned that they had

Fig. 7.7. The Week near Cottbus in 2006. Photo by the author.

a connection with a Yakima family in North America, that they visited them every other year, and that through those visits they had learned much about songs and dances. He went to their clubhouse, which he described as akin to a museum, the walls covered with objects they had made themselves. There he talked to one of the members about a drum that had been blessed by a Madoc medicine man who had visited their club, and the hobbyist began to demonstrate a drum blessing ceremony. "That's when our dilemma began," Lucas noted, because as he set out to film the event the hobbyist objected and explained to him, "This is a religious ceremony, 'you can't film it.'" "As Indians, that was quite strange for us to hear," Lucas recalled, "because that is normally the reaction one hears from us." "But what really impressed" him and his film crew, he stated, "was their sincerity [*Aufrichtigkeit*]." Lucas and Sampson later went on to film some of the hobbyists' activities, but with a completely different perspective than they had initially intended: "What we wanted most to convey was: In order to find genuine appreciation of Indians, one has to travel to Europe" (Peipp and Springer 1997:269–70).

There are many similar examples of American Indians arriving among hobbyists with strongly mixed emotions but leaving with a generally positive impression. Most notable, perhaps, are the reactions of the Cree couple Joseph and Irene Young and the Ojibwa Barbara Daniels to a group of hobbyists in the Czech Republic, just across the border from East Germany. Their experiences among these hobbyists and their reactions to their efforts were captured in John Paskievich's film *If Only I were an Indian*. Accompanied by the Canadian anthropologist David Scheffel, these three travelers met a small group of hobbyists in their home before venturing to their group's encampment. On arriving at the campsite, they all professed that they were torn by mixed emotions: "Cry, laugh, be angry," one noted, "I was going through a struggle inside of me." As they watched the hobbyists over the next few days and engaged them in activities, however, their opinions solidified: as Frantieisek Stupak told them about life in postwar Eastern Europe and explained that they were "morally defeated people" trying to learn from the Indians; as Joseph Young showed the hobbyists how to capture the best rhythm from the drum and danced with them; as Irene Young and Barbara Daniels showed them how they make bread in a pan and watched women in a sweat, a consensus emerged. Joseph Young noted how impressed they were with these people's efforts. Barbara Daniels reflected on how watching the Czechs cook food in the ground "brings back good memories." She remarked as well that while much of her culture had been taken away by whites, "these people are different, they use our culture. These things have come alive again." She stated that the visit had taught her that "Indians are not victims, but people who have a lot to offer the world," and she argued as well that "if people in Canada and America would just have a tiny fraction of interest in native culture as these people do, things would be so different than they are." In the end, she issued perhaps the most poignant statement in the film when she commented, "If this is stealing our culture than I would be happy to see more of it" (Paskievich 1995).

What emerges from these and other, similar encounters is that hobbyists recognize their precarious position as surrogates and seek confirmation that they are "getting it right." For this reason many are eager to include American Indians in their activities, quickly ceding to them positions of authority and prestige in their subculture. There have been many incidents when the American Indians they sought out proved inadequate to the task, as during the early experiences with young servicemen lamented by Willy Linder or in the tale told by the Dakota A. C. Ross in his autobiography. While Ross was stationed in Mainz-Gonsenheim with the 505th Paratroop Brigade, his commander told him and "the other Indian boys in the company" to put on their best uniforms and prepare for a meeting. The meeting was with a group of local hobbyists who were delighted to learn that he was a Dakota from Pine Ridge and invited him to attend some of their meetings to discuss his people's history and culture with them. Ross recounted his embarrassment at realizing that these Germans knew much more about those subjects than he did, and he stated that "the incident was a great awakening for me. It planted a seed in me to start studying my own history. That's when I started a search for my roots" (Ross 1993:92–93).

In most cases, however, American Indians have something to share, and quite a few are willing to do so. Some, such as Nichols, have felt so honored and content with that position in the hobbyist movement that they have become permanent fixtures in it. Indeed, Nichols was still dancing in Germany at the age of eighty-five.[24] Others, such as the Hopi Lindbergh Namingha, who also arrived in Germany under the auspices of the U.S. military in the early 1970s and returned after leaving the military, have become integrated in the scene in more official ways. Namingha became the head of the Native American Association of Germany (NAAOG), guiding it for many years, and thus he was active on the edge of the hobbyist scene. The NAAOG evolved out of a series of different associations established in 1976 to bring American Indian soldiers stationed in Germany together, and since at least 1994 it has been made up of both American Indians and Germans, most of whom are or were hobbyists. The group is well known in Germany for hosting powwows that bring Germans and American Indians together and for bringing performers from the United States to attend and headline these events. Throughout its history, one of the chief goals of the association has been to educate Germans about American Indians and their traditions. Much like Siegfried Jahn and his Mohawk group in East Germany, the NAAOG has been engaged in damage control. Indeed, a significant amount of its resources have been dedicated to outreach with schools, and its website is replete with evaluations of books and cultural events, links to information sites, and tips about exhibitions and events related to American Indians in Germany.[25] In this association, however, American Indians have taken over the role once fulfilled by their surrogates, the hobbyists, who have now been relegated to the role of helpers.[26]

The Question

One of the central criticisms faced by most hobbyists is that, try as they might, they will never be Indians. Sometimes these arguments are essentially racial (e.g., Penny 2006). They generally come from outside the clubs, but hobbyists make this comment as well. As one hobbyist in Berlin told me in 2003, "No matter how well you play your part, your ass remains white." For many other hobbyists, however, conversion was never the goal. Revering and studying groups of American Indians, learning from their culture and history, and harnessing that knowledge to reposition themselves in their own societies and cultures is not, they remind us, the same as wanting to be American Indian. They simply want to be better people.

If we distance ourselves from the question of transformation we are still left with the problem of legitimacy, its implications, and the question posited by Jolene Rickard in 1998: "why do we think it is so unusual for Europeans to dress Indian?" Why do we assume that it is humorous and problematic rather than understandable and perhaps even instructive? And what do those assumptions prevent us from seeing? To my mind, we miss understanding interconnections between Europeans and non-Europeans that are too often overlooked by scholars, too quickly filed away under the rubric of neocolonialism, and too often assigned to the actions of "kooks," as one of my colleagues deemed them. Such uncritical evaluations certainly cause us to miss the opportunity to evaluate an alternative form of knowledge production, one that stands outside the academy and is based on often-stringent discursive readings of texts and interviews that are later circulated through oral traditions in this German/European subculture rather than through academic publications or journalistic essays. Only the most pedantic ethnologists fail to grudgingly admit that many hobbyists have become authorities on a range of issues (particularly the history and production of material culture across an impressive geographical and chronological breadth). We know that there are instances in which knowledge production has circumvented the academy before—in art, in science—and at times I cannot help wondering if the quick condemnation of hobbyist activities tells us more about academics and others doing the condemning than the people they so often refuse to take seriously. Perhaps they fear the implications of these surrogates "going Native," a rather old European fear, since transformation remains the obsession in their reports. Or perhaps they fear reflecting on themselves and their own lifeways, which often seems to be the critical subtext.

Notes

1. Much of the material for this essay stems from my recent book, *Kindred by Choice* (2013). I am grateful to the University of North Carolina Press for permission to revisit some of that material here while developing a more focused argument about surrogate Indigeneity.
2. For a refreshing alternative that follows Lott's recommendation that we seek out the political range of such performances, see Weber 2010.
3. A variety of small entrepreneurs attempted to capitalize on this interest. Not all of them were successful. See, e.g., the letter from the Department of the Interior to Assistant Attorney General Leupp dated February 14, 1908, about a suit against J. T. McCaddon, for wages owed to Paul Stands Up, Charlie Yellow Wolf, and Stephen Medicine Cloud, who were abandoned by the McCaddon Show Company in Grenoble, France. Document 11192-08-047, in RG 75, Records of the Bureau of Indian Affairs, Central Classified Files, Pine Ridge, U.S. National Archives, Washington DC.
4. The records on these transactions are extensive and are not limited to interactions with Sarrasani. The Miller brothers were contacted by most of the major circuses in Central Europe. See, e.g., the letter from Julius Gleich in Cologne to the Miller brothers expressing his interest in a "good band of Indians from Pine Ridge" for his "very big circus." Miller Brothers 101 Ranch Collection, M-407, box 1, folder 1, Western Historical Collection, University of Oklahoma, Norman. Hagenbeck and Circus Krone dealt with them as well. They were not, however, the only group that helped supply American Indian performers to German and other European organizations. The last troupe of American Indian performers to work for Sarrasani arrived in 1937.
5. J. C. Miller (JCM) to Schultze, April 19, 1926, box 41, folder 2; Schultze to JCM, January 14, 1927, box 47, folder 5; and Schultze to JCM, March 8, 1927, box 47, folder 5, all in Miller Brothers 101 Ranch Collection.
6. Hüttner, in fact, related meeting Chief Black Horn at Sarrasani's circus when he was only twelve years old, and he discussed how this inspired him and influenced the ways in which he pursued his hobby (E. U. n.d.).

7. *8 Uhr Blatt* no. 243, September 7, 1963, "Cowboy-Club Zeitungen" clipping file, Munich Stadtarchiv.

8. Unlike most renditions of the Battle of the Little Big Horn, Eber's painting places several Sioux, rather than Custer, at the center of the conflict. A copy of the painting is available at "Elk Emil Eber," Thule Italia: Galleria d'arte, http://www.thule-italia.org/Arte/eber/eber_2.jpg.

9. These paintings are well known. See "Elk Emil Eber," Thule Italia: Galleria d'arte, photograph of Eber with White Buffalo, http://www.thule-italia.org/Arte/eber/eber_5.jpg, and *Dipinto di Capo indiano* (Painting of Indian chief), http://www.thule-italia.org/Arte/eber/eber_25.jpg.

10. Stabber-Eber correspondence, in the possession of Max Oliv, Munich. I am grateful to Max Oliv for sharing these with me.

11. Sarrasani also wrote, "I cannot lay too much stress on the fact that the presence of American Indians with my show, traveling as I do over Europe has aroused tremendous enthusiasm especially amongst the cultured classes and has maked [*sic*] excellent propaganda for the great and powerful United States of America." Sarrasani to Commissioner of Indian Affairs, February 25, 1931, 18184-31, National Archives, Washington DC.

12. Stabber to Eber, May 6, 1936, in possession of Max Oliv; see also Lone Bear to Eber, December 23, 1934, and Stabber (in Brussels) to Eber, June 16, 1935, both in possession of Max Oliv. Stabber and Lone Bear were not alone in their success at establishing relationships in Germany or in their efforts to return to Germany. The Miller brothers received many letters from other Lakotas on the Pine Ridge Reservation asking for assistance in getting work in Germany, or in many cases, such as with Creeping Bear and his friend Watan, wanting to return again. Jas Sweet Grass also found ways to return to Germany once he had been there. On one occasion he returned with a circus from New York State, and on other occasions after contacting the Miller brothers and arranging a contract with one of their groups. Some families, such as the Two-Two family, stayed for long stretches at a time, and different members returned for multiple visits. Edward Two-Two, one of the most famous of the Lakota visitors, was buried at his own request in a Catholic cemetery in Dresden during a visit in 1913. Hobbyists still care for his grave. Creeping Bear to JCM, March 11, 1926, box 38, folder 2; Jas Sweet Grass to JCM, January 27, 1927, September 29, 1927, box 47, folder 6; Sarrasani to JCM, February 8, 1926, box 41, folder 1, all in Miller Brothers 101 Ranch Collection.

13. Cronau, Tagebuch I, 24–26; Cronau, Tagebuch II, 75; Cronau, "Ein verleumdete Rasse," in Tagebuch III, Cronau Nachlass, Solingen Stadtarchiv.

14. Welskopf-Henrich to Amiotte, January 1, 1969, in Welskopf, *Nachlass* (collected papers), file 173, Archiv der Berlin-Brandenburgischen Akademie der Wissenschaft.

15. Discussion with a Berlin hobbyist, December 30, 2003.

16. This transformation was not uniform, but it was ultimately consistent. The timing varied between the different regional centers of the hobbyist scene: around Cologne, Freiburg, Munich, Dresden, and Berlin. One hobbyist who had been involved with the scene during the entire postwar period, for example, stressed to me that one could track the transformation by looking at photographs of hobbyists in their regalia. The old costumes that the Dresden groups used to wear during the period after World War II were uniform, much like those of the circus Indians. That changed slowly over time. The Munich and Freiberg groups, however, changed their outfits much faster, taking their lead more from the performers working with Buffalo Bill's Wild West than from those with the circus and studying artifacts and clothing in museums much sooner. Interview with German hobbyist, Berlin, May 26, 2004.

17. The public participation of American Indian servicemen in these events was discussed openly in military newspapers. See, e.g., "Heim, Heim on the Range," *Stars and Stripes*, September 5, 1959, which discusses this explicitly, and *SACom Scene*, August 15, 1963, which shows Specialist Fourth Class Leon Martenac and Private First Class Gilbert Matthews, both from Pine Ridge, at the club.

18. "Munich Cowboy Club Starts New Building," *SACom Scene*, July 28, 1961.

19. Linder to Merrival, August 6, 1956, Records of the Tribal Council Executive Committee, 1948–1956, box 1211, RG 75, Records of BIA, Pine Ridge, U.S. National Archives, Kansas City. English in the original.

20. Copies of the artwork are located in MS-3, Charles J. Belden Collection, Harold McCracken Research Library, Buffalo Bill Historical Center, Cody, Wyoming. See also a news clipping from the *Münchner Merkur*, October 9, 1959, clipping file "Cowboy-Club Zeitungen," Munich Stadtarchiv"; Charles Trimble, interview with author, July 9, 2003.

21. "'Bill der Rancher' stirbt am Marterpfahl," *Münchner Merkur*, September 7, 1959; "Feuer und Flamme für Schundhftl," *Süddeutsche Zeitung*, September 7, 1959.

22. "Auf zum Tauschen nach Taucha! Drei Tage Hochbetrieb in Leipzigs Nachbarstadt," *Neue Leipziger Zeitung*, September 3, 1938, 12. The article reports that there were two thousand visitors dressed as Indians and "trappers."

23. For similar statements from elder George P. Lee, a Navajo, about his visit to East Germany and his impressions of the Karl May Museum versus the museums he was used to in the United States, see, e.g., "Ein Indianer im Karl-May-Museum," *Sächsische Zeitung*, June 6/7, 1987.

24. See, for example, "Nicki Buffalo Child: 85 Yrs. Old Native American," July 30, 2008, YouTube, http://www.youtube.com/watch?v=vRONUAC2fTY.

25. Native American Association of Germany, http://www.naaog.de/pageID _5606389.html; see also Peterka-Hirschfield 2000.

26. For a recent multinational German powwow, see "Powwow, Unterkirnach," April 25–26, 2009, YouTube, http://www.youtube.com/watch?v=P35gD1kuLKc.

Bibliography

Aeppel, Timothy

    1996 At One with Indians: Tribes of Foreigners Visit Reservations. Wall Street Journal, August 6.

Ames, Eric

    2009 Carl Hagenbeck's Empire of Entertainments. Seattle: University of Washington Press.

Anonymous

    1966 Wenn der Papa zum Sioux wird. Kölner Stadtanzeiger 1966. Cited in 20 Jahre Indian Councils, vol. 1, 1951–1970, Max Oliv, ed. Pp. 185. Munich: Westernbund e.V., 1988.

Belden, Charles

    1960 War Whoops in the Schwartzwald. Farm and Ranch Review, November.

Blackbourn, David, and James Retallack, eds.

    2007 Localism, Landscape, and the Ambiguities of Place: German-Speaking Central Europe, 1860–1930. Toronto: University of Toronto Press.

Bolz, Peter

    1999a Indians and Germans: A Relationship Riddled with Clichés. In Native American Art: The Collections of the Ethnological Museum Berlin. Peter Bolz and Hans-Ulrich Sanner, eds. Pp. 9–22. Berlin: G&H.

    1999b Life among the "Hunkpapas": A Case Study in German Indian Lore. In Indians and Europe. Christian F. Feest, ed. Pp. 475–90. Lincoln: University of Nebraska Press.

Bolz, Peter, and Ulrich Sanner

    1999 Native American Art: The Collections of the Ethnological Museum Berlin. Berlin: SMPK.

Borries, Friedrich von, and Jens-Uwe Fischer

    2008 Sozialistische Cowboys: Der Wilde Westen Ostdeutschlands. Frankfurt a. M.: Suhrkamp.

Brown, Dee

    1971 Bury My Heart at Wounded Knee: An Indian History of the American West. New York: Holt, Rinehart, and Wilson.

Brown, Michael F.

    2003 Who Owns Native Culture? Cambridge MA: Harvard University Press.

Calloway, Colin G., Gerd Gemünden, and Susanne Zantop, eds.

    2002 Germans and Indians: Fantasies, Encounters, Projections. Lincoln: University of Nebraska Press.

Carlson, Marta

    2002 Germans Playing Indian. In Germans and Indians. Colin G. Calloway, Gerd Gemünden, and Susanne Zantop, eds. Pp. 213–16. Lincoln: University of Nebraska Press.

Conrad, Rudolf

    1999 Mutual Fascination: Indians in Dresden and Leipzig. *In* Indians and Europe. Christian F. Feest, ed. Pp. 455–74. Lincoln: University of Nebraska Press.

Deloria, Philip J.

    1998 Playing Indian. New Haven CT: Yale University Press.

    2004 Indians in Unexpected Places. Lawrence: University Press of Kansas.

Deloria, Vine, Jr.

    1981 The Indians. *In* Buffalo Bill and the Wild West. Pp. 45–56. Brooklyn: Brooklyn Museum.

Egmond, Florike, and Peter Mason

    1997 The Mammoth and the Mouse: Microhistory and Morphology. Baltimore: Johns Hopkins University Press.

E. U.

    n.d. "Manitou" unter Radebeuls Himmel. Undated newspaper clipping number 19722000 3, Karl May Museum archive, Radebeul, Germany.

Feest, Christian F.

    1990 Europe's Indians. *In* The Invented Indian: Cultural Fictions and Government Policies. James A. Clifton, ed. Pp. 313–32. New Brunswick NJ: Transaction Publishers.

    1999 Indians and Europe. Lincoln: University of Nebraska Press.

    2002 Germany's Indians in a European Perspective. *In* Germans and Indians: Fantasies, Encounters, Projections. Colin G. Calloway, Gerd Gemünden, and Susanne Zantop, eds. Pp. 25–46. Lincoln: University of Nebraska Press.

Gilders, Adam

    2003 Ich bin ein Indianer. Walrus, October.

González, Yolanda Broyles

    1989 Cheyennes in the Black Forest: A Social Drama. *In* The Americanization of the Global Village: Essays in Comparative Popular Culture. Roger Rollin, ed. Pp. 70–86. Bowling Green OH: Bowling Green State University Popular Press.

Green, Abigail

    2003 The Federal Alternative? A New View of Modern German History. Historical Journal 46(1):187–202.

Green, Rayna

    1988 The Tribe Called Wannabee: Playing Indian in America and Europe. Folklore 27:30–55.

Grewling, Nicole

    2007 Fighting the Two-Souled Warrior: German Colonial Fantasies of North America. PhD dissertation, University of Minnesota.

Guettel, Jens-Uwe

    2007 Reading America, Envisioning Empire: German Perceptions of Indians, Slavery, and the American West, 1789–1900. PhD dissertation, Yale University.

Hagengruber, James

    2002 Sitting Bull Über Alles. Salon.com, November 27. http://dir.salon.com/mwt /feature/2002/11/27/indians/index.html.

Haible, Barbara

    1998 Indianer im Dienste der ns-Ideologie: Untersuchungen zur Funktion von Jugendbüchern über nordamerikanische Indianer im Nationalsozialismus. Hamburg: Verlag Dr. Kovac.

Heermann, Christian

    1995 Old Shatterhand ritt nicht im Auftrag der Arbeiterklasse. Dessau: Anhaltische Verlagsgesellschaft.

Jahn, Siegfried

    1994 Uhwentsya karenhata: Eintragener Gemein Nuetziger Verein aus Leipzig. Das Indianermagazin. Pp. 58–59.

Kalshoven, Petra Tjitske

    2005 "Is This Play?" Reframing Metaphoric Action on Indianist Playgrounds. *In* Plan B: When the Anthropologist Becomes Data. Nathaniel Dumas, ed. Pp. 66–88. Kroeber Anthropological Society Papers 91. Berkeley: Kroeber Anthropological Society.

    2007 Beyond the Souvenir: Replicas as "the Real Thing" in Indianist Historical Reenactment. *In* Conference Proceedings: Things That Move: The Material World of Tourism and Travel. Leeds: Centre for Tourism and Cultural Change, Leeds Metropolitan University.

    2012 Crafting "The Indian": Knowledge, Desire, and Play in Indianist Reenactment. New York: Berghahn Books.

Kinzer, Stephen

    1996 Germans in Their Teepees? Naturally. New York Times, April 2.

KKN

    1964 Kinder Manitous: Eine reportage vom Indianertag in Radebeul. Dresdener Stadt-Rundschau, October 22.

LaDuke, Winona

    1984 Journey of Peace: The 1983 Native American Delegation to West Germany. Akwesasne Notes 16(2):19–21.

Lott, Eric

    1993 Love and Theft: Blackface Minstrelsy and the American Working Class. New York: Oxford University Press.

Mayo, Lisa

    1991 Appropriation and the Plastic Shaman: Winnetou's Snake Oil Show from Wigwam City. Canadian Theatre Review 68:54–63.

Moses, L. G.

    1996 Wild West Shows and the Images of American Indians, 1883–1933. Albuquerque: University of New Mexico Press.

Neuffer, Elizabeth

    1996 Germans Make a Hobby Out of Cowboys and Indians. Boston Globe, August 6.

Niezen, Ronald

    2003 The Origins of Indigenism: Human Rights and the Politics of Identity. Berkeley: University of California Press.

Oliv, Max

    1988 20 Jahre Indian Councils, vol. 1: 1951–1970. Munich: Westernbund e. V.

    1997 20 Jahre Indian Councils, vol. 2: 1971–1990. Munich: Westernbund e. V.

Paskievich, John

    1995 If Only I Were an Indian. Zemma Pictures: National Film Board of Canada.

Peipp, Matthias, and Bernhard Springer

    1997 Edle Wilde Rote Teufel: Indianer im film. Munich: Wilhelm Heyne.

Penny, H. Glenn

    2006 Elusive Authenticity: The Quest for the Authentic Indian in German Public Culture. Comparative Studies in Society and History 48(4):798–818.

    2008 Red Power: Liselotte Welskopf-Henrich and Indian Activist Networks in East and West Germany. Central European History 41(3):447–76.

    2010 The German Love Affair with American Indians: Rudolf Cronau's Epiphany. Common-Place 11(4). http://www.common-place.org/vol-11/no-04/reading/.

    2013 Kindred by Choice: Germans and American Indians since 1800. Chapel Hill: University of North Carolina Press.

Peterka-Hirschfield, Jennifer

    2000 American "Indians" Abound in Germany. Indian Country Today, April 5.

Rickard, Jolene

    1998 Alterity, Mimicry, and German Indians. In Bavarian by Law/German Indians. Max Becher and Andrea Robbins, eds. Pp. 30–31. Syracuse NY: Light Work.

Rietschel, Hartmut

    2012 Neues aus dem Karl-May-Museum Radebeul: Elk Ebers Irokesenhäuptling. Amerindianresearch 7/3(25):167–74.

Ross, A. C.

    1993 Ehanamani "Walks Among": An Autobiography. Denver: Bear.

Rossbacher, Karlheinz

    1972 Lederstrumpf in Deutschland: Zur Rezeption James Fennimore Coopers beim Leser der Restaurationszeit. München: W. Fink.

Rothfels, Nigel

    2002 Savages and Beasts: The Birth of the Modern Zoo. Baltimore: Johns Hopkins University Press.

Rubin, Daniel

    2000 Germans Emulate American Indians. Kansas City Star, August 6:A16.

Sell Tower, Beeke

    1990 Envisioning Amerika: Prints, Drawings, and Photographs by George Grosz and His Contemporaries. Cambridge MA: Busch-Reisinger Museum.

Sieg, Katrin

    2002 Ethnic Drag: Performing Race, Nation, Sexuality in West Germany. Ann Arbor: University of Michigan Press.

Smith, Helmut Walser

    2008 The Continuities of German History: Nation, Religion, and Race across the Long Nineteenth Century. New York: Cambridge University Press.

Thode-Arora, Hilke

    1989 Für fünfzig Pfennig um die Welt: Die Hagenbeckschen Völkerschauen. Frankfurt: Campus.

Turski, Birgit

    1994 Die Indianistikgruppen der DDR: Entwicklung, Probleme, Aussichten. Idstein, Germany: Baum.

Warburg, Aby M.

    1995 Images from the Region of the Pueblo Indians of North America. Michael P. Steinberg, trans. Ithaca NY: Cornell University Press.

Weber, Alina Dana

    2010 "Indians" on German Stages: The History and Meaning of Karl May Festivals. PhD dissertation, University of Indiana.

8

The Return of Kū?

Re-membering Hawaiian Masculinity, Warriorhood, and Nation

TY P. KĀWIKA TENGAN

In 1791 the chief Kamehameha erected and consecrated the massive stone temple Puʻukoholā Heiau (on the island of Hawaiʻi) in order to fulfill a prophecy telling that all of Hawaiʻi would be his if he built a house for Kū, the god of state, male generative power, and sometimes war. By 1810 Kamehameha had unified the archipelago and established the Hawaiian Kingdom. Over the next two hundred years, though, American imperialism in the Pacific led to a prolonged settler occupation of the islands (Fujikane and Okamura 2008; Kauanui 2008a; Sai 2008; Silva 2004; Trask 1999). On the 2010 bicentennial of Hawaiian nationhood, Kānaka ʻŌiwi Maoli (Indigenous Hawaiians) lifted up new prayers for reunification and restoration. In June the last three remaining temple images of Kū stood together for the first time in nearly two hundred years at the Bernice Pauahi Bishop Museum (Honolulu) when two of the statues returned to the islands from their present homes in Massachusetts and London. This special exhibit was titled *E Kū Ana Ka Paia* (The walls shall stand upright), a line from another prophecy chant that speaks of "the loss and return of the Hawaiian government through the unification of the people to form the walls of the restored nation" (Ayau and Tengan 2002:186). That same month the ʻAha Kāne Native Hawaiian Men's Health Conference gathered over six hundred men from across the islands and the U.S. continent to discuss their roles and responsibilities as the metaphorical cornerstones of these walls. The opening ceremonies took place at the Bishop Museum, where chants, prayers, and dances invoked the mana (spiritual power and authority) of Kū. Two months later many of these same men traveled to Puʻukoholā Heiau

Fig. 8.1. Members of the Hale Mua, wearing malo (loincloths) and carrying pololū (sixteen-foot-long spears) and pāhoa (daggers), perform at the Puʻukoholā Heiau ceremonies, August 2010. Photo courtesy of Joey Corcino.

to make offerings of ritual items and embodied performance—prominent among them warrior dances with carved spears—that celebrated the completion of a four-year effort to rebuild the walls that had fallen during a massive earthquake in 2006.

These events highlight the political stakes of gender and cultural performances in Hawaiʻi. As Wolfe has noted of settler colonialism, "invasion is a structure not an event" (2006:388) and one that operates under a logic of eliminating Natives (either physically or culturally) in order to replace them with non-Natives on "emptied" lands. Hall explains that such strategies of erasure include "the deliberate destruction of non-heteronormative and monogamous relationships, the Indigenous languages that could conceptualize these relationships, and the cultural practices that celebrated them" (2008:278). While recognizing that "gender oppression has been a mode of imperialism in the history of Hawaiʻi," Kauanui points out that "the nationalist struggles over the meaning of precolonial history with regard to both gender and sexuality constitute a significant political terrain within the context of Native Hawaiian decolonization" (2008b:283). Taking these Indigenous studies and Native feminist insights as a departure point, I ask what it means for Hawaiian men to link claims of masculinity to those of sovereignty. What is gained and what is lost when the restoration of both Hawaiian nationhood and men's authority is called for in the return of Kū?

Among the core groups participating in the 2010 events was the Hale Mua (Men's House), a grassroots organization on Maui and Oʻahu that emerged out of the Hawaiian cultural nationalist movement in the 1990s with a focus on training Hawaiian men to be community leaders through the practice of Hawaiian warrior traditions. This essay draws on personal involvement and ongoing ethnographic research that I have carried out with the group since 1997, which I have published on more fully elsewhere (Tengan 2008a). My central argument here is that performances of Indigenous masculinities enact both the possibilities and the limits of decolonization. Gender performances in settler societies emerge from the conditions of colonization and the struggles of Indigenous Peoples to persist and thrive as nations on their homelands. Bodies figure centrally in the gendered work of decolonization, for it is there that alternative forms of being and acting—in the Hawaiian case, those based in ea (sovereignty, life, breath), genealogy, and mana—are re-membered. However, a failure to critique Indigenous masculinities enables the perpetuation of settler heteropatriarchy and ultimately constrains the possibilities of Indigenous freedom and sovereign expression.

This chapter begins with a brief sketch of the historical and sociological contours of the Hawaiian community and the Hale Mua on Maui.[1] I follow that with a discussion of how ceremonies that invoke Kū foreground the ideological dimensions of reclaiming Indigenous masculinity in the service of nation building. Then I focus on the Hale Mua's body-strengthening routines and their intersections with broader discourses of violence and enactments of gender and culture through dance. It is through these ritual and bodily performances that Hawaiian masculine and warrior subjectivities come to acquire new meaning. I end by considering the possibilities and problematics that these reformulated identities hold for social and political change.

A Sketch of Hawaiian History and Community

According to Hawaiian moʻolelo (stories, histories, narratives), the first Oceanic voyagers came to Hawaiʻi some two thousand years ago and eventually established a highly stratified chiefdom. Yet once Hawaiʻi was put on the global imperial map with Captain James Cook's arrival in 1778, change was much more rapid. Despite international recognition of the Hawaiian Kingdom's independence in 1843, the nation suffered an overthrow backed by the U.S. military in 1893 and an annexation in 1898—both done illegally. White American sugar barons and missionary descendants thereafter ran the Territory of Hawaiʻi like a plantation, as Hawaiian leaders worked to reverse the population collapse that saw some 90 percent of their people swept away by epidemics. World War II brought further changes, including the empowerment of second-generation Japanese American veterans and labor leaders who secured statehood in 1959 and led the political and economic shift from agribusiness to militarism and tourism (McGregor 2007).[2]

Native Hawaiians renewed their cultural pride and political consciousness during a period of renaissance and protest in the 1970s, and by the 1980s a vibrant cultural nationalist movement flourished (Trask 1999). The recuperation of old identity terms such as Kanaka Maoli (Real People) and Kanaka ʻŌiwi (People of the Bone) indexed new political and cultural claims of Indigeneity (Ayau and Tengan 2002; Blaisdell and Mokuau 1994). A protest march and rally in downtown Honolulu attended by fifteen thousand people, a People's International Tribunal (Ka Hoʻokolokolonui Kanaka Maoli), and an apology from President Bill Clinton and the U.S. government marked the 1993 centenary of the illegal overthrow. The return of lands and sovereignty seemed imminent.

However, in 2000 the U.S. Supreme Court ruling in *Rice v. Cayetano* that failed to recognize Indigenous Hawaiian claims to sovereign status fueled a backlash of "color-blind" lawsuits aimed at dismantling the few programs, entitlements, and rights that Kanaka Maoli had secured under American occupation. The U.S. senator Daniel Akaka pushed forward a bill to protect against these attacks by redefining Hawaiians as members of a Native nation; a number of activists and intellectuals contested both the "Akaka Bill" and the color-blind attacks as threats to broader claims of

Hawaiian sovereignty. In the post-*Rice* era, Kanaka Maoli and their allies throughout the islands and on the continent organized in new ways to imagine and struggle for a more just and sustainable future for all peoples of Hawaiʻi (Okamura 2008; Kauanui 2008a; Howes and Osorio 2010).

Such transformed visions of a new social order offer hope to ʻŌiwi, who experience severe economic and political marginalization in their homelands and increasing growth in the diaspora. In the 2010 U.S. Census, Kānaka ʻŌiwi numbered 527,077, some 45 percent of whom lived on the continent (Hixson et al. 2012:16). The 289,970 residing in Hawaiʻi made up 21 percent of the 1.36 million residents of the state, making them the fourth-largest ethnic group, behind whites, Filipino Americans, and Japanese Americans (Niesse 2011). In 2000 Hawaiians had the highest rates of unemployment, poverty, and incarceration of all major ethnic groups in Hawaiʻi (Kanaʻiaupuni et al. 2005:80–87).[3] They constituted the second-least-likely group "to work in a managerial or professional capacity" and the "most likely to be employed in construction, extraction, and maintenance positions and in production, transportation, and material-moving occupations" (Kanaʻiaupuni et al. 2005:84–85). Jonathan Okamura also found that "Native Hawaiian men [were] substantially underrepresented as management and business specialists" whereas Hawaiian women were "employed at parity" in these high-status jobs; conversely, Hawaiian men were over-employed in service work and women were at par (2008:47, 48–49). As far as health statistics went, Hawaiians overall had the highest rates of obesity, early morbidity, depressive symptoms, suicidal tendencies, and certain other "risky behaviors" (especially among young adults) (Kanaʻiaupuni et al. 2005:94–98, 111–13, 197–203); they also had the second-highest infant mortality rates (Kanaʻiaupuni et al. 2005:157).

At the same time, owing in part to increased self-identification as well as the ability to mark multiple races on census forms, the Native Hawaiian population grew 90.1 percent between the 1990 and 2000 censuses and another 31.4 percent in 2010 (Kanaʻiaupuni et al. 2005:29; Hixson et al. 2012:6). As Kauanui (2008a) has noted, a return to "genealogical reckoning" of Indigeneity, rather than adherence to the settler logics of blood quantum classification, has enabled Hawaiians to contest the discourses of disappearance that dominated the early twentieth-century debates over "rehabilitating" the Native. Though no longer considered a "dying race,"

Kanaka ʻŌiwi of the early twenty-first century continued to struggle in a context in which identity mattered in new and important ways. This was especially the case for Hawaiian men, who above all others were thought to be "missing" and whose "return" highlighted one of the many gendered aspects of decolonization.

Kā I Mua: Cast Forward into the Men's House

U.S. colonial discourses of incorporation in the nineteenth and twentieth centuries were heavily gendered, rendering Hawaiʻi's lands and people as the feminine "hula girl" waiting to be taken by the masculine Uncle Sam (Ferguson and Turnbull 1999; Imada 2012; Tengan 2008a:50). Hawaiian men were typically erased from this picture; if they were represented at all, it was as either overly domesticated or irreparably dysfunctional—both forms of discursive emasculation that denied them manhood in a modern society (Tengan 2008a:10–11).

In a related but different way, Native Hawaiian nationalism in the late twentieth century was also gendered as feminine. Women's leadership in the decolonization movement was noted widely (Trask 1999), even to the point that men (who had been active throughout) were perceived as absent and thus called upon to be more engaged (Tengan 2008a:12–13). The animating question of "where are the men?" led to the formation of the Hale Mua (Men's House).

Their story begins with a commemoration held at Puʻukoholā Heiau in 1991, the bicentennial of its construction in 1791. Since 1972 the heiau (temple) had been a National Historic Site under the management of the U.S. National Park Service; the 1991 event entitled Hoʻokuʻikahi (To Unify As One) sought to redefine the space as a center of Indigenous Hawaiian mana (spiritual and political power), rather than an object of U.S. imperial state power. In an effort to again petition the heavens for Hawaiian unity, a committee led by the Maui carver and storyteller Sam Kaʻai (b. 1938) conducted new ceremonies on the heiau and assembled a group of men called Nā Koa (the Warriors or the Courageous Ones). Many of the Nā Koa members later became involved in the revival of the Hawaiian fighting art known as lua, which began with a series of seminars and lua schools sponsored by the Bishop Museum. Taking up the production of carved weaponry and

Fig. 8.2. Members of the Hale Mua (*far left*) await the presentation of hoʻokupu (offerings) by other groups on the grounds below Puʻukoholā Heiau, August 2010. Visible atop the heiau is a hale (house) made using traditional thatching techniques. Photo courtesy of Joey Corcino.

the practice of martial arts, these warriors for the nation would embody the aggressive posturing of identity that came out of the cultural nationalist movement. Kaʻai explained that Nā Koa was "not about being warlike" but "being courageous enough to look at your spirit.... It's about spending yourself, and in the spending you know more about yourself, things you already are" (Meyer 1998). On Maui, Kaʻai mentored a group of Nā Koa led by Kyle Nākānelua (b. 1959), a firefighter and one of the first students of the reestablished lua schools. They returned to Puʻukoholā each year to conduct ceremonies of rededication, renewal, and remembering. Between 1997 and 1998 the group split from the lua schools and reorganized itself as the Hale Mua o Maui.

The Hale Mua takes its name from the precolonial men's eating house and domestic temple, which was a part of the ʻaikapu (sacred eating) religiopolitical system that separated men and women during eating periods. Young boys were initiated in a ceremony called kā i mua, which means "cast into the men's house" or "thrust forward," and given their first malo (loincloth). The hale mua then became a space in which boys were socialized and learned the skills and stories of fishing, farming, cooking, canoe and house building, fighting, sailing, lovemaking, fathering, and providing for the family. Those taking a functionalist approach to culture and society argue that when the ʻaikapu system and the hale mua ended in 1819, men lost their way and have remained adrift in society ever since (Nunes and Whitney 1994; Paglinawan et al. 2006:62–63; Pukui et al. 1972, vol. 2:230). This notion is problematic and works to perpetuate a colonial discourse of emasculation—ineffectual or absent men—and a gendered logic of settler elimination. The loss of the hale mua was only one of a number of factors that contributed to the social decay experienced by Hawaiian men, not all of whom were equally affected. With that said, the hale mua metaphorically serves as a useful model for action and transformation by providing an idealized space for the performance of embodied and discursive practices associated with feeding, praying, and rearing.

The basic aim of the Hale Mua on Maui was to establish a cultural foundation for Hawaiian men by creating a safe space for learning and practicing culture, engaging in the ritual process of self-transformation, and establishing networks among the men. The general premise of the group was that colonization and modernization had led to a loss of Hawaiian life and culture, especially for the men. By reestablishing a Hale Mua, men would gain a deeper understanding of their history and acquire the skills, knowledge, and courage to be more effective as members and leaders in their families and communities. With its specific focus on warriorhood, the Maui group trained its men in Hawaiian martial arts, ceremonial conduct, carving, chant, and dance. The yearly activities of the Mua typically corresponded with the precolonial Hawaiian ritual calendar that devoted eight months of the year (approximately February/March–September/October) to the activities of Kū, god of work, industry, farming, fishing, governance, and political maneuvering, including war. The remaining four months (approximately October/November–January/February) celebrated Lono, god of fertility and peace, through the Makahiki harvest festivals; all work ceased, and the people engaged in sport, games, hula, relaxation, and the giving of offerings.[4] Much of the discussion that follows references the Kū season of 2002, which included weapons-crafting workshops in February, the Wehe Kū ceremony in March, weekly meetings between April and August, the Puʻukoholā event in August, and a closing ceremony in September.

The active membership in 2002 fluctuated between twenty-five and thirty-five in any given week. Most of the men were middle class, though there were a few working- and lower-middle-class men as well; most came from working-class families and were thus upwardly mobile. The median age was in the midforties, though there was fair representation of different age groups between thirty and sixty. I assumed (incorrectly, as I discuss at the end) that all were heterosexual. Though the men held a wide range of occupations, just over half were government salaried workers. The majority of the men in the group could claim at least one ancestry in addition to Hawaiian; most could claim two or three. Most of the men felt a dual sense of alienation—from Hawaiian culture because of their Americanization and class status and from American culture because of their Hawaiian ethnic background and upbringing. A desire to find one's place was a common theme running through the discussions, as many of them had experiences of travel and mobility. Anxieties of status, education, and violence underlay men's motives for transformation and were worked out, importantly through bodily and discursive practices of re-membering.

Re-membering Hawaiian Masculinities

The Hale Mua provided its members with a ritual space that allowed them to learn and perform those 'Ōiwi traditions and practices that rooted them in a deeper genealogy of place as Hawaiian men who must live and work in a settler society—even if it was one they sought to transform—outside of the sanctuary of the Hale Mua. The body figured centrally in activities such as wearing a malo (loincloth) or dancing with a spear (which I will discuss below). As Farnell (1999) notes, bodily processes produce new forms of knowledge that exist and work in ways that both complement and go beyond the contemporary understandings of culture as symbolic system. It is this quality of embodied discursive action—the active signification, enactment, and production of identities through bodily movements and engagements—that makes groups such as the Hale Mua such potent sites for identity and self-formation.

Importantly, these practices involved an active re-membering of community—a "reaggregation of members" (Myerhoff 1982:111) connected and bound by a shared past and homeland recalled through performance. Thus the Mua's ceremonies, dances, chants, routines, and stories became fertile grounds for re-membering masculinities, which can be understood as a gendered memory work that facilities the formation of group subjectivities through the coordination of personal memories, historical narratives, and bodily experiences and representations (Tengan 2008b).

In her discussion of re-membering masculinities across Oceania, Margaret Jolly writes that such an approach seeks to "connect men's sexed bodies with individual and collective processes of memory, in continuing conversations between pasts and presents" (2008:6). Commenting on Connell 2005 and Butler 1990, Jolly notes that embodied performances of gender "can both reproduce and subvert" the "privileged scripts of culture, nation, and heterosexual desire" that are found in "hegemonic masculinities"—the models of being a man that are "broadly accepted as dominant" (2008:5). In settler societies such as Hawai'i, Indigenous "male potency emerges in relation—and sometimes in resistance—to the hegemonic forces of colonialism and contending imperial models of masculinity" (Jolly 2008:1). Yet as Vicente Diaz points out, "tackling" such formations requires careful attention to the ways that American and Native Pacific cultural elements may collude in "hypermasculinist and homophobic performances" (2011:91), particularly those of warriorhood.

For the remainder of this essay, I will focus on the ways that the Hale Mua actively re-members Hawaiian masculinity through embodied discursive action—particularly body-strengthening routines, interpersonal greetings, traditional tattoos, fighting arts, and ceremonial practices. These practices foreground mana, ea (sovereignty, life, breath), and genealogy and are central to understanding (and critiquing) the masculinities performed in the ritual invocations of Kū and the weekly meetings.

Kū Rising: Structures of Mana

The Wehe Kū (opening of Kū season) ceremonies officially began the 2002 cycle of activities for the Hale Mua. Inspired by the ceremonies at Pu'ukoholā, the Wehe Kū on Maui took place at the historically and spiritually deep heiau of Pihanakalani (Gathering Place of the Chiefs) and the chiefly complex Haleki'i (House of Images). The March 30 gathering took place at 4:00 a.m., with the men dressed in malo (loincloths) and kīhei (shoulder cloaks) and carrying the wooden spears they had carved in February. The first half of the ceremony consisted of a recitation of prayers and genealogies, a ceremonial blessing of weapons, and a greeting of the rising sun with chant. The second half involved a ritual sharing of ʻawa (kava) and food, followed by a discussion of the work that would be carried out that year in order for the men to take up their responsibilities in the family and community. The season of Kū had begun.

In the Hawaiian pantheon of gods, the Kū/Hina pair represents the male/ female duality of the sexes that organizes the universe in the cosmogonic genealogy chant the Kumulipo (Liliuokalani 1978[1897]; Beckwith 1972; Kameʻeleihiwa 1999:2–4; Valeri 1985:12). Kū, whose name means "standing, upright, erect," encompasses all the male gods (and their properties) and represents the male generating power; Hina, whose name means "to fall, topple, or lean over" and references the moon (mahina), presides over the female deities and represents female fecundity and the power of growth and reproduction (Beckwith 1970:12–13; Pukui et al. 1972, vol. 2:122; Valeri 1985:12). As Lilikalā Kameʻeleihiwa remarks, "The Hawaiian world was . . . divided into female and male domains of work, and was considered pono, correct and righteous, when there was a balance between the two. When there is balance in the world, the ancestral Akua [Gods] are pleased, and when there is perfect harmony in the universe, people are protected from all harm" (1999:4). Not only is Kū defined with and in opposition to Hina (and vice versa), but also if either is missing, the whole of society suffers. As Pukui et al. explain, "Kū, the masculine, is always accompanied by Hina, the feminine," and together the two "symbolize the balance embodied in well-being" (1972, vol. 2:128, 147).

Kanaka Maoli seeking to return well-being to the self and society have used the metaphors of duality and balance between Kū and Hina as models for thinking. One of the primary philosophies of the lua (Hawaiian fighting art) seminars was that of understanding how the balance of Kū/Hina guided not only attacks and counterattacks but also the embodiment of both the masculine and feminine in each individual; indeed, the word "lua" itself means "duality" or "two, second" (Paglinawan et al. 2006:9). As the ʻōlohe (lua master) Richard Paglinawan explained in an interview when the classes began, "Lua is in harmony with nature. You go with the flow of things, and you use it to your advantage. Lua is fluid, like hula. Hula and lua at one time were almost one and the same because men were the dancers. Lua was the 'hard' part, hula is the soft. So you could relate it to yin and yang, or Kū and Hina" (Clark 1993:10). In this frame, the masculine lua complemented the feminine hula. Kyle Nākānelua credited much of what he learned about Kū/Hina balance, and his subsequent focus on the Kū, to his experience with lua.

Importantly, the connection to the mana (spiritual power and authority) of Kū comes through the physical embodiment and performance of it in ritual and in training. As Wende Elizabeth Marshall has pointed out in her review of anthropological literature on mana, the Pacific term has been interpreted in numerous ways, including Roger Keesing's rendering of it as a "quality of efficacy manifest in visible results" (1984:149) and Brad Shore's (1989:140) association of it with a "generative potency [and] the sources [of] organic creation" (Marshall 2011:4; see also Tomlinson 2006). Highlighting the performativity of mana, Marshall Sahlins writes that it "is the creative power Hawaiians describe as making visible what is invisible, causing things to be seen" (1981:31). For Kameʻeleihiwa (1992:46–49), the route of Kū—success in politics and warfare accompanied by the construction of massive heiau—was one of the two traditional paths (the other being genealogy) to mana that would justify a chief's rule over the land. In the present-day context of the Hawaiian nationalist movement, Hawaiian mana is invoked in a number of ways as a direct challenge to American imperial power (Goodyear-Kaʻōpua 2013:207; Marshall 2011:6; Trask 1999:91–92).

As a gendered project, the effort to reinvigorate the mana of Kū ritualizes resistance to the perceived colonial emasculation of Hawaiian men and the Hawaiian nation (cf. Sinha 1995). As Nākānelua described it, "Because we're a male, masculine-oriented group, our ʻimi ʻana [searching] is towards the masculinity of the culture because there's been so much femininity. And again, not that femininity is bad; everything has its place and its time. No laila [Therefore] . . . if you believe everything has its place and time, then it should hold true to da fact that there should be a place and a time for the mana Kū. There's a time for healing, there's a time for building mana" (Nākānelua 1999). The idea of building is important here, for if decolonization entails healing, it also demands an active rebuilding of nation, place, and hale (house). Yet in the name of cultural reclamation, the project of revitalizing the mana Kū runs the risk of inscribing the Kū/Hina and male/female dichotomies with the valences of strong/weak and dominant/sub-

Fig. 8.3. The Hale Mua executes a maneuver called Kū Pololū, or "Erect the Long Spear," where the men rotate (in sync) the pololū (long spears) from a horizontal to a perpendicular position and exclaim "Kū Pololū!" The embodied discursive act at once announces and performs the rebuilding of mana Kū. Puʻukoholā Heiau, August 2010. Photo courtesy of Joey Corcino.

missive that work to support the structures of Western colonial patriarchy. Arguably, Hawaiian history has numerous examples of strong, dominant women figures, and thus the Kū/Hina duality should not be seen as absolute or even applicable in all situations. I will discuss this tension further below; here I note that invocations of Kū and Hina index strategies for balance and pono (balance, well-being) in society and in individuals as well as the perceived imbalances and needs for restoration.

Kū is also the god of governance, productivity, work, industry, upland forests, deep-sea fishing, and war. Unfortunately, the common rendering of the Kū, and most notably his manifestation of Kūkāʻilimoku (the island-snatching god), exclusively appends to him the dubious distinction of being *only* the god of war. The Puʻukoholā ceremonial events attempted to refigure that depiction, so influenced by colonial and missionary outlooks. After interviewing Sam Kaʻai, chairman of the 1991 ceremonies and elder advisor for the Hale Mua, Steve Friesen wrote, "Western historians have focused on this militaristic aspect of Ku because of their own imperialist interests. But Hawaiians, according to [Kaʻai], worship the deities like Ku who care for them. The full measure of the god's care is recognized in the full measure of names, and must be understood in that broad context" (Friesen 1992:22). These tropes of "Kū the war god" are also used to change colonial subjects into savages and bloodthirsty male warriors. The primary goal of Nā Koa was to restore courage and discipline, not violence. As Kaʻai and Nākānelua sought to decouple the concept of Nā Koa from violence and war, so too did they seek to place Kū in the larger context of his multitude of being. When men re-membered the mana of Kū, they too would be upright members of the community ready to rebuild the nation. This was precisely the goal of the Kū exhibit and the opening of the ʻAha Kāne Native Hawaiian Men's Health Conference in 2010.

Embodying Sovereignty, Ancestors, and Land

In 2002 the Hale Mua o Maui met once a week from 5:30 to 8:00 p.m. at a harborside property consisting of a meeting hall and a grassy area. When the men arrived, many wore pāʻū (waist wraparounds) and greeted each other with the honi, a traditional practice of touching of noses and exchanging breath. Training began with prayers and chants that were followed by warm-ups and stretches. A more rigorous routine of hoʻoikaika kino (body-strengthening exercises) followed, much of which incorporated the seven-foot wooden spears that members had carved. When that was finished, various dances and martial sets were covered, including those that would be performed at Puʻukoholā. The last part of practice ended in sparring, which was in preparation for an upcoming sham battle that would also take place at the heiau. Though padded spears and protective gear were utilized, the training was hard and would leave men with cuts, bruises, sprains, and sometimes broken bones. Practice ended with discussion, prayer, and a final exchange of honi.

Hoʻoikaika kino primarily works to achieve pono (balance, well-being) by strengthening the body, mind, and spirit. American ideals of beauty and health shape the ways in which preoccupations and obsessions with the body are articulated by Hawaiians today, especially since the dominant sexualized images of Kanaka men and women in the tourist industry are those that conform with Western standards of slim but shapely physiques, straight hair, and facial features that are "Polynesian" but mixed with those of Anglos and/or Asians (Desmond 1999; Imada 2012). Yet for 'Ōiwi (as is the case with many other Indigenous Peoples), the colonial experience of decimation from diseases and epidemics continues to attack the cultural and psychological immune system of the Kanaka body politic and far outweighs any concern over appearance.

The colonization of the Hawaiian body manifests itself not only in culturally defined regimes of sexuality and propriety but also in more viscerally distressing ways through obesity, diabetes, cancer, and other health-related problems (Marshall 2011; McMullin 2010). These often culminate in high mortality and suicide rates, which for Hawaiian men approach epidemic proportions (Blaisdell and Mokuau 1994; Cook et al. 2005). Likewise, the structures of late capitalism and Hawai'i's dependence on imported foods and goods (as well as the forced removal of Hawaiians from the islands) maintains this bodily malaise to such a point that for many Hawaiians disease has become something endemic to their culture. Thus the project of decolonization can proceed only by recovering and healing the body.

In the Hale Mua, as in the Hawaiian health organizations that Marshall (2011) and McMullin (2010) described, the well-being of the Hawaiian people includes as its core component the vitality of the culture, and as such, many of the activities are culturally based and include a metapragmatics of healing the nation through healing the culture, identity, and soul of the "sick" people. In addition to the process of healing, the more aggressive projects of anticolonial and nationalist resistance require assertions of strength and power, both culturally and bodily. For the Hale Mua, these are gendered as inherently masculine and essential for the remaking of Hawaiian men, particularly as their presence has been obfuscated by colonial discourse.

One of the most profound and yet understated performances of a remembered 'Ōiwi masculinity is in the honi nose greeting. While some of the older men in the group remember their grandparents greeting each other with the honi, most people in Hawai'i no longer use it. It is now practiced primarily among Native Hawaiians who have been involved in cultural revitalization activities, and particularly among men. In part, this return to the honi has been inspired by interactions with the Indigenous Māori of Aotearoa/New Zealand who had maintained that tradition; indeed, much of the project of reconstituting Hawaiian masculine subjectivities has come in a trans-Oceanic dialogue with Māori (Tengan 2008a:12–13, 63). Beyond this, though, the honi itself enacts a form of decolonial being, for the Hawaiian term "ea" that means breath and air also translates to "sovereignty," "life," and "to rise up" (Goodyear-Kaʻōpua 2013:6; Pukui and Elbert 1986:36). When members of the Hale Mua stand and exchange breath in the honi, they are also asserting their sovereign presence that settler colonialism has failed to eliminate. The act affirms their bonds of solidarity and member-ship, particularly as the honi involves a closeness and intimacy that might otherwise be disavowed in more normative settings.

Nākānelua urges members to stand up and take charge of their own health. He speaks with a conviction and authority that earn the men's respect not only because he is articulate but also because he literally embodies those qualities, ethics, and attributes that he urges others to take up. Years of training in sports, the military, martial arts, and the fire department and working in the taro patches have given him a muscular, tanned physique. Through his training as a firefighter and other training in health care, he has taken as his kuleana (area of responsibility) the health and welfare of Hawaiians on the personal, professional, and political levels; in fact, when he was a member of the sovereignty organization Ka Lāhui Hawaiʻi, he was in charge of the Maui caucus's Department of Health (Nākānelua 2002).

Nākānelua also wears a number of traditionally designed tattoos that represent his ancestral lineage and visibly mark his body as a Hawaiian one. This becomes even more impressive when one discovers that Keone Nunes, a Hawaiian tattoo practitioner who uses rituals, protocols, and handmade tools and needles, placed these markings on Nākānelua in a manner that was more painful and meaningful than if done at a tattoo parlor with a machine.[5] Many of the men come to not only respect but also identify with Nākānelua through the life experiences he shares in talk story, and a number of members over the years have followed his example and had their genealogies tapped into their skin during group tattoo workshops. As Keith Camacho notes, "Indigenous genealogies exceed American spatial and temporal parameters by recalling older and foraging newer connec-tions of peoples and places" (2011:xiii). The genealogical tattoos connect men's bodies to ancestors and islands that preceded settler occupation. It is through a kinship of lived experience and intersecting lineages that the Hale Mua infuses ea into a re-membered genealogy.

Fig. 8.4. Kyle Nākānelua (*center*) chants the opening lines of the Mahaʻū ritual dance at Puʻukoholā Heiau, August 2010. His kākau (tattoos) are visible on his leg, chest, and arms; less visible in this image are the kākau that go down the left side of his face. Photo courtesy of Joey Corcino.

Two particular aspects as they relate to bodily experience and performance are worth extended discussion here: violence and dance. It is through the gendered remaking of these practices that Nākānelua is most successful at lowering men's defenses and opening them up to new experiences.

The Violence of Modernity

The problem of violence and unusually high incarceration rates among Hawaiian men has long been a topic of great concern in the Kanaka Maoli community. In 2000 Hawaiians between the ages of twenty and forty-four had the highest rates of suicide among the major ethnic groups in Hawaiʻi (Kanaʻiaupuni et al. 2005:113). The rates of confirmed child abuse or neglect were three to four times those of the other major ethnic groups, and Hawaiians were twice as likely as others to report physical, sexual, or emotional abuse on a Department of Health Survey (Kanaʻiaupuni 2005:63–64). While representing about 20 percent of Hawaiʻi's population, Hawaiians made up 38 percent of the in-state prison population and 41 percent of Hawai'i inmates housed in out-of-state facilities (OHA 2006:171, 173). There is a danger in reproducing such data without accounting for biases in collection and other possible flaws in methodology, and I do not seek to present this as proof of endemic Hawaiian violence. Nonetheless, these are disturbing figures that unfortunately correspond to given notions of Hawaiians, which themselves serve as the source of efforts to locate alternative ways of healing and transforming (cf. O'Nell 1996). They are also relevant because, as many studies of masculinities elsewhere have shown, violence is one of the most fundamental and problematic ways in which men define and embody subjectivity (Bowker 1998; Connell 2005:81–86).

One of the more promising aspects of the reemergence of the pā lua (fighting art schools), Nā Koa (the Courageous Ones/Warriors), and the Hale Mua (Men's House) is their potential to provide men a place in which violence born of hurt, pain, and lack of cultural identity can be transformed into a more productive form of energy. It is also a place where members can see and meet other men who can help in the process of both healing and constructing a different idea of masculinity. Such a theme was prominent in the interviews I conducted with Puka Ho, a thirty-seven-year-old Maui County lifeguard. While contemplating the increase in his desire to learn about Hawaiian history and language, he also discussed his new understandings of being a man:

> HO : A lot of values dat Kyle [Nākānelua] puts out there fo da guys in da Hale Mua is, you know, basically take care your family, take care your stuff . . . do what you gotta do, do what you tink is right. And I tank him fo dat, because if . . . I nevah run into dis bunch of guys, I probably would be still drinking beer aftah work every day, and instead of tinking about what I do and how I do it.
>
> TENGAN: So you feel it's had a real positive impact on your life?
>
> HO : Well, yeah, real positive impact, because when I was younger, I grew up, my dad would drink every night, come home bust up my maddah, bus me up, you know, send my maddah to one hospital. So you know da kine role models, that's how you figure, oh, well, I goin get oldah, I goin work, come home drunk. And Nākānelua wen show dat there's anadah path fo take (Ho 2002).[6]

Significantly, Ho described seeing a different vision of mature Hawaiian masculinity that contradicted his own previously held and embodied notions. Though I would not consider Ho's experiences the norm for most of the men, he certainly was not alone. Three others in the group told me they had grown up in homes where beatings were more common than not, and one of them even left home when he was seventeen and lived on the beach for a while before he had a stable job. He didn't blame his father for that behavior, for he knew that "life was hard and that's how they were," an indication that the larger structural forces were as much (if not more) of a contributing factor as individual or cultural means for coping. He also credited Nākānelua and the Hale Mua for helping to alter his perspective.

Richard Bissen Jr., the forty-year-old chief prosecutor of Maui (now a circuit court judge), also grew up in a family where violence was "natural," though in his case it was usually among the older men, who would get into fights with each other. Family violence was even seen as predestined, since his mother's maiden name was Nākoa. Like Ho, he spoke of the way Nākānelua helped to change his ideas about warriorhood and violence:

> There's varying interpretations of [Nākoa]. The way my mom had interpreted their name . . . "the warriors" . . . was like "the fighters" because there was a lot of fighting within the family, I mean a lot of hard-headed Hawaiians who . . . were stubborn, and resorting to physical violence was a natural thing. . . . But when Nākānelua explained it he said, "You know, it doesn't have to mean 'the warrior' meaning, like the violence." The way they wanted the term to be understood was "the courageous." And, the best example they gave, which is what has stuck with me, is the courage to be a young, Hawaiian male, and to wear a malo [loincloth] in public, and to say, "This, I am not ashamed of who I am or what I stand for." And it's that you have the courage to live your belief. (Bissen 2002)

Those familiar with the feature film *Once Were Warriors* (1995) might find parallels in the discourse of transforming violence by recourse to warrior cultural traditions that inculcate discipline, pride, and self-esteem, thereby transforming violent energies into productive ones. Indeed, many men find hope for the younger generations in the Hale Mua precisely on this basis. Along these lines, Nākānelua has spoken to inmates at Maui Community Correctional Center and staff members from Child Protective Services. Others, such as Kaʻiana Haili on Hawaiʻi, have used the hale mua concept to develop full curricula for domestic violence, substance abuse, and prison programs. Among other things, Haili holds that "our male ancestors were warrior/healers" and "to be either you had to learn the balance; in order to kill we learn to heal—Kū and his many forms are balanced in both death and life." While rooting the men in the cultural practices of land steward-ship and taro culture, he also advocates a political and structural under-standing "that as long as we allow others to determine the fate of our ʻāina [land] we will be at the top of the lists." (email to author, December 26, 2006).[7] Sally Engle Merry noted this sort of discourse in the program of a Native Hawaiian pastor (also in Hilo, Hawaiʻi) who "talked about the ideal warrior as a person violent in war but not at home" and "discussed male violence from a perspective of the Hawaiian sovereignty movement as well as Christian ideas" (2006:46).

While the possibilities for positive transformation of violent masculini-ties are there, they are limited and rely largely on the tailoring of the Hale Mua model to the needs of the group. The majority of the men who were in the Hale Mua at the time of my primary research were older men with steady jobs who, as thirty-nine-year-old accountant Clifford Alakai (2002) framed it, had "structure in their lives"; they were not the at-risk youth or otherwise marginalized men who would perhaps benefit most from the community and identity the Hale Mua offered. Moreover, Nākānelua was quite clear, as Ho noted, in stating that you had to "take care your stuff" first before dedicating your time to the Mua, and he did not present the Hale Mua as the panacea for all the social ills and problems that Hawaiian men face. The issue of gendered violence will not solve itself overnight and will require approaches on multiple levels. While part of that may involve a return of sovereignty and land, it must also include interventions into the structures of domination in the domestic space.

Within the group, though, the men's embodied experiences suggested that the most effective means of reforming masculinities defined through violence was refiguring warrior and masculine subjectivities through body-reflexive practices. R. W. Connell defines this as a process wherein bodies act as "both objects and subjects of practice, . . . the practice itself forming the structures within which bodies are appropriated and defined" (2005:61).

This was precisely the appeal that lua, warrior arts, and the whole regime of physical training (hoʻoikaika kino) held for remaking masculinity in the Hale Mua. As Nākānelua explained of the training routine, "It is very Kū oriented.... It makes men feel really good—no different, no different from the formation of the karate dojos, no different from shoto-kan, or kung-fu, or anything like that. It just, it's a way for men to develop their physical prowess and their thinking abilities, their strategic abilities, to practice their leadership roles" (Nākānelua 1999). Through such body-reflexive practices, men came to perform and know themselves and their bodies in a new way. Some had familiarity from previous experience in (as well as popular stereotypes of) the martial arts, and this worked to also make the process of coordinating ʻŌiwi ideals and movements into redefined practices of "fighting." The other primary area where this was worked out was in dance.

Dancing as Men

One of the most notable changes brought about by the Hawaiian renaissance in the 1970s was the rebirth of men's dancing, largely tied to the revival of the ancient (kahiko) forms of dance. The Hawaiian scholar George Kanahele contrasted the "authentic" ancient form to the "modern or hapa haole (half-foreign)" one, which had become "an accommodation to the tourists" used to "advertise the charm of the islands" with "a smiling hula lassie" (1982:15). In ways similar to the Hale Mua's reclamation of "real" cultural traditions of warriorhood, the "return of the male dancer to his rightful place" (Kanahele 1982:15) was a refuting of the colonial feminization, commodification, and "prostitution" of the modern form in the tourism industry (Trask 1999). In 1977 Kanahele remarked, "I remember as a kid no local boy would be caught dead dancing the hula for fear of being called a sissy, but now you're likely to get popped in the mouth if you imply that a male dancer, who may be on the football team, is a sissy. Something must be happening to change this deep-set attitude" (1982:3). Two years later he added, "Male dancers have also become favorites of local audiences, both men and women, although the squeals of glee I hear when the men come on stage wearing a modern style malo [loincloth] come mostly from the wahines [women]. John Lake tells me that invariably it is the male dancers who get the biggest applause" (1982:15). It's notable that Lake, who had a

Hawaiian club at the all-boys Catholic St. Louis High School, was a part of this movement, as he later came to be the primary ritual specialist at Puʻukoholā (see Tengan 2008a: ch. 2, 3). Lake, along with others such as Darrell Lupenui and John Kaʻimikaua, did much to change the image of hula as feminine, and today men are very prominent in hula competitions, such as the Merrie Monarch Festival, held annually in Hilo, Hawaiʻi, which is televised statewide and streamed live on the web.

However, many of the men in the Hale Mua still associated hula with women and māhū (effeminate males, gay men, and/or transgendered women), as have other scholars (Robertson 1989).[8] Nākānelua was one of those football players dancing hula in school (Maryknoll, a Catholic school), but he felt that it was only because he was a starter on the team that nobody teased him. Coming from a working-class neighborhood in downtown Honolulu, he hung out with boys who defined their masculinity through toughness and fighting. He recalled that when he was invited to join a hālau (hula school), he declined because he felt he would have to "duke it out every day" with the "rugged" guys he hung out with.

It was precisely this rejection of the "feminine" form of hula that led some members to search for something more "masculine" in the Hale Mua. Jacob Kana, a thirty-one-year-old power plant worker who was raised in the rural taro farming and fishing village of Kahakuloa, recalled his discovery of the Mua as such:

I really liked the group because, first of all it's like, ah, just a bunch of men, eh, just all local braddahs just gettin' togeda and stuff. That, to me, dat's what we need, dat's what was missing, all dis time. Cause like everybody else, like da wahines li' dat, dey had hula and stuff li' dat, but to me was, I dunno, I nevah like hula. Hula wasn't my ting, was more, I dunno, I used to tink was soft. Was, and, I dunno if dat's wrong or what, but da's what I used to tink, so I nevah did like join hula. But to me nevah have notin' fo' men. (Kana 2002)

Keenly aware of this perception, Nākānelua tried to emphasize the masculine and strong aspects of dance, often by highlighting the martial aspects. He also focused on the haʻa forms, which were understood to be more sacred, serious, and rigid and thus less secular, playful, and soft. Included in his rep-

Fig. 8.5. Men of the Hale Mua perform the haʻa (ritual dance) Mahaʻū with mea kaua (traditional weaponry). Photo courtesy of Joey Corcino.

ertoire of haʻa was the Mahaʻū, a ritual dance honoring the Hawaiian pig god Kamapuaʻa that incorporates fighting techniques and weaponry. The haʻa is the cognate to the Indigenous Māori dance form of the haka, commonly thought of now as a "war dance." This form has come to be a national symbol and global commodity through its performance by the New Zealand All Blacks rugby team and its use in the marketing campaigns of the corporate sponsor Adidas (Hokowhitu, this volume; Jackson and Hokowhitu 2002). For many Hawaiians (and other Polynesians), the haka represents the archetypal performance of Polynesian warrior masculinity, and thus some cultural organizations and local football teams performed the haka before games (Tengan and Markham 2009).[9] While inspired by the haka, Nākānelua chose not to appropriate the form since for him it would represent a stealing of another people's mana and a diminishment of our own.[10]

In choreographing haʻa, Nākānelua emphasized the lua strikes and fighting techniques embedded in the dance steps. This worked extremely well for Ho, who remembered, "The first time we had to dance one hula, I was like, 'Oh, brah, I no dance hula!' I mean, nothin wrong wit hula, but dat's not fo me. But when I seen them doin 'em, I was like, 'Whoa, dis buggah get plenty martial moves,' I could see in 'em. And dat's what wen' kinda attract me to dat. . . . I mean I no like dance da hula, but oh, dat buggah look like one good technique or sometin'" (Ho 2002).

The concerted effort to redefine dance was a reaction to the continued appropriation of the hula as a commodity spectacle and the consequent performance of it as such. The latter includes a cultivation of homogeneity of body types, appearances, and movements in groups that perform in tourist venues and in local competitions. Jane Desmond argues that a "physical foundationalism" operates in touristic discourse and posits the body as "that which is really 'real,' a repository of truth" through bodily performances (1999:xiv). She notes that "bodies function as the material signs for categories of social difference, including divisions of gender, race, cultural identity and species" (1999:xiv). Bodily performances serve as the final authenticator of the commodity of difference, and thus the industry highlights the "centrality of the performing body, binding notions of 'facticity,' presence, naturalism, and authenticity together under the sign of spectator corporeality" (1999:xv). At sites such as the Merrie Monarch Festival, which has become a spectacle visited by tourists and locals alike, both male and female dancers are heavily sexualized. The young, muscular males evoke the "squeals of glee . . . from the wahines." This body type corresponds to the touristic image of the domesticated and sexualized beach boy and Duke Kahanamoku (see Desmond 1999; Ferguson and Turnbull 1999:38; Tengan 2008a:ch. 1; cf. Walker 2011). For the middle-aged, heavier men in the Mua who came from a tough upbringing and contested such touristic images, the "deep-set attitude" against the popular visions of hula remained.

While many of the men may have kept their distance from what they considered feminine dance, Nākānelua nonetheless maintained hula forms in the repertoire of movements he taught, though with a "masculine" emphasis. Such was the case with the Moloka'i Ku'i. Nākānelua learned the dance when he was in intermediate school at Maryknoll, where he performed it as a courting dance in which the boys would chase the girls across the stage. In the Hale Mua he changed it to reflect more of the tough, aggressive positioning that would speak to other men:

> If you talking about, you know, trying to impress a woman, then your movements are, you know, kinda gallant, yeah, and prancing. . . . If

you're a man, and you wanna make an impression on a man—whether it be a boss, or a coach, or guys on a team dat you wanna be a part of and stuff, you know—den you gotta crank up yo' testosterone, you know, you gotta show up yo' balls, you gotta be there. So, when dat 'a'ano [attitude] comes out of you, yeah, your attitude changes, your body motions change, you tend to stiffen up at different points along da way. A different emphasis on da hand. . . . your mana is projected different. (Nākānelua 1999)

Thus Nākānelua did not disavow the hula but rather sought to reclaim it as a practice done by and for Hawaiian men, not for tourists or for women. Again, the focus was on remaking masculinity and doing so through traditions and practices that were real (cf. Goodyear-Ka'ōpua 2013:219–23). Reflecting on the spear dances we had been learning, Nākānelua explained their significance for cultural and historical consciousness:

We come from a culture that was, nothing was written. So history was in the song, history was in dance, history was in the prayer. And the commemorations of things that happened are brought forth, are brought back to life, are relived . . . through the dance. . . . We thought . . . why not do a pahua [spear dance] with a traditional Hawaiian ihe [spear]? . . . So we made 'em, and den we danced wit it. And dat was it. No great show, no grand performance in front of throngs of people, just for ourselves. Just to say, we participated in it, just to say we did it, and it was done, it can be done, just for ourselves. (Nākānelua 1999)

Nākānelua was not entirely forthcoming in his statement that there is no show in our activities, for the dances at Pu'ukoholā were certainly done in front of an audience (see Tengan 2008a:ch. 3). Yet his main point about whom these activities were done for is valid: the ritual performance of dance was meant to bring about a transformation of the self by reconnecting with history and with the fellow performers of that collective story. By performing genealogy, ea, and mana, the ritual and embodied processes of the men worked to further the goals of culturally and politically remembering Hawaiian nationhood, which itself was undergoing important changes and transitions.

The Politics of Hawaiian Masculinities:
Struggling to Balance Kū and Hina

While the project of transforming and remaking masculinity through ritual holds great promise, it also presents a set of important issues that need to be dealt with. Michael Messner (1997) notes that a variety of men's movements in the United States, such as the mythopoetic men's movement, the conservative white Christian revival of the Promise Keepers, and the African American men's Million Man March are backlashes against feminism that utilize essentialist discourses to reclaim traditional (patriarchal) roles that have been lost. In racialized masculinity politics, the struggle against race and class oppression often supersedes the struggle for gender equality, and women of color suffer most. Messner argues that the transformative potential of masculinity politics is severely limited insofar as many of the movements end up working to reconstitute patriarchy (1997:73).

As Native Hawaiians move forward in the collective pursuit of reclaiming nation, it is imperative that we take seriously the gender politics that threaten to divide men and women. In an effort to situate the personal and political project of the Hale Mua within the larger context of gender imbalance, I evaluate the extent to which the Hale Mua serves to (re)inscribe a patriarchal order that is not Maoli. In his review of recent Indigenous feminist thought, Scott Lauria Morgensen notes that "Indigenous feminism is key to Indigenous criticism not just for explaining colonialism's conditioning by heteropatriarchy but because Indigenous feminist practices of articulation are methodologically crucial to transforming settler colonial power" (2011:770). A critical aspect of this evaluative project is to interrogate how masculinity is performed and toward what ends in the contexts of exclusive ritual space vs. secular space. I ask the question, What does balancing Kū and Hina mean in these different sites?

When the Hale Mua gathers for workshops, ceremonies, and training, it provides men a safe space for learning and practicing Hawaiian identity and community in ways that would not be possible in other educational institutions, in workplaces, or at home. In this way there is some resemblance to the mythopoetic men's movement, which Michael Schwalbe argues is essentially a search for communitas among middle-age, middle-class white men who have experienced a type of spiritual bankruptcy as workers in the

American capitalist society (Schwalbe 1996, 1998). In relation to the Hale Mua specifically, Morgensen has asked "to what extent [their] methods were informed by a 1990s moment in which mythopoetics addressed perceived failures in hegemonic manhood with a turn to Indigenism, as well as how Kanaka Maoli rearticulated this moment with commitments to decolonization" (2011:771). Though Nākānelua denied any knowledge of the mythopoetic men's movements, Morgensen's questions are on point. In the Hale Mua, the activities and discourse focus on men's relationships to each other and to the family and community more generally. Invocations of Kū are meant to strengthen cultural identity, reconfigure pasts marked by violence, and encourage responsibility and upright moral behavior and leadership as Hawaiian men. The Hale Mua spaces are ritually separated from the normal work and family spheres—the space of (partial) liminality between neocolonial society and the vision of a traditional Indigenous one (see Tengan 2008a:ch. 2; Turner 1969). Ritual process reorders status relationships and allows men to relate in ways that might otherwise not occur given their differences in class, education, geographic mobility, and cultural knowledge. In this context, restoring Kū is about re-membering various qualities of masculinity and manhood he represents that are inclusive of the diverse men that come to the Mua. Yet as inclusive as this space is meant to be, the articulation of decolonization with aspects of hegemonic manhood leave open the possibilities for an uncritiqued colonial heteropatriarchy to reemerge in practice.

Leaving the Hale Mua, men reenter a neocolonial order where ritual and ceremonial meanings are vacated and Kū clashes with Hina. In one particularly relevant example, Hawaiian men (not of the Hale Mua) involved in the construction of a traditional thatch house as part of an urban development project prohibited women from participating since house building was traditionally a male activity. Maria Kaʻimipono Orr, a Native Hawaiian archaeologist who was an invited guest at the groundbreaking, noted that she and another Kanaka Maoli woman who was one of the regular construction supervisors felt "put out." She exclaimed in an email, "Barring women from building hale or participating in building one, is not only a waste of potential energy, etc., but an act of oppression . . . first this seemingly innocent kapu [prohibition] . . . then what next! The White, Protestant, males weren't/aren't the only beings on this planet to be oppressive in their dominant thinking and behavior. I feel like we're taking a giant step backwards!" (Orr, email to author and others, March 20, 2001). This example represented a patriarchal assertion of power and authority, for it prevented the participation of women who contributed to the project. The rules of kapu make sense only when they operate as part of a whole structure organized by the logic of Hawaiian kapu. When they are taken out of that system and implemented only in decontextualized and abstracted pieces, friction emerges because the other pieces that made kapu pono (correct) are not there to support it.

Noenoe Silva, a professor of political science and the director of the Indigenous Politics Program at the University of Hawaiʻi, asks, "Does mana kane [men's mana] have to exclude or oppress women, or be perceived as excluding or oppressing women? What's interesting from my point of view is that the late 19th c. Kanaka men did not seem so very invested in oppressing women—they supported and appreciated the Hui Aloha ʻĀina wahine, and went on to support women's suffrage. And they wrote down those awesome stories about [goddesses] Hiʻiaka and Papa" (Silva, email to author, May 3, 2001).[11] Silva's remarks are accurate, and the historical record does in fact demonstrate that women had access to mana, rank, and power in ways that complemented men's access (Kameʻeleihiwa 1999; Linnekin 1990; McGregor 2003). It is also useful to note that the case of the Hui Aloha ʻĀina, the men and women each had their own separate organizations and kuleana (responsibilities). I would suggest that this is one of the reasons their leaders could work together when it came to making decisions and organizing mass protests.

Ideology aside, the problem for men of the Hale Mua who are being "cast forward" as leaders is whether or not, or to what extent, their assertion of authority and mana requires a diminishment of women's authority (cf. Hokowhitu 2012). Does Kū rising depend on Hina's lying down? Do they need to be separate categories? When I asked Nākānelua directly, he responded, "Does the Mua advocate for total male dominance of the society, and the suppression of females? . . . This Mua doesn't advocate for that. What . . . the Mua advocates in regards to the male sex is, it's very important for a male to have a duty and to have a responsibility. . . . It gives him a sense of well-being. That's what we're advocating. That a male pick up his responsibility . . . the advocacy is not for the suppression of the female spirit."

Though this practice sounds good in theory, we must be wary of the contexts in which "responsibilities" are defined, understood, and practiced. There are echoes here in the discourse found in the Promise Keepers, who similarly advocate for men to pick up their responsibility as men and leaders. This call then gets taken up and used by individual men in a political fashion to support antifeminist and antigay projects through fundamentalist reading of the Bible and a call to return to "traditional" family values (Messner 1997:22–35). Such a model cannot serve to cast our people forward. I find some comfort in the fact that there is no fundamentally patriarchal or homophobic discourse in the invocations of Kū and Hina, though calls for "restoration" of Kū can easily morph into ones for "elevation above" Hina.

J. Kēhaulani Kauanui, a professor of anthropology and American studies at Wesleyan University, has posed the following critical questions:

> I guess it bothers me that the Hale Mua are attempting to reach for a moment in our genealogy that is seen as more "culturally pure" and measuring it to their status now without accounting for ways they were more empowered under the colonial system than Hawaiian women. Why such a selective genealogy? . . . Am I sensing a sort of defensiveness on the part of Hawaiian men? If so, it makes me wonder about potential resentment that may be brewing. . . . Is it that men are contesting arguments that posit that Hawaiian women are seen as the primary leaders? Or, that the men agree that women are the leaders and are contesting that leadership and asserting their own? (Kauanui and Tengan n.d.)

The selectivity comes from the present context of the cultural nationalist movement as one that privileges identity and knowledge from the remembered precolonial period, precisely as a means for addressing the current malaise of the neocolonial present. The issue of how or if men have benefited from the patriarchal bargain of colonial modernity is an important one; some have, some have not. Most of the men in the Hale Mua come from working-class families, even if they are currently middle class. Yet for many who now occupy that position, their status has come with (or created) a deep sense of alienation from the community. It is this struggle to reestablish connections with other men and community that leads most of the men to look to older forms of being and acting, forms in which men could still relate in the Hale Mua of old.

However, Kauanui is correct in identifying a certain level of resentment that is brewing. In part, this is a response to women leaders' discounting of men's leadership. The level to which discourses in the Hale Mua manifest this sort of reactionary tone varies. Most talk about male leadership tends to be along the lines of claiming responsibility in family and community, and men are less concerned with discrediting women than they are with validating men. There have been times, however, when men have made statements such as "Wahine need to step aside." This discourse assumes that leadership in the community is a zero-sum game, wherein the emergence of male leadership requires the removal of female leadership. This amounts to an assertion of patriarchy and reproduces the same structures of oppression and hierarchy that disempower individuals along the lines of race, class, gender, sexuality, age, body, and so forth. When it emerges, it suggests that patriarchy is what is needed to right society. In my experience, this kind of talk is less frequent than the concern with work, family, and community, but its presence is a cause for concern.

The oppositional nature of discourse on gender works against the establishment of balance and complementarity that we need. On the part of the Mua, one of the shortcomings of focusing only on Kū in the men's discursive practices is that the Hina in each of us is disavowed. The space of the Hale Mua is almost completely heteronormative. In response to my query about the issue of homophobia in the group, Nākānelua responded,

> I've seen serious cases of homophobia, and I have not seen that in the Mua. . . . We've had homosexuals in the Mua, bisexuals in the Mua, we have metrosexuals in the Mua—we got a pile of them in there and that's ok too. And I haven't heard anybody speak against it. I'll tell you what though . . . there was certain issues addressed in regards to understanding homosexuality and certain individuals had a need to understand it, personal issues. . . . We discussed it, and it was addressed from a cultural point of view utilizing certain kino lau [manifestations] of certain akua [gods]. For example, you got this whole māhū thing going on, like taro is one male plant, but yet get babies. . . . Well, what I look at is culturally . . . our kūpuna looked at that as one higher state of being. So, if

we're studying this and we're taking a look at this, how is there a fear for homosexuality? You know I don't see it, I don't see it.

His mention of "homosexuals" in the group surprised me, as I assumed all members were heterosexual; however, the fact that they remained closeted suggests that the openness of the Mua was more on an individual than a collective basis. At the 'Aha Kāne Native Hawaiian Men's Health Conference in 2006 (see Tengan 2008a:22), one of the keynote speakers was Hina Wong (later Hina Wong-Kalu), a māhū (transgendered woman) who has emerged as a vocal and visible leader in the Hawaiian education movement and other realms of activism and politics. I was glad that the committee brought her in to physically remind the five hundred men gathered there that Kū did not need to exclude Hina. Yet the reception was mixed; some were enthusiastic, others were put off and walked out. The problems of heterosexism and homophobia (as well as transphobia) in our community are real, even if they are not as pronounced as those in other areas that do not share a (transformed) tradition of acceptance (Tengan 2003). While the 2010 'Aha Kāne succeeded in increasing the participation of young boys, it failed to provide a space for māhū. However, the 2012 'Aha Kāne saw the return of Hina (in body and in discourse), as a panel discussion on māhū featured Hina Wong-Kalu, her Tongan partner Hema Kalu (who identified as a straight male), and me. Participants there expressed their gratitude for having a space for talking about alternative genders and sexualities, which were still being marginalized but at least were being acknowledged.[12]

I began this exploration of Indigenous performances of masculinity and warriorhood with prophecies that tell of nation building through embodied ritual and cultural action. By reconnecting to these histories and practices, the Hale Mua seeks to re-member ways of being based in mana, ea, and genealogy. I end this essay with another story, also from an earlier time and place (Pukui 1995:8). When Kū the god was living as a human, famine had brought his family to the brink of starvation. He told his wife, Hina, that the only way their children would survive was if he went on a journey. He then stood on his head and disappeared into the earth. Her tears watered that spot, and from it grew the 'ulu (breadfruit) tree whose fruits saved the people. The three Kū images that were reunited in 2010 were carved from this very wood. As Sam Kaʻai noted, "These are the fragments that went away and survived. It would be a great occasion to admire and become familiar again with that which was shaped by our ancestors" (Tengan 2010:14). The return of Kū perhaps signals a new reshaping of our men in the image of our forbears, one that stands tall to provide for the survival and pono (well-being) of our nation.

Still, the ʻŌiwi community has a long way to go toward achieving a real balance of Kū and Hina. Arguments over who has been oppressed more have become unhelpful; both men and women suffered, and differently. The strength of the Hale Mua lies in the work it does with men and the transformations of self in a social context of and for men. The extent to which new understandings of the balance between Kū and Hina may emerge is questionable. Perhaps the metaphors being used are the wrong ones to begin with. Kū and Hina were only two of the forty thousand gods. The hale mua of old was in fact dedicated to Lono, the god of peace and fertility. He too took many forms, including Kamapuaʻa, the pig god and chief the Hale Mua men also dance of in the Mahaʻū. In practice and in ideology, the group has begun to also look toward the different models for thinking offered by male deities other than Kū, such as Lono, Kāne (god of life and freshwater), and Kanaloa (god of the ocean). Hopefully the group will begin to celebrate female deities such as Pele and Hiʻiaka as well. The Hawaiian community as a whole has always recognized and celebrated the diversity of being that is manifested in the different body forms of the gods, people, and land, and the fact that moves have already been made in the Hale Mua to explore this diversity is encouraging. Kū and Hina are useful to the extent that they help Hawaiians to reflect on the ever-present struggle to seek balance and complementarity. True, many men feel there is a long way yet to go before men's places or roles are restored, however the nation defines them. Perhaps when the work of rebuilding Kū is done, Kanaka men will be ready to move on to a new embrace of Hina.

Notes

1. In this essay I focus only on the Maui group. Around 2005 a group of Hale Mua members living on Oʻahu who were originally a part of the Maui group formed their own organization called the Hale Mua o Kūaliʻi, which I am a part of. We participated with the Maui group in all of the events described here.

2. Teaiwa (1999) coined the term "militourism" to highlight the articulation of militarism (which secures American state power and secures Hawai'i as a place that is open for business) and tourism (which works to both disguise U.S. military occupation and profit from it).

3. While data from the 2010 Census is still being analyzed, the social, economic, and health trends do not appear to have changed drastically since 2000 (Kamehameha Schools 2011a, 2011b).

4. This calendar is organized primarily around male gods and the chiefly religion of the 'aikapu (sacred eating) that privileged them; women's worship, such as that of Pele on Hawai'i Island, did not adhere to this structure. Some variation in counting the months and celebrating Makahiki has also been noted across the islands. Makahiki today is commonly observed beginning in November and going through February. For more on the Hawaiian division of the year, see Malo (1951:30–36, 141–59). For a political analysis of the juxtaposition of Kū and Lono in the year, see Kame'eleihiwa (1992:44–49).

5. In 2003 the documentary *Skin Stories: The Art and Culture of Polynesian Tattoo* aired on PBS. Nākānelua and Nunes (and a number of others from the Mua) were featured in the segment on Hawai'i. The PBS companion site for the film included Nākānelua's own story and his discussion of the Hale Mua (Pacific Islanders in Communication 2003).

6. The more common vernacular used in the islands and by most of the men in the Hale Mua is called Pidgin, officially Hawai'i Creole English (HCE). Emerging from the plantation camps and from the need to communicate across language barriers, Pidgin has become a marker of "local" (typically nonwhite, working-class) identity for people who were raised in Hawai'i. Okamura's (2008:119) survey of 126 University of Hawai'i students found that men claimed to speak Pidgin more frequently than women. This supports my assertion that for men, Pidgin marks a similarly ethnic and "tough" vision of local masculinity. Pidgin has acquired a number of valuations, many of them negative (e.g., Pidgin as "broken" or "bad" English) (Sato 1991; Tamura 2008). However, Pidgin is a legitimate language, and a number of scholars and writers have put enormous effort into validating and maintaining its integrity (Da Pidgin Coup 2008). Most of the men I spoke with used Pidgin to varying degrees, reflecting the HCE continuum today (Sato 1993). For those who spoke Pidgin in interviews, such as Ho, I used an "eye dialect" spelling approach, which is a modified English writing system (the alternate is the Odo orthography, which is a phonetic spelling system).

7. By "top of the lists" Haili means the top of the lists of poor life conditions resulting from poverty, described above.

8. The translation of "māhū" is difficult, for the term is used colloquially (and not consistently) to refer to effeminate males, transgendered persons, gay men (and

sometimes lesbians), and physical hermaphrodites. My usage, derived from the way men in the Hale Mua usually think of the term, is primarily in reference to effeminate males, gay men, and transgendered women (male-to-female); however, the term may also be applied to transgendered men (female-to-male). In their *Hawaiian Dictionary*, Pukui and Elbert define the term as "homosexual, of either sex; hermaphrodite" (1986:220). Debates over the conceptualizations and place of māhū split the Native Hawaiian community in the months preceding the November 2013 passage of the Hawaiʻi Marriage Equality Act, leading *Mana* magazine to run a cover story on māhū in its February/March 2014 issue (Snow 2014). In the essay, Kaumakaiwa Kanakaʻole states that the appeal of the creative arts and hula for some māhū (including herself) is that "it's the closest we as a third gender can get to procreation" and that it is a space marked as "noa (free, not taboo)" where certain genres allowed people to "be a little more outlandish . . . and acceptedly so" (Snow 2014:27).

9. Such appropriations do not go uncontested, though, either in Aotearoa or in Hawaiʻi. In a fashion that ironically mirrored the All Blacks' struggles with intellectual property rights over the "Ka Mate" haka they had traditionally performed (Hokowhitu, this volume; Jackson and Hokowhitu 2002; Tengan 2002), the University of Hawaiʻi football team, over half of whose players are Samoan or Hawaiian, found itself in a legal and moral quandary at the end of their 2006 season when it was forced to abandon its use of the All Blacks' new haka that had been developed and copyrighted directly in response to the Ngāti Toa tribe's contestation of the All Blacks' use of their ancestor's haka (Tengan and Markham 2009). Also, the narrow definition of the haka as a war dance is a mischaracterization; "haka" is a generic term for dances. This mirrors the misidentification of Kū as only "the god of war." See Linnekin 1997 for discussion of other forms of commodified hypermasculinity, especially on T-shirts sold to both locals and tourists.

10. Such a sentiment has been repeated by others who find that the comparison to and emulation of Māori forms has gone so far that Hawaiians try to hoʻomaori (act like a Māori). Interestingly, there is less anxiety surrounding the use of the Marquesan Mahaʻū; I would suggest that this has partly to do with the fact that Marquesans are not held up as the exemplars of Polynesian masculinity in the same way Māori are.

11. The Hui Aloha ʻĀina was a Hawaiian patriotic league with both men's and women's auxiliaries that was active in organizing against American annexation between the years 1893 and 1898. The epic stories of Hiʻiaka and Papa appeared in Hawaiian nationalist newspapers in the nineteenth century. See Silva 2004.

12. In April 2014 a documentary on Wong-Kalu titled *Kumu Hina* (Hamer and Wilson 2014) made its world premiere in Honolulu.

Bibliography

Alakai, Cliff

    2002 Interview with author. Honolulu, November 30.

Ayau, Edward Halealoha, and Ty Kāwika Tengan

    2002 Ka Huakaʻi o Nā ʻŌiwi: The Journey Home. *In* The Dead and Their Possessions: Repatriation in Principle, Policy, and Practice. C. Fforde, J. Hubert, P. Turnbull, and D. Hanchant, eds. Pp. 171–90. London: Routledge.

Beckwith, Martha Warren

    1970 Hawaiian Mythology. Honolulu: University of Hawaiʻi Press.

    1972 The Kumulipo. Honolulu: University Press of Hawaiʻi.

Bissen, Richard, Jr.

    2002 Interview with author. Wailuku, Maui, May 2.

Blaisdell, Kekuni, and Noreen Mokuau

    1994 Kānaka Maoli, Indigenous Hawaiians. *In* Hawaiʻi: Return to Nationhood. U. Hasager and J. Friedman, eds. Pp. 49–67. Copenhagen: International Work Group for Indigenous Affairs.

Bowker, Lee H., ed.

    1998 Masculinities and Violence. Thousand Oaks CA: Sage.

Butler, Judith

    1990 Gender Trouble: Feminism and the Subversion of Identity. New York: Routledge.

Camacho, Keith L.

    2011 Transoceanic Flows: Pacific Islander Interventions across the American Empire. Amerasia Journal 37(3):ix–xxiv.

Clark, Jeff

    1993 Hawaiian Martial Art Enjoys Resurgence. Ka Wai Ola: The Living Water of OHA. November, 10.

Connell, R. W.

    2005 Masculinities. 2nd ed. Berkeley: University of California Press.

Cook, Bud Pōmaikaʻi, L. Tarallo-Jensen, K. Withy, and S. Berry

    2005 Changes in Kanaka Maoli Men's Roles and Health: Healing the Warrior Self. International Journal of Men's Health 4(2):115–30.

Da Pidgin Coup

    2008 Pidgin and Education: A Position Paper. Educational Perspectives 41(1–2):30–39.

Desmond, Jane C.

    1999 Staging Tourism: Bodies on Display from Waikiki to Sea World. Chicago: University of Chicago Press.

Diaz, Vicente M.

    2011 Tackling Pacific Hegemonic Formations on the American Gridiron. Amerasia Journal 37(3):91–113.

Farnell, Brenda

1999 Moving Bodies, Acting Selves. Annual Reviews of Anthropology 28:341–73.

Ferguson, Kathy E., and Phyllis Turnbull

1999 Oh, Say, Can You See? The Semiotics of the Military in Hawai'i. Minneapolis: University of Minnesota Press.

Friesen, Steven J.

1992 Pu'ukoholā: Something Old and New in Hawaiian Spirituality. Paper presented at the 1992 International Congress, Melbourne, July 15.

Fujikane, Candace, and Jonathan Y. Okamura, eds.

2008 Asian Settler Colonialism: From Local Governance to the Habits of Everyday Life in Hawai'i. Honolulu: University of Hawai'i Press.

Goodyear-Ka'ōpua, Noelani

2013 The Seeds We Planted: Portraits of a Native Hawaiian Charter School. Minneapolis: University of Minnesota Press.

Hall, Lisa Kahaleole

2008 Strategies of Erasure: U.S. Colonialism and Native Hawaiian Feminism. American Quarterly 60(2):273–80.

Hamer, Dean, and Joe Wilson (producers/directors)

2014 Kumu Hina. Documentary. 60 min. Honolulu: Pacific Islanders in Communications and ITVS.

Handy, E. S. Craighill, and Mary Kawena Pukui

1972 The Polynesian Family System in Ka'ū, Hawai'i. Rutland VT: C. E. Tuttle.

Handy, E. S. Craighill, Elizabeth Green Handy, and Mary Kawena Pukui

1972 Native Planters in Old Hawai'i: Their Life, Lore, and Environment. Honolulu: Bishop Museum Press.

Hixson, Lindsay, B. B. Hepler, and M. O. Kim

2012 The Native Hawaiian and Other Pacific Islander Population: 2010. U.S. Census Brief. http://www.census.gov/prod/cen2010/briefs/c2010br-12.pdf, accessed June 18, 2012.

Ho, Wayne Puka

2002 Interview with author. Wailuku, Maui, April 18.

Hokowhitu, Brendan

2012 Producing Elite Indigenous Masculinities. Settler Colonial Studies 2:23–48.

Howes, Craig, and Jonathan Kay Kamakawiwo'ole Osorio, eds.

2010 The Value of Hawai'i: Knowing the Past, Shaping the Future. Honolulu: University of Hawai'i Press.

Imada, Adria L.

2012 Aloha America: Hula Circuits through the U.S. Empire. Durham NC: Duke University Press.

Jackson, Steven J., and Brendan Hokowhitu

2002 Sport, Tribes, and Technology: The New Zealand All Blacks Haka and the Politics of Identity. Journal of Sport and Social Issues 26(2):125–39.

Jolly, Margaret

    2008 Moving Masculinities: Memories and Bodies across Oceania. Contemporary Pacific 20(1):1–24.

Ka'ai, Sam Kaha'i

    1999 Interview with author. Makawao, November 7.

Kaeppler, Adrienne L.

    1995 Visible and Invisible in Hawaiian Dance. *In* Human Action Signs in Cultural Context: The Visible and the Invisible in Movement and Dance. B. Farnell, ed. Pp. 31–43. Metuchen NJ: Scarecrow Press.

Kame'eleihiwa, Lilikalā

    1992 Native Land and Foreign Desires: How Shall We Live in Harmony? / Ko Hawai'i 'Āina a me Nā Koi Pu'umake a ka Po'e Haole: Pehea lā e Pono Ai? Honolulu: Bishop Museum Press.

    1999 Nā Wāhine Kapu: Divine Hawaiian Women. Honolulu: 'Ai Pōhaku Press.

Kamehameha Schools

    2011a Ka Huaka'i Snapshot: Physical Well-Being. Honolulu: Kamehameha Schools, Research and Evaluation Division. July.

    2011b Ka Huaka'i Snapshot: Social/Cultural Well-Being. Honolulu: Kamehameha Schools, Research and Evaluation Division. November.

Kana, Jacob

    2002 Interview with author. Waihe'e, Maui, June 28.

Kanahele, George S.

    1982 Hawaiian Renaissance. Honolulu: Project WAIAHA.

Kana'iaupuni, S. K., N. Malone, and K. Ishibashi

    2005 Ka Huaka'i: 2005 Native Hawaiian Educational Assessment. Honolulu: Kamehameha Schools, Pauahi Publications.

Kauanui, J. Kēhaulani

    2008a Hawaiian Blood: Colonialism and the Politics of Sovereignty and Indigeneity. Durham NC: Duke University Press.

    2008b Native Hawaiian Decolonization and Gender. American Quarterly 60(2):281–87.

Kauanui, J. Kēhaulani, and Ty P. Kāwika Tengan

    n.d. Mana Wahine, Mana Kane: Decolonizing Hawaiian Gender. Unpublished manuscript in author's collection.

Keesing, Roger M.

    1984 Rethinking Mana. Journal of Anthropological Research 40(1):137–56.

Liliuokalani

    1978[1897] The Kumulipo: An Hawaiian Creation Myth. Kentfield CA: Pueo Press.

Linnekin, Jocelyn

    1990 Sacred Queens and Women of Consequence: Rank, Gender, and Colonialism in the Hawaiian Islands. Ann Arbor: University of Michigan Press.

1997 Consuming Cultures: Tourism and the Commoditization of Cultural Identity in the Island Pacific. *In* Tourism, Ethnicity, and the State in Asian and Pacific Societies. M. Picard and R. E. Wood, eds. Pp. 215–50. Honolulu: University of Hawai'i Press.

Malo, David
1951 Hawaiian Antiquities (Moolelo Hawai'i). Nathaniel B. Emerson, trans. and ed. Honolulu: Bishop Museum Press.

Marshall, Wende Elizabeth
2011 Potent Mana: Lessons in Power and Healing. Albany NY: SUNY Press.

McGregor, Davianna Pōmaika'i
2003 Constructed Images of Native Hawaiian Women. *In* Asian/Pacific Islander American Women: A Historical Anthology. S. Hune and G. M. Nomura, eds. Pp. 25–41. New York: New York University Press.
2007 Nā Kua'āina: Living Hawaiian Culture. Honolulu: University of Hawai'i Press.

McMullin, Juliet
2010 The Healthy Ancestor: Embodied Inequality and the Revitalization of Native Hawaiian Health. Walnut Creek CA: Left Coast Press.

Merry, Sally Engle
2006 Transnational Human Rights and Local Activism: Mapping the Middle. American Anthropologist 108(1):38–51.

Messner, Michael A.
1997 Politics of Masculinities: Men in Movements. Thousand Oaks CA: Sage.

Meyer, Melanna Aluli (producer, director, and writer), and John Keola Lake (writer)
1998 Ho'oku'ikahi: To Unify as One. Video recording. 47 min. Honolulu: Native Books & Beautiful Things.

Morgensen, Scott Lauria
2011 *Review of* Making Space for Indigenous Feminism, Native Americans and the Christian Right, Native Men Remade, and Mapping the Americas. *In* Signs: Journal of Women in Culture and Society 36(3):766–76.

Myerhoff, Barbara
1982 Life History among the Elderly: Performance, Visibility, and Re-membering. *In* A Crack in the Mirror: Reflexive Perspectives in Anthropology. Jay Ruby, ed. Pp. 99–117. Philadelphia: University of Pennsylvania Press.

Nākānelua, Kyle Ka'ohulani
1999 Interview with author. Lākini, Wailua, Maui, November 26.
2002 Interview with author. Kahului, Maui, December 29.

Niesse, Mark
2011 Native Hawaiians Increase Numbers by One-Fifth. Honolulu Star-Advertiser, online edition, June 17. http://www.staradvertiser.com/news/breaking /124067829.html, accessed June 17, 2011.

Nunes, Keone, and Scott Whitney
1994 The Destruction of the Hawaiian Male. Honolulu Magazine, July:43, 59–61.

OHA (Office of Hawaiian Affairs)

    2006 Native Hawaiian Data Book. Prepared by the Office of Board Services, Lea K. Young, Research Specialist. Honolulu: OHA.

Okamura, Jonathan Y.

    2008 Ethnicity and Inequality in Hawai'i. Philadelphia: Temple University Press.

O'Nell, Theresa DeLeane

    1996 Disciplined Hearts: History, Identity, and Depression in an American Indian Community. Berkeley: University of California Press.

Pacific Islanders in Communications

    2003 Tattoo Stories: Excerpts from an Interview with Kyle Nakanelua. *In* Skin Stories: The Art and Culture of Polynesian Tattoo. http://www.pbs.org/skin stories/stories/nakanelua.html, accessed June 12, 2011.

Paglinawan, Richard Kekumuikawaiokeola, Mitchell Eli, Moses Elwood Kalauoka-lani, and Jerry Walker, with Kristina Pilaho'ohau'oli Kikuchi-Palenapa

    2006 Lua: Art of the Hawaiian Warrior. S. K. Bowman and T. L. Moan, eds. Honolulu: Bishop Museum Press.

Pukui, Mary Kawena, and Samuel H. Elbert

    1986 Hawaiian Dictionary. Rev. and enl. ed. Honolulu: University of Hawai'i Press.

Pukui, Mary Kawena, E. W. Haertig, and Catherine A. Lee

    1972 Nānā i ke kumu (Look to the Source). 2 vols. Honolulu: Hui Hānai.

Pukui, Mary Kawena, with Laura C. S. Green

    1995 Folktales of Hawai'i: He Mau Ka'ao Hawai'i. Honolulu: Bishop Museum Press.

Robertson, Carol E.

    1989 The Mahu of Hawai'i. Feminist Studies 15(2):312–26.

Sahlins, Marshall

    1981 Historical Metaphors and Mythical Realities: Structure in the Early History of the Sandwich Islands Kingdom. Ann Arbor: University of Michigan Press.

Sai, David Keanu

    2008 The American Occupation of the Hawaiian Kingdom: Beginning the Transition from Occupied to Restored State. PhD dissertation, Department of Political Science, University of Hawai'i at Mānoa.

Sato, Charlene J.

    1991 Sociolinguistic Variation and Language Attitudes in Hawai'i. *In* English around the World: Sociolinguistic Perspectives. J. Cheshire, ed. Pp. 647–63. Cambridge: Cambridge University Press.

    1993 Language Change in a Creole Continuum: Decreolization? *In* Progression and Regression in Language: Sociocultural, Neuropsychological, and Linguistic Perspectives. K. Hyltenstam and A. Viberg, eds. Pp. 122–43. Cambridge: Cambridge University Press.

Schwalbe, Michael L.

1996 Unlocking the Iron Cage: The Men's Movement, Gender Politics, and American Culture. New York: Oxford University Press.

1998 Mythopoetic Men's Work as a Search for Communitas. *In* Men's Lives. M. S. Kimmel and M. A. Messner, eds. Pp. 565–77. Boston: Allyn and Bacon.

Shore, Brad

1989 Mana and Tapu. *In* Developments in Polynesian Ethnology. A. Howard and R. Borofsky, eds. Pp. 137–73. Honolulu: University of Hawai'i Press.

Silva, Noenoe K.

2004 Aloha Betrayed: Native Hawaiian Resistance to American Colonialism. Durham NC: Duke University Press.

Sinha, Mrinalini

1995 Colonial Masculinity: The "Manly Englishman" and the "Effeminate Bengali" in the Late Nineteenth Century. Manchester: Manchester University Press.

Snow, Jade

2014 Beyond the Binary: Portraits of Gender and Sexual Identities in the Native Hawaiian Community. Mana: The Hawaiian Magazine, February/March:22–29.

Tamura, Eileen H.

2008 Hawai'i Creole (Pidgin), Local Identity, and Schooling. Educational Perspectives 41(1–2):3–5.

Teaiwa, Teresia K.

1999 Reading Gauguin's Noa Noa with Hau'ofa's Nederends: Militourism, Feminism and the "Polynesian" Body. UTS Review 5(1):53–69.

Tengan, Ty P. Kāwika

2002 (En)gendering Colonialism: Masculinities in Hawai'i and Aotearoa. Cultural Values: Journal for Cultural Research 6(3):239–56.

2003 *Review of* Ke Kūlana He Māhū: Remembering a Sense of Place. *In* Contemporary Pacific 15(1):231–33.

2008a Native Men Remade: Gender and Nation in Contemporary Hawai'i. Durham NC: Duke University Press.

2008b Re-membering Panalā'au: Masculinities, Nation and Empire in Hawai'i and the Pacific. Contemporary Pacific 20(1):27–53.

2010 The Return of Kū. *In* E Kū Ana Ka Paia: Unification, Responsibility and the Kū Images. Pamphlet for the Bernice Pauahi Bishop Museum exhibit. Honolulu: Bishop Museum.

Tengan, Ty P. Kāwika, and Jesse Makani Markham

2009 Performing Polynesian Masculinities in American Football: From Rainbows to Warriors. International Journal of the History of Sport 26(16):2412–31.

Tomlinson, Matt

2006 Retheorizing Mana: Bible Translation and Discourse of Loss in Fiji. Oceania 76:173–85.

Trask, Haunani-Kay

    1999 From a Native Daughter: Colonialism and Sovereignty in Hawai'i. Rev. ed. Honolulu: University of Hawai'i Press.

Turner, Victor

    1969 The Ritual Process: Structure and Anti-structure. Chicago: Aldine.

Valeri, Valerio

    1985 Kingship and Sacrifice: Ritual and Society in Ancient Hawai'i. Chicago: University of Chicago Press.

Walker, Isaiah Helekunihi

    2011 Waves of Resistance: Surfing and History in Twentieth-Century Hawai'i. Honolulu: University of Hawai'i Press.

Wolfe, Patrick

    2006 Settler Colonialism and the Elimination of the Native. Journal of Genocide Research 8(4):387–409.

9

Bone-Deep Indigeneity

Theorizing Hawaiian Care for the
State and Its Broken Apparatuses

GREG JOHNSON

> This complaint is based on the failure of Kawaiahaʻo Church and various
> public entities to fulfill their legal obligations pursuant to HRS Chapter
> 6E, the public trust doctrine, Native Hawaiian rights, and HRS Chapter
> 343. In this instance, government entities have failed to act with a level of
> openness, diligence and foresight commensurate with the high priority
> commanded under the laws of our state.
>
> DANA NAONE HALL, Complaint, Civil No. 09-1-1828-01, Hawaiʻi First
> Circuit Court, 2009

The new world disorder of drained economies and exhausted governments
is revealing a novel dynamic in some performances of Indigeneity, one in
which Indigenous citizens become caretakers of law amid the failings of
states. I have been following how this is taking shape in Hawaiʻi with regard
to burial laws, and I have observed similar dynamics unfolding in a number
of American Indian contexts. Comparative studies of Indigeneity suggest
that shared structural realities and broadly common Indigenous interests
may produce similar, if uneven, results elsewhere (see Niezen 2003; Povinelli 2002; de la Cadena and Starn 2007). First Nations Peoples and the
Maori, for example, have long-term experience shoring up nation-state
shortcomings (Maaka and Fleras 2005).

Native Peoples have worked long and hard for political and legal gains
within democratic nation-states over the past forty years, if not far longer.
Of necessity, many Indigenous actors have pursued their goals through
the avenues and channels of tedious administrative law. For them, the

key questions have been (1) how to get "good" laws on the books and (2) how to work with these laws effectively once they are there. Now an altogether new question has emerged: How to manage in a context in which the machinery of law seems to be halting and failing? One reaction is a return to strong versions of sovereignty arguments; in Hawai'i, however, a handful of committed people are taking a more practical if less romantic approach to the crisis. They are rolling up their sleeves to fix the state of the law, taking on the responsibility of monitoring its functions and functionaries. The results of such efforts are not yet clear; yet the very existence of these efforts demonstrates that we must reconsider the relationship of Indigenous Peoples to the state. Direct action of this kind—in which people struggle not only for specific issues but for the integrity of law and process in general—should push us to ask, How do we begin to recognize and theorize performances of Indigeneity vis-à-vis broken states?

In order to address the questions I have set out, I pursue an argument about the dialectical nature of performances of Indigeneity in settings framed by direct engagement with the state, taking religiously grounded burial law conflicts in Hawai'i as my example. At the outset, I acknowledge that asserting the dialectical nature of performances of Indigeneity is not a particularly novel point. The relevance of this point, however, is frequently underappreciated, particularly when religion is involved. For all of their claims to high seriousness, religious practitioners regularly engage in considerable performativity—religion is dramatic in the extreme. This is so for formal reasons. Religious discourse and action are predicated on a "greater than" positioning vis-à-vis everything else. Thus religious claims point beyond worldly authority and construct themselves as sharing in greater-than-worldly authority (Lincoln 1996). Persuading oneself and others of the greater-than-worldly authority of one's traditions takes some doing and a well-stocked theatrical repertoire. Many scholars of religion have long known this, and the lion's share of our attention has been pulled in just this direction. This has resulted in fascinating studies of religious drama, but also in a frequently narrow fixation on otherness in exotic manifestations. Consequently, our peripheral vision has become lazy-eyed and unclear. I worry that we have become unable to detect significant religious and cultural happenings that are performed in a lower

Fig. 9.1. Performers at Lā Hoʻihoʻi Ea (Restoration Day), an annual celebration of Native Hawaiian culture and sovereignty at Thomas Square, Honolulu, Oʻahu. Photo courtesy of the author (2009).

key. My aim in what follows is to push for a redirection of our attention to such understated moments for analytical reasons, but also because these are the kinds of "performances" making a tremendous impact in Hawaiʻi today.

Revising Dialectical Theories of Performance

I am not particularly fond of the category "performance." It has unlimited potential to offend and leaves so much out of consideration. That said, I resonate with the concept of social drama and have a Shakespearian inclination to regard us all as actors, if with varying degrees of intention, agency, and opportunity, and with highly variable skills (see Goffman 1982[1967], 1974). I also recognize that "performance" has entered our shared analytical parlance and has the ability to shed new light on a range of enduring and novel issues germane to understanding Indigeneity, as is so powerfully demonstrated throughout this volume. I am also inclined toward "performance" for its Aristotelian resonances that point simultaneously to drama, metaphor, ethics, and, indeed, the conjunction of these. In the Hawaiian burial protection context, for example, Antigone and her tragic struggles with the state and family are familiar and powerfully suggestive.

For all of its richness, "performance" has fallen short in my field tests of the category. Consider three highly visible and influential Hawaiians: Kekuni Blaisdell, Dana Naone Hall, and Halealoha Ayau.[1] Respectively, they are: a hard-core sovereignty activist who has staged major public protest events; a poet whose works are widely known and studied; and a famous repatriation activist who has been incarcerated for his defiance of court orders and who has testified in the first person as an ancestor (Johnson 2007, 2011).[2] They are all top-tier "performers" of Hawaiian Indigeneity. I am convinced, however, that any effort to analyze their significance and successes by means of a narrow frame of performativity would misconstrue their work and their profound effectiveness. Each has a life less visible and modes of acting less detectable than their "stage" presences would let on. Kekuni Blaisdell is a renowned physician who has devoted years to Native Hawaiian health care. Dana Naone Hall is a burial protection activist versed in administrative procedure. Halealoha Ayau has a law degree and spends many of his days writing grant materials.

These less visible selves inform, shape, and undergird their performative alter egos. In this way, each of these individuals exemplifies a more general pattern discernable in the dialectics of contemporary Indigenous performativity. In some respects this insight mirrors other binary ways of conceiving social drama (e.g., onstage/offstage; public transcript/hidden transcript), as well as theories about discursive code switching and layered identities (see Scott 1990; Collins 1998; Feldman 1991). It also draws upon and echoes now-familiar ideas about cultural elites being educated, skilled, and vocal across lines of class, race, and culture. However much these various conceptual schemas have purchase, I would insist that they require recalibration in view of the ways the current economic-cum-political crisis of late modernity is shifting the relationship between more and less visible modes of Indigeneity. The workaday side of things is carrying a heavier load now.

I would like to establish some further groundwork for a dialectical

Fig. 9.2. Dr. Kekuni Blaisdell greeting the author. Nuʻuanu Valley, Oʻahu. Photo courtesy of Kari Robinson (2010).

theory of Indigeneity by attempting to specify the relationship between more and less dramatic, more and less theatrical, and more and less flamboyant modes of performance.[3] Heuristically, I will call the more flamboyant performances "skin" and the less dramatic ones "bones." I understand that this construct is potentially inflammatory and may cause some readers to assume I am making a value judgment about the relative worth of these modes of social representation. I might also be accused of trafficking in dubious biological metaphors susceptible to racialist ends. This is not my intent. Rather, I wish to draw attention to what scholars of religion and others too frequently miss: the underlying skeletal frameworks that make more visible forms of social life possible. Previous generations of scholars looked to such things as kinship, economics, and historical diffusion, for example, as explanatory keys to the riddle of culture; my finger points to unexpected investments and prowess in feats of administrative cross-checking. I don't claim to have solved the riddle of Hawaiian culture with my observations, but I would insist that caring for the dead—in precisely the kinds of law-heavy atmospheres I will describe—is one pillar of Hawaiian religion in the present (see, e.g., Nihipali 2002). I should note, too, that many Native Hawaiians find deep meaning in bone metaphors.

"Skin" and "bones" are meant to stand as loose markers for the ends of an imagined performative spectrum running from self-conscious and amplified at one end to unmarked and unremarked on the other. Rough homologues might include declarative and substantive, surface and core, and so forth. For my analytical purposes, and because I am dealing with burial issues, I'll stick with skin and bones. Roland Barthes (1957[1972]) and others taught us to read outward, skin-level signs of performance, and Maurice Merleau-Ponty (1945[2012]) has given us a phenomenology of the flesh; now we might take a Hawaiian lead and root metaphors in bone. Whatever the case, most performances have elements of skin, flesh, and bones, and few performances inhabit either end of the spectrum in any simple sense. My central point is not only about *where* any given performance falls on an imagined spectrum but also about *how* performances interact in their social unfolding.

In many contexts of Indigenous cultural articulation, skin and bone performances stand in dialectical relationship to one another as a strategy—self-conscious or not—of managing perceptions of and reactions to Indigeneity in putatively multicultural democracies. The former establish the ongoing presence of a group as an internal "other" and thus serve to ground and sustain political claims (to special programs and legislation, for example) based in cultural difference and historical marginality; the latter serve in a more workaday capacity to implement gains made possible by the former, which necessarily entails working within the system and terms of the dominant society. This often has the effect of domesticating Indigeneity—the more involved in the system actors become, the less distinct they appear. In this way, "bone" performances risk enacting their own erasure. Therefore, working against passive assimilation as these performances do, the relevance of staged, emphatically marked "skin" performances remains central to Indigeneity. For this dialectical theory to have explanatory power in the present, however, it must grapple with the crumbling condition of state apparatuses and performances of Indigeneity relative to this phenomenon.

Repertoires of Performance and the
Burial Protection Movement

The burial rights and repatriation movement is a cultural and political domain that bridges skin and bone realms of Hawaiian Indigeneity. Some activities in this context are rather local and almost invisible, like an aunty tending to an ancestor's grave. Other activities, like activists penetrating the Bishop Museum to reclaim objects, have occasioned considerable media attention and public commentary (Johnson 2009). Indeed, up to the present, Hawaiian repatriation and reburial activities have relied heavily on flamboyant modes of skin performance, especially when issues are playing out at state and federal levels. Ritual offerings in hearings, chanting prayers, genealogical recitations, and other similarly dramatic performances have punctuated the movement (see, e.g., Johnson 2003). Now quite a different mode of engagement is predominant in the form of tedious monitoring of legal processes.

As in North American Indian contexts, repatriation and reburial issues in Hawai'i have flared since at least the 1960s. But it was not until the 1980s, when increased numbers of Native people had gained a voice in political, legal, and scholarly circles, that concrete legal remedies were established at the state and federal levels. At the federal level, Hawaiian representatives were vocal in establishing the Native American Graves Protection and Repatriation Act (NAGPRA, 1990) and are now leaders in its implementation (Ayau and Tengan 2002). At the state level, the burial protection movement emerged as part of a widespread Hawaiian cultural renaissance. Pivotal in this process were the events at Honokahua, Maui, in the late 1980s, where eleven hundred ancestral remains were disturbed in the course of a hotel construction project (Naone Hall 2010). Hawaiian activists and cultural experts rallied around the desecration at Honokahua and formed a burial protection community, establishing a range of neotraditional reburial protocols in the process. Individuals awakened to burial protection also agitated for a new state burial law (HRS 6E-43), which established island burial councils to be constituted by a Native Hawaiian majority. There are five councils and each meets monthly, producing minutes and transcripts of their proceedings. These councils enable the local Native community to have a voice in development policies and practices. However, the state apparatus for supporting burial laws and the burial councils has begun to collapse in the wake of recent fiscal crises.

The Department of Land and Natural Resources (DLNR), which oversees implementation of burial protection laws, has been particularly hard hit. A range of mishandled cases suggests the magnitude of this crisis, including burial disturbances at a large-scale commercial property in downtown Honolulu and a road-widening project that has not been subjected to proper cultural and historical review. Widespread frustration with the state came to a head in 2008 when a number of Hawaiians petitioned the federal government to conduct an oversight review of the state burial protection process. Community meetings were held, emotions were vented, and a scathing report was published (Conrow 2010). To the dismay of the burial protection community, this reprimand has not translated into action for the very reasons that the system is failing in the first place—resources are simply too thin. Some Hawaiians are taking up the challenge directly. The following examples explore four contexts of contemporary bone-deep Indigeneity.

A House on Graves

In early July 2010 I arrived on Kaua'i for the first leg of a five-week research trip. My aim was to get an on-the-ground sense of what was happening at the Brescia property, a homesite on the North Shore at Naue.[4] The property is situated on a stunning coastal point where a ridgeline meets the ocean. A developer from California proposed and then built a home on what is clearly an ancestral Hawaiian burial ground. More than thirty sets of human remains have been documented on the one-acre oceanfront property (Hoerman and Dega 2010). Of these, eight *iwi kūpuna* (ancestors') graves are within the footprint of the house itself. Brescia's builders took care not to place pilings directly through the known graves, but one can easily enough begin to imagine why this house has offended local Hawaiians and their supporters. Beyond the raw emotions the dispute has laid bare, the conflict is pivotal in the context of state burial law for the way it has shown the weaknesses of island burial councils. The Kaua'i and Ni'ihau Islands Burial Council has changed its position on reinterment versus in situ protection and on the building plan in general, which has been before the committee in numerous drafts (see, e.g., KNIBC 2008). The DLNR has been inconsistent in the degree to which it has acted on or ignored the council's findings, and the courts have further eroded the apparent clout of the council.[5] At stake, then, is not only the sanctity of one burial ground. Some observers suggest that this dispute may establish precedents that will either shore up the legal standing of burial councils or, conversely, undercut them significantly.

Through this process of legal wrangling, the Brescia dispute has attracted considerable popular and media attention, occasioning its fair share of performativity on a variety of stages. Burial council meetings are one such stage, as are the courtrooms in which aspects of the dispute have been heard. Most visible has been Native Hawaiian presence at the site. Native Hawaiians are vigilant in protecting the space and memory of their ancestors. In the case of the Brescia property, locals from Kaua'i were quick on the scene. They engaged in several highly visible skin activities. They ministered to the site and to the ancestors through *pule* (prayer), *ho'okupu* (offerings), and the construction of *ahu* (shrines).

These activities took place around and on the property itself, which constituted acts of trespass. Cognizant of this, some Hawaiian activists and religious leaders reconfigured their presence as one of emphatic political protest. Aware that their actions were being observed and recorded (initially by curious bystanders and a documentary filmmaker, then by media representatives, and finally by the police), many of the protesters engaged in a range of dramatic acts, which included amplification of their prayers and other ritual gestures and placement of torches to locate and call attention to the dead. Finally, when a considerable police presence was marshaled, they engaged in a classic form of resistance, binding their hands through sections of PVC piping and defying orders to leave. Numerous arrests resulted. More significantly, video of this event quickly made its way to the public sphere through YouTube. The events of that day went from ritual performance to direct action to media event in remarkably quick succession. Then the video itself became subject of legal contestation (ACLU of Hawai'i 2009).

All of this had piqued my interest, and I was curious about what remaining traces of performance and presence I could detect at the site. Taking advantage of the slow pace of state and legal machinery, Brescia had simply forged ahead with his house. By July 2010 it was all but done. When I arrived it was being landscaped. The only suggestions of drama were strategically placed Keep Out signs and a few discrete ahu (shrines) placed just *ma kai* (seaward) of the property setback line. This, however, is not to say that the dispute had been conceded by Hawaiian activists. Numerous burial law activists, including Dana Naone Hall, Halealoha Ayau, and Alan Murakami, an attorney from the Native Hawaiian Legal Fund, were pushing back.[6] They regard this as a crucial moment to act, to take up the full measure of the law lest it be eroded beyond recognition. This dynamic— the movement from on-the-ground protest to legal challenge—interests me a great deal. Sometimes the players remain the same across this transition; other times the cast shifts. At times this transition is smooth; other times it is bumpy and contentious. Those people who occupy a site and pay the legal price for doing so often exert a moral claim upon the place, a claim that is threatened when experts from other islands take up the cause in rarified venues, in legal discourse, and with painfully slow results.

Knowing that the Brescia dispute had been going through just such a transition, I was curious to gain an ear for how these tensions were being construed and represented by various parties. I had thus scheduled my visit to correspond with the timing of a Kauaʻi and Niʻihau Islands Burial Council meeting. Alas, one nonperformance trumped all others. Due to economic constraints and ongoing personnel issues, the State Historical Preservation Division (SHPD) canceled the meeting a day before it was to be held. This scuttled my plans but sensitized me to another issue that I have long considered but had not adequately fathomed. Namely, when space for Indigenous political and legal performances are established and sanctioned by the state—such as burial council meetings—these performances are thereby constrained in any number of ways. Sunshine laws (laws that mandate open meetings), *Robert's Rules of Order*, audio recordings: all such things shift and shape how performances will emerge or be silenced. But the most profound silencing of all is the most obvious and blunt. Namely, no meetings results in no voices being expressed or registered. In this way the postsecular state (a state making room for Indigenous and other voices announced in a religious key) has run headlong into the bankrupt state.

A Hotel on Graves

Quite distinct from the Brescia dispute I have just described, with its You-Tube fame and media visibility, is a case that began unfolding on Maui in 2010. Now settled, it never generated media attention or a public outcry, and this is precisely what I find analytically engaging about it. Not a single news report preceded or emerged from a court hearing in Wailuku, the county seat of Maui, on July 22, 2010.[7] Only a handful of people were present: the judge, attorneys from both sides, one claimant, two defendant representatives, a court reporter, and four members of the public, including me. This is a rather small cast of characters for what I take to be a significant episode in the context of legal matters concerning construction planning, burial laws, and, ultimately, due process.

I describe this as a significant moment because one Native Hawaiian claimant took on a major development company, the County of Maui Planning Commission, and the SHPD and prevailed, if in a narrowly constrained way. But it is also a battle that should not have needed to be fought, as the legal issues in question had been settled in Hawaiians' favor more than twenty years earlier. This, then, is an example of Hawaiians being caught up in a Kafkaesque situation whereby they appear again and again to argue for their standing and for the seriousness of their claims. Their willingness to do so is keeping their causes alive and the law functioning.

The case at hand concerns one of the most luxuriously developed coastlines in Hawai'i, an area known as Wailea. Many international hotel chains have prominent properties in Wailea, including Marriot and Four Seasons. The Grand Wailea Hotel is in the heart of Wailea and is the largest hotel built in the region. It is truly gigantic, with 780 rooms. The hotel was built just prior to the passage of Hawai'i's modern burial laws. Thus the Grand Wailea is one of the last hotels built on Maui without special protection for burials located on the property. As with so many of Hawai'i's oceanfront hotels, the building site was over dunes, which precolonial Hawaiians favored for burial purposes. As building ensued, 344 sets of human remains were disinterred and scattered.

Hawaiian sensibilities about the dead have heightened over the past twenty years as increasing numbers of Hawaiians have become educated in traditional religious practices, one focus of which is responsible care for the ancestors' memories and remains. So it was that a member of the local community paid close attention in 2008 when a developer proposed to expand the Grand Wailea by 310 rooms. The proposed construction would entail a significant enlargement of the hotel's footprint.

When Dana Naone Hall learned of this construction proposal, she set to work. Among the most experienced Hawaiian burial rights activists, Naone Hall has a longtime affiliation with the Wailea region of Maui. She has served on the Maui and Lana'i Islands Burial Council as its chair and vice chair and has been instrumental in making sure developers and governmental agencies abide by state and federal burial laws (Johnson 2007). With her command of Hawaiian tradition, legal acumen, street smarts, and fierce oratorical style, Naone Hall is a force to be reckoned with. She works in concert with her husband, Isaac Hall, a well-known environmental and Native rights attorney. This duo has been at the forefront of Hawaiian rights for decades, so the corporate representatives must have been uneasy when they learned who was paying close attention to their development plans.

The story I am telling is not about a showdown encounter over redevelopment of the hotel itself. That was settled through mediation in 2011, with Naone Hall's concerns about burial disturbance being addressed to her satisfaction. My point here is to explore a crucial early step on the way to this victory. Almost from the outset, and contrary to law and precedent, Naone Hall was shut out of the planning process for the hotel expansion. The legal issue in question was about her standing to participate in a contested case proceeding before the Maui County Planning Commission. Members of the general public are allowed to speak at such meetings, but time is limited to three minutes and they may not introduce evidence into the record or cross-examine other parties. Those deemed to have special standing beyond that of the general public have recourse to these entitlements. Hawai'i state law has made amply clear that Native Hawaiian burial experts have special standing in such contexts. Increasingly, however, this standing is ignored; Dana Naone Hall and Isaac Hall were out to challenge this broken state of affairs.

Naone Hall had been denied standing at a meeting in 2009. Her intention had been to push for a thorough archeological inventory survey (AIS), which is mandated by law but was not included in the county's or the developer's plans. These plans included a new wing of the hotel to be located in

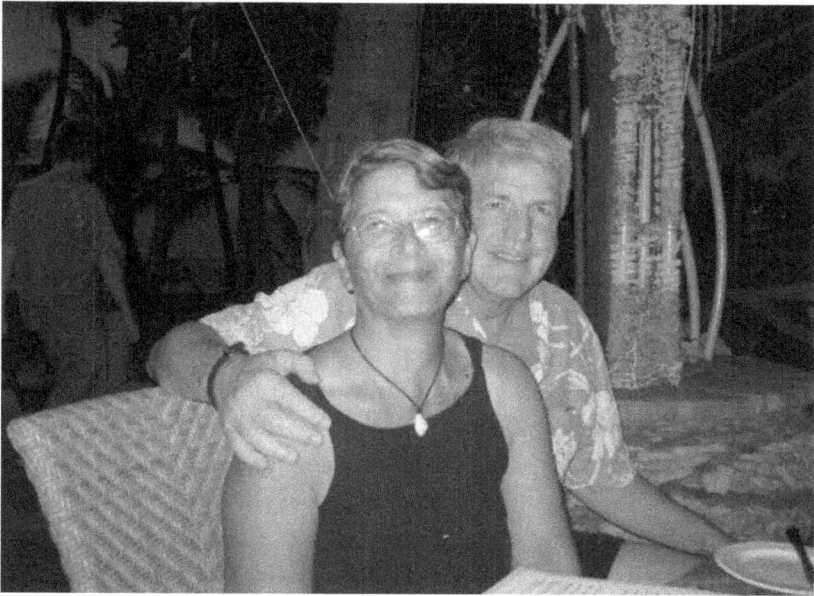

Fig. 9.3. Dana Naone Hall and Isaac Hall celebrating near Paʻia, Maui. Photo courtesy of Dana Naone Hall (2011).

a sand dune area just inshore, precisely the kind of location where ancestral Hawaiian burials are often located. Subsequent to these meetings, the developer was issued a Special Management Area building permit and the SHPD issued a "no effect" statement (a summary conclusion that no substantial disturbance would occur), which unburdened the developer from needing to complete a comprehensive AIS prior to construction work. Astounded by this neglect of legal and administrative process, Naone Hall filed a suit against the Maui County Planning Commission for violating her rights to due process. She sought an injunction on the building permit and petitioned for the process to be reset to the public meeting stage and for her standing to be recognized in that context (Dana Naone Hall, Petition to Intervene, Maui Planning Commission, filed September 8, 2009).

In his opening remarks at the hearing, Isaac Hall provided a thorough history of state law with regard to the question of Native Hawaiian standing in cultural contexts in general and with specific reference to burial contexts. He detailed his wife's long history as a burial expert and as a reburial ritual practitioner. Representatives of the planning commission were far less polished and coherent. Theirs was the epitome of a circular argument: administrative bodies reserve the right to self-define procedural protocols, including recognition of standing, for purposes of efficiency and relevance. In the case at hand, Naone Hall was said not to have an interest beyond that of the general public and to have not established her credentials as a burial expert, and, it was said, her testimony would slow down a process that needed to move forward with due haste for obvious economic reasons.

The judge was not patient with the planning commission. He lectured them about setting the clock back twenty years. He asked, What is the point of law if administrative bodies constantly reinvent its framework to suit their immediate needs? He apologized to Naone Hall and Hall for the cost to them in time and effort and acknowledged that were it not for such efforts, burial laws—and even county planning procedures—would not function as they should. He ruled in favor of Dana Naone Hall. He invalidated the building permit and required that the planning meeting be revisited, with Naone Hall enjoying full standing as a Native Hawaiian burial expert. Dana Naone Hall and Isaac Hall left with half smiles—half pleased that they "won" and half chagrinned that they had to stage their performance at all (see Perry 2010).

A Hill of Graves

For two years Dana Naone Hall has been alerting me to issues surrounding a large parcel of land in upcountry Maui called Kula Ridge. The site, she says, "could be as pivotal to implementation of burial and cultural protection laws as Honokahua was to establishing those laws" (Naone Hall, personal communication with author, July 21, 2010). This is no small claim. Based on her letters to SHPD and to members of the Maui and Lanaʻi Islands Burial Council, I could see the intensity of Naone Hall's engagement with the dispute and the scope of the conflicts encapsulated by it (Naone Hall, letter to DLNR and SHPD, September 21, 2009). When she offered to take me to the site in early August 2010, I was ready to go.

Upcountry Maui is a legendary place. It is a land of considerable cultural and agricultural productivity, a place of gigantic views—to Kahoʻolawe, Lanaʻi, Molokaʻi, and beyond—and it is a place of bones. The Kula region is all of this, especially the latter. In Hawaiian, one designation for "homeland" is *kula iwi*, which literally means "bone plain." In Hawaiian thinking the key point here is that home is where the ancestors are; making a home is, therefore, intertwined with caring for the bones, which can include making offerings, building shrines, and offering prayers. Other aspects of such care are subtler and include proper bodily and social comportment when in proximity to graves. Ultimately, the most important aspect of caring for the dead is the least marked, until it is triggered. This is protection of the ancestors' space—their burials and surroundings—from violation, especially direct physical disturbance of the bones. Antigone's sensibilities loom large.

Perhaps the minimum claim one can make about Kula is that it would likely not be named as such if it were not a burial ground of some significance. Herein lies the rub. In 2008 a developer bought the land and began paperwork for the governmental approval process to build a housing project. One aspect of the process is State Historic Preservation Division review of an AIS. The way in which this process was handled is what catalyzed Naone Hall's involvement in the dispute. Specifically, she found implausible the following discrepancy: the AIS lists 1,218 archaeological features but designates none of these as burial sites or places of worship. Naone Hall leapt into action, crafting multiple documents addressed to the developers and relevant state and county offices. She included lengthy discussions of Hawaiian history and cultural practice, arguing that it is inconceivable that the land would not have burial and religious features, especially because the site was a known area of high agricultural productivity, which for Hawaiians correlates with religious practice. Naone Hall also drew attention to the remarkable cultural features of the site, which include numerous walls, terraces, enclosures, and unusual tower-like structures.

The site runs along both sides of a prominent gulch. Even from our parking spot a quarter mile away, I could see that this was a culturally configured space of generationally worked land. We could also detect another feature Naone Hall had wanted me to see. It was at the very edge of a road cut that had been bulldozed earlier in the year during the first phases of construction and well after Naone Hall had written her warning letters. Covered by a blue tarp, but not otherwise marked, this iwi kupuna (ancestor) was the reason the construction had come to a halt.

The human remains were "inadvertently discovered" during the access road grading. Naone Hall is now using this episode as a means to chal-

Fig. 9.4. The proposed location of the Kula Ridge project is an open midland on the broad slope of Haleakalā, Maui's highest mountain. A recently graded access road on the south side of the 272-acre project area exposed a traditional Hawaiian burial and sliced through numerous terrace walls. Photo courtesy of Masako Cordray (2011).

lenge further construction at the site. Naone Hall is also making the Kula Ridge situation central to her ongoing attempt to reform implementation of state burial law. Her primary campaign is to have SHPD revisit and revise its issuance of "no effect" letters. This hinges on proper, thorough AIS reports. The relevance of her point is not hard to find. Several weeks earlier I attended a Maui and Lana'i Islands Burial Council meeting at which two other instances of the problem were discussed. A week prior to that I saw the same with reference to several sites on O'ahu. The Brescia case on Kaua'i was bedeviled by similar problems. The issue at stake is as crucial as it is banal, and it amounts to abrogation of burial law by means of administrative ineptitude and stated desires for "efficiency."

A Church on Graves

I will close by demonstrating my point about the depth of bone convictions and actions through discussion of a final example, the implications of which are momentous for a variety of reasons. In this case, performances of many sorts have played out on various stages. Once again, however, the issue turns on substantive performances focused on maintaining the integrity of law. The dispute concerns Kawaiaha'o Church, a famous Congregationalist church in downtown Honolulu. It is often referred to as the "Westminster Abbey of Hawai'i" and has been guided by Native Hawaiian leadership since 1918. The church has long been a site of significant Hawaiian cultural performances, including royal weddings and burials. King Lunalilo's mausoleum, for example, occupies a prominent spot in front of the sanctuary. The nation-state has also laid claims on the church's significance, designating it a National Historic Landmark and placing it on the National Register of Historic Places. This is not an average church and this is no simple story about Hawaiians vs. Christians. It is a complex and unfinished epic about the ways diverse groups of Hawaiians are struggling over the meaning of the past in the present and the ways in which law supports or fails to support various agendas therein (Greer 2013; Johnson 2013).

In 2004 the church announced plans to build a new multipurpose facility. Constricted as it is by the developed nature of its location, the church made plans to build over a portion of its cemetery. The congregation was consulted and an application was made to the State Department of Health for a mass disinterment permit so that burials could be moved as necessary within the boundaries of the cemetery to make room for the new footprint of the building. State burial law allows for this kind of activity within known, maintained cemeteries. However, the building plans included various infrastructure elements that entailed digging outside of the cemetery boundaries. This area, as documented by oral tradition and earlier archaeological surveys, is known to contain Hawaiian burials that predate the church. This component of the plan should have triggered state-level review and a thorough archaeological inventory survey. The church bypassed this legal requirement and began work in early 2009. Shortly thereafter, in the course of initial trenching for a sewer line, sixty-nine iwi kūpuna (human remains) were encountered and disinterred.

This event provoked a number of Hawaiian burial activists into action, including Dana Naone Hall and Halealoha Ayau, both of whom have connections to ancestors buried in the cemetery. They and others announced objections to the church's plan on moral, religious, and legal grounds, which resulted in a highly public and visible dispute process. The *Honolulu Star-Advertiser* and *Honolulu Weekly* have run a number of stories, as have television news channels.[8] Several protests have been staged at the church, some of which have been video recorded, and the videos now circulate on the Internet.[9] A prominent Indigenous activism radio show hosted by Wesleyan University anthropology professor Kēhaulani Kauanui ran a program on the dispute.[10] *Issues that Matter*, a television production of the anthropology program at Hawaii Pacific University, aired a feature episode on the conflict.[11] Much of the press reporting and Internet coverage focused on flamboyant aspects of the dispute, with attention centering on the arrest of two protesters, Paulette Kaʻanohi Kaleikini and Kamuela Kalaʻi.

Less attention has been paid to the relentless efforts of Dana Naone Hall, who has pursued legal and administrative channels to challenge the church, SHPD, and DLNR. In 2009 she filed a suit for injunctive relief to have the construction project halted (Civil No. 09-1-1828-08, Hawaiʻi First Circuit Court, 2009; see also Wu 2009). In early 2011 she was denied standing in the case. In the same case, the judge declared Halealoha Ayau to be an unreliable witness regarding Hawaiian burial practices, despite the fact that he has long been recognized in the Hawaiian cultural community as a leading figure in the burial protection movement and was trained by widely recognized elders in relevant ritual protocol (Sakamoto ruling, *Hall v.* DLNR, Civil No. 09-1-1828-08, Hawai'i First Circuit Court, October 11, 2011). After Naone Hall's legal case was rejected, she began to prepare her appeal, which is currently being reviewed by the court. Additionally, she mounted an ongoing campaign to have the Office of Hawaiian Affairs (OHA) audit a grant of one million dollars that it awarded to the church for the construction project. Her point is to call attention to the tension between OHA's support for this project and the stakes of the project for protection of the iwi kūpuna. Beyond raising this large-order moral and cultural question, Naone Hall alleges that the church has improperly expended the grant funds and that, by contract, OHA can recall the funds (Naone Hall, letter to Office of Hawaiian Affairs, February 24, 2011).

Naone Hall's persistent efforts appeared to be yielding results by April 2011. Behind closed doors, the church leadership began meeting with Naone Hall, Ayau, and a few other Hawaiians in order to attempt cultural mediation known as *ho'oponopono*. This process required numerous long meetings, regular interisland travel for Naone Hall and Ayau, and huge amounts of emotional energy. It also required negotiation skills and plain hard work. Ultimately, ho'oponopono failed to yield a settlement, so the parties continue to struggle through media and legal venues. Skin and bones activists are working in conjunction for the protection of the iwi kūpuna. Meanwhile, the church has forged ahead. By August 2012 the remains of more than 570 individuals had been "recovered," to quote the language of the church's archaeological report (Cultural Surveys Hawai'i 2012).[12]

Bone-Deep Chicken Skin

I have argued that performances of Indigeneity in contemporary Hawai'i have a dialectical quality, and I have distinguished between skin and bone modalities of such performances. This heuristic device has enabled me to place the workaday efforts of various Hawaiians in stark relief and to argue that it is precisely these mundane but intense efforts that are propelling Indigenous interests vis-à-vis various manifestations and failures of governance. Again, my point has not been to denigrate skin performance; it has been to redirect attention to the less flamboyant labors on which these depend for continued cultural vitality. I have insisted that neglecting to account for the bone-level performance of Indigeneity would be to miss so much of what makes it work, and I provided four examples of how I see this dynamic unfolding in Hawai'i today.

Now I hope to re-join what I have divided, playfully suggesting that socio-poetic selves are, of course, not so neatly separable. Sometimes you can feel chicken skin to the bone.[13] Consider two poetic-political utterances by Dana Naone Hall. The first is excerpted from a 1985 poem, the second from testimony before the Office of Hawaiian Affairs trustees regarding the Kawaiaha'o controversy in February 2011. Her words serve as my coda.

LOOKING FOR SIGNS

Aunty Alice said it first
there had been ho'ailona
ever since we took up
trying to keep the old road
from being closed in Mākena
on the island where Maui
caught the sun in his rope.
The foreign owners of a half built
hotel don't want their guests
to taste the dust
of our ancestors in the road.
(Naone Hall 1985:33)

Good morning Trustees. Thank you, thank you for this opportunity, because you know it is forums like this that allow us to receive more information on difficult issues, but with information we can make better decisions. . . .

Just to show you how little process there is . . . this is a October 22, 2010 letter . . . it is basically the disinterment permit itself. You'll notice that the application has date of death "unknown," full name of deceased "unknown," place of death "unknown," age at time of death "unknown," sex "unknown," race "unknown." Everything on this application is "unknown." So they are not giving the people buried at Kawaiaha'o the dignity of being anything other than an unknown burial which they can excavate at will. Now this is the letter, the disinterment permit: a one-paragraph statement. That's how our kupuna get excavated in 2011 after the lessons of Honokahua and the hurt and pain our people have endured? (Naone Hall 2011; see also Magin 2011)

Acknowledgments

I would like to thank Glenn Penny and Laura Graham for their productive editorial suggestions as this chapter took shape. I would also like to express my profound appreciation for the time and energy given over by Dana Naone Hall and Halealoha Ayau in the effort of helping me understand current issues in the implementation of burial protection law in Hawai'i.

Notes

1. The category "Hawaiian" is framed in at least five ways in contemporary academic and political discourses. I use the category here as a general label, intended to signal not a geographical but a cultural identity, referring to people who have a shared identity with the inhabitants of the islands prior to 1778, the year of Captain James Cook's arrival in Hawai'i. I use "Hawaiian" and "Native Hawaiian" (favored in federal contexts) interchangeably, which reflects common local usage. Other frequently used designations include "native Hawaiian" (often indicating a narrower, blood quantum–based definition), "Kanaka Maoli" ("real people," a designation favored by some sovereignty-focused groups), and "Kanaka 'Ōiwi" ("people of the bone," often used in Native academic and religious contexts).

2. In 1993, for example, Blaisdell coordinated a massive event known as Ka Ho'okolokolonui Kānaka Maoli (Peoples' International Tribunal Hawai'i). This involved hearings on each island regarding the ways the United States has violated Hawaiian sovereignty. For a video recording of the event, see *The Tribunal* (Nā Maka o ka'Āina 1993).

   Naone Hall is perhaps most well known for her edited volume *Mālama: Hawaiian Land and Water* (1985). Her poetry has been included in numerous volumes, including Bird and Harjo 1997.

3. On Indigenous representation generally, see, e.g., Clifford 2001; Collins 1998; Graham 2002; Murray 1991; Sahlins 1992; Sider 1987. For Hawai'i, see, e.g., Aikau 2012; Friesen 1996; Linnekin 1991; Halualani 2002; Kauanui 2008; Tengan 2008.

4. For a detailed cultural history of the North Shore, see Andrade 2008.

5. See, e.g., *Brescia v. North Shore Ohana*, Supreme Court of Hawai'i, no. 27211, July 12, 2007.

6. See, e.g., Naone Hall's testimony in *Brescia v. Chandler*, Hawai'i Fifth Circuit Court, Civil No. 08-1-0107, 2008. See also Naone Hall, letter to DLNR and SHPD detailing problem with state procedures, June 16, 2009.

7. Hawai'i Second Circuit Court, Civil No. 09-1-0901(1).

8. E.g., Conrow 2011; Gomes 2011; see also KITV, "Native Hawaiians Oppose Kawaiaha'o Church Project," February 14, 2011, YouTube, http://www.youtube.com/watch?v=y4usVw0sXtk.

9. E.g., "Hawaiians Protest Kawaiaha'o Church," Justice for Hawaiians, February 20, 2011, http://www.justiceforhawaiians.com/kawaiahao-church-2/hawaiians-protest-kawaiahao-church; "Arrested for Trespassing at Kawaiaha'o Church, Sunday, March 13," MaoliWorld (blog), March 15, 2011, http://maoliworld.ning.com/profiles/blogs/arrested-for-trespassing-at-1.

10. To listen, see "Stop Kawaiaha'o Church! Protect Hawaiian Burials!" *Indigenous Politics: From Native New England and Beyond* episode 6, WESU, Middletown CT, March 15, 2011, http://www.indigenouspolitics.org/audiofiles/2011/3-15%20Desecration%20at%20Kawaiaha%27o.mp3.

11. See Pono Kealoha, "Issues that Matter—Kawaiaha'o," March 9, 2011, YouTube, http://www.youtube.com/watch?v=YuYEnXGUjjo.

12. As this chapter was going to press, three rulings shed some light on the status of Hawai'i's burial law in general and on the Kawaiaha'o conflict in particular. On August 24, 2012, the Hawai'i Supreme Court announced its decision concerning archaeological survey processes in the context of a major Honolulu rail project (*Kaleikini v. Yoshioka*, SCAP-11-0000611), affirming the significance of archaeological inventory surveys under the law and underscoring the fact that HRS 6E-43 is clear in setting out the procedural priority of such surveys (i.e., that they should be completed before any construction activities commence). On September 28, 2012, the Intermediate Court of Appeals of the State of Hawai'i granted Naone Hall's second motion for preliminary injunction pending appeal in the matter of Kawaiaha'o Church (CAAP-12-0000061). Relying on the Supreme Court's position in *Kaleikini v. Yoshioka*, the court ordered the church to cease construction activities pending conclusion of the appeal process and indicated that Naone Hall's appeal has a likelihood of prevailing on its merits. On December 4, 2013, the Hawai`i Supreme Court upheld the Intermediate Court of Appeals ruling (SCWC-12-0000061).

13. "Chicken skin" is Hawaiian Pidgin for "goose bumps."

Bibliography

ACLU of Hawai'i
    2009 ACLU of Hawaii Invokes "Media Shield" Law in Defense of Documentary Filmmaker. News release. June 30. http://www.aclu.org/free-speech/aclu-hawaii-invokes-media-shield-law-defense-documentary-filmmaker.

Aikau, Hokulani

    2012 A Chosen People, A Promised Land: Mormonism and Race in Hawai'i. Minneapolis: University of Minnesota Press.

Andrade, Carlos

    2008 Hā 'ena: Through the Eyes of the Ancestors. Honolulu: University of Hawai'i Press.

Ayau, Edward Halealoha, and Ty Kāwika Tengan

    2002 Ka Huaka'i O Na 'Oiwi: The Journey Home. *In* The Dead and Their Possessions. C. Fforde, J. Hubert, and P. Turnbull, eds. Pp. 171–89. New York: Routledge.

Barthes, Roland

    1957[1972] Mythologies. Annette Lavers, trans. New York: Hill and Wang.

Bird, Gloria, and Joy Harjo

    1997 Reinventing the Enemy's Language: Contemporary Native Women's Writing of North America. New York: W. W. Norton.

Burlingame, Burl

    2000 Group Picked to Bring Remains Instead Gives 205 Sets to State. Honolulu Star-Bulletin, December 30. http://archives.starbulletin.com/2000/12/30/news/story2.html.

Clifford, James

    2001 Indigenous Articulations. Contemporary Pacific 13:468–90.

Collins, James

    1998 Understanding Tolowa Histories: Western Hegemonies and Native American Responses. New York: Routledge.

Conrow, Joan

    2010 Cut to the Bones. Honolulu Weekly, July 17, 2011. http://lauhala.com/hinano/20130902-015708-Cut-to-the-bones.pdf.

    2011 Cultural Grounds: Uncertain Future for Remains at Kawaiaha'o Church. Honolulu Weekly, January 26.

Cultural Surveys Hawai'i

    2012 Weekly Report on Excavations at Kawaiaha'o Church for the Week of June 4–9. Submitted by David Shideler to SHPD; copy in possession of author.

de la Cadena, Marisol, and Orin Starn, eds.

    2007 Indigenous Experience Today. Oxford: Berg.

Feldman, Allen

    1991 Formations of Violence: The Narrative of the Body and Political Terror in Northern Ireland. Chicago: University of Chicago Press.

Friesen, Steven

    1996 The Origins of Lei Day: Festivity and the Construction of Ethnicity in the Territory of Hawaii. History and Anthropology 10:1–36.

Goffman, Erving

    1974 Frame Analysis: An Essay on the Organization of Experience. Cambridge MA: Harvard University Press.

1982[1967] Interaction Ritual. New York: Pantheon.

Gomes, Andrew

    2011 Burials Are "Kapu," Public Tells Church. Honolulu Star-Advertiser, February 10. http://www.staradvertiser.com/business/20110210_Burials_are_kapu_public_tells_church.html.

Graham, Laura

    2002 How Should an Indian Speak? Amazonian Indians and the Symbolic Politics of Language in the Global Public Sphere. *In* Indigenous Movements, Self-Representation, and the State in Latin America. Kay B. Warren and Jean E. Jackson, eds. Pp. 181–228. Austin: University of Texas Press.

Greer, E. Sunny

    2013 Kawaiaha'o: Recolonizing the Borderlands of the Native Hawaiian Body. Hūlili: Multidisciplinary Research on Hawaiian Well-Being 9:115–31.

Halualani, Rona Tamiko

    2002 In the Name of Hawaiians: Native Identities and Cultural Politics. Minneapolis: University of Minnesota Press.

Hoerman, Rachel, and Michael F. Dega

    2010 Preservation Component of a Burial Treatment Plan for Multiple Burials Discovered on a 18,106 Square Foot Parcel in Wainiha Ahupua'a, Hanalele'a District, Island of Kaua'i, Hawai'i. Honolulu: Scientific Consultant Services, Inc.

Johnson, Greg

    2003 Ancestors before Us: Manifestations of Tradition in a Hawaiian Dispute. Journal of the American Academy of Religion 71(2):327–46.

    2007 Sacred Claims: Repatriation and Living Tradition. Charlottesville: University of Virginia Press.

    2009 Social Lives of the Dead: Contestation and Continuities in the Hawaiian Repatriation Context. *In* Culture and Belonging in Divided Societies. Marc Howard Ross, ed. Pp. 45–67. Philadelphia: University of Pennsylvania Press.

    2011 Courting Culture: Unexpected Relationships between Religion and Law in Contemporary Hawai'i. *In* After Secular Law. Winnifred Sullivan, Robert Yelle, and Mateo Taussig, eds. Pp. 282–301. Stanford CA: Stanford University Press.

    2013 Varieties of Native Hawaiian Establishment: Recognized Voices, Routinized Charisma, and Church Desecration. *In* Varieties of Religious Establishment. Winnifred Sullivan and Lori Beaman, eds. Pp. 55–74. Burlington VT: Ashgate.

Kamakawiwo'ole, Israel

    1995 The Man and His Music. DVD. Honolulu: Mountain Apple Company.

Kauanui, Kēhaulani

    2008 Hawaiian Blood: Colonialism and the Politics of Sovereignty and Indigeneity. Durham NC: Duke University Press.

KNIBC (Kaua'i and Ni'ihau Islands Burial Council)
2008 Minutes. State of Hawaii, State Historic Preservation Office. November 6. http://www.state.hi.us/dlnr/hpd/bcd/minutes/kani-minutes-081106.pdf. Copy in author's possession.

Lincoln, Bruce
1996 Theses on Method. Method and Theory in the Study of Religion 8:225–27.

Linnekin, Jocelyn
1991 Text Bites and the R-Word: The Politics of Representing Scholarship. Contemporary Pacific 3(1):172–77.

Maaka, Roger, and Augie Fleras
2005 The Politics of Indigeneity: Challenging the State in Canada and Aotearoa New Zealand. Dunedin, New Zealand: University of Otago Press.

Magin, Janis L.
2011 Kawaiaha'o Church Misses OHA Grant Reporting Deadline. Pacific Business News, May 13. http://www.bizjournals.com/pacific/print-edition/2011/05/13/kawaiahao-church-misses-oha-grant.html.

Merleau-Ponty, Maurice
1945[2012] Phenomenology of Perception. Donald A. Landes, trans. New York: Routledge.

Murray, David
1991 Forked Tongues: Speech, Writing, and Representation in North American Indian Texts. Bloomington: Indiana University Press.

Nā Maka o ka'Āina
1993 The Tribunal. DVD. 84 min.

Naone Hall, Dana
1985 Mālama: Hawaiian Land and Water. Honolulu: Bamboo Ridge Press.
2010 Sovereign Ground. In The Value of Hawai'i: Knowing the Past, Shaping the Future. Craig Howes and Jon Osorio, eds. Pp. 195–201. Honolulu: University of Hawai'i Press.
2011 Testimony before the Trustees of the Office of Hawaiian Affairs. Honolulu, February 17. Transcription by author. Video available at http://www.youtube.com/watch?v=JP-Alz1Hj5M.

Niezen, Ronald
2003 The Origins of Indigenism: Human Rights and the Politics of Identity. Berkeley: University of California Press.

Nihipali, Kunani
2002 Stone by Stone, Bone by Bone: Rebuilding the Hawaiian Nation in the Illusion of Reality. Arizona State Law Journal 34(1):28–46.

Perry, Brian
2010 Grand Wailea Interveners to Get Second Look. Maui News, September 17. www.mauinews.com/page/content.detail/id/540562.html.

Povinelli, Elizabeth

    2002 The Cunning of Recognition: Indigenous Alterities and the Making of Australian Multiculturalism. Durham NC: Duke University Press.

Sahlins, Marshall

    1992 The Economics of Develop-Man in the South Pacific. Res: Anthropology and Aesthetics 21:12–25.

Scott, James C.

    1990 Domination and the Arts of Resistance: Hidden Transcripts. New Haven CT: Yale University Press.

Sider, Gerald

    1987 When Parrots Learn to Talk, and Why They Can't: Domination, Deception, and Self-Deception in Indian-White Relations. Comparative Studies in Society and History 29(1):3–23.

Tengan, Ty Kāwika

    2008 Native Men Remade: Gender and Nation in Contemporary Hawai'i. Durham NC: Duke University Press.

Wu, Nina

    2009 Kawaiaha'o Church Project Hit with Second Suit. MaoliWorld (blog), August 28. http://maoliworld.ning.com/forum/topics/kawaiahao-church-project -hit.

10

Haka

Colonized Physicality, Body-Logic, and Embodied Sovereignty

BRENDAN HOKOWHITU

"Can the Subaltern Speak?" . . . Spivak's answer to her own question is a qualified "no." A primary condition of subalternity, she argues, is, in fact, a lack of position of speaking. For subalterns, the condition of being post-colonial is one of being relentlessly constituted in the discourses of power that control their situation and that lie beyond their agency . . . a warning about the limitations of the intellectual endeavour of postcolonialism, and a challenge towards its transformation.

SIMON FEATHERSTONE, *Postcolonial Cultures*

The most globally recognizable example of mediated appropriation of Māori culture (and perhaps of any Indigenous culture) is of the *haka*, titled "Ka Mate," used in prematch entertainment by New Zealand's national rugby-union team, the All Blacks. In general terms, and as defined by Māori scholar Nathan Matthews, haka as a performing art "is a posture dance accompanied by chanted or shouted song. . . . One of the main characteristics of haka are that actions involving all parts of the body are used to emphasize the words" (2004:9). While there is a vast array of haka, the most renowned is "Ka Mate." New Zealand's sporting icons, the All Blacks, use "Ka Mate," composed in the 1820s by the famous Ngāti Toa chief Te Rauparaha. In brief, prior to each game and immediately following the respective national anthems, the All Blacks form a semicircle at midfield facing their opponents. At this point "Ka Mate" is performed as an entertainment spectacle, supposedly serving as an expression of cultural identity, as a motivational tool, and to intimate the opposition. Tīmoti Kāretu points out, however,

Fig. 10.1. Prematch entertainment: All Blacks perform "Te Kapa o Pango" (The Dance of Black) vs. France, World Cup Final, October 23, 2011. Photo: www.flickr.com.

that when "Ka Mate" was composed it was intended as a *ngeri*. Ngeri "are short haka to stiffen the sinews, to summon up the blood, but unlike haka taparahi, have no set movements, thereby giving the performers free rein to express themselves as they deem appropriate" (Kāretu 1993:41). Kāretu expresses his concern with the popularized version of "Ka Mate," which has "become the most performed, the most maligned, the most abused of all haka. Jumping is not a feature of either haka taparahi or ngeri and it is these irritating perpetrations that lead to a lot of discord" (1993:68).

From its initial synthesis with rugby, haka has functioned to allure sporting crowds and, more recently, has aided in branding the All Blacks by the New Zealand Rugby Union (NZRU) in conjunction with major global corporations (including sponsors Adidas, Iveco, and MasterCard) and the media conglomerate News Corporation (Hope 2002; Hokowhitu and Scherer 2008).[1] The taking over of the All Blacks' primary sponsorship by the global sports clothing company Adidas signified a mass wave of marketing based on selling the exoticism of "traditional" Māori masculine culture. At the time, the marketing campaign led to questions by Māori regarding intellectual property rights and the misappropriation and commodification of Indigenous culture.[2] Mass billboards appeared in sites such as London's Time Square prior to the 1999 Rugby World Cup, displaying dramatic images, including a massive black-and-white billboard featuring various All Blacks performing "Ka Mate" surrounded by Māori warriors. Another immense billboard contained a close-up image of the head of a *moko*-clad (facially tattooed) warrior ominously glaring, with only the Adidas trifoil logo and the NZRU trademark silver fern subtly located beneath (see Jackson and Hokowhitu 2002). Synonymously, Adidas unleashed a dramatized version of racially selected All Blacks performing "Ka Mate" (notably, the All Black footage focused on Māori players such as Taine Randell and Kees Meeuws and Pacific Island players Tana Umaga and Jonah Lomu) juxtaposed against a tempestuous Māori warrior with full facial moko, dressed in only a *piupiu* (flax skirt), holding a *taiaha* (close-quarters-combat staff), and backdropped by bubbling mud pools (Primal Team 1999). According to advertising giant Saatchi & Saatchi's Howard Greive, "We always wanted to create a sort of primal scary ad" (Primal Team 1999:22). Greive suggests Adidas was looking for something unique in order to brand its products and believed it could capture this via the passion elicited through the All Blacks performance of "Ka Mate":

> You have to go back to: why did Adidas come in and pay all that money for the All Blacks? It's because the All Blacks can deliver something to their brand that no other team or individual can in sport. Which is they are playing a very, very physical game—it has been called the last warrior sport in the world. Not only that, but they play it with intensity and the easiest way to judge that intensity is through the haka. That is exactly what Adidas wanted in terms of what the All Blacks could bring to their brand. (Primal Team 1999:22)

Over the last decade in particular, the branding of the All Blacks via Indigenous imagery has helped make it one of the most recognizable sporting teams in the world. Such is the power of the All Black brand to draw crowds that in November 2009 the All Blacks were able to attract eighty thousand Italian fans, who packed the San Siro Stadium in soccer-mad Milan. At the same time, the increased visibility of "Ka Mate" in the global public domain has liquidated any tacit sanctions surrounding its performance. Over the last decade in particular a host of companies have picked up on the marketability of haka, leading to the commodification of "Ka Mate" through products as diverse as Fiat and Lego. Also, a raft of seemingly unrelated sporting teams, including American high school and college football (gridiron) teams (see Tengan and Markham 2009), now perform haka prior to games in emulation of the supposed advantage their performance has for the All Blacks. Moreover, "Ka Mate" has become a masculine national anthem, religiously performed, typically as a mark of public respect, at significant national and local events, such as funerals.

The ill-informed normalization of "Ka Mate" within "Kiwi" masculine culture means the complexities of postcolonial history and the problematics surrounding, for example, the commodification of Indigenous culture go conveniently uncensored. The full version of the haka narrates Te Rauparaha's search for refuge from a pursuing *taua* (war party) led by Tauteka. Although not entirely welcomed by Chief Te Wharerangi, Te Rauparaha was concealed in an empty *kumara* (sweet potato) pit by Te Wharerangi's wife, Te Rangikoaea, who sat over the entrance. As the taua approached, they recited incantations to essentially draw Te Rauparaha out of his hiding place. Te Rangikoaea's function in sitting above Te Rauparaha was due to her *mana* (esteem) as a chieftainess and her ability to protect him from these incantations. That is, female genitalia had the power to neutralize the solicitous incantations performed by the pursuing taua. Although there are many verses to the haka that fully describe Te Rauparaha's transpiring affection as events come to pass, the verse made famous by the All Blacks begins as the pursuers enquire about Te Rauparaha's whereabouts when they arrive at Te Wharerangi's *kāinga* (residence). During the conversation between Tauteka and Te Wharerangi, Te Rauparaha mutters under his breath, "Aha ha. Ka Mate, Ka Mate. Ka ora, ka ora. Ka Mate, Ka Mate." (I die, I die. I live, I live. I die, I die.) Finally, when he hears his pursuers leave, he exclaims, "Ka ora, ka ora. Tenei te tangata puhurupuhuru nana nei i tiki mai whakawhiti te ra." (I live, I live. For this is the hairy person who has fetched the sun and caused it to shine again.) As he takes his first two steps out of the pit he says, "Hupane, kaupane" (An upward step, another), and as he stands clear he shouts, "Whiti te ra" (The sun shines) (Kāretu 1993).[3]

Connotations of feminine power and protection in "Ka Mate" illustrate the immense disparity between how it is popularly conceived and its original epistemology. Such is the chasm that few New Zealanders are willing to accept the leap. For instance, one of New Zealand's most celebrated sportswriters, Spiro Zavos, denies the possibility of an Indigenous epistemology in deference to the national importance of the All Blacks and conceptions of "classical" Māori culture: "It does not ring true to Maori tradition. . . . Maori culture is male hegemonic. . . . It seems implausible that the All Blacks . . . would embrace a haka that had such embarrassing connotations. . . . The hairy man in this haka is an archetype of strength, a figure of power, capable of bringing about the triumph of life over death. . . . When the All Blacks chant their haka . . . they will lead their great team, and the nation that identifies with it, into the sun that shines" (1998:71–73).

Beyond the comic element of such misrepresentation, of more interest to the present chapter is the way that dominant discourses weave themselves through the performance of Indigenous culture, indicating the function that rugby culture, for instance, historically played in the violent synthesis of "Kiwi culture."[4] Renowned New Zealand historian Sir Keith Sinclair outlines this neatly: "Rugby stimulated national pride and national feeling. It brought the nation together, providing a focus for a feeling of unity. It brought Pakeha and Maori together" (Zavos 1992:79).[5]

The performance of "Ka Mate" by the All Blacks signifies a particular expression of masculine patriotism, commonly expressed as a synthesis of the best of the nation's culture. The expression of nationalism in this way is important because the cross-sectional representation of "all New Zealanders," as embodied by the contemporary All Blacks as least (i.e., the team typically includes Pākehā, Māori, and New Zealand–resident "Pacific Islanders"), through an Indigenous performance signifies the modernity of a synthesized nation. That is, it signifies a nation propelling itself forward under the banner of meritocracy. "Ka Mate" as performed by the All Blacks is thus a powerful symbol of the neocolonial nation.

In *Postcolonial Cultures* Simon Featherstone lays the groundwork for interpreting popular culture, which would contemporarily include *kapa haka* (Māori haka group) performance as both a commodified text and part of the postcolonial ethnic formalization of Māori culture. While most dominant representations of haka consider it a "traditional" and relatively fixed aspect of Māori culture, it is in reality a fluid concept that, because of its discursive nature, offers a critical lens for appreciating the contested and contradictory nature of power in the postcolonial condition. Haka is one of those postcolonial sites that power has run through in unimaginable synergies. The particular importance of Featherstone's quote that begins this chapter lies in its acknowledgement of the lack of Indigenous agency that is produced by the relentless reformulation of Indigeneity (and how an Indigenous person performs Indigeneity), as the above discussion concedes. Yet what does this mean for postcolonial criticism and, specifically, how should we understand the Indigenous body within such analyses? As this chapter explains, the establishment of haka (i.e., an Indigenous performance) as a symbol of nationalism stemmed from a complex integration of the Māori masculine "body," sport, and ethnic formalism through a developing and perverse understanding of Māori culture within the nation. The aim of this chapter is to discuss the competing discourses surrounding haka and its "body logic" by, first, providing a genealogy of postcolonial haka, from its rendering as "savage" by early travelers to its marking as a postcolonial identity marker. Second, this chapter introduces the possibilities of haka in terms of what I refer to as "embodied sovereignty," including the existential and everyday properties of Indigenous culture—that is, what culture "feels like" as opposed to the antiquation of Indigenous culture, which enables the temporal dislocation of Indigenous Peoples away from the present.

Genealogy: Haka, Synthesis, and the Indigenous Body

When one thinks of Homi Bhabha's conception of "third culture," it is easy to romanticize the performance of "Ka Mate" (an Indigenous "artefact") by the All Blacks as an example of a neocultural formation: a performance that signifies a cultural expansion, which serves to unsettle the binary between colonizer and colonized. Nevertheless, as the introductory section of this chapter highlights, the synthesis of Indigenous culture within such dominant frames has been a violent one, beginning with the collision of epistemologies in the colonial context, in which loss of Indigenous knowledge (i.e., of "being") was central to the imperial process. Having said this, it is important to not fall into the trap of suggesting that performances of haka today are less "authentic" or less "traditional" then those performed in that precolonial imaginary, which haunts the *telos* of decolonial studies.

Haka boggled the minds of early colonists and came to signify "savagery"—a state of unenlightenment in which reason was ruled by impulses and superstition and often transcribed into physical terms. For instance, during James Cook's third voyage (1776–80) Thomas Edgar wrote, "The War dance or Heva consists of a variety of violent motions and hideous contortions of the limbs, there is something in them so uncommonly savage and terrible, their eyes appear to be starting from their head, their tongue hanging down to their chin" (Best 1976:86). In 1863 Frederick Maning likened haka to a "dance and capper" performed by "mad-monkeys" (Maning 1956:44). In his narrative of haka, trader Joel Polack used words such as "howling," "demonical," "distorted," and "grimace," contrasting the heathen physical practice with his civilized scientific knowledge of the body: "Yelling, howling, loud and loud, that threaten hard to destroy the auricular organs." Polack went on to describe "rolling the eye-balls to and fro in their sockets . . . as the most diabolical appearance" (1840:86–87).

The importance of the visible appearance of haka and its tithing to moral deficiencies cannot be underestimated, from its genealogical construction through to the representation of haka today. The colonial conception of what it meant to be Indigenous (or perhaps "passionate") was in large part a visual phenomenon: "With all the political and ideological force that the seemingly naturalness of the body as the locus of difference can claim . . . [a] cultural training that quite literally teaches the eye not only how but what to see" (Wiegman 1995:22). Allegorically, it is crucial to make the connection between the rationality of the European and the body of the colonized Other. As David Theo Goldberg outlines, the eighteenth-century resurrection of classical values of beauty was (like "classical economic theory") based on geometrical features of the body, such as "proportion, symmetry, and refinement," so that "beauty was established in terms of racial properties: fair skin, straight hair, organthous jaw, skull shape and size, well composed bodily proportions, and so on. To fail to possess these traits was considered a fault of inheritance" (Goldberg 1993:30). The corporeal "reality" of the asymmetrical performance of the Indigenous body within haka undoubtedly naturalized colonial endeavor and subjugation, allowing colonialist claims to moral superiority dependent on what Robyn Wiegman refers to as "bodily fictions," which "unproblematically reflect the natural meaning of flesh" (1995:21). Here Pierre Bourdieu is useful, as he conceives of the body metaphorically, as "the bearer of symbolic meaning and values and a key site through which social differences are created, perpetuated and reinforced" (Edwards 2006:145).

The process involved what I refer to throughout this chapter as "synthesis." That is, the violent amalgamation (authentification) of one culture into another, which typically involved encompassing and reconfiguring the incomprehensible into comprehensible forms, the classification of Indigenous forms of knowing into Western ontological catalogs, or simply the denial that many practices even existed. The authentication element in this devolution is crucial because from the premise of Enlightenment reason, knowledge was authentic only if it was known to the mind. That is, Indigenous practices like haka, which conjured up horror and boggled the minds of the European, had to be either banned or made comprehensible to Western thought. The first principle of colonizing the Indigenous body, then, was to bring the philosophical underpinnings of the savage under the logic of the colonizer, to authenticate the inauthentic (see Hokowhitu 2008a).

Augustus Earle's early description of haka thus authenticated the physicality of the savage in a way not dissimilar to Charles Marlow's account of the frailty of European mental capacity to comprehend its own recesses, in Joseph Conrad's *Heart of Darkness*: "They soon work themselves up to a pitch of frenzy; the distortions of their face and body are truly dreadful, and fill the mind with horror" (Earle 1909:62). The incomprehensibility of haka to early colonists led to the outright banning of haka by missionaries and later by the colonial state. In 1845 the missionary William Brown described Māori haka but noted with pride that "amongst the missionary natives they are entirely discontinued" (Best 1925:15). Accordingly, haka became obsolete in some *iwi* (large genealogical social groupings). For instance, following Sir Apirana Ngata's initial "renaissance" period, one iwi had to be taught haka by another so that they were able to host the 1934 Waitangi celebrations.[6]

In this genealogy of epistemological collision and void, it is obvious that Descartes's (1996) mind/body dichotomy is pertinent. Māori did not conceive of haka as a physical activity, leisure pursuit, or "pastime," as classified by the early twentieth-century ethnographer Elsdon Best, for example. The physical realm was not divorced from other realms, such as the mind (*hinengaro*) or spirituality (*mauri/wairua*). Within the universe of

Enlightened rationalism, however, it was assumed that reason (i.e., European reason) could differentiate between truth and falsehood and, thus, the world was inherently knowable. Indigenous epistemologies challenged that knowable world. Enlightenment reason, as the determinant of truth, was applied to the untranslatable—the epistemologies of other cultures.

In relation to Edward Said's (1978) *Orientalism* Bhabha points out, "Said is aware when he hints continually at a polarity or division at the very centre of Orientalism. It is, on the one hand, a topic of learning, discovery, practice; on the other, it is the site of dreams, images, fantasies, myths, obsessions and requirements. It is a static system of 'synchronic essentialism,' a knowledge of 'signifiers of stability' such as the lexicographic and the encyclopaedic" (1983:24–25). This "synchronic essentialization" of the Other fundamentally involved the synthesis of Indigenous epistemologies within Western ways of understanding the world. And this ontological imperialist project was inherently violent, as Madan Sarup argues: "In Western philosophy, when knowledge or theory tries to understand the Other, then the alterity of the Other vanishes as it becomes part of the same. In all cases it involves violence towards the Other" (1996:68). Similarly, Robert Young outlines, "Ontology amounts to a philosophy of power, an egotism in which the relation with the Other is accomplished through its assimilation into the self" (2004:45).

If the reader has ever witnessed a "noncommodified" performance of haka, its subversive nature is immediately apparent. Indeed, in many ways haka is embodied sovereignty, which will be discussed later. For now, however, the apparent subversion of haka was not lost on the colonists, who for much of the twentieth century domesticated it through classification and schooling and by incorporating bastardized versions of it within rugby games. Colonization, in New Zealand at least, did not attempt to drive the subversive savagery out of Māori, realizing this was impossible given the immutability of the savage. In 1867, for instance, the *Wellington Independent* reported on a meeting of the "races" at Wairoa where

> thither flocked most of the white population to witness the Hakas with which the hosts and visitors were entertaining one another. The less said the better on this subject of this species of Maori diversion. Forty years of civilization ought to have taught these people the decency, but scrape

a Maori, the most civilised, and the savage shows distinctly underneath. The "Haka" is an *exposé* of the evil which really lies at the root of their present prostrate condition, an exhibition of the substratum of utter immorality, depravity, and obscenity, which forms the ground work of their race; and spite of the veneering with which we clumsily cover the rough wood, we shall do nothing until we alter their entire character, by taking in hand the education, *per force*, of the young growing saplings. (Wellington Independent 1867:6)

Foucault's (2008) conception of biopower, in which individuals become aware of themselves and their place in the world through the disciplined nature of their own body, speaks to the quote above and to the material depth of colonization. As the quote intimates, nothing was more powerful in the materialization of dutiful Indigenous colonial citizens than schooling, in which, again, haka was to play an important role.

Māori culture was synthesized into mainstream culture in recognizable and cognizable forms, typically underpinned by "physicality," including war exploits, physical labor, physical education, sport, and haka: haka being that faculty of Māori life, domesticated and classified to explain "Māori Rhythm." For example, the introduction of token aspects of Māori culture into Native schools (i.e., schools in rural locales for Indigenous students, with a specialized "nonprofessional" curricula) included only its nonthreatening aspects, such as "song, crafts, art, story, and dance" (New Zealand Department of Education 1941:190). A large part of the Māori content taught in Native schools was considered "physical education." Māori culture was perceived as a "doing" culture and, consequently, physical education was deemed an appropriate subject area for cultural integration, as outlined by the New Zealand state education pamphlet the *Education Gazette*:

The play interval is devoted to agility exercises and games, including Maori games such as homai, stick games, top spinning, and string games. . . . At the end of the afternoon, when the children are becoming mentally tired, we have a further fifteen-minute period for gardening, or pois [a ball connected to a string to practice supple and dexterous use of the wrists and hands], action songs . . . to offset the mental fatigue and to release of the pent-up physical energy. . . . In terms of modern educational theory the Native craft work fits into the "doing" programme, the appealing and important aspect of any school. . . . As a "golden fringe" to the busy activities come the poi, haka, and the action songs. All of these exhibit remarkable rhythmic features. (New Zealand Department of Education 1941:195)

The acknowledgment of Māori physicality and "rhythm" aided the colonial project by providing a bridge for Pākehā to recognize some good in their darker brethren. In an article titled "Maori Rhythm," Phillip Smithells (1941), the inaugural dean of the School of Physical Education at the University of Otago, Dunedin, New Zealand, demystifies the properties of Māori physical practices via a scientism discourse that cut across holistic understandings of haka: "By countless years of experience, trial and error these rhythmic activities have evolved with the purpose of giving quickness of hand and eye, rhythm, anticipation, and the strengthening of certain muscle groups. Besides the direct physical effects of greater motor control, there is the joy and exhilaration that comes from such control and from the body moving rhythmically, whether in the wild sweeps of the taiaha, the staccato beat of homai, or the continuous smooth rhythm of the stick games."

Such classification demonstrates how the subversive nature of haka was assimilated into the service of imperialism itself. The process of colonization did not mean Māori were to reach the echelons of enlightened reason, however; rather, what was imperative to the colony was the domestication of their physicality, the suppression of their passions, and the nobilization of savagery so viscerally performed via haka. Ideologically, colonization demanded the domestication of Māori physicality. As the widely used education resource series Imperial Readers hopefully stated in 1899, "Maori were savages but noble savages" (Whitcombe &Tombs 1899:83).

Foucault's determination of the body's passivity as a symbol of the contested terrain can be translated to describe the colonized Indigenous body and, in particular, Indigenous bodily practices such as the haka, in which "they incest it, mark it, train it, torture it, force it to carry out tasks, to perform ceremonies, to emit signs" (1995:25). In summary, then, the profound weave of mind/body duality into the fabric of colonialism has in part enabled the "biopolitical management of life" as an assimilatory, synthesizing force. The colonial production of the Indigenous/non-Indigenous,

Self/Other dialectic has, in part, functioned through the performances of Indigenous bodies. What it means or meant to be an authentic and tradition-abiding Indigenous subject was materialized and reified by bodily practices, including haka. Importantly, this construction of colonial power accounts for Hegel's (1899) modernity in that it speaks to how the Indigenous subjects became self-conscious and constituted themselves as social subjects within the colonized Self/Other dialectic, through and because of their body and body practices. The above genealogy suggests that the increasing popularization of masculine haka and the ritualized and patriotic performance of haka by men at events of national, provincial, and local importance is but one example of the profound and unimaginable synergies at play in the production of postcolonial citizens.

For the Māori subject, the rationale was impassioned. Indeed, it has been said that Māori located thought in their gut. As this chapter develops, then, it is important to keep re-evoking the way the Indigenous world has been classified, interpreted, and defined via Enlightenment rationalism and, as a consequence, how we might reinterpret Indigenous bodily practices using the notion of "body-logic." The movement away from the dependency on what we consider "rational thought" is summed up in Robert Young's critique of the state of postcolonial studies in relation to nonsecular thought. He writes, "Despite its espousal of subaltern resistance, [postcolonial theory] scarcely values subaltern resistance that does not operate according to its own secular terms" (2001:338). Thus I invite the reader to question the way Western epistemic knowledge "preserves the boundaries of sense for itself" (Bhabha 1983:24) and to imagine the idea of a body-logic underpinning practices such as haka.

Performing Indigenous Masculinity

Looking at haka as "popular culture" through the lens of masculinity helps elucidate the way that power constructs meaning that, in turn, makes possible the conditions for a national sports team's performance of an Indigenous "artefact" as an evocative symbol of hetero-patriarchal patriotism. In serving two essentialised binary masters (i.e., colonized/colonizer and woman/man), the study of Indigenous masculinities provides for a model that speaks to the complexity of the postcolonial condition. Rather than serving a simple hierarchical master/slave binary model of power, the multiple analysis of binaries helps describe a flatter conception of power, in which postcolonial ontological constructions of gender are discursive, in that they avoid the prescription of one binary. The dominance of colonized man over the Indigenous man, and man over woman, means the Indigenous heterosexual patriarch is simultaneously both oppressor and oppressed. He cuts an ambivalent figure, admired in his moments of mimicry, yet increasingly abhorred and held in contempt in moments of slippage, that is, in moments of reversion back toward savage physicality (see Hokowhitu 2008b).

Ann Oakley's (1972) *Sex, Gender and Society* and Sandra Bem's (1974) famous studies of androgyny both challenged the biological determinism surrounding sex. These seminal works argued that biological sex had little, if anything, to do with gender and, therefore, in the present context masculinity is simply a set of culturally constructed qualities. Beyond the somewhat pointless dialectic of "nature versus nurture," the present chapter presupposes the historical contingency of gender. Generally, then, masculinity does not exist, other than through "historically constructed performance" (Edwards 2006:109), with the qualification that the discursive construction of masculinities nevertheless produces very real men, who inhabit history and who embody and thus make "true" the discursive field. A genealogy of gender constructions in the colonies makes both the constructed and the material nature of masculinity clear. In precolonial times, androgyny was the marker of uncivilized cultures. Gail Bederman (1995) outlines how in the late nineteenth century clear gender roles were an essential component of civilization; advanced civilizations were identifiable by the degree of sexual differentiation. Savagery was signified by androgyny, while civilized cultures had evolved pronounced sexual differences: "Civilised women were womanly—delicate, spiritual, dedicated to home. And civilised white men were the most manly ever evolved—firm of character; self-controlled; protectors of women and children. In contrast, gender differences among savages seemed to be blurred. Savage women were aggressive, carried heavy burdens, and did all sorts of masculine hard labor. Savage men were emotional and lacked a man's ability to restrain their passions. Savage men were creatures of whim . . . who even dressed like women in dresses and jewellery" (Bederman 1995:25). Today, with the so-called crisis of masculinity (see Edwards 2006), it seems that the savage masculinity of yesteryear (i.e., a combination of masculine and feminine traits) is again in vogue. Ironically, however, the postcolonial Indigenous male is barred ontological access to being "the new man" because of his tendency to violence, patriarchy, and general hypermasculinity (see Hokowhitu 2003a).

One of the symptoms of Indigenous masculinity's mimicry of invader masculinity was the divestment of the feminine out of the masculine. In a Lacanian sense, a masculine subject position was seen to be a rejection of the feminine subject in unconscious terms (see Doyle 2001). The mimicry of colonial masculinity by Indigenous men and its subsequent reinterpretation as "traditional Indigenous masculinity" has meant that "authentic" forms of Māori masculinity have largely been defeminized. Such polarity has led to ritual displays of physical manliness and hypermasculinity, along with the traditionalization of heterosexuality, homophobia, and patriarchy within postcolonial Indigenous masculine cultures. And here patriarchy is defined as including crude acts of aggression, but more importantly as "men's control of women's bodies and minds . . . deeply entrenched in rituals, routines and social practices" (Beynon 2002:85). For example, the gendered form of haka seen today is a colonial construction. When haka was revived in the 1920s it came to resemble the colonial physical education practice of the time. That is, physical education or "drill" was performed in strict and uniform lines marked by a stringent gender division, with females lined in rows in the front and males lined in the back. Furthermore, androgynous components of precontact haka became gendered. For example, the androgynous "poi" ball came under the domain of women because of its aesthetic nature, while virulent haka came to be dominated by men.

Bourdieu (2000) is useful in thinking of the Indigenous masculine body via "physical capital" as a historical materialism–oriented analysis. The Indigenous body symbolized the physical realm and, thus, was employed for its physical labor, observed for its performativity, and humanized through physical pursuits such as sport and haka. For many Indigenous men of my parents' generation, Bourdieu's analysis is important because of its concern with the body in relation to the working class, the members of which, through bodily cognition as a necessary effect of a physically intensive life, acquired different relations to their bodies than the middle or dominant classes. Thus, in many Indigenous communities, masculine subcultures developed throughout much of the twentieth century and were based on relationships with a physically laboring body that, in turn, came to symbolize an ontologically authentic Indigenous man. For instance, the relationship between physical labor, sport, and the Māori male body has determined a traditional Māori masculinity symbolically reified within the physical realm (see Hokowhitu 2003b, 2004).

The late New Zealand historian Michael King once suggested, "Apart from warfare, the national activity to which Maoris contributed in a measure resembling their full potential was rugby football" (Zavos 1992:78). This is a discourse that has, unfortunately, been evoked, embodied, and replicated by Māori themselves, as Hemi Nikora, a Māori sports historian, outlines: "Rugby is one sport where Maoris succeed. It is the sport in which the natural instincts of the individual complements team combatant skills. It is said that rugby is the natural outlet or activity substituting for the days of tribal warfare" (1988:35).

The naturalization of the synergy between Māori masculinity and sport began with colonial schooling. Inspired by the character-building notions of the English public schools, sport in private boys' schools in the colonies was "one of the most important aspects of British imperialism.... The lessons of the playing field were designed to be the lessons of life.... The public school games ethic was supposed to teach courage, endurance, assertion, control and self-control" (Dimeo 2002:80). The development of school rugby culture was associated with "muscular Christianity," which "helped shape the Victorian notion of sportsmanship" (Pringle 2003:49), including fair play, modesty, and adherence to rules. Sport thus became an important cog in the machine of British imperialism. Throughout Britain's imperial era "there was a wide-spread view that great empires of the past had fallen because the ruling classes had grown luxurious and effeminate" (Collins 1998:4).

In New Zealand it was no coincidence that colonial authorities attempted to create a Māori gentry modeled on their British counterparts via the creation of Māori boys' private boarding schools, where rugby in particular played a central role in producing a certain form of heterosexual masculinity, an "old-boy" masculinity, and, in particular, a burgeoning form of hybridized masculine leadership that would enable more effective assimilation (Hokowhitu 2004, 2005, 2009b). Rugby, as a form of "muscular

Christianity," became readily promoted in all private Māori boys' schools to impart desirable attributes of manly virtue. For example, in describing one of these schools, Finlay MacDonald suggests the school presents "an extraordinary blend of various colonial legacies. Over the past 120 years, Anglicanism, Māoritanga [Māori culture] and rugby have combined to form a unique New Zealand institution ... [in which Māori] families sent their chosen sons to be educated in a replica of the nineteenth century English boarding school" (1996:13–14).

Many of the Māori gentlemen who came out of private boys' schools became leaders in their communities" strong, competent, eloquent, and able to function between both worlds. Later, as a testament to the extent that elite Māori masculinity mirrored the British gentry's dominant masculinity, Viscount Bledisloe (one of New Zealand's most respected governor-generals) said at the centenary of the Kaiapohia (Kaiapoi) Pa (communal gathering space) that a Māori (i.e., a Māori gentleman) "could at least vie with his British comrade in loyalty, dignity, refinement, athletic achievement and eloquent speech" (Slatter 1970:170).

The discursive synergy between Māori masculinity and sport was a constant throughout postcolonial history, with many of Māori masculinity's most popular memories centering on the feats of Māori players on the rugby field. As is evident in the introduction to this chapter, the unnatural alignment of symbols of Māori masculine culture has become so imbibed within New Zealand rugby culture that it is difficult to envision the synergy's inauthenticity. For instance, along with the performance of "Ka Mate" by the All Blacks, many other sporting franchises are encoded with Māori imagery. The New Zealand rugby league team that plays in the Australia-based National Rugby League competition is named the New Zealand Warriors and has a *whakairo upoko* (carved head with protruding tongue) as its motif. The Waikato Super 15 rugby franchise (located in the heavily Māori-populated areas of Waikato and the Bay of Plenty) is suitably named the Waikato Chiefs, while its motif features a hand clasping a traditional *patu* (club-like weapon).[7]

In sum, the traditions and the material conditions of postcolonial life have led to the construction of an authentic Māori masculinity that is hyper-masculine, aggressive, violent, and patriarchal, represented by a figure who establishes his masculinity through bodily acts, including performances on the sports-field. Such a figure is neatly imagined in "Jake-the-Mus" in the film *Once Were Warriors* (Tamahori 1995), a character who is working class (underclass), has an inability to find a mature (civilized) voice to deal with the complexities of his home life, and, as a consequence, flies into violent rampages. Entirely governed by his passions, Jake is unable to find ways of expressing himself other than through physical violence. Indeed, everything about Jake is physical: his ferocity, his sexuality, his being, even his nickname, "the Mus." From slurping oysters to his brutality, Jake emanates an uncivilized physicality, void of mature expression. When Beth (his wife) suggests to Jake that he "talks with his fists," she provides a succinct analysis of colonized Māori masculinity, devoid of mature communication and overreliant on physicality (see Hokowhitu 2007). The contemporary normalization or privileging of the brutal masculine haka as a symptom of "traditional" Māori masculinity is thus unsurprising.

Postcolonial Māori masculinity has struggled to find a voice that is assertive yet not violent, constructive and yet not submissive. When Māori men do become assertive in the Pākehā world, savage discourses are often called upon to mislocate that assertion, while the assumption of gentleman-like British qualities (i.e., stoicism), associated with the Māori gentry's version of humility, has led to a degree of submissiveness to neocolonial desires. In essence, the subversive, constructive, creative, typically feminine voice of Māori men has been largely silenced, leading to a profound void and anger that resonate most vividly through haka as a gender construction. In a sense, haka is the space where the embodied anger of colonization seeps/weeps.

Haka and Ethnic Formalization

"There is always, in Said, the suggestion that colonial power and discourse is possessed entirely by the colonizer, which is a historical and theoretical simplification. The terms in which Said's Orientalism is unified—the intentionality and unidirectionality of colonial power—also unify the subject of colonial enunciation. This is a result of Said's inadequate attention to representation as a concept that articulates the historical and fantasy (as the scene of desire) in the production of the 'political' effects of discourse" (Bhabha 1983:24–25).

Much of what has been discussed thus far reflects a typical deconstruction of postcolonial Indigenous identity. In particular, I have outlined a genealogy that made possible the inauthentic synergy between the performance of masculine patriotism by a national sports team and symbols of Indigenous culture. In the remainder of this chapter I would like to take this analysis beyond historical deconstruction to understand the political and ethical possibilities of haka via the coined notions of "embodied sovereignty" and "body logic." The excursion toward embodied sovereignty cannot be a romanticized one, however, as the Bhabha quote immediately above suggests. Such honest self-criticism involves less concentration on the deconstruction of dominant discourses and more focus on the violent process of Indigenous postcolonial identity formation in relation to Indigenous choice and responsibility.

The postcolonial definition of Indigenous subjectivity relates to the processes of "ethnic formalization," particularly through the concepts of authenticity, tradition, and culture. The cultural insecurity, the unprincipled, immoral, unethical, anarchical cultural void left in colonization's wake, necessitated the search and desire for classical Indigenous culture. Unmistakably, then, a sense of loss and a desire for origin were colonization's etch on the Indigenous psyche. Postcolonial Indigenous identities were and are made distinct by their constitutional opposition to the annexation and subjugation of their unique lands and cultures. In other words, the renaissance of classical Indigenous culture involved the search for a precolonial authentic culture and reconstruction of precolonial Indigenous language and culture as "unpolluted," as "pure," as "traditional," and, importantly, as lacking an alterity that might threaten or challenge such an authentic self.

The formalization of Indigenous identity is marked by an economy of violence. The strategic cultural essentialism that occurs at the interstitial space of postcolonial identity formation is necessarily one underpinned by discrimination, by exclusion of various Indigenous subjectivities that disobey "tradition" and "authenticity." Postcolonial Indigenous identity is, therefore, "threatened by what it cannot integrate in itself—haunted by the negated, the neglected, and the unforeseeable" (Hägglund 2004:47). According to Robert Niezen a simple logic underpins such violent essentialism: "The more human groups are displaced, removed from familiar relationships and strategies of power-accumulation and peacemaking, the more they will attach themselves to leaders, organizations, and social movements that offer stability and self-esteem through the reinventions of their past, often making social belonging more exclusive and sharply defined" (2009:176). In partial agreement, it is with disquiet that I have witnessed the increasing "ethnic formalization" of Māori culture that has taken place over the last two decades in particular. The glue of Indigenous identity markers such as land, language, and performance of culture has, as a consequence, bound Indigenous resistance movements.

In New Zealand such cultural essentialism has led to a number of "Māoriness" scales being published by Indigenous scholars, closely related to the earlier anthropological scales produced by James Ritchie (1963) and Joan Metge (1976). Hana O'Regan, for instance, outlines the quantification of "Māoriness" as an enabler of social reality: "By accepting that people may possess varying levels or degrees of identity we engage in a process of redefining and revaluing the criteria of cultural identity in order to accommodate the social and cultural reality" (2001:91). Similarly, Mason Durie suggests, "the concept of a secure identity rests on definite self-identification as Māori together with quantifiable involvement in, and/or knowledge of, whakapapa, *marae* participation, whānau, whenua tipu (ancestral land), contacts with Māori people, and Māori language" (1998:58). In relation to these, Durie (1998) goes on to list "secure," "positive," "notional," and "compromised" identity profiles as descending categories. Central, then, to the ethnic formalization process is demarcation that excludes those Indigenous subjectivities that threaten the "security" of an imagined authenticity. For both O'Regan and Durie the formalization of Māori ethnicity is undoubtedly a strategy to enable Indigenous Peoples to gain a stronger foothold to say "I am Māori." The cost of this ontological revelation is, of course, the death of those Indigenous subjectivities that threaten strategic traditionalism. The pursuit of decolonization—that is, the pursuit of "Indigenous rights"—has meant "defining in particular terms who is the beneficiary of those rights and who is not . . . [and] calls for clearly defined subjects attached to specific communities" (Niezen 2009:10).

Foucault's theorization suggests that "the body is not only caught up within this set of relations, but its meaning becomes entirely constituted by them" (Edwards 2006:144). Such an analysis takes us back to the ideas of Spivak outlined in the epigraph to this chapter, in which "the condition of being postcolonial is one of being relentlessly constituted in the discourses of power that control their situation and that lie beyond their agency" (Featherstone 2005:10). As Linda Smith points out, "For Maori people . . . the cultural institutions which encouraged oral debate and the sense of injustice which fuelled the debates made politics the basis of everyday life" (1999:110). Here I take "everyday life" to refer to the materialization of the political that, for instance, is reflected in the increased uptake of *moko kauae* (feminine chin tattooing) as a political signifier of Indigenous self-determination (see Higgins 2004).

This politicized cultural formalism includes haka as a mainstay of an authentic and traditionalized form of culture. In ontological terms, haka signifies a worthy bodily exercise in the pursuit of "being Māori." Stated more positively, haka has been a critical component in the makeup of a strategically essentialized ontological construction of postcolonial Māori identity. An important contemporary marker of "being Māori," then, is involvement with kapa haka communities. For instance, on many application forms for financial educational assistance provided by Māori fiduciary entities, attempts to establish the "authenticity" of the applicant are included via questions surrounding "community involvement" that commonly list "kapa haka" as one example. Thus haka is one cultural form that identifies "who is the subject of rights": "Indigenous peoples have therefore drawn new cultural boundaries, redefined themselves as nations, and, by implication, redefined the foundation of belonging for their individual members not only as kinship or shared culture but also as distinct citizenship, as belonging to a distinct regime of rights, entitlements, and obligations" (Niezen 2009:40).

The integration of haka into a Māori ontology is not surprising, for it mimics the narrow definition of "culture" as a derivative of modernity, that is, "as the objects of aesthetic excellence ('high art')" (Sim 2001:218). One of the biggest events on the "Māori calendar" is Te Matatini, formerly known as the New Zealand Polynesian Festival and then the Aotearoa Traditional Māori Performing Arts Festival, the national kapa haka competition, a culmination of earlier provincial competitions that in 2011 included two thousand performers and twenty-five thousand spectators (Mana Magazine 2011:12). The question of culture is central to the politics of recognition, for as Spivak argues, the biopolitical production of postcolonial Indigeneity reflects a "re-orientalization," while the eventualities of Indigenous resistance movements have in many cases produced unhealthy and prolonged cultural essentializations that have led to an Indigenous form of necro-politics (Mbembe 2003).

On the flip side of the above critique of ethnic formalism is the concern that such theorization hastens Indigenous people's discarding of those political notions of culture at the forefront of Indigenous rights, "the very identities, narratives and analytical tools that had charged a long history of popular anti-colonial struggles" (Featherstone 2005:18). Spivak's notion of "strategic essentialism" is important in the figuring of haka as a political tool because of the critique offered by Paul Gilroy, who refers to antiessentialist stances as "premature pluralism" in the context of black studies programs, "a postmodern evasion of the need to give historical specificity and complexity to the term *black*, seen as linked racial formations, counter histories, and cultures of resistance" (Clifford 1994:319). Similarly, Arif Dirlik argues that postcolonialism has had a tendency to undermine effective anticolonial praxis by unraveling "the traditional tools of a radical analysis of the postcolonial condition—history, causality, identity—and installing instead concepts that are much more amenable to the forces of global capitalism—the now canonic theoretical repertoire of hybridity, diaspora and anti-essentialism" (Featherstone 2005:13).

Perhaps a more constructive way to frame this ongoing essentialist/nonessentialist debate, which plagues postcolonial theory in general, is to reanalyze it through Indigenous sovereignty, in which Indigenous sovereignty refers to the way Indigenous Peoples choose to represent their worlds, whether that be through hybrid or essentialist notions of culture, both forms remaining critical to strategic decolonization and fluid epistemologies. Rather than focusing on the detrimental effects of diluting essentialized Indigenous culture versus the violence that occurs as Indigenous cultures are produced to be "authentic," the key is to concentrate on the choice and responsibility of Indigenous communities to represent themselves as they see fit, flanked by processes of critical self-reflexivity.

Underpinning this critical self-reflexivity is asking, when do such essentialisms stop being strategic and become inhibitive, and what do the cultural essentialisms Indigenous people have clung to through the violent torrent of colonization resemble today? That is, what do they signify and, indeed, are they strategic representations? For example, at what point does the notion of haka as gendered "tradition" serve to rejuvenate and when does it serve to restrain? In sum, what is the cost of recognition? In the act of desiring recognition, what choices do Indigenous Peoples lose? Or do we simply lose choice? When we presume, for instance, that the global recognition afforded Māori culture via the All Black's performance of "Ka Mate" can only but benefit Māori, we fail to conceive of the costs of recognition.

Embodied Sovereignty

> The tongue is the avenue whereby the thoughts of the mind is conveyed.... It is, therefore, correct that the tongue should be so honoured as it is in carvings of male ancestors.... Like pükana [dilation of the eyes], whëtero [protrusion of the tongue] is used to emphasise certain words, phrases or references.
>
> TĪMOTI KĀRETU, *The Dance of a Noble People*

One of the key problematics this chapter puts forward is the epistemological reconstruction of a "body logic" in particular relation to Indigenous material existentialism (see Hokowhitu 2009a). Indigenous theorists' current preoccupation with the idea of "decolonization" has led to a schizophrenic envisioning of an authentic Indigenous self located in a precolonial past and thus divorced from the materiality of the present (see Hokowhitu 2010). Robert Young suggests that the oppressive process of colonization in and of itself has initiated a "distinctive postcolonial epistemology and ontology" (Coulthard 2007:454). Here Young is suggesting that resistance to colonization has produced a postcolonial consciousness within Indigenous Peoples—which in turn has led to Indigenous claims to distinctive rights—that seldom recognizes that such demands are themselves framed by modernity's tradition of dissent (see Spencer 2001) and desire a "classical" form of Indigenous culture that never universally existed. This critique suggests that when contemporary culture is reframed in terms of the renaissance of classical practices lost due to colonization, and when this supposed cultural renaissance is underpinned by an inherent resistance to the dominant colonial ideology, then an ontological blunder occurs that divorces what it means to be Indigenous from the *present*. Indigenous people lose their existential self: the immediacy of just being, of living, of doing. There is nothing more *immediate* than the body.

Here I want to remind the reader of Young's critique of postcolonial studies' disregard of nonsecular Indigenous ways. Although postcolonial theory readily deconstructs Cartesian dualism as a civilizing factor of colonization, seldom is any space for analyses allocated to those Indigenous bodily practices that inherently undermine the mind/body binary. While many Indigenous scholars have challenged the mind/body dichotomy by describing holistic Indigenous epistemologies that typically include the physical, spiritual, mental, and material reality of place, almost without fail such holistic theorizing seeks to authenticate an Indigenous tradition in opposition to the imposition of mind/body dualism. Hence, I want to evoke the importance of strenuous analyses into the existential possibilities of the Indigenous body, into the *immediacy* and political nature of Indigenous bodily practices such as haka.

Indigenous body performances can produce a radical alterity that resides beyond "rational thought." Here C. L. R. James's analysis of Caribbean cricket is important to reconsider. Featherstone explicates,

> For [James], the body in movement was a dynamic sculpture shaped by a dialectical tension [between] individual will and desire, and the forms and constraints of its social environment at a particular historical moment. Whilst the body has always been at the painful centre of colonial and imperial history, it was James who first articulated its capacity for expression and resistance, not through violence necessarily, but through the detailed aesthetics of the body's response to stimuli at a particular moment in history. The political theatre of movement occurs in various and unexpected places by no means limited to traditional definitions of "art" or rebellion: in a batman's stroke in cricket. (2005:27)

Here Indigenous studies can take the lead from feminist cultural studies, in which scholars consciously established a position beyond the Western masculine intellectual tradition of mind/body dualism: "an approach which refuses to privilege mind over body . . . and which assumes that the body cannot be transcended" and an approach that "emphasizes contingency, locatedness, the irreducibility of difference, the passage of emotions and desire, and the worldliness of being" (Ahmed and Stacey 2001:3).

Indigenous embodied sovereignty, then, refers to a critical bodily practice that brings into question those subjugating forces written upon the Indigenous body, that is, the very materiality of Indigenous existence, while affirming the complexity, diversity, and multidimensional ways of being Indigenous. Moreover, practices of embodied sovereignty must be aware of the way that discourses of Indigenous authenticity and tradition haunt them. As a consequence, part of the study of embodied sovereignty should be an analysis of how the specter of tradition remains written upon the Indigenous body: how, for instance, the location of Indigeneity in the primitive past marks the Indigenous body in tourist sites and in commodified versions of Indigenous culture, such as the All Blacks' rendition of "Ka Mate."

It is in the genealogical inscription upon the everyday material reality of the Indigenous body that the complexity of the historical and contemporary Indigenous condition must be analyzed. Predominantly, such an analysis should be driven toward an Indigenous existentialism that confronts and theorizes the everyday materialism of the Indigenous body, while encouraging an epistemological leap in which a body logic is made possible. Rather than haka, for instance, being constructed as a "traditional" performance to be viewed by an audience, its impassioned bodily properties in conjunction with its often politically verbalized cultural elements should be recognized. *Ihi*, *wehi*, and *wana*, as overarching concepts of haka, help explain a body logic, as outlined by Nathan Matthews: "*Haka* is comprised of both physical and spiritual aspects. The spiritual aspects of *haka* and its performance are linked to various cultural concepts contained in the Māori world-view. These include the concepts of *ihi* (authority, charisma, awe-inspiring, psychic power), *wehi* (fear, awe, respect) and *wana* (thrill, fear, excitement, awe-inspiring)" (2004:10). It is said that when these aspects are achieved in tandem it effects a physiological response, such as the raising of the hair on the back of one's neck. Here, then, body logic refers to what culture "feels like" as opposed to the production of Indigenous culture to be viewed or Indigenous knowledge to be "preserved." The focus is on haka's existential properties as a cultural practice of "the everyday," as opposed to a reflection of "culture" as "high art."

In the condition of postcoloniality it is difficult to disengage with a mind/body duality, and it is at this fundamental level that theorizing toward epistemological transformation must begin: with the thinking body, the conceptualization of the body as a material producer of thought, the body as a holistic notion in which physiology and the interplay between history, present, and future interact to produce social meaning, which may be freeing and/ or disciplinary. Such conceptualizations enable a move beyond the limits of constructionism (e.g., the agencyless body described by Foucault's biopower) and essentialism (e.g., biological determinism). For Indigenous people, such an approach makes possible Indigenous existentialism because it suggests that the morphing body through time both is changed and can change its facticity, yet its practices must be open to deconstruction and scrutiny, especially in the ways it produces gender and reifies tradition and cultural essentialisms. The foremost question should be, then, how has haka come to be naturalized as an activity to be performed on stage? Why is it not just an everyday bodily practice? Haka is an ideal avenue for embodied sovereignty because of its disciplined passion, evocative passion, and political voice.

The colonial project "limited the identity of the colonized to the materiality of their bodies" (Featherstone 2005:65–66), meaning that the project of embodied sovereignty must be at once deconstructory and existential, for it would be dangerous to merely foreground the possibilities of embodied sovereignty. We need to tread carefully, for no better reason than that it was the naturalization of biological racism through the scientific age that gave credence to the atrocities of colonization and imperialism. Bourdieu argues, "If it is quite illusory to believe that symbolic violence can be overcome with the weapons of consciousness and will alone, this is because the effect and conditions of its efficacy are durably and deeply embedded in the body in the form of dispositions" (2001:39). This reflects an underpinning concept similar to Fanon's decolonial recourse to violence in that Fanon could not envisage existential "decolonization" without the materiality of violent revolution to effect an epistemological "break" from the subjugation of colonialism (Fanon 1967).

Indigenous theorizing cannot fully develop without the possibility for existential agency, for I do not want to believe that the atrocities of colonization were the defining point at which the existential potential of the Indigenous body remains scarred indeterminately. Indigenous existentialism must materialize beyond such embodied and genealogical pain. The endurance of somatic and psychosomatic pain may not be a choice, but Indigenous people can choose to live beyond the genealogical scarring inflicted by colonization. That is, we must strategically recognize the importance of the Indigenous body for the possibilities of Indigenous existentialism and sovereignty without "collapsing into a form of biological or fatalistic essentialism" (Edwards 2006:151). The project also calls for the full weight of Bhabha's analysis, in which he suggests that European rationalism preserves "the boundaries of sense" for itself. That is, the seemingly simplistic idea of "body logic" will probably make little sense to most.

The snippets of savagery the mainstream media edit into their coverage of haka mean that haka is currently used as a vehicle to reproduce the conditions of power. Moreover, the neocolonial reproduction of patriotism via the performance of haka by national and high school sporting teams and the use of Māori imagery in general by global conglomerates aid in the neocolonial reconstitution of the Indigenous body. Yet this chapter calls on Indigenous people to be responsible in the production of haka; for instance, some critical strategic analyses into the gendering that occurs in haka must be considered. This analysis also values haka's proliferation as an enactment of "embodied sovereignty," in which haka has the potential to be transformative and in which haka is a site where Indigenous bodies exude a political presence that moves Indigenous liberation beyond rational thought. The *immediate* materiality of the Indigenous body is inescapable, and thus there is potential for the concept of an Indigenous body logic to move beyond historical constructions and the "rational," so as to reorient a focus away from what Indigenous cultures "look like" and toward how "culture feels" in the moment. That is, it allows for the existential and everyday properties of Indigenous culture, an idea that moves beyond the categorization of Indigenous cultures within the premodern, "traditional," and/or "to be preserved" frames, a vital logic to the temporal decolonization of the Indigenous body.

Notes

1. In 1888, four years prior to the formal formation of the New Zealand Rugby Football Union, the first New Zealand team, referred to as the "New Zealand Native Football Representatives," toured Britain and Australia (Phillips 1987; Ryan 1993). A player on the tour, Tamati Erihana or Rangiwahia "Tom" Ellison (of Ngāi Tahu descent) introduced haka to rugby, more than likely as a pregame entertainment spectacle to attract British crowds to the Native games, the tour largely being a pro-

fessional exercise. However, it was the tour of one of New Zealand's most famous teams, the 1905 All Blacks (now referred to as "the Originals"), that marked the first official use of the "Ka Mate" haka within a sporting context (see Hokowhitu 2005).

There have been a number of criticisms concerning the exploitation of Ka Mate as it is linked to popular cultural spectacles, such as the mock performance by the Spice Girls during a promotional tour of Bali in 1997.

2. The appropriation and use of Māori culture by the likes of global conglomerates such as Adidas is outlined clearly. Māori lawyer and Treaty of Waitangi claimant Maui Solomon points out how the very use of a colonial legal tradition to evaluate and judge cultural and intellectual property rights (IPR) is fraught with contradictions:

> the intellectual property rights system is totally inadequate to recognise and protect Māori cultural values and cultural rights, for example, the IPR system was developed to protect private economic rights that came out of the Industrial Revolution, but when you talk about Māoritānga [Māori culture], cultural heritage rights, these are collective by nature so they don't belong to one individual, they belong to the whānau [family], the hapū [clan] or the iwi [peoples]. . . . Increasingly . . . you've got major corporates who are drawing upon Māori branding, Māori imagery and Māori icons to promote their products. Now if they're going to do that they've got to go to Māori and make sure that they have the proper authority that they are doing the right thing, that they are using those images and icons in a culturally appropriate way. And if there is going to be a commercial return then what share of those benefits will Māori get? (Backchat 2000)

3. For a fuller description of the genesis of the "Ka Mate," see "The Kata, Its Meaning and Origin," http://www.kawhia.maori.nz/haka.html, accessed March 1, 2011.

4. When I employ the terms "violent/violence," I refer to the inherent discrimination that must occur when broad cultural identities are formed. Whereas certain aspects of culture become "cultural traits," other aspects of identity are discriminated against as not being "authentic" to a particular identity construction.

5. In reality, the rhetoric of egalitarianism was a smoke screen for an unofficial but accepted segregation, both in rugby and in broader New Zealand society. In New Zealand's developing imperial nation, Britain's class system was transported to the antipodes and transformed so that New Zealand became largely segregated along racial lines. Here an "inferior" Native race was accommodated in the margins of a superior white settler society. From 1840 (when New Zealand's founding document, the Treaty of Waitangi, was signed) until the late 1950s (i.e., during the period of mass Māori urbanization), the largely rural Māori population were free to retain a number of their cultural vestiges but were able to perform these practices only in segregatory fashion. That is, as token gestures within broader society (e.g., the haka performed prior to All Black games) or on unmarked rural reserves (i.e.,

on marae [communal gathering places]). Given this situation, authentic Māori culture was wholly segregated from Pākehā society, while tokenistic performances were held up as signifiers of a racially inclusive imperial nation.

6. The Waitangi celebrations commemorated the signing of the 1840 Treaty of Waitangi between Māori and Pākehā. The Treaty of Waitangi is recognized as New Zealand's founding document.

7. The Super 15 is a professional rugby union competition in which teams from New Zealand, South Africa, and Australia participate.

Bibliography

Ahmed, Sara, and Jackie Stacey, eds.
  2001 Thinking through the Skin. Transformations: Thinking through Feminism. New York: Routledge.

Backchat
  2000 Who Owns the Haka? Gordon Harcourt, host. Series 3, program 16. Television One, June 18.

Bederman, Gail
  1995 Manliness and Civilization: A Cultural History of Gender and Race in the United States, 1880–1917. Chicago: University of Chicago Press.

Bem, Sandra
  1974 The Measurement of Psychological Androgyny. Journal of Consulting and Clinical Psychology 42:155–62.

Best, Elsdon
  1925 Games and Pastimes of the Maori. Wellington: Board of Maori Ethnological Research for the Dominion Museum.
  1976 Games and Pastimes of the Maori. 2nd ed. Wellington: Government Printer.

Beynon, John
  2002 Masculinities and Culture. Buckingham, UK: Open University Press.

Bhabha, Homi
  1983 The Other Question. Screen 24(6):18–36.

Bourdieu, Pierre
  2000 Distinction: A Social Critique of the Judgement of Taste. London: Routledge and Kegan Paul.
  2001 Masculine Domination. Stanford CA: Stanford University Press.

Clifford, James
  1994 Further Inflections: Toward Ethnographies of the Future. Cultural Anthropology 9(3):302–38.

Collins, Tony
  1998 Rugby's Great Split: Class, Culture and the Origins of Rugby League Football. London: Frank Cass.

Coulthard, Glen

2007 Subjects of Empire: Indigenous Peoples and the "Politics of Recognition" in Canada. Contemporary Political Theory 6:437–60.

Descartes, René

1996 Meditations on First Philosophy. Melbourne: Cambridge University Press.

Dimeo, Paul

2002 Colonial Bodies, Colonial Sport: "Martial" Punjabs, "Effeminate" Bengalis and the Development of Indian Football. International Journal of the History of Sport 19(1):72–90.

Doyle, Laura, ed.

2001 Bodies of Resistance. Evanston IL: Northwestern University Press.

Durie, Mason

1998 Te Mana, Te Kāwanatanga: The Politics of Māori Self-Determination. Auckland: Oxford University Press.

Earle, Augustus

1909 A Narrative of a Nine Months' Residence in New Zealand in 1827. Christchurch: Whitcombe & Tombs.

Edwards, Tim

2006 Cultures of Masculinity. New York: Routledge.

Fanon, Frantz

1967 The Wretched of the Earth. C. Farrington, trans. Harmondsworth, UK: Penguin.

Featherstone, Simon

2005 Postcolonial Cultures. Jackson: University Press of Mississippi.

Foucault, Michel

1995 Discipline and Punish: The Birth of the Prison. A. Sheridan, trans. New York: Vintage Books.

2008 The History of Sexuality. Vol. 1. Camberwell, UK: Penguin.

Goldberg, David Theo

1993 Racist Culture: Philosophy and the Politics of Meaning. Oxford: Blackwell.

Hägglund, Martin

2004 The Necessity of Discrimination: Disjoining Derrida and Levinas. Diacritics 34(1):40–71.

Hegel, Georg

1899 The Philosophy of History. J. Sibree, trans. New York: Colonial Press.

Higgins, Rawinia

2004 "He tanga ngutu, he Tuhoetanga te mana motuhake o te ta moko wahine": The Identity Politics of *Moko Kauae*. PhD thesis, University of Otago, Dunedin, New Zealand.

Hokowhitu, Brendan

2003a Māori Masculinity, Post-Structuralism, and the Emerging Self. New Zealand Sociology 18(2):179–201.

2003b Race Tactics: The Racialised Athletic Body. Junctures: The Journal for Thematic Dialogue 1:21–34.

2004 Tackling Māori Masculinity: A Colonial Genealogy of Savagery and Sport. Contemporary Pacific 15(2):259–84.

2005 Rugby and Tino Rangatiratanga: Early Māori Rugby and the Formation of Māori Masculinity. Sporting Traditions: Journal of the Australian Society for Sports History 21(2):75–95.

2007 Māori Masculinity: Overcoming Discourses of Savagery in Working with Māori Men. Special issue, "Working with Male Clients," New Zealand Journal of Counselling 27(2):63–76.

2008a Authenticating Māori Physicality: Translations of "Games" and "Pastimes" by Early Travellers and Missionaries to New Zealand. International Journal of the History of Sport 25(10):1355–73.

2008b The Death of Koro Paka: "Traditional" Māori Patriarchy. Contemporary Pacific 20(1):115–41.

2009a Indigenous Existentialism and the Body. Cultural Studies Review 15(2):101–18.

2009b Māori Rugby and Subversion: Creativity, Domestication, Oppression and Decolonization. International Journal of the History of Sport 26(16):2314–34.

2010 A Genealogy of Indigenous Resistance. In Indigenous Identity and Resistance: Researching the Diversity of Knowledge. B. Hokowhitu, N. Kermoal, C. Andersen, M. Reilly, P. Rewi, and A. Petersen, eds. Pp. 207–25 Dunedin, New Zealand: University of Otago Press.

Hokowhitu, Brendan, and Jay Scherer
2008 The Māori All Blacks and the Decentering of the White Subject: Hyperrace, Sport, and the Cultural Logic of Late Capitalism. Sociology of Sport Journal 25:243–62.

Hope, Wayne
2002 Whose All Blacks? Media, Culture & Society 24(2):235–53.

Jackson, Steve, and Brendan Hokowhitu
2002 Sport, Tribes and Technology: The New Zealand All Blacks Haka and the Politics of Identity. Journal of Sport and Social Issues 26(2):125–39.

Kāretu, Tīmoti
1993 The Dance of a Noble People. Auckland: Reed Books.

MacDonald, Finlay
1996 The Game of Our Lives. Auckland: Penguin.

Mana Magazine
2011 Bring It On. 98:12–13.

Maning, Fredrick
1956 Old New Zealand. Christchurch: Whitcombe & Tombs.

Matthews, Nathan

2004 The Physicality of Māori Message Transmission: *Ko te tinana, he waka tuku kōrero*. Junctures 3:9–18.

Mbembe, Achille

2003 Necropolitics. L. Meintjes, trans. Public Culture 15(1):11–40.

Metge, Joan

1976 The Maoris of New Zealand. London: Routledge and Kegan Paul.

New Zealand Department of Education

1941 Native Education. Education Gazette 20(10):189–208.

Niezen, Ronald

2009 The Rediscovered Self: Indigenous Identity and Cultural Justice. Montreal: McGill-Queen's University Press.

Nikora, Hemi

1988 Maori Rugby: Otaki and Districts. Historical Journal (Otaki Historical Society) 11:35–42.

Oakley, Ann

1972 Sex, Gender and Society. London: Temple Smith.

O'Regan, Hana

2001 Ko Tahu, Ko Au: Kai Tahu—Tribal Identity. Christchurch: Horomaka.

Phillips, Jock

1987 A Man's Country? The Image of the Pākehā Male—A History. Auckland: Penguin.

Polack, Joel

1840 Manners and Customs of the New Zealanders, with Notes Corroborative of Their Habits, Usages, etc., and Remarks to Intending Emigrants, with Numerous Cuts Drawn on Wood. London: James Madden.

Primal Team

1999 Admedia 14(9):22–23.

Pringle, Richard

2003 Doing the Damage? An Examination of Masculinities and Men's Rugby Experiences of Pain, Fear and Pleasure. PhD dissertation, University of Waikato, Hamilton, New Zealand.

Pringle, Richard, and Pirkko Markula

2005 No Pain Is Sane after All: A Foucauldian Analysis of Masculinities and Men's Experiences in Rugby. Sociology of Sport Journal 22:472–97.

Ritchie, James

1963 The Making of a Maori—A Case Study of a Changing Community. Wellington: AH&AW Reed.

Ryan, Greg

1993 Forerunners of the All Blacks. Christchurch: Canterbury University Press.

Said, Edward

1978 Orientalism. New York: Vintage Books.

Sarup, Madan
  1996 Identity, Culture, and the Postmodern World. Edinburgh: Edinburgh University Press.
Sim, Stuart, ed.
  2001 The Routledge Companion to Postmodernism. London: Routledge.
Slatter, Gordon
  1970 On the Ball: The Centennial Book of New Zealand Rugby. Christchurch: Whitcombe & Tombs.
Smith, Linda
  1999 Decolonizing Methodologies: Research and Indigenous Peoples. London: Zed Books.
Smithells, Phillip
  1941 Maori Rhythm. Education Gazette 20. Unpaginated inset.
Spencer, Lloyd
  2001 Postmodernism: Modernity and the Tradition of Dissent. *In* The Routledge Companion to Postmodernism. S. Sim, ed. Pp. 158–69. London: Routledge.
Tamahori, Lee, dir.
  1995 Once Were Warriors. Culver City CA: Columbia TriStar Homevideo.
Tengan, Ty, and Jesse Markham
  2009 Performing Polynesian Masculinities in American Football: From "Rainbows to Warriors." International Journal of the History of Sport 26(16):2412–31.
Wellington Independent
  1867 The Great Native Meeting at Wairoa. Rōrahi XXII, Putanga 2508, 20 Paengawhāwhā 1867. P. 6. http://paperspast.natlib.govt.nz/cgi-bin/paperspast?a=d&d=WI18670420.2.15&l=mi&e=————-10—1——0—, accessed March 2, 2011.
Whitcombe & Tombs
  1899 The Imperial Readers. Christchurch: Whitcombe & Tombs.
Wiegman, Robyn
  1995 American Anatomies: Theorizing Race and Gender. Durham NC: Duke University Press.
Young, Robert
  2001 Postcolonialism: An Historical Introduction. Oxford: Blackwell.
  2004 White Mythologies. 2nd ed. New York: Routledge.
Zavos, Spiro
  1992 Kea Kaha. Metro Magazine 127:77–80.
  1998 Ka Mate! Ka Mate! New Zealand's Conquest of British Rugby. Auckland: Viking.

11

Genders of Xavante Ethnographic Spectacle

Cultural Politics of Inclusion and Exclusion in Brazil

LAURA R. GRAHAM

On December 2, 2009, during a public hearing at the Commission on Human Rights of the Federal Senate in Brasília, Brazil, Tuira Kayapó stepped up to the podium in front of TV cameras, photographers, and international journalists. Her hands richly blackened with body paint, she shook her fist as she publicly harangued officials from the National Indian Foundation (FUNAI). Tuira passionately spoke against government plans to construct the Belo Monte hydroelectric dam on the Xingu River. Her words echoed those that she and two other Kayapó women—Kokomu and Paipunu—had blasted at representatives of the Brazilian state's hydroelectric company (Electronorte) in 1990, in a protest at Altamira that became an icon of Native Amazonian political protest and assertions of Indigenous rights. Tuira especially captured national and international media attention when she dramatically swiped her machete across the face of the Electronorte representative (see, e.g., Beckman 1989; O'Connor 1995).

The Kayapó women's brief words, and Tuira's performance in particular, were remarkable since heretofore women had not been prominent in Native Amazonian public displays of Indigeneity. Moreover, if and when women appeared in expressions of Native Amazonian Indigenous identity directed to non-Indigenous audiences, they tended to be silent (Gal 1991, 1989).[1] These women's fleeting, but prominent, appearances stood out, calling attention to ways that the decidedly masculine and masculinized gendered pattern of these displays was beginning to shift to reflect the complexity of gender roles, relations, and ideologies of life internal to communities. In more recent demonstrations against the Belo Monte Dam Indigenous women feature prominently and some, such as Yasani Kalapalo from the Xingu area, now volubly advocate for Indigenous rights.[2] In a session on human rights at the United Nations in Geneva on March 11, 2014, Sonia Guajajara, coordinator of Brazil's Association of Indigenous Peoples (APIB), publicly condemned the Brazilian government for its failure to respect indigenous rights in the construction of large hydroelectric dams (Instituto Socioambiental 2014).

In contemporary Indigenous movements, where stakes are extremely high, leaders and organizers tend to strategically emphasize cohesion rather than internal diversity and heterogeneity (see Jackson 1995; Warren 1998). Identity-based assertions and claims to difference that are articulated against dominant social orders almost inevitably erase or flatten social distinctions, power differentials, and hierarchies, including those based on gender. Similarly, with few exceptions, scholars have paid minimal attention to gender in Indigeneity and to ways that the concept of Indigeneity erases difference, presenting an Indigeneity that is homogenous and usually masculine (see Hodgson 2002:1045).[3] They also have given little attention to the ways that various forms of social heterogeneity that exist within any Indigenous group are masked, both in these movements and in public displays of Indigeneity. The gender politics of Native Amazonians' public performance of Indigeneity, as well as its scholarly analysis, fit this general pattern.[4] The Kayapó women's public appearances, along with several other cases, such as that of Yasani Kalapalo and Sonia Guajajara, suggest, however, that the highly masculine presentation of Indigeneity is in flux. Their words and actions highlight that Native Amazonian women appear with increasing frequency and also speak in public displays of Indigeneity. They provoke further thought and analysis concerning the gender politics of Amazonian Indigeneity and the contexts in which women assume prominent, even speaking roles. Ultimately they bring attention to ways that Native Amazonian gendered patterns of engagement with Others beyond local communities are changing.

Xavante are another central Brazilian Indigenous People who—like the Kayapó—are exceptionally visible and audible in Brazilian Indigenous politics and in the national imaginary. Until very recently Xavante have consistently presented themselves in hypermasculine ways; their image in the Brazilian national imaginary is similarly hypermasculine. Yet, like Tuira, Kokomu, and Paipunu Kayapó, some Xavante women are beginning to appear in cultural display and also to speak in public spaces. These women are breaking the pattern of Xavante's public hypermasculinity and men's exclusive control over externally oriented performance and cultural display.

This chapter directs attention to the cultural logics and conditions that give rise to various innovations in Xavante performances for non-Indigenous publics, including changes in participation and the inclusion and exclusion of gendered expressive forms and speaking roles. I demonstrate that male-centric practices and ideologies of performance combined with men's traditional management of exogenous relations inform the outreach work of two Xavante communities, Eténhiritipa Pimentel Barbosa and Idzö'uhu Abelinha (Little Bee), that recently have been particularly active in outreach work.[5] The externally oriented "autoethnographic" (Pratt 1992) projects of these two communities are especially interesting because they differ markedly in terms of gender.

The work of both communities accommodates the creative innovations entailed in recontextualizations of expressive forms for non-Indigenous publics. I argue that an emphasis on aesthetics in the work of Pimentel Barbosa affirms and reinforces Xavante's male-centric "symbolic economy of alterity" (see, e.g., Viveiros de Castro 1992) and men's dominance of contemporary cultural outreach, including its exclusive use of men's expressive forms. In the case of Abelinha, however, the traditionally male-centric model of managing exogenous relationships provides a path for gender innovation. I suggest that, by positioning cultural display within a "male-imported" global discourse of environmentalism, organizers of Abelinha's work open a space for the incorporation of female expressive forms and women's participation in outreach. Female participation in this outreach is, however, predicated on male mediation, not an alternative to it. Thus, although their innovative and creative projects for managing exogenous relationships through performance diverge significantly, an underlying cultural logic—indeed, one that embraces women's participation in engaging alterity—unites them. Ultimately, the contrast between these Xavante communities' outreach presents an ideal opportunity for thinking about gender in Indigeneity as well as about gender in relation to Native Amazonian ideologies and orientations to alterity, and specifically what happens when Native Amazonian cosmologies meet global identity politics (see also Ball in press).

Forms of public spectacle and performance construct Indigeneity as displays of difference within intercultural spaces (Myers 2002) or contact zones (Clifford 1997).[6] Such cultural displays are political and self-reflexive and, however serious, also involve forms of play (Sherzer 2002). Moving forms of expressive culture to new contexts, through processes of "decontextualization" and "recontextualization," directs attention to expressive forms as objects, to performance conventions, and to participation.[7] Like the ways that play languages or puns disrupt conventional grammar and bring attention to language form (see Sherzer 2002) and speakers, moving expressive forms into new representational contexts presents opportunities for organizers and performers to objectify, think about, and play with culture and expressive performance in new and creative ways. The contrast between Pimentel Barbosa's and Abelinha's outwardly directed performances offers an ideal opportunity for exploring how individuals and groups who mediate performances for extralocal audiences, and who are themselves situated within fields of power, differentially respond to the reflexivity entailed in moving forms of cultural expression out of traditional locales and into new contexts.

It is important to emphasize at the outset that, for members of both Pimentel Barbosa and Abelinha, the process of recontextualizing expressive performance for non-Indigenous publics is inherently "traditional," for Xavante tradition is, as it is elsewhere in Native Amazonia, fundamentally creative (see, e.g., Green 2009; Oakdale 2009b; Santos-Granero 2009; Chernela 2012b; Oakdale and Course 2014).[8] Recontextualizing expressive performance is at once creative, innovative, and essentially "traditional."

Before turning to an exploration of ways that people from Pimentel Barbosa and Abelinha have been "playing with," objectifying, and engaging in politics of ethnographic display in recent years, it is important to have some ethnographic background and context regarding ideas of Xavante within the Brazilian national imaginary. These provide a backdrop for understanding ideologies of performance as well as the politics of gender, and also age, that inform these two communities' cultural outreach projects.

The Hypermasculine Indian: Xavante in the Brazilian National Imaginary

Xavante are a central Brazilian Gê-speaking people who today number approximately 15,315. Traditionally seminomadic, they now live sedentarily in more than two hundred autonomous communities dispersed across defined Indigenous territories in Mato Grosso state (Instituto Socioambiental 2013; see fig. 11.1).

Xavante are one of Brazil's most high-profile Indigenous Peoples. They became famous in the 1940s as part of a highly symbolic and ideologically loaded state-sponsored mass-media campaign mounted to justify state control of the hinterland—including its inhabitants—as part of a patriotic agenda (Garfield 2001; also see Maybury-Lewis 1967). In this campaign the group figured as heroic icons of a romanticized Noble Savage. Journalists embedded in the "pacification team" regularly reported to a national audience on the targeted group's fierce resistance to state attempts at "pacification" and championed Xavante for their bravery, heroism, and indomitable spirit. This mass media campaign created for Xavante a highly public and very masculine profile that has persisted to the present.

During the 1940s through the early 1980s, the very name "Xavante" signified positively valued masculine qualities: bravery, heroism, endurance, and resistance. It became fashionable within Brazilian popular culture to adopt "Xavante" to assert and emphasize these manly characteristics. Soccer teams (see Grêmio Esportivo Brasil-Xavante 2010), a bus company, and even musical groups (see Pena Branca e Xavantinho 2006, 2010) took the name "Xavante" to highlight their masculine qualities. Perhaps the best example of the semiotic valence that "Xavante" carried is the moniker applied, in 1970, to the Brazilian Air Force EMB-326, "Xavante," Brazil's first nationally manufactured fighter jet. Fittingly baptized to celebrate nationalism and the nation's industrial progress, the name "Xavante" underscores the nation's native aeronautics industry and its military capabilities (see Embraer Historical Center 2010).[9]

In the 1970s and 1980s, during Xavante's fight to recoup some of the territory that had been stolen from them in the landgrab that followed the media-celebrated "Xavante contact," leaders capitalized on the group's positive masculine image as daring, courageous, and assertive warriors.[10]

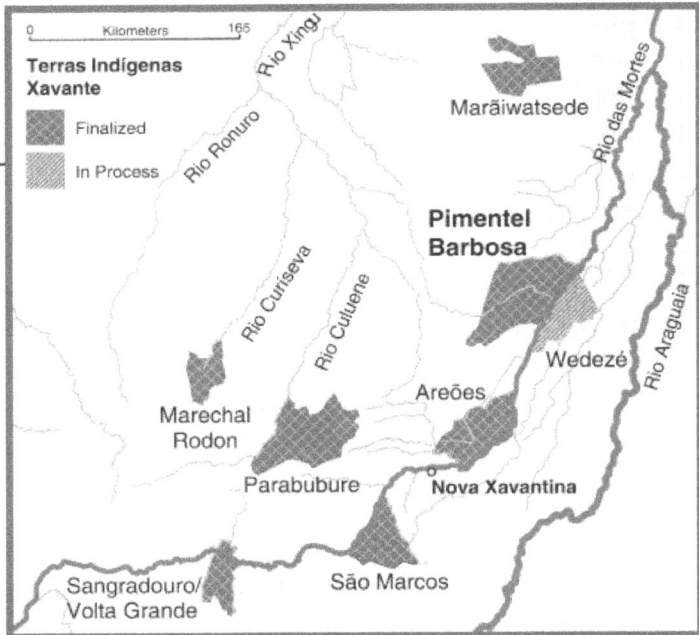

Boldly painted and armed with bows, arrows, and war clubs, Xavante men regularly appeared in Brasília, in the offices of the National Indian Foundation (FUNAI) and the Ministry of the Interior, where decisions affecting Indigenous Peoples were made. They staged aggressive oratorical displays in attempts to intimidate high-level government officials. One leader in particular, Mario Juruna from São Marcos, won national and eventually international acclaim for his use of cultural spectacle, new media technologies (a cassette-tape recorder), and resistance to corrupt government officials during Brazil's military regime.[11] Juruna and other Xavante men repeatedly deployed aspects of masculine culture to attract media attention and win public support. Their displays reinforced the group's celebrity and its highly masculine warrior image and helped Xavante to achieve concrete goals, especially legal rights to portions of their land.

Xavante's positive, male-dominated image held firm in the national imaginary through the early 1980s but declined rapidly after Juruna entered formal politics and as Xavante men unrelentingly continued to press demands on FUNAI.[12] From the mid-1980s through the 1990s, national media mobilized the negative trope of the Noble Savage narrative to overturn the positive image of Xavante that it had previously helped to construct. It overwhelmingly portrayed Xavante in pejorative ways, depicting men as belligerent ruffians who invaded the nation's capital and other cities with excessive appetites and demands (see Graham 2001). Xavante leaders were, in fact, attempting to establish productive social relationships that would ensure fulfillment of basic social services for their communities: primary health care, clean water and basic sanitation, and means to transport the infirm to clinics and hospitals.[13] Negative media depictions effectively undermined popular support for this once-championed group and destroyed lingering remnants of Xavante's formerly positive image. Throughout these media manipulations of both positive and negative extremes of the Noble Savage trope, Xavante's image remained consistently highly masculine.[14]

Xavante's rapid demise, like the swift downfalls of celebrity Indigenous leaders like Mario Juruna and Payakan Kayapó, serves as a potent remind-

Fig. 11.1. (*opposite*) Location of Xavante territories. Maps by Angela Collins. From Graham et al. 2009.

er of Indigenous Peoples' particular susceptibility to image manipulation, especially when their fame rests on outsiders' imaginaries, ideas, and idealized images (see Conklin and Graham 1995; Conklin 2002, 2006; Ramos 2003; Graham 2011). Their case exemplifies the double binds of idealized Indigeneity (see Heatherington 2010:10; see also Fortun et al. 2010:227).

Throughout this mass-mediated history Xavante men have stood as metonyms for the larger social whole within the national imaginary, despite the occasional special-interest story featuring Xavante women. Xavante men derive their metonymic status, which media configured into a hypermasculine profile for all Xavante, from the fact that historically men have served as the primary "transactional" as well as "representational go-betweens" (Metcalf 2005);[15] men mediate relations between Xavante communities and the world beyond and incorporate masculine representational strategies into their transactions with Brazilian nationals. Thus, within the national imaginary, Xavante were, and in fact still are, a hypermasculine and masculinized Indigenous group.

Gender, Alterity, and Mediating Worlds

Men's status as mediators between worlds is deeply rooted in social and political practice and Xavante cosmology, what Eduardo Viveiros de Castro (1992)—building on the work of Joanna Overing (1977, 1983–84; see also Santos-Granero 2009)—calls a "symbolic economy of alterity" (see also Vilaça 2010; Ball in press). The notion of symbolic economies of alterity draws attention to the ways in which Amazonian societies place particular emphasis on difference, focusing less on identity and more on difference in domains such as kinship, religion and spirituality, subsistence, and warfare. Amazonian symbolic economies of alterity privilege connections with Others and incorporation of the Other as a basis of the self and collective (see, e.g., Perrone-Moisés, this volume). Some scholars criticize the original model's formulation as overly male-centric and predatory, as well as for its underestimation of daily life and intimate spheres (e.g., McCallum 1999, 2013, in press). The Xavante case underscores that women also participate in symbolic economies of alterity, in specifically gendered ways: through nurturing, sharing, and providing in female domains. In fact, as I shall show, women's unique engagement with alterity is a fundamental part of what enables women and girls to join with men in Abelinha's cultural outreach.

Through ceremonial performance and dreaming, men mediate between Xavante and spirits who inhabit the *cerrado* (savannah) forest and between the living and the "always living" ancestors (see Graham 1995; Welch 2010). During a period of extended residence in the bachelors' hut (*hö*), preinitiate boys, known as *wapté*, receive instruction from senior mentors who prepare them for adult life and for encounters with Others, including their dream experiences and their dreams' proper expression, as *da-ño're* song and dance (see Graham 1995, 1994). In the powerful Wai'a ceremonial, considered to be extremely dangerous for women, men engage with potent spiritual beings of the cerrado forest and transfer the beings' force to Xavante (see Welch 2010).

As part of their socialization boys develop the skills to deal with powerful Others, the dangerous beings of the "outside": the forest, the supernatural, and, as Cecilia McCallum (1999:447) notes of the Cashinuá, the *city*. Since the contact, when the Vargas government transported Xavante leaders to Rio de Janeiro, the nation's capital at the time, to display them as icons of the state's triumph over the backlands, Xavante men have traveled beyond their territories to cities and, more recently in some cases, to other countries—*ö pore* (across the ocean), as Xavante say. Men have penetrated the *warazu* (non-Indigenous) world to advocate for their communities, display culture, make friends and increase their network of allies, and sometimes during the late 1960s and 1970s, to hire out for wage labor.

Beginning in the 1970s and 1980s when men traveled to Brazilian cities to advocate, first for lands and other forms of state support, they began to stage displays of Xavante culture. While cultural displays such as those pioneered by Mario Juruna in the fight to recoup stolen lands were initially staged for explicitly political purposes, men also occasionally performed for economic or material reward. Sometimes small groups of men, as few as two or even just one, put on simple displays, singing and dancing da-ño're, an expressive form to which I return below, and attempted some ethnographic explanation, if their Portuguese-speaking ability allowed (Graham 2005). Men often sang and danced in school classrooms or gymnasiums, usually without props other than their white cotton neckties, the emblems of Xavante identity, or possibly with just a swath of red *urucum* paint daubed across the forehead. On these occasions men typically performed in exchange for hand-me-down cloths, blankets or (often outdated) medicines. In several instances groups of men performed in outdoor museum spaces, usually as part of special events such as the National Indian Day (Dia do Índio) that is celebrated annually on April 19.[16] Thus, in very ad hoc ways, Xavante men have a history of staging cultural performances for non-Indigenous audiences that stretches as far back as the 1970s.

Whereas many (but not all) men enjoy traveling to Brazilian cities and sometimes beyond, thereby extending their role as mediators between worlds into foreign lands and cultures, women rarely journey beyond the Xavante region. In general, women associate travel with unpleasant experiences; sickness and death because of ill health—either their own or that of close family members whom they accompany—is frequently the motivation for their travel. Women also associate travel with social discrimination, since this unfortunately is a common experience, even in medical facilities, for any Xavante who travel in the central Brazilian region. Women's comparative lack of Portuguese-speaking ability often exacerbates the strain of regional travel.

While men mediate relations with the world "outside," women's primary concern is with domestic activities and the "inside" of Xavante social life. This simple inside/outside binary is complex, however, as it is within other Amazonian societies (see McCallum 1999). Xavante women also engage with and orient to Others, although these Others are typically on the "inside" of Xavante social life. Among Xavante—as among the Cashinuá and Araweté (McCallum 1999) and *many* other, possibly all, Amazonian groups—women cultivate gardens, collect cerrado fruits and roots, and through their culinary practices prepare and serve the foods that are exchanged with Others on the "inside" and consumed to consolidate kinship. Women also prepare raw materials, especially cotton, that are used to make items used in ceremonial exchanges and, with their bodies, nurture and manage babies and small children. McCallum's statement about gender relations among the Cashinuá and Araweté holds well for Xavante: "Women's activities endlessly constitute the inside, the space of living . . . [while] men are the inside's 'outsiders'—the hunters, warriors, in-marrying sons-in-law, [who] also represent communities to foreigners" (1999:448).

The Xavante version of an Amazonian symbolic economy of alterity is thus highly gendered.[17] Men manage exogenous relations, especially inter-actions with Others that take place "outside" of Xavante communities—in dreams, ceremonial activity, the forest, or the city—then selectively bring their knowledge and experiences of Others into "interior" space, where it is subject to comment, engagement, and potentially to transformation. Women, on the other hand, manage many aspects of alterity on the "inside" of Xavante social life through provision and nurturance. And, as we shall see through the case of Abelinha, women may engage with and also trans-form elements from the "outside" once these enter their "interior" domain.

Gender Ideologies and Performance Practice

Public ceremonial life in the community primarily revolves around male-centered ritual activities whose cyclical periodicity organizes the ceremo-nial lifecycle and also creates and expresses social formations and meaning in social life. During ceremonials, as in other central Brazilian Indigenous communities (see, e.g., Gregor 1977), the central plaza becomes a public stage where multiple sensorial modalities converge to intensify dramatic and emotional effect: fragrant and visually dramatic body paint, feather ornaments, repeated choreographed movements, and the sounds of many voices—in either song or other socialized acoustic arrangements—often including the vibration of many pounding feet.

In contrast to men, Xavante women appear infrequently in public cer-emonials, that is, ceremonials that take place in arenas that are visibly and acoustically accessible to all members of the community. Most women's activities, through their association with the domestic sphere, are not con-sidered to be appropriate for attracting public audiences. Women's expres-sive practices—weaving baskets, cooking, or stringing beads, for example—are generally appreciated for their utility and association with intimate life, and women's engagement in these activities is not considered audience worthy; their activities are not deemed intrinsically beautiful, inherent-ly worth looking at or listening to. This contrasts with ideologies of male ceremonial, which both young and senior men describe as "for elders and always living ancestors *to look at*" (Graham 1995, emphasis added). Only a few public ceremonials are specifically dedicated to females and in these, females appear in public space only briefly. In the Adaba marriage ceremonial, for example, the bride (*adaba*) makes a fleeting cameo appearance in the central plaza. Young women also sing *warnaridobe* as part of male initiation, but women play no other major publicly visible or audible role in this male-focused ceremonial complex that is a centerpiece of Xavante ritual and social life. Even in the women's naming ceremony, Pi'ō-ñitsi, the only public ceremony that is dedicated specifically to females, women publicly appear very briefly.[18]

Women and girls also participate in ceremonial sporting events, such as the *uiwede* log race and *wa'i* wrestling matches, but much less than boys and men. And, unlike their male counterparts, women and girls do not join members of their age-set cohort to sing and dance da-ño're around the village after these activities. Women and girls sing *heza*, hymns that are led by a single man, and when senior men call on them, they join men in impromptu collective da-ño're performances in the *warā* central plaza. On these occasions women sing and dance da-ño're *with* men. Thus, although they are rarely the visual or acoustic focus of public life, women are often audible in public space through, for example, tuneful laments, singing, or making aside comments or in other mediated fashion (see Graham 1993).[19] Their expressions form part of a sonorous background within an acoustic stage that centers on male expressive forms.

Da-ño're: Masculinity, Mobile Culture, and the Symbolic Management of Alterity

Much of Xavante ceremonial activity and most contemporary performances that take place outside of Xavante communities build around traditional performance genres, especially da-ño're, a collective song and dance form that men control. It is, therefore, important to have some understanding of da'ño're practice and the performance, aesthetic, and gender ideologies that inform its use in local communities. These form the context for comprehending the deployment of da-ño're in performances designed for non-Xavante spectators.

Da-ño're is a quintessentially male expressive form. Ideologies of da-ño're, performance practice, and its formal characteristics emphasize masculinity and male solidarity; moreover, da-ño're essentially expresses Xavante's male-centric symbolic economy of alterity and men's management of exogenous relations. Men control access to da-ño're through the theory that compositions are dreamed and only initiated men have earplugs (gained during male initiation), the means and therefore the ability to "receive" compositions from ancestors and spirits.[20] Men access these Others in the nether space of dreams and then, through embodied performance, bring Others' voices into Xavante social space. Women do not perform da-ño're without men.[21] Their ears are not pierced and they do not have the means to acquire dreamed songs. Senior men and the ancestors are the primary audience for da-ño're performances, although women and children see, listen to, enjoy, and comment on them. When they find a performance particularly moving, da-ño're may move elder men as well as women to weep *da-wawa*.

Da-ño're compositions are ideally suited for recontextualizations into new performance arenas because this expressive form travels within local communities. Groups of men sing and dance da-ño're on the patios of designated houses on a performance tour around the village. Groups literally move their dreamed revoicings of the Others' songs around Xavante villages when they sing: age sets from different agamous moieties travel around the village in opposite directions (see fig. 11.2). Singing groups thus circulate *within* Xavante communities such that da-ño're are displaced from one performance location to another. With da-ño're, Xavante men have a ready-made tradition of moving expressive performance into different locales.

Since da-ño're is an aesthetically valued expressive form that is mobile, repeatedly recontextualized, and "portable" within the local context, da-ño're compositions are naturally suited to travel and to move into new spaces where they can be appreciated by non-Xavante audiences.

Recontextualizing Performance in National and International Public Arenas

Eténhiritipa Pimentel Barbosa's Isari

In the mid-1990s men from Pimentel Barbosa developed several collaborative cultural projects with Angela Pappiani and Cristina Floria, two women then affiliated with the São Paulo–based Nucleu de Cultural Indígena (Nucleus of Indigenous Culture, NCI) that was brokering several development projects in the community (see Graham 2000). Among these was a

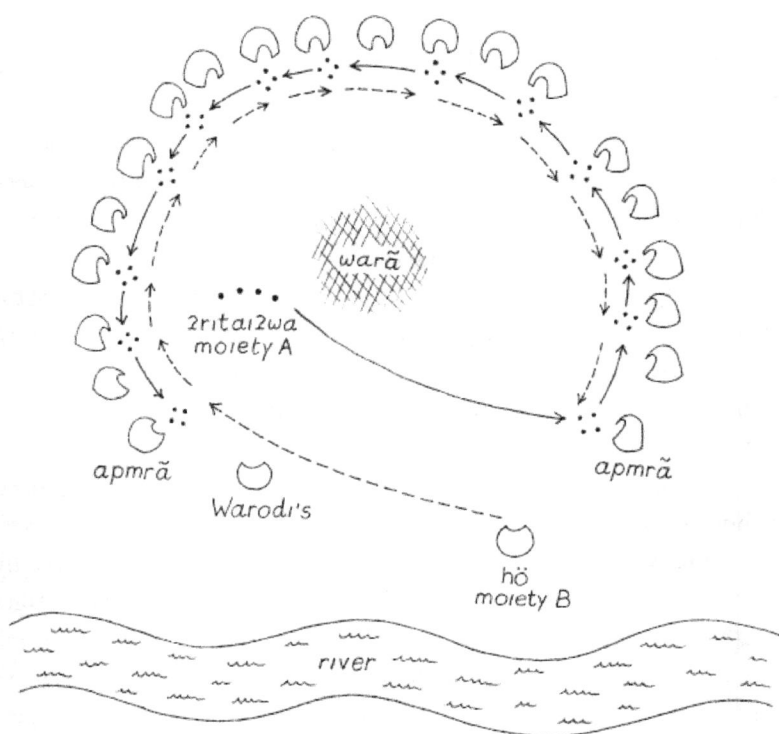

Fig. 11.2. Agamous moieties move in opposite directions around the community on their da-ño're performance tours. The hö is the bachelors' hut for moiety B. From Graham 1995.

professionally choreographed performance piece called *Isari* (Roots) that they first presented in 1998 as part of a World Music and Dance Festival in São Paulo.

Aside from the immediate rewards and gratification that come in the form of stipends, media attention, appreciative crowds, travel, and making new friends, leaders from Pimentel Barbosa have two main intangible objectives when they engage in cultural performances for non-Xavante audiences (Graham 2005). One is to project Xavante culture outward— "horizontally"—across space and cultural borders, to achieve what I have called "existential recognition." By reclaiming "representational sovereignty," they seek to make others aware of their existence and of the beauty and importance of their culture and knowledge.[22] The other objective, a primary concern of younger leaders, is to "improve Xavante's image," based on their awareness, which has come with increasing interaction with non-Indigenous Brazilians and domestic travel, that Xavante currently have a particularly poor image in the national imaginary. Elder men's humanistic desire for their knowledge and traditions to be known more broadly and younger leaders' concern with Xavante's "negative" image motivate elders and leaders to present the expressive forms that they consider to be most aesthetically pleasing. They showcase what they deem to be the most worthy, viewable, and audible expressions of Xavante culture. These are, not surprisingly, the male performance traditions that all Xavante, both men and women, so highly esteem.

In consultation with Pappiani, men selected a diverse range of expressive forms that they thought would be compelling for urban audiences. First they thought only of da-ño're, the "default" traveling form, but then, following Pappiani's suggestions, they chose a range of expressive practices that have distinctive acoustic, visual, and choreographic character and that all Xavante appreciate for their aesthetic value (Paulo Supretaprã and Suptó, personal communication, 2000). Performers change some elements of *Isari* from year to year, as Paulo explained, "to make it interesting for us [performers]." Certain expressive forms, however, consistently anchor the *Isari* spectacle. In addition to the highly masculine form, da-ño're, the dance of the Pahöri'wa is a stunning performance that appears in all *Isari* performances I have seen. Part of the elaborate male initiation ceremonial, this dance is highly appreciated for its precisely coordinated movements and for the remarkable synchronicity exhibited by the two adolescent dancers who perform it. These are occupants of the honored Pahöri'wa role. With their heads wrapped in turbans of spun cotton ornamented with two macaw feathers, the youth and the elements of costume incorporate the combined spiritual and physical essence of human beings and game animals.[23] Their dance, which is executed without musical accompaniment, represents the duality of this convergence and honors the vitality of the rising sun.

For months before the ceremony, these youth practice in seclusion with two senior Pahöri'wa, who teach them the dance movements and choreography. The senior incumbents drill the youth until they move as one. From a crouched stance, the two dancers rhythmically tap one heel, then dramatically twist their upturned heads from one side to the other as they gaze toward the sky, gracefully leaping in tandem.

During the initiation ceremony in which the Pahöri'wa is normally performed, the dancers are two adolescents. They are members of the same age set and always perform the dance as an age-matched pair. In *Isari* performances for non-Indigenous audiences, however, Pahöri'wa dancers do not necessarily belong to the same age set. In 1998, 2000, and 2001, for example, the Pahöri'wa dance was executed by a father-son team. The two performed spectacularly but their age differential violated the local performance conventions that make the dance socially intelligible and give participation its meaning in traditional contexts.

In some *Isari* performances, following a suggestion from Pappiani (Paulo, personal communication, 2000), men sometimes move what would normally be considered a "backstage" activity onto center stage. When men from Pimentel Barbosa performed as part of a multicultural bricolage called Rito de Passagem in 2000 (see Graham 2005), performers stopped their singing and dancing partway through their show to apply (more) paint to each other's bodies. In Xavante communities, preparing the body for public performance—through bloodletting, the application of body paint, and other forms of ornamentation—is not considered appropriate for public viewing. These activities take place "inside," within (or near) houses, or out of sight, in sheltered areas apart from social space.

Recontextualized performances for non-Indigenous audiences, however, have prompted men to think of body painting as an activity that, at least for warazu (non-Xavante, non-Indians), is worthy of viewing. Indeed, when non-Indigenous people visit Xavante communities, they are fascinated with body painting and take a lot of photographs. Their behavior denaturalizes the Xavante routine and causes men to think about body painting and other "nonspectacular" activities as admirable in their own right, and therefore worthy of inclusion in their externally oriented ethnographic displays.

In fact, a number of elements in *Isari* disturb local performance conventions. These disruptions indicate that when men move expressive forms—like da-ño're and Pahöri'wa—into new arenas, they think about, indeed play with, them in new and creative ways. Men are comfortable disrupting certain conventions, such as those associated with age (although only of *initiated* men), that regiment participation and create meaning in local contexts. They even incorporate some behaviors, like body painting, that—within Xavante communities—are not meant to be publicly seen.

On the other hand, men have not readily embraced the idea that women could participate in *Isari* or in other forms of externally oriented display. I submit that this is because they do not think of women's practices as worthy of audience attention. Although warazu visitors sometimes photograph women's quotidian behaviors, Xavante do not typically think of these as inherently admirable. Women's behaviors (like their bodies) are not designed, performed, or thought of as spectator-worthy activities; they are not thought of as intrinsically admirable, worthy of "being viewed" or "listened to" by elders, or the always-living ancestors, as are da-ño're and other male expressive behaviors.

In 2000 I asked an elder, Serebu'rã, if he thought women should participate in *Isari*. His wife overheard our conversation and chimed in, stating that she would. But Serebu'rã quickly dismissed the idea out of hand, stating, "Women don't know how to travel!" He had naturalized the idea that only male culture is worth viewing and believed that men naturally are the ones to travel and present.

In December 2008 three women, accompanied by Paulo Supretaprã, traveled to São Paulo for the premiere screening of the film *Pi'õ höimanazé: Mulher Xavante em sua arte* (Women's traditions: Xavante women and their art).[24] Directed by Christina Floria, the film follows twelve women at different lifecycle phases through the activities of their daily lives and across seasons. Floria, Paulo Supretaprã, and a TV station manager presented the film: they spoke about the production, how the filming was organized, and the women's participation in the process.[25] According to Floria, "[The women] had no desire to speak. Paulo [Supretaprã] spoke in their names and, as a leader and chief, in the name of the community" (personal communication, July 6, 2012). All twelve women featured in the film attended a subsequent screening in the town of Canarana, some one hundred miles from the Pimentel Barbosa Indigenous Territory. As in São Paulo, no women spoke and, in contrast to programming associated with the launching of cultural products that feature male culture, no cultural presentations formed part of either screening event (Floria, personal communication, July 5, 2012).

While both the film and the screening events were instigated and executed through Floria's initiative, men and women were enthusiastic about the projects and women's participation in them. Each activity demonstrates to Xavante men, and also to women, that women and women's culture can and does attract significant public attention and admiration in the national arena. They also show, *pace* Serebu'rã, that women can travel for cultural events. Even though these women were reluctant to speak at the screenings and despite their reported preference that a man "speak for them," their participation interrupts the pattern of men's exclusive control over outreach into domains beyond Xavante communities. However, to date women from Pimentel Barbosa have not subsequently participated in other outwardly directed activities; it appears that most Xavante people continue to naturalize men's control over externally oriented speech and cultural display and the use of male expressive forms in these activities.

Idzô'uhu Abelinha

The community of Idzô'uhu Abelinha, located in the Sangradouro Indigenous Territory (see fig. 11.1), stages representational projects that are very different from those of Pimentel Barbosa. Its programs are run by the Associação Xavante Warã (Xavante Warã Association, henceforth "Warã"), a Xavante NGO founded in 1996 to support sustainability projects in Abelinha.[26] Warã frames its campaigns within a broader politics of environmental conservation and this, I propose, opens a space for presenting a diversity of perspectives, actors, and expressive practices in performances staged for non-Indigenous audiences, including those of women and girls.

Xavante women's embrace of environmental discourses echoes women's adoption of the language of environmentalism in many regions throughout the globe. Although scholars have noted that global environmental discourses tend to flatten or essentialize the diversity within Indigenous groups (see, e.g., Braun 2002; Conklin 2006; Heatherington 2010), in many places ecological movements provide women an opportunity to bring their voices into public debates about the environment (see, e.g., Shiva 1988; see also Agarwal 1997; Tsing 1997; Garb 1997; Sturgeon 1997; Heatherington 2010).[27] The outreach work of Abelinha demonstrates further that positioning spectacles of Indigeneity within the discursive space of environmentalism presents opportunities for organizers to reflect differently on local conventions of outreach and cultural performance, including the gender associations these entail. This positioning inspires experimentation and new ways of thinking about who can perform and about which cultural practices and types of knowledge are worthy of being seen and heard by non-Indigenous audiences. It can also provide a platform from which women can speak. In Abelinha, the link to environmentalism opens space for displaying and affirming women's as well as children's specific cultural knowledge, practices, and voices.

Warã's mission, "to preserve *'ro,* the Xavante world that encompasses both the cerrado environment and Xavante culture" (Associação Warã 2010), aims to promote Xavante knowledge and ways of living in the central Brazilian cerrado and conservation of this unique biome, which Conservation International designates as one of the world's "environmental hotspots."[28] Tsõ'rebonã Ró Hã: Salve O Cerrado (Save the Cerrado), one of Warã's major campaigns, aimed to bring visibility to Xavante's sustainable lifestyle and knowledge of cerrado resources, as well as to the destruction of the cerrado resulting from the astonishing proliferation of unregulated capitalist soy agro-industry during the Amazon region's most recent economic "boom."[29] Publicity for the campaign quotes two elders, Adão Top'tiro and Thiago Tseretsu:

> The Xavante depend on the cerrado and the cerrado depends on the Xavante. The animals depend on the cerrado and the cerrado depends on the animals. The animals depend on the Xavante and the Xavante depend on the animals. This is Ró. Ró signifies everything for Xavante hunters: the cerrado, the animals, the fruits, the flowers, the fauna, the river and everything else. We want to preserve the Ró. Through the Ró, we guarantee the future of new generations: our food, wedding ceremonials, our rituals, and the strength to be Xavante.... The spirits helped us discover the secrets that are hidden within the Ró.... Xavante women continue to love the Ró; they know that as long as it exists they will be able to wed and their sons and daughters will be able to marry. (Associação Warã n.d.b; quotes given in 1999, translation mine)

In this quotation Top'tiro and Tseretsu speak the language of the "global dreamtimes of environmentalism" (Heatherington 2010). They mention the cerrado's natural and spiritual resources and people's relationship to these, thus appealing to members of a global ecological imaginary (Conklin and Graham 1995) and Occidentalist (Coronil 1997) idealizations of Indigeneity.[30] Notably, their discourse underscores that distinct sectors of Xavante society—hunters (men) and women, and also sons, daughters, and future generations—have specific relationships to 'ro.[31] Their use of environmentalist discourses underscores the diversity within Xavante society, emphasizes that distinct segments of the society relate to 'ro in different ways, and highlights Xavante's unique relationship to the cerrado. It provides a frame for talking about the cerrado and Xavante people's relationship to it in ways that are accessible and even appealing to non-Indigenous audiences. Thus, while in other contexts global environmentalist rhetorics may tend to erase the diversity among Indigenous Peoples (see, e.g., Conklin 2006) and efface the heterogeneity within Indigenous groups, Xavante from Abelinha use the language of environmentalism as a platform for showcasing internal social and cultural differences and Xavante's unique relationships to the environment. In the process, leaders and organizers go beyond typical male-centered patterns of engaging Others outside of local communities and disrupt Xavante's hypermasculine image. They present new and more complex images of Xavante people and culture to broader publics.

Hiparidi Top'tiro, Warã's founder and its leading intellectual driving force, is the primary vector for the influx of environmentalist discourses into this community. For over a decade Hiparidi lived in São Paulo, where he attended the University of São Paulo (USP), consulted with environmental NGOs (ENGOs) such as Greenpeace, took modeling and acting jobs for cash, and founded Warã and then managed its projects.[32] Hiparidi became well versed in the global language of environmentalism and is intimately familiar with romanticizations and "Occidentalist" stereotypes of Indigeneity, as well as the double binds that these entail (see Graham 2014; see also Oakdale 2009a). Hiparidi developed a discourse that champions Xavante's coexistence with the threatened cerrado habitat and opposes the destruction wrought by unregulated capitalist soy agribusiness (see Top'tiro 2009). Under Hiparidi's leadership Warã drew on this discourse to secure funding for Abelinha's projects from ENGOs, including Rainforest Action Network (RAN), and from "green businesses" such as the domestic cosmetics company FitoErvas.

Among individuals Hiparidi credits for inspiration and significant influence is his mother, Batika Dzutsi'wa. She, along with several other female relatives, helped shape Warã's vision to include female perspectives, concerns, and activities. These women, as well as several dedicated non-Indigenous women, have been instrumental in a number of projects that validate women's knowledge and practices in relation to the cerrado.[33] Flores e Frutas do Cerrado (Cerrado Fruits and Flowers) documented women's knowledge and practices related to cerrado foods and plants and sought to recoup these for future generations. The Parteira project focused on midwives, specifically their knowledge and use of cerrado plants and herbs in pregnancy, gestation, and birth (Gomide and Lima n.d.).

For political and tactical inspiration Hiparidi credits Mario Juruna, the famous leader from São Marcos who, in the 1970s and early 1980s, strategically coupled political demands with theatrical cultural display during the fight for land and earned national and international celebrity. Like Juruna, Hiparidi is pragmatic about cultural display but cautious about celebrity's potential to "seduce" and sidetrack from Warã's guiding political mission. Since the beginning of the new millennium, Hiparidi is taking on nothing less than the powerful multinational agro-industry and the Brazilian state—seeking protections for Xavante and the environment and more land.

Hiparidi and other leaders from Abelinha envision cultural display as a powerful didactic instrument, especially for youth, and as an effective way to attract public attention that can then be used as a platform to educate non-Indigenous audiences about Abelinha, Xavante culture, and sustainable lifestyles.[34] Having achieved the spotlight, they can advocate for Warã's campaigns and political causes while simultaneously disseminating information about the cerrado environment and the challenges that Xavante and other contemporary Indigenous peoples face. Thinking pragmatically about cultural spectacle and display, Hiparidi sometimes uses these as means to earn money for projects.

Relocating expressive performance within Warã's environmental and cultural politics has led Hiparidi and others from Abelinha to think in novel ways about which Xavante practices are appropriate for presentation to Brazilian audiences, as well as who should participate. Rather than automatically defaulting to those practices that Xavante think of as spectacular or "audience worthy," as in Pimentel Barbosa, the men and women of

Abelinha start with their use of cerrado resources. They then contemplate what practices and whose "culture" showcase their relationships with these resources. As a result, gender, and also age, figure into Abelinha's cultural performances for non-Indigenous audiences in completely differently ways than in displays staged by other Xavante groups.

Whereas Pimentel Barbosa's performances feature initiated (adult) men and male culture almost exclusively and never (at least to date) present children, Abelinha's performances include women and women's culture whenever possible, and often also children. In 2003, at the University of São Paulo's 2003 Environment Week (Semana do Meio Ambiente), women from Abelinha held two of the most popular and well-attended public workshops: one on cerrado herbs and medicinal treatments, the other on Xavante basket weaving. Even though the senior women who held these workshops speak little Portuguese, they spoke by and for themselves. Without men acting as spokespersons, translators, or mediators, they demonstrated their elaborate knowledge and unique use of cerrado resources. The women ably interacted with participants and communicated their messages. Hiparidi's sister, Bernadete, who has a master's degree in Indigenous education and is a teacher in Abelinha, spoke in one of the meeting's academic sessions. This was the first time that a Xavante woman had participated in an academic panel at a major university. Her participation represents a major departure from typical gender protocols. Xavante men and women also sang and danced da-ño're at the opening act for Environment Week's final event: a large open-air concert featuring the nationally famous singer Marlui Miranda.

Organizers from Abelinha also make a point of including children in cultural outreach as much as possible (see also Goodman 2005). According to Hiparidi, these experiences are important opportunities that enable Xavante children to understand the contemporary world they live in. He and other leaders view these experiences as essential to the formation of a new generation of leaders. "Ai'utéto: Brincadeiras de criança: Um intercâmbio cultural entre crianças" (Children's Games: A Children's Cultural Exchange), held in the city of Goiânia, Goias in 2001, was one of Warã's early outreach activities; this program complemented a Warã-designed museum exhibit, *Viver a vida Xavante* (Living the Xavante life), that featured Xavante's use of cerrado resources. Xavante children demonstrated games using cerrado resources and then played these with city children, who could also have their faces painted with Xavante designs. According to the event's brochure, "Using cultural exchange, this pedagogical activity for children seeks to awaken interest and respect for Brazil's cultural and environmental diversity" (Associação Warã n.d.a).

In 2002 Warã installed another museum exhibit in Jataí, Goiais.[35] Again Xavante boys and girls traveled to the city along with men and women. In a week-long series of activities coordinated by educational psychologist Xanda de Biase, Xavante children learned about city life.[36] They visited a park and a water treatment facility, reflected on the contrasting organization of social space in urban versus Xavante communities, and contemplated why parks and water treatment are important in urban zones.

The Xavante kids also shared typical children's games and activities with school groups that visited the museum exhibit. They taught their city counterparts to play a stick game in which two individuals grasp and pull, in opposite directions, forked sticks that are hooked together. In tug-of-war fashion opponents attempt to drag each other over a line drawn in the dirt. In one especially lively match a Xavante girl hauled a much larger non-Indigenous boy across the line. Their match prompted a great deal of gender teasing on both sides and was great fun for all participants and spectators (see fig. 11.3). The children also played the *oi'o* club fight and, even though oi'o is traditionally played only by boys, the organizers included girls as well. The children's cultural exchange was designed to demonstrate to urban audiences, especially children, that Xavante children live and play in the cerrado, using cerrado resources. Throughout the week girls and boys also sang and danced da-ño're together with men and women.

The people of Abelinha/Warã frequently locate cultural spectacles in "unexpected" urban spaces (Deloria 2004), and this also distinguishes Abelinha's work from that of Pimentel Barbosa, which uses a professionally designed set and lighting to create a simulacra of village space (see Graham 2005). Hiparidi intentionally creates "cultural disjunctures" to disrupt romanticized notions that locate Indigenous Peoples in remote, "natural" contexts. Disrupting romanticized images of Indigenous people is a tactic for avoiding the "double binds" of idealized Indigeneity or the pitfalls of the "authenticity trap."[37] Hiparidi exploits this potential to its fullest.

Fig. 11.3. Tseredzadze Gonçalino Xavante drags a Brazilian boy in a forked-stick tug-of-war match as part of a children's event in Jataí, Goias. Photo by the author (2004).

Among the most striking and disruptive displays of Indigeneity that Warã staged was an event that Hiparidi coordinated in São Paulo in 2004 and repeated in 2005. Xavante from Abelinha challenged a group of Krahô, another Gê group from the neighboring state of Tocantins, to a ceremonial log race. Instead of running the log from the forest into the community's central plaza, however, the barefoot runners cantered down the Avenida Paulista, the South American equivalent of Wall Street.[38] Avenida Paulista is the financial heart of Brazil, South America's largest economy, and home to some of the world's largest financial institutions. As the symbolic hub of South American capitalism, the point where multinational capital converges in Brazil, this was an ideal spot for Indigenous activists to bring attention to their complaint against the internationally financed agricultural industry, the soy industry in particular. At the site of this financial epicenter, barefoot Xavante and Krahô runners, decorated with body paint and other adornments and carrying two-hundred-pound tree trunks, shouted encouragement as they ran through the shadows of towering skyscrapers that housed huge multinationals.

Xavante women as well as men shared the media spotlight at the Avenida Paulista event. Women ran their own log race and, like the men, attracted journalists' microphones and cameras during their preparations. After the races—which, to the Xavante's chagrin, the Krahô won—the men sang and danced. The Krahô sang first; then Xavante performed daño're.[39] Surrounded by curious onlookers, several of the younger women nursed their babies as they watched the men perform. An advocate then stepped up to the stage and spoke out against agro-industry and environmental destruction.

Since the late the 1990s, Warã outreach projects have included women and children almost annually. Whereas the focus on aesthetics and authenticity prompts leaders in Pimentel Barbosa to default to male-centric expressive forms and practices for managing exogenous relations, the discourse of environmentalism adopted by leadership in Abelinha stimulates people to rethink conventional gender roles and forms of cultural expression as well as participation in public outreach work. Women, girls, and boys envision their practices and knowledge as "culture" that is worthy of display. They also see themselves as cultural ambassadors and advocates for Xavante as well as for 'ro.

These experiences, in which "nontraditional" performers travel to Brazilian cities to participate in exchange activities and displays of cultural forms that—in local contexts—are not thought of as "spectator worthy," are changing ways that people from Abelinha think about travel, cultural spectacle, and outreach. Women, girls, and boys look forward to future opportunities to represent themselves and Xavante culture to non-Indigenous Brazilians and to engage with Others in new arenas. Betina, a nine-year-old girl, told me in 2004 that she had been on two trips, one to Goiânia and another to São Paulo. "Wa za mo duré!" (I will go again!), she added enthusiastically. How different her experiences are from those of Serebu'rã's wife in Pimentel Barbosa, whose desire to travel and participate was dismissed out of hand. Betina's remarks echo those of many other women and children from Abelinha with whom I spoke. She fully expects to participate and to represent her community to warazu in the future. Her participation, along with that of other girls, boys, and women, contributes to painting a more complex and diverse profile that contrasts with Xavante's highly masculine profile in the national imaginary. It also paints a more complex eth-

Fig. 11.4. Hiparidi Top'tiro speaks with a reporter at the Warā-sponsored log relay race competition against the Krahô that took place in 2004 on Avenida Paulista in São Paulo's financial district. Photo by the author (2004).

Fig. 11.5. Xavante and Krahô racers relay two-hundred-pound logs along São Paulo's Avenida Paulista. Photo courtesy of Sylvia Caiuby Novaes (2004).

Fig. 11.6. Dilza Xavante, from Maria Auxiliadora village in the Sangradouro/Volta Grande Indigenous Territory, runs the uiwede log race along São Paulo's Avenida Paulista. Photo courtesy of Sylvia Caiuby Novaes (2004).

nographic portrait of Xavante interactions with the cerrado, for it depicts different sectors of the society engaging 'ro in very distinct ways. Finally, it suggests that females may begin to play more prominent roles in presenting and re-presenting Xavante and to engage with non-Xavante Others in new and different ways.

Situating performance within the context of environmentalism breaks the default pattern of Xavante male-dominated ethnographic performance and men's exclusive management of relationships outside of the local context. It provides a space that enables women to enter into new contexts and relationships and to represent and speak for themselves in new arenas, and it offers the opportunity for community members to showcase a diversity of actors as well as expressive practices and social forms. Together, men, women, boys, and girls present a complex and heterogeneous profile of Xavante to the world beyond and also to themselves. As people from this community shift toward new modes of engaging non-Xavante Others, they are altering Xavante's hypermasculine image in the national imaginary, and possibly among other Xavante as well.

In recent years native lowland South American women have gained increasing presence in national and even international arenas. Some women have achieved prominent leadership roles in national politics. In the Bolivarian Republic of Venezuela, for example, Noeli Pocaterra (Wayuu) and Maria Andarcia (Kariña) hold seats in the national Congress.[40] Nicia Maldonado, who is Ye'Kuana, is Venezuela's minister of Indigenous Peoples. In Ecuador native Amazonian women have significant presence in public demonstrations for environmental protections and rights, especially against oil (see Sawyer 2004).[41] In Brazil women are also increasingly active in Indigenous organizations; a number have achieved significant prominence and assumed important leadership roles. Sônia Bone Guajajara, for example, is coordinator of the Association of Brazilian Indigenous Peoples (Articulação dos Povos Indígenas do Brasil, APIB), a leading Indigenous organization, and Miriam Terena, director of the Conselho Nacional de Mulheres (National Women's Council), has organized multiple Indigenous women's meetings (see Instituto Socioambiental 2003). As this book goes into production, Almerinda Ramo's (Tariana) election to the presidency of the Federation of Indigenous Organizations of the Rio Negra (FIORIN) (Crítica Amazônia 2012) has just been announced. These women, among others, represent new forms of Native Amazonian women's leadership and novel ways of engaging with the world "outside."[42]

Since the mid-1990s people from Pimentel Barbosa and Abelinha have developed highly innovative cultural outreach projects that underscore Xavante's willingness and ability to engage in self-reflexive practices and connect with Others outside their communities in new and creative ways. These projects differ in significant respects, particularly in relation to women's participation, the showcasing of women's culture, and also women's participation in speaking roles.

The work of each community is, nevertheless, informed by a dynamic interplay between male-centered ideologies and practices for the mediation and management of alterity that intersects with men and women's creative, dialogic engagement with the new ideas, knowledge, discursive and expressive forms, and technologies (and sometimes Other beings) that men selectively bring into Xavante communities. Initiated men venture out into spaces inhabited by Others, at least initially, and, as in the case of dreamed da-ño're songs, bring elements of the Other into local communities. Once "imported" to the "inside," expressive resources, new forms of knowledge, technologies, discursive forms, and ideas, including Others' ideas of Xavante, are subject to reflection, comment, engagement, and transformation by both men and women together.

The emphasis on aesthetics and existential recognition in Pimentel Barbosa has led to creative innovations and the generation of new cultural images in the presentation of male culture. In Abelinha, the flexibility and readiness to incorporate new "outside" elements generates even more than new cultural images: it changes the conditions of possibility for who among Xavante may incorporate new cultural forms and knowledge and how, as well as who may reach out, and in what ways. This creates new opportunities for women to expand into new arenas, and in unprecedented ways.

Male-imported environmentalist discourses in Abelinha have opened a space for women, as well as men, to engage these discourses, and also to reflect on their specific relation to the cerrado and its resources as "Xavante culture." Furthermore, even though reaching out to Others beyond local communities is not the norm for women, as the work of Pimentel Barbosa suggests, because women do orient in Other-centric ways within communities, they also may readily adapt to presenting new cultural images and images of culture to novel Others. Women's participation in Xavante's Other-centric logic even entails the possibility for women to establish new positions from which to speak, as Bernadete and other women from Abelinha demonstrate.

Men and women from Abelinha adopt the language of environmentalism not because of its connection to any "ethnic essence" but because of its relational appeal. Through it, men and women forge connections and linkages with novel Others and enter into new and broader communities, Indigeneity, and the "global ecological imaginary." Ultimately environmental discourse opens space for men and women from Abelinha to engage non-Indigenous publics in new ways, to showcase a diversity of actors, and to present new and more complex images of their "culture" to Others, as well as to themselves. These performances are beginning to change Xavante's hypermasculine image in the national imaginary. As part of this innovative process women are finding new positions for speaking. All of this is possible because of Xavante creativity and fundamentally Other-centric ways of being.

Acknowledgments

My research on Xavante cultural outreach has been generously supported with a fellowship from the National Endowment for the Humanities and a University of Iowa Global Scholar Award. I am indebted to Grant Arndt, Christopher Ball, Janet Chernela, Tracey Heatherington, Jean Jackson, Glenn Penny, T. M. Scruggs, and anonymous reviewers for careful readings and helpful comments on previous drafts of this chapter. I have also greatly benefited from comments and discussions on earlier versions and issues raised in this chapter at talks presented at the University of California campuses at Davis and Berkeley, at the University of Texas at Austin, and at the annual meetings of the American Anthropological Association. Most of all, I deeply appreciate the patience, insights, and friendship of Xavante people who have been my interlocutors and collaborators over the years.

Notes

1. Gal is careful to point out the cross-cultural multivalence of such silence, cautioning against universalizing feminist interpretations of powerlessness.

2. When she was twelve years old Yasani Kalapalo and her family moved to the city where Yasani pursued her formal education. She speaks both Kalapalo and Portuguese. Tuira made her protest speeches in Kayapó. For discussion of the politics of language choice, speech, and Indigeneity, see Graham 2002.

3. With regard to gender and Indigeneity in the Latin American context, Diane Nelson (2001, 2006) suggests that women serve as "prosthetics" in the Guatemalan Maya cultural rights movement. Stéphanie Rousseau (2011) and Patricia Richards (2004) demonstrate that Indigenous women have advanced their causes in Bolivia and Chile, respectively, through collaboration with national women's movements. For discussion of gender politics in the Zapatista movement in Chiapas, see Stephen 2005:282–323; Speed et al. 2006; see also Speed 2008:118–35. Guzmán (2013:30) observes that women are now at the forefront of the Brazilian Indigenous movement.

4. One possible explanation for the lack of scholarly critique may be scholarship's potential to be cited and used against these often-fragile movements in attempts to undermine their legitimacy (see Brosius 1999:180–81). Further, at least in the case of the Brazilian Amazon, where Indigenous Peoples have been prolific in their displays of difference, scholars themselves may also uncritically accept that men's roles as leading mediators between worlds naturally translate to male dominance in autoethnographic display and representation to the world "outside."

5. For the remainder of this chapter I adopt the Portuguese names for these communities, which Xavante use in interactions with Brazilian nationals: Pimentel Barbosa for Eténhiritipa and Abelinha for Idzö'uhu. The referent of Eténhiritipa Pimentel Barbosa is complicated by the fact that the original Eténhiritipa, known in Portuguese as Pimentel Barbosa, fissioned in 2007. Two distinct communities now claim the name Eténhiritipa, and the new community even legally registered itself as Eténhiritipa. Since most of the research for this study was carried out before the establishment of the new community, I here refer to the original community that encompassed members of what are now two distinct villages.

   With regard to the spelling of other Xavante words, there is no standardized Xavante orthography and different communities adopt their own versions. For proper names I use the spelling used by named individuals and their associated communities. For other terms, such as *warazu/waradzu*, I adopt the form used in Pimentel Barbosa. The exception is my use of *ñ*, for nasal alveolar stop, which Xavante consistently write as "nh." My choice here is guided by consistency, as I have used *ñ* in my other English publications.

6. On Indigeneity as display of difference, see, e.g., Hall 1997; Conklin 1997; Comaroff and Comaroff 2009; see also Hodgson, this volume.

7. In discussing decontextualization and recontextualization of expressive performance, I draw on linguistic anthropologists' use of these terms for discussing the movement of discourse and texts (see Bauman and Briggs 1990; Silverstein and Urban 1996). Others, such as Myers (2002), discuss similar processes in the movement of material culture, such as visual arts.

8. Recognizing the complexity of the notion of "tradition" (see, e.g., Hobsbawm and Ranger 1984), I use the term here to refer to socially situated practices that Xavante perform repeatedly to create a sense of continuity, even as each new performance is itself a creative act that embodies the potential for change (see Graham 1995). Xavante identify such practices as "da-höimanazé" and translate this term into Portuguese as "tradition" or "culture" (see Graham 2005:629).

9. According to Embraer, "The name [Xavante] was given in honor of *the pre-Columbian* native Brazilian warrior tribe" (Embraer Historical Center 2010, emphasis added).

10. The media-celebrated contact focused on the Indian Protection Service's efforts to enter into peaceful relations with a single Xavante group, the one that resided in the area near what are now the Indigenous Territories of Pimentel Barbosa and Wedezé. The entire Xavante contact spanned nearly twenty years. For excellent descriptions of the entire contact, see Lopes da Silva 1992; see also Garfield 2001; Gomide 2008.

11. In 1982 Juruna was elected to the national congress and became the first, and so far only, Indigenous leader to hold national office in Brazil. For further discussion of Juruna, see Juruna et al. 1982; Maybury-Lewis 1991; Conklin and Graham 1995; Ramos 1998; Graham 1995:46–47, 2011; Garfield 2004; Hemming 2003.

12. In the late 1970s and 1980s the state implemented monoculture (rice) agricultural projects to justify the return of portions of Xavante lands and to demonstrate that these would contribute to the region's capitalist economy. These projects were an immense failure: they drained the state of substantial financial and human resources, stimulated the division of Xavante communities, and increased Xavante dependence on the state. The projects terminated in the late 1980s. For more extensive discussion of the "Xavante Projects," see Graham 1995:44–61; Garfield 2001:187–221; Coimbra et al. 2002:86–87, 175–78, 183–84.

13. Inspired by Hugh-Jones's (1992) proposal that making such demands is constitutive of social relations in the Colombian Vaupés (see also Ball 2012, in press; Rodriguez 2012), I understand Xavante men's demands as fulfilling a strategy of elicitation not of goods first but of exchange relations through which services can be articulated. Ball (2012) examines how similar processes operate in interactions with representatives of international development agencies. He argues that complaint and ideological processes that structure Wauja exchange relations often clash with national and international development ideologies that are relatively more focused on ends and results. A similar clash is evident in media coverage of Xavante appetites and demands for goods and services (see Graham 1995:58, 2001).

Basic social services such as sanitation, basic health care, and elementary education are sorely lacking in many and virtually nonexistent in most Xavante communities. Infant mortality is substantially above the national average in areas where studies have been conducted. Only 86 percent of children survive to age ten (Sousa and Santos 1999:16; see also Ávila-Dresser 1993:10). For further discussion of health conditions in Xavante communities, see Coimbra et al. 2002.

14. Elite media's treatment of Xavante exemplifies its manipulation of both elements of the Enlightenment-derived Noble Savage trope according to elite agendas. For discussion of other examples, see Conklin and Graham 1995; Graham 2011; Slater 2010. For discussion of mass media and its affiliation with elite business, see Smith 1997; see also Graham 2011.

15. Metcalf (2005) categorizes go-betweens into three types: physical or biological go-betweens create material links and include carriers of plants, animals, and disease and bearers of children of mixed race; transactional go-betweens are individuals who facilitate social interaction and include translators, culture brokers, and negotiators of various sorts; representational go-betweens are those who represent the "other" culture through texts, words, or images (see 2005:12 specifically). Metcalf observes that, in many cases, these categories overlap.

16. In one exceptional and highly visible performance organized by Mario Juruna in 1975, a group from São Marcos performed at the Teatro Nacional (National Theater) in São Paulo.

17. Gender is a fundamental organizing principle for Xavante notions of and management of alterity, *pace* Vilaça (2011:244), who asserts that gender plays "a much more central role in the anthropological understanding of Melanesian sociality"

than it does in Amazonia, where the human/nonhuman distinction encompasses gender (see also McCallum 2013, in press).

18. In most communities the female naming ceremony Pi'õ-ñitsi, which involves extramarital relations, has been abandoned. Missionaries discouraged it and non-missionized communities gradually ceased practicing it in postcontact years. I observed parts of it in 1987 when it was last performed in Pimentel Barbosa, the only community that had continually maintained it since contact. Pi'õ-ñitsi is now experiencing a revival in some communities, such as Abelinha. Camilia Cerqueira de Gauditano (2006) documents the women's recollections of their naming ceremonies in Pimentel Barbosa.

19. Unlike some Native Amazonian societies in which women use specific expressive forms—such as lament, song, and "back talk" (Briggs 1992, 1993; Chernela 2003, 2011, 2012a) or aside commentary on chiefly discourse (Ireland 2008)—to publicly make social critiques, there is no gender-specific expressive form or context available to Xavante women. Women do not participate in warã men's council meetings. Like men, women sing da-wawa tuneful laments and, although these are publicly audible, they are associated with the most intimate spheres of social life and do not transmit propositions (see Graham 1986).

20. Men explain that earplugs are "like antennae" (see Graham 1994, 1995). For further discussion of da-ño're and its formal characteristics, ideology, and performance practice, as well as how these constitute and display masculinity and male solidarity, see Graham 1994, 1995; see also Aytai 1985; Fuscaldo 2011.

21. In nearly thirty years of fieldwork in Xavante communities, I have witnessed only one extraordinary event in which women performed a woman's dreamed da-ño're (Graham 2003).

As part of the male initiation ceremonies, women perform *wanaridobe* without men, as mentioned above, but this is not a dreamed song. Xavante ancestors appropriated wanaridobe from the Karajá, whom they spied performing it the night before a surprise attack (Hiparidi Top'tiro, personal communication, 2006). Xavante's incorporation of the Karajá wanaridobe into their expressive repertoire is a Xavante articulation of Amazonian perspectivism or symbolic economy of alterity, their way of incorporating an element of the Other into the collective (Viveiros de Castro 1992; Vilaça 2010).

22. Considering the importance of multiple sensorial modalities in Xavante moves to assume control over ways their image circulates in public spaces, I expand Raheja's (2010) formulation of Native American moves to reclaim "visual sovereignty" in film.

23. The ornaments added to the human body signify physical and spiritual animal essence. Dancers in *Isari* are not fully adorned with all elements of the Pahöri'wa regalia.

24. Xavante practice sororal poloygamy. The three women who traveled to São Paulo for the film premiere are sisters and Paulo Supretaprã's wives.

25. They presented the film at CineSece, a movie theater run by a state-funded public arts and leisure venue known as SESC TV. SESC's manager joined Floria and Supretaprã to present the film.

26. Since its founding, the scope of Warã's projects and objectives have expanded significantly. It now works to benefit people in all Xavante territories.

27. Environmental disruption and conservation efforts have profound effects on gender relationships (see West et al. 2006:260–61). Ecological destruction and preservation campaigns often provide opportunities for women to form new alliances, step outside of local frameworks that define self and identity, and create platforms for women to constitute themselves in new ways (see, e.g., Sundberg 2004; West et al. 2006). Well-documented examples are women's involvement in campaigns in India to stop deforestation and construction of a dam in the Chipko region (see, e.g., Shiva 1988; Srinivasan 2004).

28. According to Conservation International, environmental hotspots are "the richest and most threatened reservoirs of plant and animal life on Earth" (Conservation International 2011).

29. The Amazonian region has a long history of economic boom-and-bust cycles, each accompanied by devastating social and environmental consequences (see, e.g., Weinstein 1983; Grandin 2009). For further discussion of the soy boom and its effect on Xavante and other Indigenous people in Brazil's cerrado, see, e.g., Top'tiro 2009; Graham 2009.

30. "Occidentalism" is the term coined by Fernando Coronil (1997:xi) to refer to "representational practices whose effect is to present non-Western peoples as the Other of a Western self." Alcida Ramos aptly applies this term to notions of Indigeneity (2003:356).

31. "Sons' and daughters'" weddings depend on the cerrado's abundance because wedding ceremonials involve the exchange of gendered foods, such as game and corn cakes, that represent the contributions that each party will bring to the new couple's family.

32. For further biographical information on Hiparidi and his autobiographical reflections, see Graham 2014.

33. Among influential non-Indigenous women who have worked with Hiparidi and on Warã campaigns are Xanda de Biase, Mariana Kawall Leal Ferreira, Helena de Biase, Daniela Lima, Maria Lucia Gomide, and me.

34. Howard Morphy (2006) observes similar practices among Australian Aboriginals.

35. Hiparidi chose Jataí because, like Goiânia, it is a hub of cattle ranching and agroindustry.

36. Xanda de Biase was Hiparidi's wife at the time.

37. Beth Conklin (2006) notes that another way that Indigenous Peoples avoid "the entrapments of idealized environmental visions" is to reframe themselves as bearers of unique knowledge as opposed to environmental stewards, especially when

Indigenous Peoples act in ways that environmentalists see as ecologically destructive.

38. Warã organized this log-race challenge for two years during the mayorship of Marta Suplicy (2001–4), a member of the Workers' Party. During her term, Suplicy closed traffic along Avenida Paulista on Sundays and opened it for cultural activities. Warã obtained permission to hold the log-race challenge and had access to a public stage for musical activities as part of its event (see "Marta Suplicy," Academic Dictionaries and Encyclopedias, http://en.academic.ru/dic.nsf/enwiki/508312, accessed June 24, 2010).

39. Because no Krahô women attended the event, the Xavante women divided into two teams that ran against each other (carrying slightly less heavy logs than the men carried). No Xavante women spoke directly to journalists and only a few of the senior men, who spoke relatively good Portuguese, entertained journalists' questions.

40. The constitution of the Bolivarian Republic of Venezuela designates seats specifically for Indigenous people.

41. Michael Cepek (personal communication, 2012) notes that he has witnessed many protests "in which equal numbers of Huaorani, Cofán, Siona, Secoya, and Napo Runa men and women are present" but none in which women have special prominence or leadership roles. There is precedent for Native women's participation in Ecuadorian national civic life: several Indigenous women from the Andean region, such as Nina Picari, occupy important positions in national Indigenous movements and in government. The context of environmentalism may well be, as I suggest below, more relevant to these women's involvement in public events than the participation of Andean women in Ecuadorian civic life.

42. Sônia Bone Guajajara, from Maranhão state, is recognized as a powerful spokeswoman for Brazil's Indigenous movement (see, e.g., Amazon Watch 2014). Prior to becoming the national coordinator of Brazil's Association of Indigenous Peoples (APIB) she was vice coordinator of the Network of Indigenous Organizations of the Brazilian Amazon (Coordenação das Organizações Indígenas da Amazônia, COIAB). In addition to Guajajara a number of other women are now among nationally visible Indigenous leaders in Brazil. Tracey Devine Guzmán (2013:254n12) notes (in alphabetical order by first name) Azelene Kaingang, Eliane Potiguara, Graça Graúna, Lúcia Fernanda Kaingang, Yasani Kalapalo. Janet Chernela (2012a, in press) underscores the importance of the Association of Women from the Upper Rio Negro (Associação das Mulheres do Alto Rio Negro, AMARN), founded in 1982 by Tukanoan women living in Manaus, where they worked in domestic service. She notes that AMARN has the significant distinction of being the oldest official Indigenous association in Brazil that is still in existence and that women from AMARN were also active in the creation of COIAB in 1989 and were a driving force in establishing COIAB's Department of Women (Departamento de Mulheres Indígenas da Amazônia Brasileira, DMI-AB). See Chernela 2012a:107; Bernal 2003; Trindade Serra 2008.

Bibliography

Agarwal, Bina

1997 Gender Perspectives on Environment and Action: Issues of Equity, Agency, and Participation. *In* Transitions, Environments, Translations. Joan Scott, ed. Pp. 189–225. New York: Routledge.

Amazon Watch

2014 Profiles: Sônia Guajara, a Powerful Voice for Brazil's Indigenous Peoples. March 10. http://amazonwatch.org/news/2014/0310-sonia-guajajara-a-powerful -voice-for-brazils-indigenous-peoples, accessed March 24, 2014.

Associação Warã

2010 Associação Warã website. http://wara.nativeweb.org/associacao.html, accessed June 11.

n.d.a Ai'utéto: Brincadeiras de Criança. Publicity flier.

n.d.b Tsõ'rebõnã Ró Hã: Salve o Cerrado. Publicity for a campaign and exhibit held in Parque Agua Branca, São Paulo, November 20, 1999–January 2000.

Ávila-Desser, N.

1993 Projeto de assistência medico-sanitária e de formação de agents communitários de sáude para tribos Xavante e Bororo: Estado de Mato Grosso, Brasil, Nova Xavantina e Barra do Garças. Unpublished report. Rio de Janeiro: Médicos Sem Fronteiras.

Aytai, Desiderio

1985 O Mundo Sonoro Xavante. Museu Paulista, Etnologia, vol. 5. São Paulo: Universidade de São Paulo.

Ball, Christopher

2012 Stop Loss: Developing Interethnic Relations in Brazil's Xingu Indigenous Park. Journal of Latin American and Caribbean Anthropology 17(3):413–34.

In press Exchanging Words: Language, Ritual, and Relationality in Brazil's Xingu Indigenous Park. Unpublished manuscript.

Bauman, Richard, and Charles L. Briggs

1990 Poetics and Performance as Critical Perspectives on Language and Social Life. Annual Review of Anthropology 19:59–88.

Beckman, Michael (director and producer)

1989 Kayapó II: Out of the Forest. In collaboration with consulting anthropologist Terence Turner. Grenada Films.

Bernal, Roberto Jaramillo

2003 Indiens urbains: Processus de reconformation de l'identité ethnique indienne à Manaus. PhD dissertation, Ecole des Hautes Etudes en Sciences Sociales, Université de Paris.

Bianchi, Sergio (director)

2000 Cronicamente Inviável. 101 min. http://www.osfilmes.com.br /cronicamente/, accessed June 29, 2010.

Braun, Bruce

2002 The Intemperate Rainforest: Culture and Power on Canada's West Coast. Minneapolis: University of Minnesota Press.

Briggs, Charles

1992 "Since I am a woman, I will chastise my relatives": Gender, Reported Speech, and the (Re)production of Social Relations in Warao Ritual Wailing. American Ethnologist 19(2):337–61.

1993 Personal Sentiments and Polyphonic Voices in Warao Women's Ritual Wailing: Music and Poetics in a Critical and Collective Discourse. American Anthropologist 95(4):929–57.

Brosius, Peter

1999 On the Practice of Transnational Cultural Critique. Identities 6(2–3):179–200.

Bruner, Edward, and Barbara Kirshenblatt-Gimblett

1994 Maasai on the Lawn: Tourist Realism in East Africa. Cultural Anthropology 9(2):435–70. Reprinted in Edward M. Bruner, Culture on Tour: Ethnographies of Travel, pp. 33–70. Chicago: University of Chicago Press.

Cerqueira, Camila Gauditano de

2006 Zöomo'ri: A construção da pessoa e a produção de gênero na concepção Xavante; Wederã, Pimentel Barbosa, Etenhiritipá. MA thesis, Anthropology Department, Faculdade de Filosofia, Letras e Ciências Humanas, Universidade de São Paulo.

Chernela, Janet

2003 Language Ideology and Women's Speech: Talking Community in the Northwest Amazon. American Anthropologist 105(4):1–13.

2011 The Second World of Wanano Women: Truth, Lies, and Back-Talk in the Brazilian Northwest Amazon. Journal of Linguistic Anthropology 21(2):193–210.

2012a Indigenous Rights and Ethno-Development: The Life of an Indigenous Organization in the Rio Negro of Brazil. Tipití: Journal of the Society for the Study of Lowland South America 9(2):92–120.

2012b Mascarading the Voice: Texts of the Self in Brazilian Northwest Amazon. Journal of Anthropological Research 68:315–38.

In press Directions of Existence: Indigenous Women Domestics in the Paris of the Tropics. Journal of Latin American and Caribbean Anthropology.

Clifford, James

1997 Routes: Travel and Translation in the Late Twentieth Century. Cambridge MA: Harvard University Press.

Coimbra, Carlos E. A., Jr., Nancy M. Flowers, Francisco M. Salzano, and Ricardo V. Santos

2002 Xavante in Transition: Health, Ecology, and Bioanthropology in Central Brazil. Ann Arbor: University of Michigan Press.

Comaroff, Jean, and John Comaroff

2009 Ethnicity Inc. Chicago: University of Chicago Press.

Conklin, Beth A.

1997 Body Paint, Feathers, and VCRs: Aesthetics and Authenticity in Amazonian Activism. American Ethnologist 24(4):711–37.

2002 Shamans versus Pirates in the Amazonian Treasure Chest. American Anthropologist 104(4):1050–61.

2006 Environmentalism, Global Community, and the New Indigenism. In Inclusion and Exclusion in the Global Arena. M. Kirsch, ed. Pp. 161–76. London: Routledge.

Conklin, Beth A., and Laura R. Graham

1995 The Shifting Middle Ground: Amazonian Indians and Eco-Politics. American Anthropologist 97(4):695–710.

Conservation International

2011 "Biodiversity Hotspots," "Where We Work: Cerrado," and biodiversity map. http://www.biodiversityhotspots.org/Pages/default.aspx, http://www.conservation.org/where/priority_areas/hotspots/south_america/Cerrado/Pages/default.aspx, and http://www.conservation.org/where/priority_areas/hotspots/Documents/CI_Biodiversity-Hotspots_2013_Map.pdf, accessed June 28.

Coronil, Fernando

1997 The Magical State: Nature, Money, and Modernity in Venezuela. Chicago: University of Chicago Press.

Correio Brasiliense

1987 Indian Fight Costs FUNAI Dearly: Xavante Depart but Leave Bills to Be Investigated by Federal Police. September 20.

1996 Armed Xavante Invade FUNAI. October 23:1, 7.

Coy, Martin

2006 Gated Communities and Urban Fragmentation in Latin America: The Brazilian Experience. GeoJournal 66(1–2):121–32.

Crítica Amazônia

2012 Indígena mulher é eleita para dirigir a Foirn. November 9. http://acritica.uol.com.br/amazonia/Manaus-Amazonia-Amazonas-FOIRN-Indios-Almerinda_Ramos-Indigena-mulher-eleita-dirigir-Foirn_0_807519323.html, accessed September 17, 2013.

Cultural Survival Quarterly

2012 New Wedezé Indigenous Reserve Affirms Xavante Rights to Land in Brazil. 36(2):18–19.

de la Cadena, Marisol, and Orin Starn

2007 Indigenous Experience Today. Oxford: Berg.

Deloria, Philip

2004 Indians in Unexpected Places. Lawrence: University Press of Kansas.

Economist

2001 Bullet-Proof in Alphaville. August 18.

Editoria Abril

2010 Editoria Abril website. http://portalexame.abril.com.br/revista/exame
/edicoes/0849/economia/m0080017.html, accessed June 12.

Embraer Historical Center

2010 Aircraft History: EMB 326 Xavante. http://www.centrohistoricoembraer
.com.br/en-US/HistoriaAeronaves/Pages/EMB-326-xavante.aspx, accessed February 12.

Floria, Christina (director)

2009 Pi'õ höimanazé: Mulher Xavante em sua arte. São Paulo.

Fortun, Kim, Mike Fortun, and Steve Rubenstein

2010 Editors' Introduction. Special issue, "Emergent Indigeneities," Cultural
Anthropology 25(2):222–34.

Fuscaldo, Arthur Iraçu Amaral

2011 Rowapari Danho're: Sonhar e pegar cantos no xamanismo a'uwẽ. Master's
thesis, Universidade Estadual Paulista "Júlio de Mesquita Filho," Campus de São
Paulo, Instituto de Artes.

Gal, Susan

1989 Language and Political Economy. Annual Review of Anthropology 18:345–
67.

1991 Between Speech and Silence: The Problematics of Research on Language and
Gender. *In* Gender at the Crossroads of Knowledge: Feminist Anthropology in
the Postmodern Era. M. Di Leonardo, ed. Pp. 175–203.

Garb, Yaakov

1997 Lost in Translation: Toward a Feminist Account of Chipko. *In* Transitions,
Environments, Translations. Joan Scott, ed. Pp. 273–84. New York: Routledge.

Garfield, Seth

2001 Indigenous Struggle at the Heart of Brazil: State Policy, Frontier Expansion,
and the Xavante Indians, 1937–1988. Durham NC: Duke University Press.

2004 Mario Juruna: Brazil's First Indigenous Congressman. *In* The Human Tradition in Modern Brazil. Peter M. Beattie, ed. Pp. 287–304. Wilmington DE: SR
Books.

Gomide, Maria Lúcia

2008 Marãna Bödödi—A territorialidade Xavante nos caminhos do Ró. PhD dissertation, Faculdade de Filosofia, Letras, e Ciências Humanas, Universidade de
São Paulo.

Gomide, Maria Lúcia, and Daniela Lima

n.d. Livro das parteiras. Unpublished manuscript.

Goodman, Jane E.

2005 Berber Culture on the World Stage: From Village to Video. Bloomington:
Indiana University Press.

Graham, Laura R.

1984 Semanticity and Melody: Parameters of Contrast in Shavante Vocal Expression. Latin American Music Review 5(2):161–85.

1986 Three Modes of Shavante Vocal Expression: Wailing, Collective Singing, and Political Oratory. *In* Native South American Discourse. Joel Sherzer and Greg Urban, eds. Pp. 83–118. Berlin: Mouton.

1993 A Public Sphere in Amazonia? The Depersonalized Collaborative Construction of Discourse in Xavante. American Ethnologist 20(4):717–41.

1994 Dialogic Dreams: Creative Selves Coming into Life in the Flow of Time. American Ethnologist 21(4):719–41.

1995 Performing Dreams: Discourses of Immortality among the Xavante Indians of Central Brazil. Austin: University of Texas Press.

2000 Xavante Wildlife Management: Lessons in Collaboration. *In* Indigenous Peoples and Conservation Organizations: Experiences in Collaboration. Ron Weber, John Butler and Patty Larson, eds. Pp. 47–72. Washington DC: World Wildlife Fund.

2001 Os Xavante na Cena Pública. *In* Povos Indígenas no Brasil-95/00. Aconteceu Especial. Pp. 693–97. São Paulo: Instituto Socioambiental.

2002 How Should an Indian Speak? Brazilian Indians and the Symbolic Politics of Language Choice in the International Public Sphere. *In* Indigenous Movements, Self-Representation, and the State in Latin America. Jean Jackson and Kay Warren, eds. Pp. 181–228. Austin: University of Texas Press.

2003 Take Back the Night: Subverting Gendered Symbolic Dominance through Song. Paper presented at the Annual Meeting of the American Folklore Society, Albuquerque NM, October 8–12.

2005 Image and Instrumentality in a Xavante Politics of Existential Recognition: The Public Outreach Work of Eténhiritipa Pimentel Barbosa. American Ethnologist 32(4):622–41.

2009 The Tractor Invasion. Cultural Survival Quarterly 33(2):21–37.

2011 Quoting Mario Juruna: Linguistic Imagery and the Transformation of Indigenous Voice in the Brazilian Print Press. American Ethnologist 38(1):164–82.

2014 Fluid Subjectivity: Reflections on Self and Alternative Futures in the Autobiographical Narrative of Hiparidi Top'tiro, a Xavante Transcultural Leader. *In* Fluent Selves: Autobiography, Person, and History in Lowland South America. Suzanne Oakdale and Magnus Course, eds. Lincoln: University of Nebraska Press.

Graham, Laura R., Caimi Waiassé, and David Hernández Palmar

2009 Owners of the Water: Conflict and Collaboration over Rivers. Watertown MA: Documentary Educational Resources.

Grandin, Greg

2009 Fordlandia: The Rise and Fall of Henry Ford's Forgotten Jungle. New York: Metropolitan Books.

Green, Shane.

    2009 Customizing Indigeneity: Paths to a Visionary Politics in Peru. Stanford CA: Stanford University Press.

Gregor, Thomas

    1977 Mehinaku: The Drama of Daily Life in a Brazilian Indian Village. Chicago: University of Chicago Press.

Grêmio Esportivo Brasil-Xavante

    2010 http://www.sonico.com/gebxavante, accessed May 11.

Guzmán, Tracey Devine

    2013 Native and National in Brazil: Indigeneity after Independence. Chapel Hill: University of North Carolina Press.

Hall, Stuart

    1997 The Work of Representation. In Representation: Cultural Representations and Signifying Practices. S. Hall, ed. Pp. 13–74. London: Sage.

Heatherington, Tracey

    2010 Wild Sardinia: Indigeneity and the Global Dreamtimes of Environmentalism. Seattle: University of Washington Press.

Hemming, John

    2003 Die If You Must: Brazilian Indians in the Twentieth Century. London: Macmillan.

Hobsbawm, Eric, and Terence Ranger

    1984 The Invention of Tradition. Cambridge: Cambridge University Press.

Hodgson, Dorothy

    2002 Introduction: Comparative Perspectives on the Indigenous Rights Movement in Africa and the Americas. American Anthropologist 104(4):1037–49.

    2008 Cosmopolitics, Neoliberalism, and the State: The Indigenous Rights Movement in Africa. In Anthropology and the New Cosmopolitanism: Rooted, Feminist and Vernacular Perspectives. Pnina Werbner, ed. Pp. 215–30. Oxford: Berg.

    2011 Being Maasai, Becoming Indigenous: Postcolonial Politics in a Neoliberal World. Bloomington: Indiana University Press.

Hugh-Jones, Stephen

    1992 Yesterday's Luxuries, Tomorrow's Necessities: Business and Barter in Northwest Amazonia. In Barter, Exchange and Value: An Anthropological Approach. C. Humphrey and Stephen Hugh-Jones, eds. Pp. 42–74. Cambridge: Cambridge University Press.

Instituto Socioambiental (ISA)

    2003 Mulheres Terena ralixzam primeiro encontro. News release. December 26. http://pib.socioambiental.org/en/noticias?id=10654, accessed January 10, 2014.

    2013 Xavante. Povos Indígenas no Brasil. http://pib.socioambiental.org/pt/povo /xavante, accessed April 15.

2014 Governo brasileiro é denunciado na ONU por violação de direitos indígenas. News release. March 11. http://www.socioambiental.org/pt-br/noticias-socio ambientais/governo-brasileiro-e-denunciado-na-onu-por-violacao-de-direitos -indigenas, accessed March 12, 2014.

Ireland, Emilienne
2008 When a Chief Speaks through His Silence. POLAR: Political and Legal Anthropology Review 16(2):19–28.

Jackson, Jean
1995 Culture, Genuine and Spurious: The Politics of Indianness in the Vaupés, Colombia. American Ethnologist 22:3–27.

Journal do Brasil
1988 Xavante Take Hostages at FUNAI. March 18.

Juruna, Mario, Antonio Hohlfeldt, and Assis Hoffman
1982 O Gravador do Juruna. Porto Alegre: Mercado Aberto.

Li, Tania Murray
2000 Articulating Indigenous Identity in Indonesia: Resource Politics and the Tribal Slot. Comparative Studies in Society and History 42(1):149–79.

Lopes da Silva, Aracy
1992 Dois séculos e meio de história Xavante. In História dos índios no Brasil. Manuela Carneiro da Cunha, ed. Pp. 357–78. São Paulo: Editora Schwarcz.

Maybury-Lewis, David
1967 Akwé-Shavante Society. Oxford: Clarendon.
1991 Becoming Indian in Lowland South America. In Nation-States and Indians in Latin America. Joel Sherzer and Greg Urban, eds. Pp. 207–35. Austin: University of Texas Press.

McCallum, Cecilia
1999 Consuming Pity: The Production of Death among the Cashinahua. Cultural Anthropology 14(4):443–71.
2013 Intimidade com Estranhos: Uma Perspectiva Kaxinawá sobre Confiança e a Construção de Pessoas na Amazônia. Mana 19(1):123–55.
In press Trustworthy Bodies: Cashinahua Cumulative Persons as Intimate Others. In Intimacy, Trust, and the Social: Tensed Relations. Vigdis Broche-Due and Margit Ystanes, eds. Oxford: Berghahn.

Metcalf, Alida
2005 Go-Betweens and the Colonization of Brazil: 1500–1600. Austin: University of Texas Press.

Morphy, Howard
1983 "Now You Understand"—An Analysis for the Way Yolngu Have Used Sacred Knowledge to Retain Their Autonomy. In Aborigines, Land and Rights. Nicolas Peterson and Marcia Langton, eds. Pp. 110–33. Canberra: Australian Institute of Aboriginal Studies.

2006 Sites of Persuasion: Yingapungapu at the National Museum of Australia. *In* Museum Frictions: Public Cultures/Global Transformations. Ivan Karp, Corrine Kratz, Lynn Szwaja, and Tomás Ybarra-Frausto, eds. Pp. 469–99. Durham NC: Duke University Press.

Myers, Fred R.

2002 Painting Culture: The Making of an Aboriginal High Art. Durham NC: Duke University Press.

Nelson, Diane

2001 Stumped Identities: Body, Image, Bodies Politic, and the Mujer Maya as Prosthetic. Cultural Anthropology 16(3):314–53.

2006 The Cultural Agency of Wounded Bodies Politic: Ethnicity and Gender as Prosthetic Support in Postwar Guatemala. *In* Cultural Agency in the Americas. Doris Sommer, ed. Pp. 93–120. Durham NC: Duke University Press.

Oakdale, Suzanne

2009a The Culture-Conscious Brazilian Indian: Representing and Reworking Indianness in Kayabi Political Discourse. American Ethnologist 31(1):60–75.

2009b Ritual and the Circulation of Experience. *In* Ritual Communication. Gunter Senft and Ellen Basso, eds. Pp. 153–70. New York: Berg.

Oakdale, Suzanne, and Magnus Course

2014 Introduction. *In* Fluent Selves: Autobiography, Person, and History in Lowland South America. Lincoln: University of Nebraska Press.

O'Connor, Geoff

1995 Amazon Journal. New York: Filmakers Library.

Overing, Joanna

1977 Orientation for Paper Topics. Acts of the 42nd International Congress of Americanistes 2:9–10.

1983–84 Elementary Structures of Reciprocity: A Comparative Note on Guianese, Central Brazilian, and North-West Amazon Socio-Political Thought. Antropológica 59–62:331–48.

Pena Branca e Xavantinho

2006 Warner 30 anos: Pena Branca e Xavantinho. http://www.vagalume.com.br /pena-branca-e-xavantinho/discografia/warner-30-anos-pena-branca-xavantinho .html, accessed May 11, 2010.

2010 Pena Branca & Xavantinho. Last. fm. http://www.last.fm/music/Pena +Branca+&+Xavantinho, accessed May 11.

Pratt, Mary Louise

1992 Imperial Eyes: Travel Writing and Transculturation. London: Routledge.

Raheja, Michelle H.

2010 Reservation and Reelism: Redfacing, Visual Sovereignty, and Representations of Native Americans in Film. Lincoln: University of Nebraska Press.

Ramos, Alcida

1994 The Hyper Real Indian. Critique of Anthropology 14:153–71.

1998 Indigenism: Ethnic Politics in Brazil. Madison: University of Wisconsin Press.
2003 Pulp Fictions of Indigenism. *In* Race, Nature and the Politics of Difference. D. S. Moore, J. Kosek, and A. Pandian, eds. Pp. 356–79. Durham NC: Duke University Press.

Redford, Kent
1990 The Ecologically Noble Savage. Orion Nature Quarterly 9(3):25–29.

Richards, Patricia
2004 Pobladoras, Indigenas, and the State: Conflicts over Women's Rights in Chile. New Brunswick NJ: Rutgers University Press.

Rodriguez, Juan
2012 The Interplay of Greetings and Promises: Political Encounters between the Warao and the New Indigenous Leadership in the Orinoco Delta, Venezuela. Pragmatics 22(1):167–87.

Rousseau, Stephanie
2011 Indigenous and Feminist Movements at the Constituent Assembly in Bolivia: Locating the Representation of Indigenous Women. Latin American Research Review 46(2):5–28.

Salomão, Alexa e Felipe Seibel
2005 Os 10 novos pólos do agronegócio. Exame, August 8.

Santos-Granero, Fernando
2009 Hybrid Bodyscapes: A Visual History of Yanesha Patterns of Cultural Change. Current Anthropology 50(4):477–512.

Sawyer, Suzana
2004 Crude Chronicles. Durham NC: Duke University Press.

Sherzer, Joel
2002 Speech Play and Verbal Art. Austin: University of Texas Press.

Shiva, Vandana
1988 Staying Alive: Women, Ecology and Development. London: Zed Books

Silverstein, Michael, and Greg Urban
1996 Introduction: Genre, Performance, and the Production of Intertextuality. *In* Natural Histories of Discourse. Michael Silverstein and Greg Urban, eds. Pp. 1–14. Chicago: University of Chicago Press.

Slater, Candace
2010 Metaphors and Myths in News Reports of an Amazonian "Lost Tribe": Society, Environment and Literary Analysis. *In* Environmental Social Science: Methods and Research Design. Ismael Vaccaro, Eric Alden Smith, and Shankar Aswani, eds. Pp. 157–87. Cambridge: Cambridge University Press.

Smith, Anne-Marie
1997 A Forced Agreement: Press Acquiescence to Censorship in Brazil. Pittsburg: University of Pittsburg Press.

Sousa, L. G., and Ricardo V. Santos

1999 Mortalidade, fecundidade, e padrão de assentamento dos Xávante de Sangradouro-Volta Grande, Mato Grosso (1993–1997). Working papers, 2. Porto Velho: Universidade Federal de Rondônia, Centro de Estudos em Saúde do Indio da Rondônia e Escola Nacional de Saúde Pública, Departamento de Endemias S. Pessoa.

Speed, Shannon

2008 Rights in Rebellion: Indigenous Struggle and Human Rights in Chiapas. Stanford CA: Stanford University Press.

Speed, Shannon, R. Aída Hernández Castillo, and Lynn M. Stephen, eds.

2006 Dissident Women: Gender and Cultural Politics in Chiapas. Austin: University of Texas Press.

Srinivasan, Bini

2004 The Taming of a River: Gender, Displacement and Resistance in Anti-dam Movement. New Delhi: WISCOMP, Foundation for Universal Responsibility of His Holiness the Dalai Lama.

Stephen, Lynn M.

2005 Zapotec Women: Gender, Class and Ethnicity in Globalized Oaxaca. Durham NC: Duke University Press.

Sturgeon, Noël

1997 Strategic Environmentalism. In Transitions, Environments, Translations. Joan Scott, ed. Pp. 285–94. New York: Routledge.

Sundberg, J.

2004 Identities in the Making: Conservation, Gender and Race in the Maya Biosphere Reserve, Guatemala. Gender, Place and Culture 11(1):43–66.

Top'tiro, Hiparidi

2009 My Cerrado. Cultural Survival Quarterly 33(2):38–40.

Trindade Serra, Juscimeire

2008 Depoimento. In Estigmatização e território: Mapeamento situacional dos indígenas em Manaus. Alfredo Wagner B. Almeida and Glademir Sales dos Santos, eds. Pp. 132–35. Manaus, Brazil: Universidade Federal do Amazonas.

Tsing, Anna

1997 Transitions and Translations. In Transitions, Environments, Translations. Joan Scott, ed. Pp. 253–72. New York: Routledge.

Vilaça, Aparecida

2010 Strange Enemies: Indigenous Agency and Scenes of Encounters in Amazonia. Durham NC: Duke University Press.

2011 Dividuality in Amazonia: God, the Devil, and the Constitution of Personhood in Wari' Christianity. JRAI, n.s., 17(2):243–62.

Viveiros de Castro, Eduardo

1992 From the Enemy's Point of View. Chicago: University of Chicago Press.

Warren, Kay

1998 Indigenous Movements and Their Critics: Pan-Maya Activism in Guatemala. Princeton NJ: Princeton University Press.

Weinstein, Barbara

1983 The Amazon Rubber Boom, 1850–1920. Stanford CA: Stanford University Press.

Welch, James R.

2010 Hierarchy, Symmetry and the Xavante Spiritual Lifecycle. Horizontes Antropológicos (Porto Alegre, Brazil) 16(34):235–59.

West, Paige, James Igoe, and Dan Brockingham

2006 Parks and People: The Social Impact of Protected Areas. Annual Review of Anthropology 35:251–77.

12

Showing Too Much or Too Little

Predicaments of Painting Indigenous
Presence in Central Australia

FRED MYERS

This essay considers a predicament foundational to the most famous genre of Aboriginal art–Western Desert acrylic painting—in Central Australia. Begun at the Papunya Aboriginal Settlement in 1971 as a translation of ritually based designs for ground, body, and rock paintings into a new medium, the acrylic painting movement has gained international success that attests to its recontextualization from "ritual" to "art" (Thomas 1991). While acrylic painting in Central Australia is a contemporary social practice, its origins and the objects are embedded in complex histories and social fields. It is widely known that most Western Desert painters represent the events of their "country" (*ngurra*) that are understood to have occurred in the mythological period known as The Dreaming and that the form of these representations draws on the ceremonial tradition of images and iconography as well as the culturally rendered landscape itself. Rendered in acrylic and on canvas and produced for sale to an art market that is both national and international, such paintings are valued, locally and interculturally, by virtue of their connection to geographically grounded "Dreaming-places."

The predicament that concerns me here is more specific, about "showing" or "performing" Indigenous value while also maintaining control of it—the problem of "showing too much" or "showing too little." While some of the iconography in the early paintings from Papunya Tula Artists (as the first cooperative is known) was later considered inappropriate to circulate (even to the modern art world that is famously founded on decontextualization), the acrylic paintings have continued to be exhibited and are considered to be authentic forms of presenting Indigeneity. Western Desert painters have always insisted that these paintings reveal Indigenous claims to identification with the land as well as enunciations of their distinctive ancestral world; yet changing styles of painting and increasingly abstract representation have made these dimensions *less* apparent to outsiders. Recently, painters in the arts cooperative have begun to say that uninitiated community members should not be allowed to see some of these early works because they contain images that may be seen only by properly authorized (i.e., initiated) men.

In this essay I explore implications of these intersecting and sometimes competing concerns for the continued exhibition of Aboriginal acrylic paintings, whether in private collections or in public arenas such as museums and art galleries (and more generally of these circumstances themselves). Using the example of Australian acrylic paintings, I ask how Indigeneity is performed or managed in the cultural field called "art," when its revelation conflicts with local protocols.

There are two principal points I am making. First, I argue that the performance of Indigeneity is almost necessarily a problematic or contradictory act—crossing, intersecting, and perhaps challenging social, political, and/or cultural boundaries and regimes of value. Such performances can be powerful and unsettling, especially when concealment and revelation, and their concomitant aesthetics, are not only characteristics of the intercultural boundaries but are also constitutive of Indigenous practice itself. In this argument, I draw in part on Alfred Gell's conceptualization of artworks as extensions of the agency of their makers (Gell 1992, 1998) and on my own previous arguments about the significance of "objectifications" in Western Desert social life (Myers 1986, 2001, 2002). Relatedly, then, as a second point, ultimately I suggest that claims over art, a form of cultural property, are linked to the desire for what was once called "self-determination"—combining political recognition and the pursuit of "sovereignty."

Exhibitions such as the ones I discuss here are often characterized by the instabilities of meaning that come from culture making across cultural boundaries. Thus I am particularly concerned with the preparation of one recent traveling exhibition, *Icons of the Desert: Early Aboriginal Paintings from Papunya*, held at three venues in the United States.[1] *Icons of the Desert* was an exhibition of some fifty paintings, mainly from the early inaugural period of acrylic painting from the Aboriginal-owned cooperative Papunya Tula Artists. The works were entirely drawn from the collection of New York collectors John and Barbara Wilkerson and were curated into an exhibition by the Australian art historian Roger Benjamin, who also edited the catalogue (Benjamin 2009). I was a consultant and sometimes informal adviser in the organization and development of the exhibition, which involved paintings from the communities and period of my own ethnographic research, and was more intimately involved in the installation and programming and publicity at one of the venues, New York University's Grey Art Gallery.

The Early Acrylic Art Movement: Implications Unforeseen

The acrylic painting movement began at the Central Australian Indigenous community of Papunya, 160 miles west of Alice Springs, in 1971. Here a government policy aimed at Aboriginal assimilation brought together a community of recently settled, formerly seminomadic hunter-gatherers. The older men of the community responded with excitement and enthusiasm to the unusual interest of a new schoolteacher, Geoffrey Bardon, with the transposition of ceremonial practices and iconography (traditionally applied to the body or the ground or in the form of ritual objects) into the new medium of two-dimensional acrylic paintings. In recent years painters from the cooperative that began at Papunya, Papunya Tula Artists, have won national art awards in Australia, been exhibited internationally, and had their work collected by major art museums, particularly in Australia.[2] In this essay, however, I am concerned not with that success but with recent objections to the exhibition of the early paintings—the "early Papunya boards," as they are sometimes known—that arose in the planning of an exhibition of privately held works.[3]

As the painters of these works insisted to me, from the time I first knew them in 1973, these are not just "pretty pictures" and their value does not lie simply in their appearance; rather, it derives from their origin in what Pintupi people call Tjukurrpa, The Dreaming. Drawing on a repertoire of forms deployed in body decoration, ceremonial objects, sand designs, and so on, the paintings are held to be images that iconically and indexically represent The Dreaming, the invisible realm occupied by Ancestral Beings in which the visible world acquired its shape and structure. The features and topog-

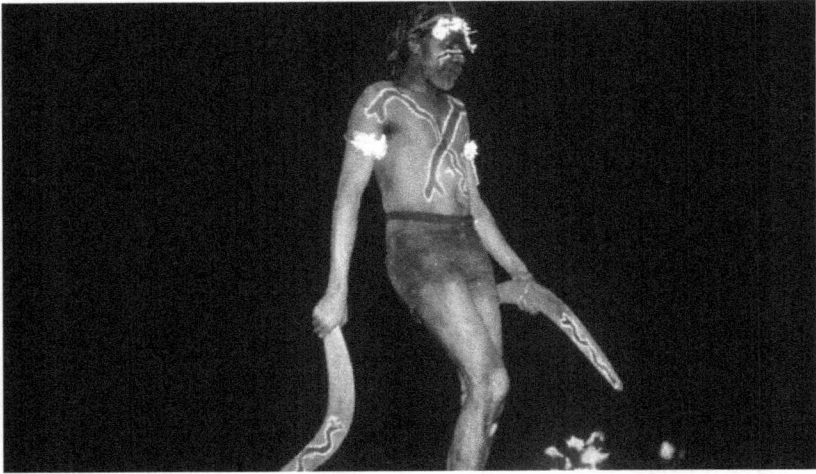

Fig. 12.1. Jeffrey James Tjangala in the Rain Dreaming Ceremony. Photo by the author, Northern Territory, 1974.

raphy of the land are understood as object forms that make visible (*yurti*) and knowable these otherwise unknown powers. This process of making visible or sensorily present—objectifying—is a fundamental component of Indigenous cultural practice, organized in the transmission or exchange of this value in the making or producing of social persons and identities.

Following local objections to their being seen, one might ask what it would mean to remove the early Papunya paintings from circulation in art arenas, given their extraordinary capacity to reveal the foundations and inspiration at the heart of both the earlier and later work. For one thing, such a removal would demonstrate the continued religious power of the stories that provide meaning in local contexts, subordinating the *creativity* of the works to other values, particularly the association of certain images with restricted ceremonial practices in which they are revealed only to initiates. This would assert, of course, the authority and power of Indigenous custodianship. It would also protect the painters from recrimination and possible retribution in their own communities.[4]

Additionally, these concerns challenge the status of paintings as "commodities," objects whose value derives solely from exchange. Perhaps the final disposition of these paintings is not as commodity. If this is so, as Aboriginal people who object to their exhibition maintain, should private collectors have to attend to meanings attached to these objects beyond their commercial and artistic values? Are these meanings part of the commodity and artistic value the paintings have acquired?

For those of us whose relationships to the communities and painters are of principal concern, the obligations are perhaps different from those of collectors who have purchased the paintings for their aesthetic qualities and who desire to exhibit them. For non-Australians, to take another category of participant in the intercultural space (Myers 2002) surrounding these paintings, the sway of national heritage laws protecting Indigenous protocols may be inconvenient but not binding—and their moral histories with respect to Indigenous people of lesser concern than would be the case for non-Indigenous Australians. But as the paintings move across these cultural boundaries and these distinct regimes of value with accelerated speed, and as the relative power and knowledge of the painters and others involved in their circulation shifts, the arrangements governing such movement are increasingly unsettled.

Are there theories that can render these complexities more comprehensible? In a well-known essay challenging the boundaries of art and artifact, the late Alfred Gell (1996) proposed a movement away from nineteenth-century aesthetic theorizations of art. He proposed a post-Duchamp framework as a guide for responding to a whole range of objects—such as "nets" and "traps"—as art objects. These kinds of human constructions, he wrote, had much in common with late twentieth-century art forms—as extensions of the human mind, embodying ideas and conveying meanings (Gell 1996:36).

In his subsequent book, *Art and Agency* (1998), Gell elaborated a view of the art object as an index—or agentive extension—of the maker, a projection of his or her agency toward a viewer. The object (in the Indigenous Australian case, the acrylic painting) is, in this sense, an objectification of the subjectivity of the maker, a performance or bringing forth of the agent into a variety of social spaces. A concrete material object may, of course, have different properties in time and space than an embodied practice, but it also shares many other properties of enactment with these, especially for paintings so closely associated with fundamental rituals. In these terms I explore how these acrylic paintings "perform"—that is, instantiate, bring into being or copresence, for observers—and even extend local Aboriginal identities and how this shapes their circulation.

The Border Zone: Unsettled Business

As paintings moved from ground and body to canvas or board, they also became objects for sale, not just simulacra of ritual objects. Sometimes they presented ritual almost directly, as in examples of the painter Kaapa Tjampitjinpa's work where the power of symmetry itself is a sign of the ordering power of Tjukurrpa and its fascination for those in the grip of this tradition.[5] Paintings like some of those by another Anmatyerre painter, Clifford Possum, can be seen as attempts to communicate to viewers an understanding of The Dreaming—an emanation of this world from the Dreaming realm and actions that are its foundation.

Other paintings from the broad Central Desert painting movement beyond Papunya seem to engage viewers with various effects of the extension of Tjukurrpa power into the world—or its haptic presence on the bodies of women dancers.

Still others present themselves to be engaged with the optical effect, similar to the flashing effect of moving body paintings illuminated by the flickering fire.

Sociologically, however, the paintings are what I have called "unsettled business" (Myers 2002, 2004). "Business" is the Aboriginal English word for ritual, and I use the phrase to draw attention to the way these objects occupy a border zone of performance. This is the border zone along which I have been working—to ensure respect for the painters' claim that these are not just "pretty pictures," as the Pintupi painters said, "made up by human beings." Instead these images are "true, from The Dreaming." At the same time, I have tried to argue that their ascension to the status of "fine art" as they circulate to museums and into the hands of collectors is deserved and appropriate (Myers 1994, 1999, 2002). This ascension has elevated the cultural status of their makers and contributed to political concern about their rights to land.

The "recognition" of this art form appeared at one time to raise issues of appropriation and authenticity as immediate questions (Fry and Willis 1989), questions much discussed under the false certainties of the "Primitivism" debates of the 1980s. My interest as a scholar has been not so much to decide on the virtues or iniquities of intercultural activities but rather with delineating the process of circulation itself, with the significance of the

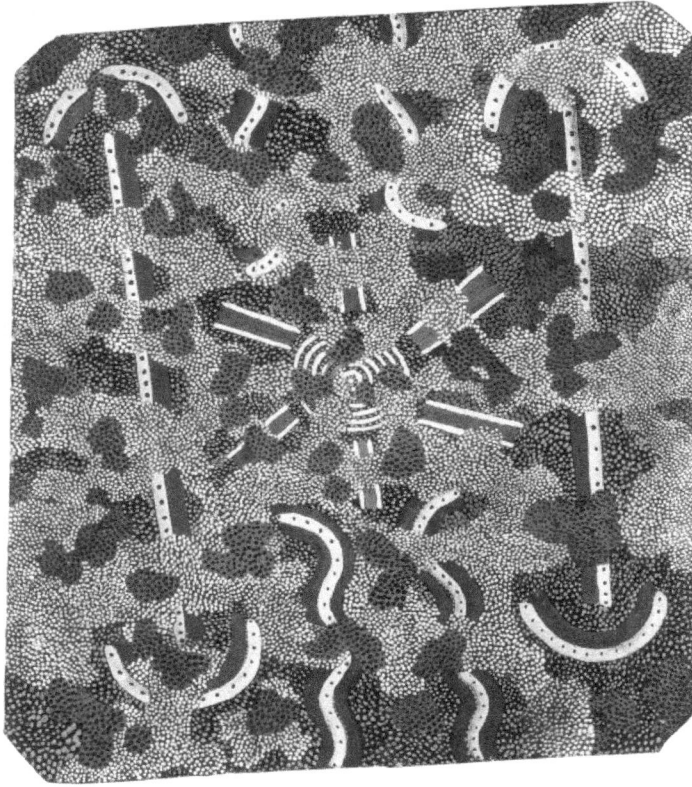

Fig. 12.2. Clifford Possum Tjapaltjarri, *Women's Dreaming about Bush Tucker "Yarlga,"*
1972. 64.45 x 55.56 cm. Collection of John and Barbara Wilkerson. © Clifford Possum
Tjapaltjarri 2014. Licensed by Aboriginal Artists Agency Ltd.

movement of objects and/or practices between such distinctive "regimes of
value" (Appadurai 1986). The cultural work along these boundaries remains
an interesting site because the status and value of objects are often unsettled. Border zones are characterized by instability; it is not clear on whose
territories, on whose land one is standing—and therefore whose values
should predominate.[6]

These paintings, regarded by their producers as revelations of inalienable value, are nonetheless sold and bought, exhibited and seen by Western
outsiders. They represent a movement of Indigenous cultural forms from
one regime of value into another, and this recontextualization is the source

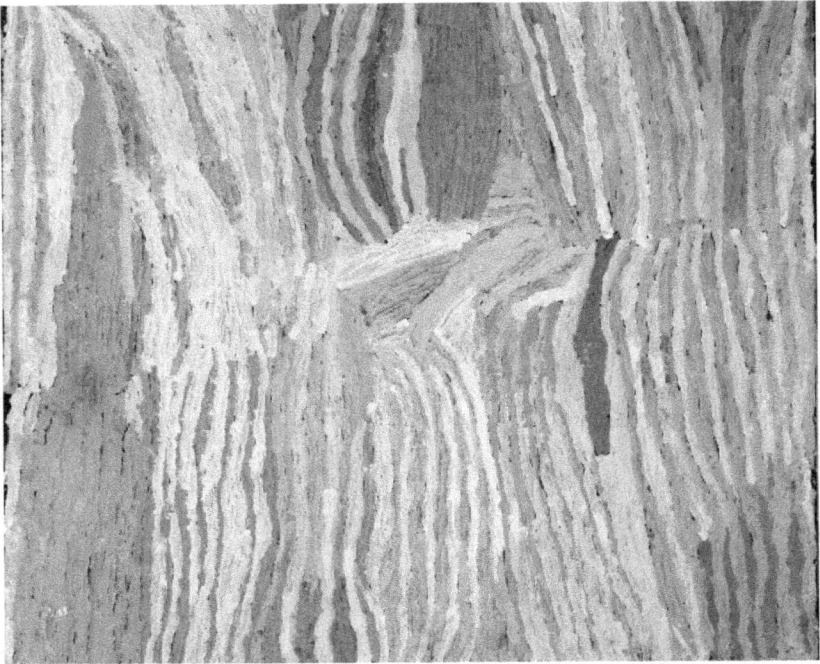

Fig. 12.3. Makinti Napanangka, *Lupulnga*, 2006. 120 x 107 cm. Image courtesy of Makinti Napanangka and Papunya Tula Artists. © Makinti Napanangka 2014. Licensed by Aboriginal Artists Agency Ltd.

of much of the instability and anxiety in their status as "high art." Indeed, one considerable complexity in this regard has been the status of paintings as market commodities—exchangeable for money. Although the paintings were considered "from the Dreaming," the painters were, in fact, ecstatic with the initial sales of their paintings in 1971. Bardon reported that the first sales were "a sensation" and that the "Aboriginal men were jubilant" (Bardon 1991:34). As he wrote, the "first painting sales [were] a source of hope for Aboriginal people. There had been a terrible lack of dignity and self-esteem in the black men, and the money they were earning made me believe that much of this would change, if only the people could stand up and be themselves. The painting movement had brought forth an enormous passion in the desert people to develop their own style and their own sense of self" (Bardon 1991:41–42). However, this market value did not (does not) represent the place of the paintings in the local system of value.

Fig. 12.4. Simon Tjakamarra, *Tingarri Camp at Pillintjina*, 1988. 120 x 180 cm. Courtesy of Kluge-Ruhe Aboriginal Art Collection of the University of Virginia. © Simon Tjakamarra 2014. Licensed by Aboriginal Artists Agency Ltd.

A Revelatory Regime of Value

It may be useful to think of regimes of value as at least semiautonomous spheres of social life in which the capacity of [art] objects *to mark difference* is articulated. The ways in which the Indigenous iconography participates in a system of differences remain very important—a "revelatory regime of value." This regime distinguishes *those with a right to see or learn* about these designs (initiated men and sometimes, more particularly, those from a particular local group) *from those who are still learning* and all of them *from females (who have their own exclusive ritual traditions) and uninitiated males.* In this revelatory regime, structures of visibility and invisibility provide the mechanics of Indigenous visual culture, in which control over the visual—over what can be seen and by whom—is central. The fundamental concern is to limit dispersal, to control the potential manifestations of Tjukurrpa, objectifications of ancestral power identified with persons and groups. A particular set of objects, designs, and performances in ceremony is considered too valuable ("dear") or too "dangerous" to show to uninitiated persons. Yet representations of precisely such forms were often present in the initial years of the Papunya painting movement in the "early Papunya boards." The painters did not imagine that their work would remain within the sensory world of their own communities and that its circulation into the whitefella domain would be exempt from local prohibitions.

Despite concerns about the imagery, the paintings have continued to be exhibited. Their materiality as permanent objects—unlike the temporary constructions of body painting, sand design, or ritual objects or the very closely controlled permanent sacred objects—has allowed them to exist and circulate far beyond their producers' communities. Indeed, if the painters were right in seeing their paintings—like the images of ritual practice—as being generative of social relationships, they did not imagine the ways in which the market and mechanical reproduction could detach these signs from those who make and initially circulate them. The painters draw on a framework that is not particularly concerned with the usual sources of value for cultural objects marked as "art" in the West. This circulation represents, in fact, the movement of acrylic paintings into the purview of Western viewers and patrons in terms that challenge the ways in which cultural objects are familiarly formulated for us, in terms of an ontology and set of practices drawn from the world of Aboriginal cultural production, imagining or asserting their circulation to be articulated in the terms of that local economy of exchange that I have marked as a revelatory regime of value. The paintings, it was sometimes said, were being given "to Canberra," understood as the site or country of the Australian federal government, on whom they were dependent, which by virtue of this "giving" or "revelation" was thereby drawn into a relationship of monetary obligation or moral identity.

From the earliest exhibition of the paintings, there was concern from other Aboriginal people about revealing certain iconography—not so much to whites, but to inappropriate Aboriginal people. Apparently, at the neighboring settlement of Yuendumu in 1972, questions were raised that led painters at Papunya to remove overt visual references to sacred objects and designs that could not be seen by the uninitiated—principally these involved ritual objects and paraphernalia that were commonly represented in paintings of the period 1971–73. After consultation with descendants of the painters, at the *Icons of the Desert* installation in 2009 at the Grey Art Gallery at New York University, paintings of this sort were placed in a separate room downstairs, with a warning to visitors.

While some of the painters at Papunya disagreed with the assessments of what could appropriately be revealed (see Johnson 1994), because their own language group's practices were less restrictive than the practices of those who criticized them, by 1973 the painters of Papunya Tula Artists had become much more careful. As part of their response to the challenges I have described, the painters largely restricted themselves to a particular portion of the mythological cycle—Tingarri Dreamings and those classed as similarly acceptable—that knowledgeable Pintupi men say are less dangerous for uninitiated people to see.[7] As a result, distinctive styles of painting emerged, especially the development of certain grid structures built out of the circular icons that typically represent hills, waterholes, and named country.

Freddy West's 1975 painting (fig. 12.5, *Kirrpinnga*) is an example of this change in the organization of a basic grid structure of named places. In this example the cave Wartunumanya is represented by the circle in the center. As the flying ants (known as *wartunuma*) rose through a hole in the top of a cave, marking the beginning of spring with their glittering wings, they saw other countries in the distance—the Ancestral Rock Pythons depicted in travel by the meandering lines above the center, and the poisonous King

Brown snakes at the top moving on past Lake Mackay. As they saw these Ancestral Beings, they sang. And this song enacts what happened. Showing the body designs of Tingarri ritual, the form of the painting may also hide as much as it shows.

Concealment and Display

As I learned, these images still contained many references to sacred objects and practices that were restricted. Indeed, difficulties still remained. For example, when Pitjantjatjarra men visiting Perth in 1974 saw the exhibition of Pintupi paintings in the Tingarri tradition, they insisted that the paintings be turned toward the wall, as they were inappropriate for exposure. Subsequently they demanded and received compensation from the Papunya Pintupi painters, because the acrylic designs were images that belonged to them jointly (Kimber 1995, personal communication), as part of the same "songline," and they had not given permission for these designs to be exposed or divulged.

Such examples illuminate the ways in which these objects—although they have entered into the world of commoditization, being bought and sold and exhibited as "art"—still bear the traces of their standing in local, Indigenous regimes of value. In this way, for example, the images have continued to embody forms of collective identity—as "belonging to all the people of the Tingarri story." Further, painters long regarded work that represented the same story as having equivalent value—it all represented the "same Dreaming," after all. At the same time, this experience and these restrictions have shaped the formal practice of painting, toward abstraction and ambiguity. Pintupi painters have further made this acceptable by masking or omitting the more esoteric and secret elements of the Tingarri tradition, giving their work perhaps some of its characteristically cerebral and formal focus on design. Finally, the separation of acrylic image from ritual practice has intensified a segregation of painterly practice from the social life of ceremony.

The concern with concealment and display is not only part of Western Desert tradition. Let me take a moment to be explicit. It is, as many readers will know, a constitutive condition of much contemporary performance—and circulation—of Indigeneity. In *The Cunning of Recognition*, Elizabeth Povinelli (2002) has illuminated this condition in a way that has devel-

Fig. 12.5. Freddy West Tjakamarra, *Kirrpinnga*, 1975. Collection of Fred Myers. ©
Freddy West Tjakamarra 2014. Licensed by Aboriginal Artists Agency Ltd.

oped a following in Indigenous politics. She shows how the Australian settler state's process of recognition has "demanded" that Indigenous people
perform themselves in acceptable terms of "authenticity" or "tradition," as
defined by the state. Povinelli sees this dynamic of the liberal state as one
demand that subordinates the Indigenous to a higher authority even while
it recognizes that it constitutes the framework within which Indigenous

performers strategically reveal and conceal. Art and politics, in this regard, are inseparable. Nicholas Thomas (1999) has made similar arguments about the relationality of Indigenous art and settler society, with more attention to New Zealand Aotearoa.

In analyzing the particular forms of relationality, some recent considerations of First Nations Canadian art have drawn on an exchange model resonant with what I am arguing for Papunya Tula art. Especially Charlotte Townsend-Gault's (2004) focus on the circulation of Northwest Coast aboriginality in evanescent form—considering the case of crest designs on copper-colored tissue paper or stylized killer whales on canvas tote bags— made the case that these are "declarations that are also disguises." That is, these are political declarations. Withholding while giving (modifying Annette Weiner's famous [1992] discussion of "keeping-while-giving"), these forms and their makers make tangible (i.e., they objectify) a recent shift in Native–non-Native relations and Canadian multiculturalism. Complicated stances are performed in these extensions of Indigenous presence, and Townsend-Gault's interpretations offer a model for understanding the relationship between object form and agency.[8] In Australia, and surely in the Northwest Coast region of Canada as well, experience with this dialectic of showing while withholding surely predates the colonial moment.

Performing Authority

Thus painting practice changed. But the older paintings were in the marketplace, selling for high prices at auction houses such as Sotheby's, and they were prized objects for collecting in national galleries in Australia— in Adelaide, Melbourne, Sydney, and Canberra. As owned by various collectors, too, they could be exhibited or the rights to their reproduction (in books, catalogs, calendars, postcards) could be granted by their subsequent owners (private or museum), with possibly unenforceable insistence on obtaining the permission of the artists themselves. Some cases of their deployment have been challenged legally, in well-known copyright cases, but there is no question that in many instances, the painters (or their families) have agreed to their being shown. Insofar as previous rights-holders had agreed to such circulations of these images, they have flowed everywhere— in reproductions, in books, on the Internet, and so on—sometimes without copyright compensation for the artists, as well. As commodities, objects for sale, whatever their capacity to objectify Indigenous points of view as cultural heritage, they have escaped local control as others acquire them and reproduction intensifies.

Nonetheless, the connection between painting and other traditions of Indigenous performance of authority and presence is claimed and clearly marked by painters, as illustrated in the remarks of Michael Nelson Tjakamarra, a Warlpiri painter from Papunya:

> White people don't fully understand this sacred ground and the law that constrains our interaction with it. We've been trying to explain it to them, to explain what it means to us. For the sake of all Australians, we try to show them that this is our land. We try to show them our dreamings, which are part of this country that we all live in. But white people don't even recognize our ownership of it. We paint all these pictures and they still can't understand. They want them as souvenirs to hang on their walls but they don't realize that these paintings represent the country, all of this vast land. (Michael Nelson Tjakamarra, quoted in Nairne 1987:221)

Having seen so many of the early paintings published in catalogs and exhibited, by the early 2000s I had assumed that the question of exhibiting those with overt religious material had somehow been settled. Recently, however, painters representative of this movement in the arts cooperative have begun to say that *these* early paintings should not be seen by the uninitiated. As the *Icons of the Desert* exhibition itself was being contemplated a few years ago, at least a few of the men from Papunya Tula expressed opinions ranging from *reservations* about the exhibition of such images to declarative statements that they ought not be shown to uninitiated people—although it is still not quite clear whether they meant just women and children or *everyone*, including non-Indigenous men, for example. Yet these very paintings had been made and sold as commodities, and their sale was "experienced jubilantly" as success by the painters and their communities. What are the implications of such proposed restrictions on the right to see and the right to exhibit for those who have purchased such work, from national museums to collectors?

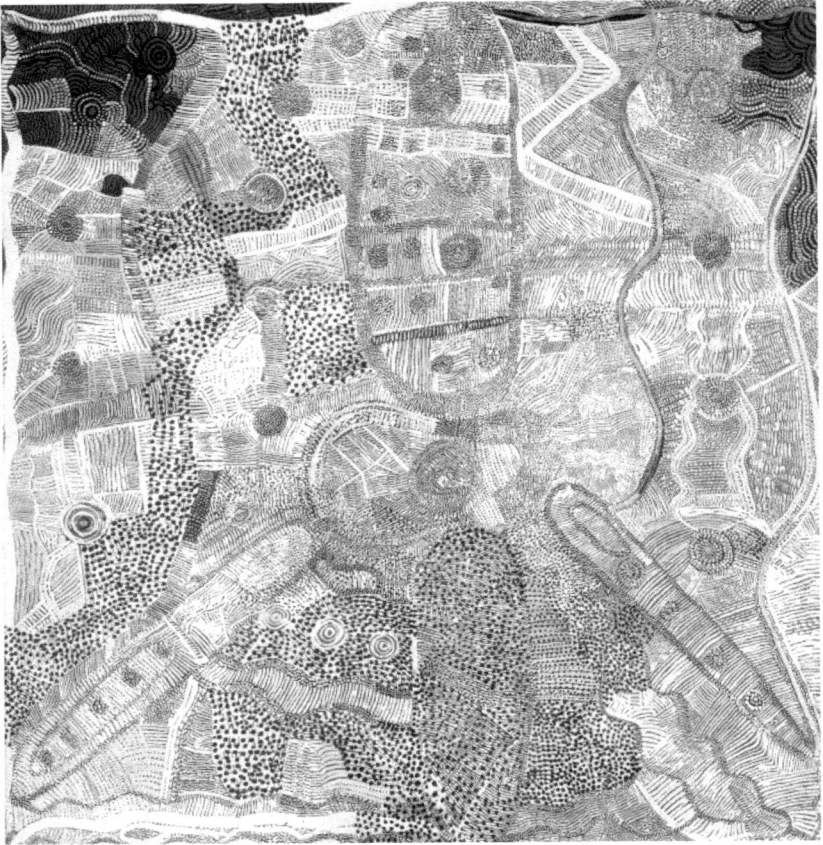

Fig. 12.6. Johnny Warangkula Tjupurrula, *Water Dreaming at Kalipinypa*, 1972. 80.65 x 75.57 cm. Collection of John and Barbara Wilkerson. © Johnny Warangkula Tjupurrula 2014. Licensed by Aboriginal Artists Agency Ltd.

For Indigenous Australians, participants in an oral culture, such embodied practice has been a principal context for cultural transmission—extending, as many of my anthropological colleagues have observed, into contemporary frameworks of intercultural exchange, protest, and display.[9] In two earlier essays (Myers 1994, 2006), I have considered directly the performance of Indigeneity that is embodied in the presence of Aboriginal painters or participants in museum settings, drawing out some of the ambiguities, complicities, and productivities of their concrete enactments of their culture and personhood. The concern of critics of such performances has been with the enframement of the performance within hegemonic systems of representation—especially in various "Primitivist" tropes or insistence on "authenticity" and "tradition"—reinforcing and/or reproducing asymmetries of power.

Despite the popularity of such critiques, it seems to me that the engagements of performance are often more complex and productive than expected. Diana Taylor has argued for "taking 'performance' [as an embodied praxis] seriously as a system of learning, storing, and transmitting knowledge" (2003:16). While her emphasis on embodied practice would seem to deny acrylic painting a status as "performance," I want to insist that the activities of acrylic painting are, equally, a medium of performing Indigeneity—or more specifically, Indigenous identity.

In many respects, what we call the "circulation" of acrylic paintings, and their prior objectification of ritual practice and knowledge into a material form, must be seen as sharing family resemblances with other materializations of performing culture. Like ritual performances, the paintings project knowledge of Dreaming traditions into observable form, and like those performances they may be selective in concealing and revealing different levels and dimensions of knowledge. As a performance, too, they "enact"—bring into being for the purposes of the present—an existing scenario or potential. In the activity of painting, too, as I have argued for the case of Linda Syddick (Myers 2004), painters themselves claim to be enacting a general and specific Indigenous identity through the exercise of recognized rights to represent certain stories and places. Unlike ritual performances, however, but like some versions of ritual performed for filming, the objectification continues to exist in external form beyond the actions of the makers. Indeed, the object forms of acrylic paintings are made to be bought and sold and therefore to exist beyond any present moment of viewing and exchange. In this way they extend the risk subjects take in "showing" esoteric knowledge to others, challenging protocols that delineate—if they do not ensure—appropriate revelation.[10]

Transposed Art

In fact, the early Papunya paintings have been regularly published and exhibited over the years. Dick Kimber delineated the style of the earliest stage succinctly: "The earliest of the transposed art was executed on any and every scrap of flat wood, art-board or linoleum that came to hand. Finger-width strokes were common, artists' brushes were invariably reversed or discarded in favor of traditional Aboriginal brushes made by chewing and abrading a small branch. The design was often vivid against the generally dark priming which Geoff Bardon had taught" (1981:8).

Much of this work involved exquisite "fine detail" (Kimber 1981:8), "meticulously miniaturized details, and usually a compendium of the contents of ceremonial activity: relevant designs, perhaps the decorated participants and props, sacred boards, . . . and the like" (Crocker 1987:25). For example, a large number of paintings were exhibited in the comprehensive and celebratory 2000 exhibition at the Art Gallery of New South Wales, *Papunya Tula: Genesis and Genius*. The paintings selected had been cleared in consultation with the artists' cooperative. However, by 2006, the understandings that had held in earlier consultations were under reconsideration, raising the question of how one might approach restricting the paintings' exhibition.

Aside from sexually explicit representations, restrictions on showing images are not very common in the Western art world—although the liberal-secular regime has become increasingly subject to challenge by religious actors (as in the Danish cartoon case, recently). What we see in the Aboriginal case, however, is a change of mind, long after the paintings have been sold and circulated to private collectors and museums.

Cultural Heritage: The Performance of Protocol

In the spring of 2006, during a consultation about protocols for movable cultural heritage, whatever accommodation to allow noninitiates to view restricted images that had held sway began to fall apart. The consultant was a woman who, along with me, had been involved as a scholar to participate in the *Icons* exhibition involving early Papunya paintings. As she opened her laptop, however, an image that was likely going to be in the planned exhibition came on the screen, a painting that happened to be one painted by the deceased father of the man to whom she was talking—Bobby West, son of the painter Freddy West Tjakamarra. Bobby reacted viscerally, indicating that this image ought not be shown. Based on his reaction, we estimated at least ten of the fifty paintings in the exhibition containing similar design elements could be problematic.

My colleague faced a particularly difficult problem. The men who were responsible for the decisions about ritual questions ought not discuss these matters with her, as a woman, so she had to retire from the conversation, but this led to further discussions with a senior painter, Long Jack Phillipus, the last of the early Papunya painters and an impressive figure. These deliberations were described for me in a letter from another colleague, who wrote,

The writer took sizable photographic images of early paintings held by the [Northern Territory] museum to Long Jack to obtain his opinion.... Without the slightest prompting one way or another . . . , he ruled out, in their entirety, the displaying of any of the Pintupi and Pintupi-related boards at all, and said that no one other than initiated men should be able to view them. His sons suggested that those painted by him should be returned to Long Jack, so that they could be sold at modern prices, but Long Jack was adamant that this was "not on," and that they should be kept in Darwin. . . . I asked him about the possibility of displaying them in a "men-only" display area, and he accepted this as reasonable, so long as it was completely closed off and strictly controlled. . . . Long Jack said that he alone being left of the original artists of the Pintupi group, he had to take responsibility for not only his paintings, but also all others done by the early Pintupi artists. . . .

It is likely to be a widespread view among at least Pintupi and Warlpiri that any early workings containing depictions of sacred boards . . . and certain other sacred elements should not be placed on open public display. [June 13, 2006.]

The writer added, we were relieved to know, that "On the basis of what the few men consulted said, there should be no problems with having a public exhibition in New York, but there might well be problems with a publication or video that eventually reaches Papunya/Kintore/Kiwirrkura . . ."

Interestingly, the focus is clearly on public exposure:

Long Jack, Michael and Barney don't have problems with overseas sales of early works. Even when they were created while singing the songs, and are loaded with power, the senior artists inherently or subconsciously know that they are still not really as powerful as the land-forms and tju-runga. They know that all other people outside of their cultural world are essentially ignorant of it. . . .

The comments that the men made are that private individuals can purchase any early painting and display it in their home.

An informal email inquiry to some of the art galleries (museums) with such paintings in their collection left me unclear as to what the current practice should be. One curator said they were following the protocol estab-lished in 2000 with the twenty-five-year retrospective at the Art Gallery of New South Wales, *Papunya Tula: Genesis and Genius*, namely that if noth-ing was written to identify images, that viewers wouldn't know.[11]

Nonetheless, I understood that the recent revelations were leading to further meetings on the question and some paintings might be removed from exhibition. At another museum, more closely connected geographi-cally and therefore more likely to have Indigenous visitors, a review was taking place to address this kind of issue.[12] One suggestion has even been for the government to buy up all the paintings and place them in storage for five hundred years!

In 1971 Papunya Tula painters shared their work with white buyers in an arrangement along the lines of a long-standing accommodation or assimi-lation of whites to equivalent standing with Aboriginal men or a view of whites as standing outside the meaningful boundaries of the Aboriginal domain. The exposure to us was harmless to their system, and possibly ben-eficial, as they strove to inform the dominant white community about their culture and what they valued. The circulation of paintings staged, wherever they were shown or seen, a declaration of Indigenous presence and identi-fication with place. The recognition of the paintings as valuable, expressed in cash but also in attention to the painters, was a source of pride and—in the long term—an effective strategy in some ways. The paintings could be said to have extended the agency of the painters into far-off places, stand-ing in for performances of Indigenous presence to those who may never have met an Indigenous person. In 2000 the same Bobby West who in 2006 questioned the exhibition of the early paintings had told interview-ers (and me) how proud he was to see the works of his father and other senior relatives at the retrospective in the Art Gallery of New South Wales.

Subsequently, however, men like Bobby West and Long Jack Phillipus expressed concern about the showing of these images and regret that the images had escaped their domain of control.[13] The field of black-white relations and power has changed, certainly within Australia, and museums might well decide to restrict exhibition of these paintings—in recognition of their trust or custodial relationship to Indigenous heritage, but also in recognition of these objects as extensions of Indigenous protocols. But the paintings have circulated as commodities, and many are in the hands of private collectors who have no such relationship to the painters or their communities. There are many ironies in the arc of this story. It took many years to establish Papunya painting as a fine art, and the prices paid for the early paintings in auction have surely fueled the value perceived in more recent work—which depends in part on the paintings' capacity to be exhibited.

James Clifford's (1988) well-known diagram of the "art-culture system" provides a grid with which to conceptualize the changing cultural status of objects within what he maintained was the prevailing schema, and it might be helpful for us to lay out the movement or recontextualization of Aboriginal acrylic painting in these terms. I would insist that these have to be understood not in abstract cultural terms but as a template organized in relation to existing institutions in a field of cultural production (art museums and galleries, natural history museums, and heritage collections as well as material practices such as art markets, catalogs, textbooks, and educational curricula) that affect circulation and reception of these objects.

In the instance of the exhibition planning that brought these issues back into visibility, the organizers of the *Icons* exhibition made a direct attempt to address the concerns of the originating community. At my suggestion, they developed a consultation with current members of Papunya Tula Artists to determine which imagery could and could not be shown. The consultation was undertaken especially with descendants of those who painted the images (see Kimber 2009). This recognized the artists' rights and knowledge but also their possible accountability to others with rights to these stories. As Dick Kimber's contribution to the *Icons of the Desert* catalog (Benjamin 2009) makes clear, and as I found on my own consultation with some descendants of the original painters, the local Indigenous consultants agreed that paintings with explicit representation of sacred objects ought not be exhibited in Australia, but they said it was accept-

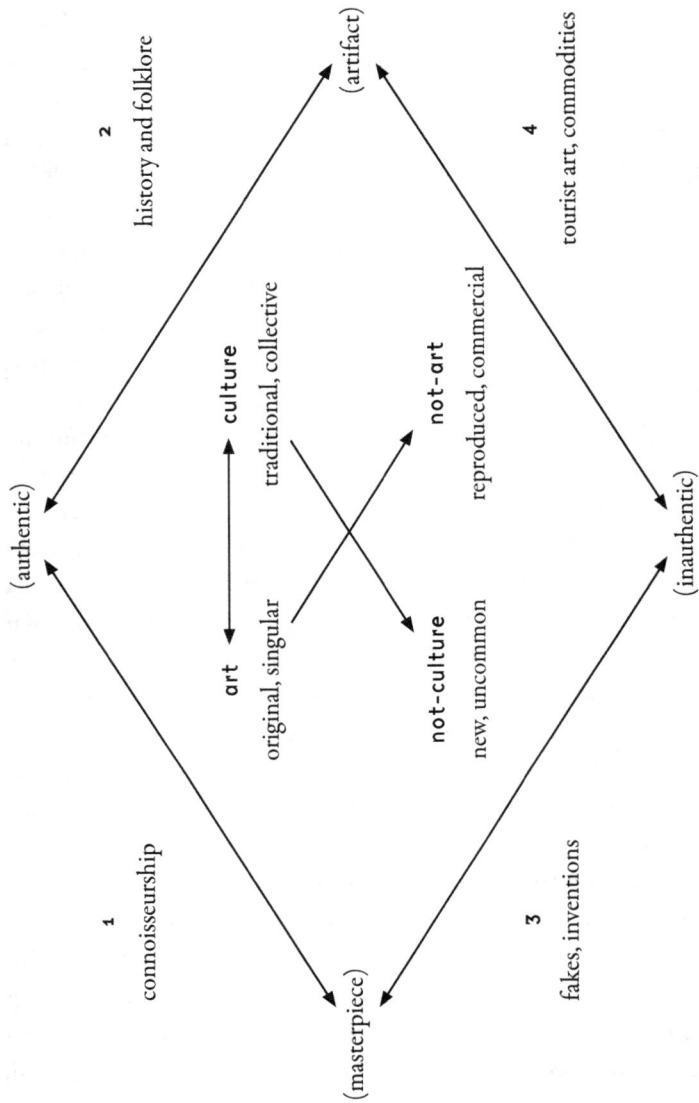

Fig. 12.7. The art-culture system (after Clifford 1988:224).

able to exhibit them overseas. In fact, some images that *we* (as part of the organizers) thought might be objectionable were found to be acceptable to the consultants, being seen to represent "open" dimensions of the stories. The Papunya Tula representatives also asked that the problematic or restricted images not be reproduced in catalogs that could circulate back to Australia. That decision was negotiated in the catalog by putting the restricted images into a supplement inserted in the American edition but removed from copies that might be sold in Australia.

In Performance

Of course this mystery surrounding early Papunya art lies at the heart of its appeal. The first boards, with their finely painted symbols and scenes from ceremony, have become, as [curator of *Icons* Roger] Benjamin writes, "fetish objects" for collectors. They are rare and beautiful, they stand at the beginning of an art tradition that has expanded in the most dramatic fashion to reshape the nation's understanding of indigenous culture and of the desert landscape's lurking depths.

More than this, they seem to harbour a sacred force: many of those who seek them out and compete for them at auction believe they hold some clue to the deep essence of the desert dreaming, the tjukurrpa, the spiritual core of things. For Benjamin, the most potent of the early paintings possess a kind of ritual authority, an aura, that adds to "the visual power that these small jewel-like works project."

This sacred register not only intensifies the pull of the Papunya boards, it complicates the task of displaying them, and indeed it almost scuppered this exhibition. There were plans for the Wilkerson collection to be shown by east coast Australian state institutions: they were shelved as the depth of opposition in desert communities to the display of much of the work became plain.

NICOLAS ROTHWELL, "From the Desert, Artists Came," *Australian*, February 13, 2009

This, however, was not fully the end of the performance problem. As the exhibition approached, in early 2009, one of the major Australian writers on Aboriginal art, Nicolas Rothwell—the Northern Territory correspondent for the newspaper the *Australian*—interviewed Roger Benjamin, guest curator of the show, and published an essay on the catalog (Benjamin 2009) with lavish praise. Rothwell's article lauded both the quality of the paintings as representative of the early period of the movement and equally what he regarded as Benjamin's "fearless proclamation of autonomy" in "claiming the right for the mainstream audience to look and interpret with responsive freedom: we are witnessing not just a new beauty but a new chapter in Aboriginal art criticism" (Rothwell 2009).

The acknowledgment of the essential mystery of this work, for lack of adequate knowledge, is recuperated in part to this end through recourse to a sacred register that intensifies its pull. At the same time as he celebrates this freeing of the objects from anthropology and for art, however (a dichotomy that I reject and that mainly serves to empower art critics), Rothwell also discussed the difficulties that threatened the exhibition and suggested that such exhibitions might be impossible in the future because of restrictions:

> The wheel has turned: the images inscribed on the early boards, which emerged from concealment at a crucial point in the history of the Australian frontier, are moving back into the shadows. It is most unlikely, despite the present urgent efforts of at least two big public galleries to mount Papunya board exhibitions, that anything like informed consent from the senior custodians of the desert for their display will be forthcoming in future years. The gems of the Wilkerson collection, on view in distant gallery spaces, half a world away from the place of their creation, are not just the tokens of an artistic renaissance: they are like the pale, precious light, revealed only for a moment, that floods from the sun in eclipse. (Rothwell 2009)

Rothwell conveyed one of the themes of the exhibition and something of the pathway of its interpretation as Benjamin constructed it. In this image of a "pale, precious light, revealed only for a moment," Rothwell offered a view of the early period of painting—the "early Papunya boards"—as the more authentic indicator of Indigenous imagination and mystery.

But what perspective does this view represent? What does it make of the later paintings of Papunya Tula Artists? The accession to the fetish-like character of "early Papunya boards"—consistent with other of Rothwell's essays—unfortunately may relegate more recent painting production, more restricted in its revelation, to a lesser category, implying a lesser knowledge or commitment. Indigenous painters of the present, by this view, may be seen to have lost some of the mystery that clings to their predecessors. How could he possibly know this? Their predecessors may only seem more mysterious than they should to some in the present because of linguistic and cultural incapacity on the part of recorders. Indeed, when I recorded Bobby West discussing the show, as presented in our video at the exhibition, his words were almost identical to what I heard his father and others say thirty years ago: "We hold this law for the next generation and pass it on to them."[14] Where should the fetishism, the mystery, lie—since Indigenous revelatory practices themselves play on mystery? Concealment and revelation are partly matters of performance, tactic, and strategy, and this is part of the intended effect of the paintings.

The problems of concealment and revelation, however, are no less in the present. At the exhibition's venue in Ithaca, New York—at Cornell University's Herbert Johnson Museum of Art—three Pintupi painters came to prepare a large groundwork during the week of February 9, 2009. This ground design, similar to those executed in Sydney at the Art Gallery of New South Wales in 2000 and a few other venues, used *wamulu* (dried "bush daisy" flowers worked into a kind of cotton) on a sand surface to produce a design very like those on painted surfaces—and one having a certain relationship to ground paintings executed for ceremony. In this instance the three painters—Bobby West Tjupurrula, Ray James Tjangala, and Joseph Jurra Tjapaltjarri—did a design that they identified to the viewers who attended as "Kiwirrkura, Tjukurrpa." It was the Tingarri Dreaming at the site of Kiwirrkura, the location of their current community. In explaining the meaning of this work to the viewers, whose physical copresence demanded further engagement, Bobby extended his comments. The central circle, he said, was Kiwirrkura–that is, the place in the landscape. The surrounding circles were Tingarri men who were there in The Dreaming. Back to the central circle, Kiwirrkura. He said this was a "desert oak." Desert oak (*kurrkapi* in Pintupi) is a tall tree that grows in sandhill country like that at Kiwirrkura. For some reason, Bobby felt he needed to say more. Perhaps the description did not clarify the value of what they had shown in their work. He elaborated on the reference to the "desert oak" to the somewhat mystified audience. "The desert oak," he said, "like this one," and he pointed to the painting of "Medicine Story" behind him, done by Long Jack Phillipus, with a clear representation of the penis of an ancestral trickster character known as "the Old Man"! I knew that he meant that the "desert oak" in the Kiwirrkura story was also part of Tingarri ceremonies and the penis of the other painting was another manifestation of this object, but the desert oaks of Kiwirrkura are "Tjurkurrtjanu," from The Dreaming.

The next day, at the end of a symposium on Papunya Tula painting, a public event was scheduled in which Bobby West had been scheduled to explain the groundwork, to provide the public with a context for the other paintings on the walls. Again, Bobby discussed the desert oak in the center of the image. This time, instead of pointing to Long Jack's painting, he pointed over to one of the restricted and rather explicit ceremonial paintings of Kaapa Tjampitjinpa, one of those we had excluded from the catalogue proper. It is not appropriate for me to discuss his explanations here, and their specifics do not matter.

Rather, I want to draw attention to the complex workings of the secret and the restricted. Some of the non-Aboriginal participants had expressed concern over the painters' possible response(s) to the display of the nine excluded paintings, but I heard no comment about these paintings and saw no apparent discomfort. Indeed, in the face-to-face experience of explaining the significance of the groundwork they had done, Bobby West felt the necessity of connecting the abstract image to the ceremonial traditions that continue to inform their lives and construct their authority and identity. It did not seem, at least to me, that "the pale, precious light" would be revealed only for one moment and never again. Bobby explicitly marked the connection between the contemporary painting, practice, and lives of the middle-aged artists and the jewels or icons on the walls of the exhibition space. This interruption of the fetish of the collection of the rare artifacts of the past was a claim surely of a more important Indigenous continuity and authority and *a claim of the right* to conceal or reveal. Concealment and control lie at the heart of an Indigenous performance that seeks to impress us with its value without accepting the dominance of those who view.

Concealment, Control, and Negotiation:
So, Who Owns Native Culture?

The question of how to recognize claims over the display, performance, and circulation of culture has become a significant concern with Indigenous people (Zipf and Rao 1997; Coombe 1998; and Brown 1998, 2003). As we know, these questions had considerable visibility in the Indigenous communities of the Anglo settler nations—Australia, the United States, Canada, and New Zealand Aoteroa—before they gained academic focus. As a result of Indigenous claims, various "cultural protocols" have been developed, with varying legal standing. Going back to the 1970s Indigenous communities, leaders and artists themselves have voiced concerns about inappropriate revelation, problems with published cultural material and photographs returning back to local communities. One case, for example, *Foster v. Mountford and Rigby Ltd.* (14 ALR 17 [1976]), set the Pitjantjatjarra against the publication of C. P. Mountford's magnum opus, *Nomads of the Australian Desert* (1976)—a case that the Pitjantjatjarra won. It raised questions about the possible reach of Indigenous laws and protocols beyond the local context.

In *Who Owns Native Culture* (2003), anthropologist Michael Brown moved away from a simple advocacy position to ask some difficult questions about protocols that employ the concept of cultural property to regulate the circulation of culture. While his considerations of the *pragmatics* of instituting a judicial regime have been regarded as a productive contribution to scholarship, there is something ultimately disturbing about taking cultural property claims just on their face value. His analysis neglects or ignores the cultural logics behind many Indigenous claims and thereby reduces Indigenous claims to essentialist notions of property. The underlying logic of many Indigenous claims to "property," it seems to me, is not always or not simply to establish a barrier to circulation but rather to insist on the acceptance or recognition of local cultural protocols. In Australia, frequently, I have found that people are concerned that their relationship to cultural material be acknowledged. This acknowledgement would typically take the form of being "asked" (consulted) for permission to use or deploy cultural material someone regards as identified with him or her, as "his (or her) own" (Myers 1986). Asking constitutes recognition of one's rights. The trajectory of the *Icons of the Desert* consultation illustrates this point. This exhibition mobilized a confrontation between two sets of protocols— between Western protocols for viewing and knowledge, on the one hand, and Indigenous Australian protocols, on the other. This has happened in other exhibitions about men's art and women's art and culture, of course, posing questions about whether particular categories of viewers can visit and view material culture objects or performances. In the case of this exhibition, however, with the warrant from the contemporary painters to exhibit all the paintings in the United States, the organizers were reluctant to exclude the early paintings altogether. These paintings are, after all, foundational—part of the history of how this work came to be what it is. For those people who are interested in history, which is Westerners in particular, this is an essential part of the story. Therefore, it was not necessary to give absolute priority to one or the other of the protocols of viewing, as long as the exhibition did not produce too much discord between them. Thus, in the installation at the Grey Art Gallery, in New York, the warning label and the restricted paintings were put in a downstairs room of the gallery but were accessible to any viewers who chose to go.

If this seems a temporary compromise, I believe it to be preferable to static regulation when, very likely, the local protocol has itself been available in practice to contextual variation—as illustrated in Bobby West's decisions at the Herbert Johnson Museum venue at Cornell. Our objective overall in planning *Icons* had been to promote a *face-to-face negotiation*. Rather than the implementing a law or establishing an objective set of rules to regulate the terms of what could and could not happen, for this exhibition we decided to respect the agency, if you will, or custodianship of the Indigenous makers who were absent or distant parties in this negotiation. Such negotiation demands that the Indigenous parties be consulted and their needs be addressed. Although distant, they were fully participating actors in the decision-making process. Making decisions on the basis of these relationships (to viewing and to each other) opens people to accountability and responsibility. With regard to Central Australia, at least, this is a return, to some extent, of the kind of accountability that people have in their own society, an accountability that I suspect is common in many if not most Indigenous societies.[15] Indeed, this was the problem faced by Terry Yumbulul in a famous copyright case in Australia, in which other clan custodians of a design held him responsible for the usage of one of his paintings on a postage stamp. These are personal accountabilities, not ones that are protected by lawyers and the law.

Museums may not like to depend on negotiation, because it is costly and inefficient for them—it takes time—and also because the outcomes are not necessarily clear. In developing this process, however, the exhibition organizers and consultants intended to set a precedent for other private collectors to follow, who are not subject to many regulations and the accountability that state museums might have.[16]

For any exhibition, of course, it is not *easy* to consult in this way, and it puts a lot of pressure on those who want to consult. Nonetheless, I think that mechanisms for negotiation on the use of "culture" should be encouraged and would prove superior to instituting a bureaucratic legal regime. While the regulatory approach provides protection, it threatens to establish a true commodification, in which such cultural objects are profoundly removed from people's agency. Negotiation, in contrast, recognizes people's humanity—as persons who must be accepted, as active agents in exchange.[17]

Thus while Michael Brown and I probably share a suspicion of the legal regime's capacity to represent the fundamental conflict, I find his (2003) discussion of "who owns native culture?" to be problematic. It gives short shrift to the aspirations that Native Peoples embed in property claims. Brown treats the goal of using property-like regulations straightforwardly in legal terms as a means of controlling a resource. I see the pursuit of control over culture in terms of an underlying logic in which "property" forms the basis of a relationship and thereby makes claims for recognition: gaining access to cultural material would be predicated on establishing a relationship. Ownership, at least in Pintupi culture as I have come to understand it (see Myers 1982, 1986), involves fundamentally the expectation of recognition, of having one's identity-bearing rights recognized by others. As Audra Simpson (2006) and others are arguing more broadly, claims over cultural property have a link with the pursuit of "sovereignty"—of political recognition.[18] One might extend this to advocate for ethnographically informed understanding of Indigenous stakes in making property claims.

Such distinctions have a place in legal considerations of property. Therefore, the view I am taking of "property" in this regard is resonant with the performative orientation in the work of feminist legal scholars Barbara

Rose and Margaret Radin or Rosemary Coombe (1998), who regard property as an "identity-bearing" form. Brown's careful and commonsense critique of a utopian juridicalization is misleading in focusing so insistently on the means of these claims—some kind of propertization—rather than considering culture as a basis of recognition.[19] The emphasis on recognition could be easily argued for Northwest Coast (or for many Melanesian) people, where it extends cultural ontologies into the present.[20] I take this to be Jennifer Kramer's point in her discussion of Nuxalk attitudes toward museums and the government. "I think," she writes, "that the accusations of 'theft' directed at the British Columbian and Canadian governments, which took land and material objects from Native peoples, is a demand for self-determination and control" (Kramer 2006:11). In the contested field of art, claims are linked to the pursuit of "sovereignty" and self-determination: "In the same way that Nuxalk political leaders fight for the return of their land and resources, Nuxalk artists fight for the right to express cultural knowledge and to control the construction of Nuxalk national identity" (Kramer 2006:11).

There is not, of course, a singular solution to the problems of concealment and revelation, any more than there is a singular history. For Nuxalk people, according to Kramer, the dialectic of revelation and concealment has a different history and a different structure. She describes distinctive tensions whereby elected chiefs favor the development of art as a basis of economic growth and encourage exhibition and sharing of knowledge while "hereditary chiefs fear the 'cultural prostitution' that results from selling Nuxalk art to non-Native people." (Kramer 2006:11). The point is that negotiation is more sensitive to shifting and potentially contradictory tensions in Indigenous societies that cannot be reduced to bureaucratic rules.

Of Censorship

As I have argued elsewhere (Myers 2002), these objects cannot be understood simply as products of local tradition. In the canons of the old "primitive art," this would have relegated them to the category of the impure, the products that James Clifford likes for "going crazy" but that were regarded as somehow lacking in authenticity. This is where the primitivism frameworks that for so long constrained the view of local traditions were so misguided.

Rather, as I have indicated, these objects and their makers have been in dialogue with an external world, with its standards and expectations, and also in dialogue internally, in reassessing local conventions of ownership, of restraint, of revelation. This is why the claims of the primitivism debates were so very unilluminating about these works, leading to a fixation either on unchanging authenticity or on overacceptance of the claims of the Euro-Australian art worlds.

Even when these paintings look like our own kind of objects, even when they resemble abstract expressionism, for example, they are not what they seem. They are the creative products of a very different practice, history, and set of social relations that make them profoundly interesting in many, many ways, including their capacity to provincialize Western art histories. The implications of this recognition are quite broad. On the one hand, this would allow us to return to Gell's discussion of art as providing "conceptual traps"—traps that, in this case, might remind us why the qualities and lives beyond the canvas actually matter. One can only really understand—and appreciate—these works for what they are when one sees the trajectory of which they are a part. On the other hand, Gell's argument in *Art and Agency* is equally germane. These objects are extensions of the agency of their makers, having effects far beyond their physical life and immediate world—an agency that can extend, as in this case, to limiting the regard of the art world, asserting a change in the hierarchy of protocols of viewing. It is also an agency that can continue to require responsibility and accountability on the part of painters when their works circulate beyond their control. William Pietz (1986) regarded the "fetish" as a concept referring to objects at the borders between cultural worlds, objectifying irreducible cultural difference. But one person's fetish is another's communication. Cultural difference is only irreducible for those who don't want to take the time and make the effort to understand how and why things—like these paintings—might be different.

Acknowledgments

This paper is a revision and development of an earlier paper, focused more on the problem of censorship. I thank Faye Ginsburg and Jane Anderson for commenting on various versions of the paper, Glenn Penny and Laurie Graham for suggestions, and also participants in the Performance of Indigeneity Conference for their comments and criticisms. I am grateful to Roger Benjamin, Vivien Johnson, Dick Kimber, John Wilkerson, and Andrew Weislogel for their part and varied contributions in developing the consultation process of the exhibition and to Lynn Gumpert and Lucy Oakley for including me in the Grey Gallery's installation.

Notes

1. The exhibition began at Cornell University's Herbert Johnson Museum of Art (January 10–April 5, 2010), moved to the Fowler Museum at UCLA (May 3–August 2), and ended at New York University's Grey Art Gallery (September 1–December 5).

2. In many respects one can compare the example of Papunya Tula Artists and Western Desert painting with other cases of Indigenous art in settler societies in the twentieth century. In the Southwest of the United States (Wade 1985; Mullin 2001; Babcock 1995), and previously in California (McLendon 1993, 1998; Cohodas 1999), as in the Canadian north (Graburn 2004; Glass 2006), various networks of artists and artisans, dealers, patrons, anthropologists, museums, and others operated to produce intercultural objects that articulated with prevailing notions of art and craft. A growing body of work shows how typically, in the twentieth century, these were developed to provide income for indigent Native peoples first and later became articulated with representations of national identity of these societies (see Myers 2001, 2002).

3. For a discussion of the category "early Papunya boards" in historiographic terms, see Roger Benjamin's (2009) recent essay. The term refers to the fact that the paintings were often done on masonite or composition board, rather than canvas or cardboard-backed canvas, but also alludes to a similarity with traditional sacred objects—often referred to as *churinga*, from the Arrernte designation—carved in wood.

4. In the famous case of Terry Yumbulul's painting of the "Morning Star" ceremonial pole, which came to be considered protected under copyright law, the extent to which Yumbulul was responsible to other custodians in caring for and reproducing a sacred image was a significant point. See French 1991.

5. I have not shown images of Kaapa's work precisely because of questions about whether his depictions of ritual objects should be shown in public.

6. In my view, a focus on intercultural movement as the *boundary (the unusual or "marked") condition* for visual art's consideration is misleading. Instead, I believe one should begin with "intercultural" objects and activity—that is, one should consider cultural forms and practices that circulate not only through boundaries

of cultural difference conceived of in ethnic terms but also through those of "difference" conceived under the sign of cultural hierarchy. Both trajectories involve the movement of objects through distinctive institutions and social fields that classify them, giving them their meaning and value. The needed framework is one that focuses on *circulation* (or movement), *institutions*, and culture making, rather than relatively static cultural categories. In this framework, Indigenous—local—conventions concerning the nature of images have come to be acknowledged, if not completely incorporated, in cultural property considerations, in exhibition practices, and in art critical responses to the work itself.

7. Even this view has, at times, been challenged by authoritative members of related communities. This is not surprising when new forms of evaluation are applied to protocols that had been grounded in a given set of practices and expectations. For the case of Pitjantjatjarra viewers, see my later discussion in this chapter.

8. The properties of glistening, copper-colored tissue, Townsend-Gault (2004) argues, convey and transmute something about coppers (like crests, markers of social transactions on the Northwest Coast), and in this sense the tissue-paper designs are not simply a degradation of the emblematic idea of copper for Northwest Coast people. These forms—the miniature, the mimetic, the mechanically reproduced—are not just the inauthentic; they are not simply commercial kitsch.

   In a brilliant and subtle analysis of the meanings embodied in the evanescent forms themselves, Townsend-Gault explains the complicated stances performed in these extensions of Indigenous presence and substantially increases our understanding of the relationship between object form and agency. Against the sense that extreme circulation is the worst situation, the objects (1) provide an agency *disturbing* to the *spectatorial* regime intrinsic to "not-yet post-colonial relations," a regime of display in which "conflicted political relations were subsumed into looking relations"; and further, (2) as a form of action, the visual *deflects* attention from, or masks, conflicts present (Townsend-Gault 2004:189). In this regard, Townsend-Gault's description is similar to Jennifer Kramer's (2004) concept of "figurative repatriation." According to Kramer, "'artist warriors' forcibly recover . . . First Nations objects on display in foreign settings and reinscribe meaning at the level of the personal and the communal. They make objectified assertions of native identity that reclaim the right to self-definition" (2004:161). This circulation is not just a mask, or should it be said that "masking" is also a form of presentation, a form of being visible and therefore present? Indeed, the metaphor of the mask surely resonates with traditions of masking in the Northwest Coast, of performing identities of power.

   It seems, however, that insisting on presence *through* the visual might not be adequate to reclaim Indigenous presence and being. Townsend-Gault's insight takes seriously the potentials that come from interrupting the dominance of the visual, and she stakes a particular claim for the Indigenous value of the other sensuous modes deployed by the evanescent forms. If overprivileging of the visual is understood as constitutive of the *reduction* of Indigenous Peoples, then movements to the sensuous and immediate could provide an arena for the more confident expression or indication of Indigenous identities and epistemologies. These forms also work against the domination of the visual, reinstating this sensorium, reprivileging touching and smell, and in this mode they reflect on the intensified circulation of forms of mechanical reproduction.

9. Performance has been a central element of Indigenous activism and protest in Australia. I have discussed this elsewhere (Ginsburg and Myers 2006).

10. Some similar points about restrictions on photography can be found in Michaels 1994.

11. Brenda Croft explained the National Gallery of Australia's policy as follows: "I am guided by PTA (Paul Sweeney) and Hetti on this, following the research for her show, which states it is okay to put the works on display as the general public cannot decipher them—nor me, nor do I want to. We have some of the early works from the Fannin collection on display right now. We follow the same with secret/sacred works from Arnhem Land and elsewhere too" (personal communication, July 25, 2006).

12. See Richards 2012 for a discussion of the 2009 conflicts at the Northern Territory Museum and Art Gallery.

13. Long Jack would be happy, he said, if they were all sent to Africa, or New Zealand—away.

14. The installation video was nearly nine minutes long, and it was entitled *Painting Culture*.

15. These paradoxical, if not contradictory, accountabilities have been given some analytic consideration in various writings, including Christopher Anderson's (1990) and Philip Batty's (2005) discussions of repatriation. They are similarly discussed, for a Northwest Coast Canadian example, in Saunders 1997. As Jeremy MacClancy underscored in his introduction to *Contesting Art*, "Regularly, the repatriation of objects to their land of origin helps to revitalize indigenes' sense of their own identity. However, it may also serve to re-kindle intra-tribal differences." Saunders, he writes, "shows that when Kwakiutl campaigned for the restitution of potlach regalia sequestered over fifty years before, the issue of their present ownership led to local division, with one group appealing to European ideas of genealogically-based inheritance and another wielding 'traditional' notions of proprietorship" (MacClancy 1997:17).

16. Laura Graham (personal communication) has suggested that things might go differently if the Indigenous people are fully in control of the objects. A relevant case is the Makah and their negotiations with museums when they allowed objects to tour to other institutional sites. See Erikson 1999.

17. See J. Anderson 2009. In this regard, and ultimately in leaning toward negotiation rather than overbureaucratized regulation, Anderson has pointed out the significance of local Indigenous "difference . . . within and between communities, families, clans, and individuals" as "the feature characterizing the failure of the [over-

arching] Labels [of Authenticity]: an ironic twist given that the effort to provide practical legal mechanisms rendered silent the diversity of Indigenous interests and positions" (Anderson 2009:208). The "differing needs, articulations, political representations and definitions of 'communities' within Australia" (209) are a prod to negotiation rather than a blanket legislation. Participants must mediate a range of concerns in allowing culture to circulate. It is, she argues, "the presumption of the *stability* of 'community' that represents the fundamental problem for developing any legislative strategy addressing communal ownership" (210).

18. On his website, Brown (2007) responded to Simpson's review of his book by claiming she had misrepresented his position: "On balance, the book is less interested in making a romantic case for a global intellectual commons, which is what Simpson alleges, than it is in making a case *against* the development of multiple, dystopian anti-commonses, even when implemented in the name of Native rights."

19. I want to make it clear that I admire Brown's presentation and analysis of the varied cases of claims surrounding cultural property. In their sweep and detail, they bring the object into sustained vision. Nonetheless, it has seemed to me that the position from which he regards the prospects of cultural property is that of how this would actually be managed, of what the implications would be within existing legal regimes, and so on. These are fair questions, but the claims of *Indigenous* people for cultural property may be distinctive from those of other minority groups. They have to be understood as moral claims on dominant settler societies, and these are claims that focus on reorganizing the relations between parties regarding the shared space of the settler nation. This is, I think, the point that Audra Simpson (2006) makes in distinguishing the history and claims of Indigenous people from those who are members of other collectivities. While these others, in liberal societies, might expect equally to have the same claims as those of any "different" group, this is certainly not the point of view that would emerge from those who begin with the condition of Fourth World people.

20. In making this point, I am reminded particularly of the extraordinary ethnographic moment in Kenneth Read's *The High Valley* (1965) in which Read learns that his main informant, Makis, is disappointed in his relationships with the white colonizers because they do not exchange with him, do not give him the opportunity to be recognized as a person on the same level.

Bibliography

Anderson, Christopher

    1990 Repatriation, Custodianship and the Policies of the South Australian Museum. COMA: Bulletin of the Conference of Museum Anthropologists 23:112–15.

Anderson, Jane

    2009 Law, Knowledge, Culture: The Production of Indigenous Knowledge in Intellectual Property Law. Cheltenham, UK: Edward Elgar Press.

Appadurai, Arjun
    1986 Introduction: Commodities and the Politics of Value. *In* The Social Life of Things. Arjun Appadurai, ed. Pp 3–63. Cambridge: Cambridge University Press.

Babcock, Barbara
    1995 Marketing Maria: The Tribal Artist in the Age of Mechanical Reproduction. *In* Looking High and Low: Art and Cultural Identity. Brenda Bright and Lisa Bakewell, eds. Pp.125–50. Tucson: University of Arizona Press.

Bardon, Geoffrey
    1991 Papunya Tula: Art of the Western Desert. Melbourne: Penguin / McPhee Gribble.

Batty, Philip
    2005 White Redemption Rituals: Reflections on the Repatriation of Aboriginal Secret-Sacred Objects. Arena Journal 23:29.

Benjamin, Roger, ed.
    2009 Icons of the Desert: Early Aboriginal Paintings from Papunya. Ithaca NY: Cornell University Press.

Brown, Michael
    1998 Can Culture Be Copyrighted? Current Anthropology 39(2):193–222.
    2003 Who Owns Native Culture? Cambridge MA: Harvard University Press.
    2007 On the Protection of Indigenous Heritage: A Response to Audra Simpson. October. http://www.williams.edu/go/native/reply_to_simpson.htm, accessed January 7, 2010.

Clifford, James
    1988 On Collecting Art and Culture. *In* The Predicament of Culture: Twentieth-Century Ethnography, Literature, and Art. Pp. 215–51. Cambridge MA: Harvard University Press.

Cohodas, Marvin
    1999 Elizabeth Hickox and Karuk Basketry: A Case Study in Debates on Innovation and Paradigms of Authenticity. *In* Unpacking Culture: Art and Commodity in Colonial and Postcolonial Worlds. Christopher Steiner and Ruth Phillips, eds. Pp. 143–61. Berkeley: University of California Press.

Coombe, Rosemary
    1998 The Cultural Life of Intellectual Properties. Durham NC: Duke University Press.

Crocker, Andrew
    1987 Charlie Tjaruru Tjungurrayi: A Retrospective, 1970–1986. Orange, New South Wales: Orange Regional Gallery.

Erikson, Patricia Pierce
    1999 A-Whaling We Will Go: Encounters of Knowledge and Memory at the Makah Cultural and Research Center. Cultural Anthropology 14(4):556–83.

French, J.
    1991 Yumbulul v. Reserve Bank of Australia and Others. Intellectual Property Review (Butterworths, New South Wales) 21:481, 490.

Fry, Tony, and Ann-Marie Willis

1989 Aboriginal Art: Symptom or Success? Art in America, July:109–17, 159–60.

Gell, Alfred

1992 The Enchantment of Technology and the Technology of Enchantment. *In* Anthropology, Art and Aesthetics. J. Coote and A. Shelton, eds. Pp. 40–63. Oxford: Oxford University Press.

1996 Vogel's Net: Traps as Artworks and Artworks as Traps. Journal of Material Culture 1:15–38.

1998 Art and Agency. Oxford: Oxford University Press.

Ginsburg, Faye, and Fred Myers

2006 A History of Aboriginal Futures. Critique of Anthropology 26(1):27–45.

Glass, Aaron

2006 Conspicuous Consumption: An Intercultural History of the Kwakwaka'wakw Hamat'sa (British Columbia). PhD dissertation, New York University.

Graburn, Nelson

2004 Authentic Inuit Art: Creation and Exclusion in the Canadian North. Journal of Material Culture 9:141–59.

Johnson, Vivien

1994 The Art of Clifford Possum Tjapaltjarri. East Roseville, New South Wales: Craftsmen House.

Kimber, R. G. (Dick)

1981 Central Australian and Western Desert Art: Some Impressions. *In* Mr. Sandman, Bring Me a Dream. Andrew Crocker, ed. Pp. 7–9. Sydney: Aboriginal Artists Agency and Papunya Tula Artists.

1995 Politics of the Secret in the Contemporary Western Desert. *In* Politics of the Secret. Oceania Monographs 45. Christopher Anderson, ed. Pp. 123–42. Sydney: University of Sydney.

2009 Relatives of the Artists Respond to the Paintings. *In* Icons of the Desert: Early Aboriginal Paintings from Papunya. R. Benjamin, ed. Pp. 71–76. Ithaca NY: Cornell University Press.

Kramer, Jennifer

2004 Figurative Repatriation: First Nations "Artist/Warriors" Recover, Reclaim and Return Cultural Property Through Self-Definition. Journal of Material Culture 9:161–82.

2006 Switchbacks: Art, Ownership and Nuxalk National Identity. Vancouver: University of British Columbia Press.

MacClancy, Jeremy

1997 Anthropology, Art and Contest. *In* Contesting Art: Art, Politics, and Identity in the Modern World. J. MacClancy, ed. Pp. 1–26. London: Berg.

McLendon, Sally

1993 Collecting Pomoan Baskets, 1889–1939. Museum Anthropology 17(2):49–60.

1998 Pomo Basket Weavers in the University of Pennsylvania Museum Collections. Expedition 40(1):34–47.

Michaels, Eric

1994 A Primer of Restrictions on Picture-Taking in Traditional Areas of Aboriginal Australia. *In* Bad Aboriginal Art: Tradition, Media, and Technological Horizons. Pp. 1–20. Minneapolis: University of Minnesota Press.

Mountford, Charles P.

1976 Nomads of the Australian Desert. Adelaide: Rigby.

Mullin, Molly H.

2001 Culture in the Marketplace: Gender, Art, and Value in the American Southwest. Durham NC: Duke University Press.

Myers, Fred

1982 Always Ask: Resource Use and Landownership among the Pintupi of Central Australia. *In* Resource Managers: North American and Australian Hunter-Gatherers. N. Williams and E. Hunn, eds. Pp. 173–95. Boulder CO: Westview Press.

1986 Pintupi Country, Pintupi Self: Sentiment, Place and Politics among Western Desert Aboriginal People. Washington DC: Smithsonian Institution Press.

1994 Beyond the Intentional Fallacy: Art Criticism and the Ethnography of Australian Aboriginal Acrylic Painting. Visual Anthropology Review 10(1):10–43.

1999 Aesthetics and Practice: A Local Art History of Pintupi Painting. *In* The Art of Place: Dialogues with the Kluge-Ruhe Collection of Australian Aboriginal Art. H. Morphy and M. Boles, eds. Pp. 219–59. Seattle: University of Washington Press.

2001 The Wizards of Oz: Nation, State, and the Production of Aboriginal Fine Art. *In* The Empire of Things: Regimes of Value and Material Culture. F. Myers, ed. Pp. 165–204. Santa Fe NM: SAR Press.

2002 Painting Culture: The Making of an Aboriginal High Art. Durham NC: Duke University Press.

2004 Unsettled Business: Acrylic Painting, Tradition, and Indigenous Being. Special issue, "Confronting World Art," Visual Anthropology 17(3–4):247–72.

2006 The Complicity of Cultural Production: The Contingencies of Performance in Globalizing Museum Practices. *In* Museum Frictions: Public Cultures/Global Transformations. I. Karp, ed. Pp. 504–35. Durham NC: Duke University Press.

Nairne, Sandy, in collaboration with Geoff Dunlop and John Wyver

1987 State of the Art. London: Chatto and Windus.

Pietz, William

1986 The Problem of the Fetish, I. RES: Anthropology and Aesthetics 9:5–17.

Povinelli, Elizabeth A.

2002 The Cunning of Recognition: Indigenous Alterities and the Making of Australian Multiculturalism. Durham NC: Duke University Press, 2002.

Radin, Margaret

 1994 Reinterpreting Property. Chicago: University of Chicago Press.

Read, Kenneth

 1965 The High Valley. New York: Columbia University Press.

Richards, David

 2012 On the Boundary Lines. Alice Online. January 3. http://aliceonline.com.au
 /2012/01/03/on-the-boundary-lines/.

Rose, Carol

 1994 Property and Persuasion: Essays on the History, Theory, and Rhetoric of
 Ownership. Boulder CO: Westview Press.

Rothwell, Nicolas

 2009 From the Desert, Artists Came. Australian, February 13.

Saunders, Barbara

 1997 Contested Ethnie in Two Kwakwaka'wakw Museums. In Contesting Art:
 Art, Politics and Identity in the Modern World. Jeremy MacClancy, ed. Pp. 85–
 130. Oxford: Berg.

Simpson, Audra

 2006 On the Logic of Discernment. American Quarterly 59(2):479–91.

Taylor, Diana

 2003 The Archive and the Repertoire. Durham NC: Duke University Press.

Thomas, Nicholas

 1991 Entangled Objects: Exchange, Material Culture and Colonialism in the Pacific. Cambridge MA: Harvard University Press.

 1999 Possessions: Indigenous Art/Colonial Culture. New York: Thames and Hud-
 son.

Townsend-Gault, Charlotte

 2004 Circulating Aboriginality. Journal of Material Culture 9:183–202.

Wade, E. L.

 1985 The Ethnic Art Market in the American Southwest, 1880–1980. In Objects
 and Others: Essays on Museums and Material Culture. George Stocking, ed. Pp
 167–91. Madison: University of Wisconsin Press.

Weiner, Annette B.

 1992 Inalienable Possessions: The Paradox of Keeping-While-Giving. Berkeley:
 University of California Press.

Ziff, Bruce, and Pratima V. Rao, eds.

 1997 Borrowed Power: Essays on Cultural Appropriation. New Brunswick NJ:
 Rutgers University Press.

13

Cities

Indigeneity and Belonging

MARK K. WATSON

Whoever sees the banks of the Seine sees our grief.

GUY DEBORD, *Society of the Spectacle*

With the words above, in 1989 the French philosopher Guy Debord (1931–94) famously spoke of his fears that Paris was losing its distinct identity amid the clamor for modernization and development. Such melancholy at seeing the city's "bulldozing" reiterated Debord's concerns during the 1960s, when he was a leading figure in the avant-garde Situationist movement, that the flattening of the world's cities would lead to the erasure of popular memories and produce "historically brainwashed" metropolises (Bonnett 2006:34).[1] "Unitary Urbanism" was the watchword for rethinking and reworking what he and other members of the collective saw as the insipid functionalism of urban architecture and environments. Of paramount concern was the production of a compliant global urban citizenry struck with amnesia (Bonnett 2006:34).

I regard Debord's anxiety as the notional backdrop to this essay, which I am writing in direct response to calls at recent United Nations–sponsored meetings for more international comparative research on Indigenous urbanization.[2] Drawing on two urban Indigenous memorials—one situated in Melbourne, Australia, the other in Tokyo, Japan—I aim to show how both—unassuming, even mundane on the surface—rework the historical narratives of their respective cities and of the lives of Indigenous Peoples in them in ways that undermine or disrupt the all-too-prevalent belief that Indigenous people do not belong or are somehow "out of place" in urban centers.

Today statistical evidence from around the world suggests that a significant proportion if not a majority of Indigenous Peoples may live in urban (or nonrural) areas rather than on traditional lands. This demographic challenges many of the foundational assumptions, such as sedentarism, isolation, and timelessness, implicit in the Western imagination that have incarcerated Native Peoples in remote, peripheral places for hundreds of years (Appadurai 1988). In this vein, I portray the two memorials as agentive in the sense that they facilitate particular actions on the part of people, actions that not only realize personal and collective struggles over what it is to be and to belong in the city but also strategically intervene in what Debord poignantly described as the city's ubiquitous "paralysis of history and memory" (Debord [1967]1983:thesis 153). As we will see, these memorials not only mark the local existence of marginalized peoples but also call attention to alternative social understandings and lived experiences of urban and suburban cityscapes. Ultimately, we find, the memorials tell stories about people and events, which in the city refigure the public face of Indigenous campaigns for land rights into more nuanced narratives over place and belonging.

Three milk crates sit at the base of a mature palm tree on the perimeter of O'Donnell Gardens, a public park located in the Port Phillip district of St. Kilda, a southern suburb of the Australian city of Melbourne. In spite of their industrial symmetry, the crates' weathered, grayish tone matches that of the dusty floor and the mottled stone wall behind. Cast in bronze, the crates do not move. Iron rods fix them in place, permanent roots reinforced by bluestone footings set in concrete. Two of the crates have inscriptions. One reads, "Alma was my sister. We used to meet in the park every day. It's not the same without her." On the second is written, "He had a heart bigger than Phar Lap."[3] On May 26, 2005, as part of a municipal event for Australia's National Day of Healing, Mayor Darren Ray unveiled the crates at a public gathering.[4] "They say to the world," he announced, "that parkies have a claim on this place" (City of Port Phillip 2005:2).[5]

Shiba Park, central Tokyo, Japan. Enter from a major intersection and you see, visually sandwiched between a tourist signpost in the foreground and Tokyo Tower in the distance, two white boxes. These are the ubiquitous canned-drink vending machines of Japan's modern-day convenience. Beside one, through the tendrils of a bush, it is just possible to make out a

Fig. 13.1. *Aunty Alma's Seats* (2005). Photo by Julie Shiels.

Fig. 13.2. Shiba Park, Tokyo. Photo by Mark K. Watson (2003).

headstone-shaped object. Move to the front to glimpse a commemorative-like stone. Etched writing records that in 1872, in the vicinity of the memorial, thirty-eight Ainu were brought down to the capital from the northern island of Hokkaido to attend an agricultural residential school.

Return here the first weekend in August and in front of this stone you will see Ainu perform a "sinrit mosir koicarpa"—a memorial for the world of the ancestors. The ceremony's principal organizer, Hasegawa Osamu, describes this as a moment of remembrance for five Ainu who died at the school but also a memorial for all Ainu who have left the homeland over time and died without returning (Ainu mosir o hanare, kaerezu shinda Ainuutari no koto mo kuyō o suru; Hasegawa 2003:11).[6]

Fig. 13.3. Memorial Stone. Photo by Mark K. Watson (2003).

Commonplace and ordinary, such small-scale monuments in public spaces are perhaps the routine adornments of today's cities. These static and fixed memorials do not excite or affect onlookers in the ways that charismatic and visually energetic displays of difference do. Their understated nature does not attract the same kind of attention as does a North American powwow or street protest. Indeed, one might ask what can be learned from comparing examples, as I do here, of such unobtrusive memorials, when more obvious occurrences of Indigenous intervention into the public urban imaginary abound?

I want to show that these discreet monuments are performative agents of social action. This means that, far from representing passive and subdued moments of fleeting reflection, the bronze milk crates in suburban Melbourne, known as *Aunty Alma's Seats*, and the commemorative stone in Tokyo act and effect change in the world by facilitating civic engagement. Of course, neither "perform" in exactly the same way. Whereas the former's utility resonates closely with Fred Myers's (this volume) interest in the art object as a projection of its creator's agency into public space (Gell 1998), the latter characterizes a more implicit form of performativity situated in the power of words to not just passively describe the world but actuate social change within it (Austin 1962). Such differences do not undermine comparison; in fact, as we shall see, they underscore how both memorials converge as performative agents transforming their respective sites in unexpected ways and, in recursive fashion, then transforming the people who use and occupy them (Savage 2009:11).

Reminiscent of historian Evan Pritchard's enduring claim that "once you see New York [City] through Algonquin eyes . . . you will never be the same" (2002:20), these memorials are the physical markers of an "Indigenous city" within the city. Yet they are also displays of social memory that testify to the power of remembrance as a means of resisting the "paralysis" of urban history. This is an important point. For most urbanites, after all, urban Indigeneity is broadly understood as an oxymoronic status because of the truism that Indigenous people do not belong, or are "out-of-place," in urban centers. However, the relationship between cities, Indigeneity, and belonging is far from anomalous. In fact, it is a critical aspect of Indigenous and metropolitan life worldwide. Bearing in mind that many cities emerged in places where Indigenous Peoples once gathered or settled, the history of urbanization is often the story not only of Indigenous displacement and removal but also of forgetting. Histories of Indigenous life in cities such as Perth (Jacobs 1996), New York (Pritchard 2002), and Seattle (Thrush 2007), for example, all speak to how the rush toward urban development and civil society meant that Aboriginals "found themselves becoming invisible . . . in the very places that had always been their homes" (Cronon 2007:ix). This historical process of amnesia pushes into the shadows of time events that may haunt collective memory all too easily. As George Morgan chillingly notes with regard to Sydney, Australia, "There is little to remind us, that the bodies of black warriors were once displayed *in terrorem* in places where bungalows stand on quarter-acre lots" (2006:ix; italics in original).

Akin to Debord's anxieties over the erasure of social history through the transformation of urban landscapes, palpable unease over the normalized opposition between city and Indigeneity points to the vital roles that small-scale memorials can play in staging historical interventions into urban life. Working through the two cases below allows us to better understand the generalities of this claim.

Aunty Alma's Seats and the Politics
of Aboriginal Emplacement

At a glance (see fig. 13.1), it is not immediately apparent how *Aunty Alma's Seats* memorializes Indigeneity in St. Kilda, suburban Melbourne. In fact, observers may interpret the bronze crates' minimalist iconography as a somewhat indifferent attempt at commemoration. The crates do not dominate the landscape or imply grandiose self-importance in the way that (as one may imagine) a nearby elevated statue of Captain Cook on the St. Kilda foreshore does. To anticipate the sight of a grander—"This Is Our Land"— statement, though, would mistake the project's purpose for monumentalizing urban Aboriginal history. *Seats* (as I shall refer to it hereafter) neither formally speaks to nor aspires toward such grandiosity. As the installation's creator, Julie Shiels, a longtime supporter of the urban Aboriginal community, puts it, "The crates represent a humble, low scale monument to a humble local community" (City of Port Phillip 2005:2).[7]

In 2002 Shiels, a local St. Kilda artist and college instructor, was seated on a plastic crate in O'Donnell Gardens next to her friend "Aunty" Alma Roach. Roach was an Aboriginal community leader, elder, and sister of the renowned musician Archie Roach. The spot was a popular place for Alma and other local Aborigines to sit, gather, and converse. It represented a key meeting place in the early 1990s, especially after municipal authorities demolished a previously used site in a neighboring park to make way for the city's grand prix track. Shiels remembers, "I remarked what good seats they were but [Alma] said she often had to hunt around to find one. I suggested that we could turn them into bronze and put them in permanently. After that, every time I saw Aunty Alma she would say, 'You got to do that, babe. Put it in bronze'" (Hart 2006:2).

At Alma's encouragement, the artist set about the demanding task of raising funds and gaining the necessary permissions to make the meeting place permanent. This turned into a three-year collaboration between the artist and the Parkie community. During this time, however, the symbolism of the project heightened. "Aunty" Alma passed away in 2003 and soon after the community also lost William "Boom Boom" Forbes, a fellow elder and leader. Suddenly Shiels realized the need to deliver funding for three seats because "everyone said that Aunty Alma would get lonely just being honoured with one" (Hagan 2005). At their unveiling, two of the crates carried inscriptions memorializing "Aunty" and "Boom Boom." This left the third crate to symbolize "the living" and the range of social interactions that link past and present, life and spirit, and that make this corner of O'Donnell Gardens an identifiable place in the urban Aboriginal community (Julie Shiels, personal communication, 2010).

History, Sociality, Emplacement

In itself, *Seats* is a practical project—the bronze installations are actually seats intended to be sat on.[8] But it is also a subversive undertaking. As the historian Bain Attwood observes, Aboriginal peoples in Australia are usually "consigned to the past, but not to history" (1996:xii). To specify, one could easily add, "particularly not metropolitan history." After all, rarely do the citizens of a particular city hold a genuine understanding of urban Indigenous experiences and their historical use of what are contemporary urban spaces. Therefore, when Mayor Ray exclaimed at the unveiling of Seats that "they say to the world that parkies have a claim on this place," one could be forgiven for assuming that such a public commitment to urban Aboriginal entitlement is characteristic of a rather radical shift in thinking. Yet for non-Indigenous Australians, as L. K. Hart (2006) remarks, such an attitude is symptomatic of a more profound angst. "White anxiety," she writes, "constructs a continuing battle against Indigenous Peoples, not for land but for *emplacement*. The settler anxiety over our inability to successfully settle into an antagonistic 'other' land, is reawakened when we see Indigenous people adapting to our (urban) landscapes" (2006:5, italics in original).

Reworking the schema of urban Indigeneity from the customary conflict over land into an everyday, relational issue about place and belonging supplants static and essentialist ideas of Indigeneity with a perspective that reveals what Marisol de la Cadena and Orin Starn note "always has been." This is to say that "indigenism . . . is a process; a series of encounters; a structure of power; a set of relationships; a matter of becoming, in short, and not a fixed state of being" (2007:11).

This relational standpoint emphasizes the configuration of ties that makes Seats part of the ongoing, creative process of becoming that is characteristic of Indigenous life (Pratt 2007). It also draws attention to the role that social memory plays in its performance. This is evident in a number of ways. First of all, in an ironic twist on colonial history, *Seats* re-creates what Hart (2006) terms the "spectre of first contact." This refers to a popular image in early colonial portraiture and the Australian imaginary: the image of an aristocratic-type gentleman approaching a group of Aboriginal men seated under a tree. In spite of its evocative colonial imagery of the upright, civilized European dominating the partially dressed, passive Natives, the retelling and daily reenactment of "first contact" by users of *Seats* makes a powerful statement: it signifies prior occupation of the land on which the city now stands by Aboriginal peoples.[9] Simultaneously it refers to the subsequent displacement of Indigenous Peoples from their traditional homelands. As Hart (2006) points out, this symbolic performance contravenes the dominant narrative of Aboriginal peoples as outsiders to the city and latecomers into white urban space. It also animates the encounter between Aboriginal and colonial society that followed Europeans' arrival. It offers a narrative on the present state of how and why things are the way they are.

Second, the *Seats* installation succeeds in evoking an idea of "historical time" (Debord [1967]1983: thesis 143) in which history is neither benign nor passive but an active agent of change. By this I mean that in formally marking an Aboriginal place in urban, public space, *Seats* speaks of personal experience and oral history. Particular reference is made to the experiences and narratives of the elders who were children of the "Stolen Generation." For them the city represents their forced removal from families and life under a government policy aimed at their assimilation into white society.

Furthermore, *Seats* plays on the idea of "stolenness"; it recalls that the original milk crates were also appropriated locally and therefore points to what is at stake in claiming a place for oneself in the city (Hart 2006:3). In this way, *Seats* narrates a new urban history. Whereas in the past the indentations left by the crates in the earth, the only evidence of their users' presence, would quickly disappear (along with the crates!), Aboriginal gathering and socializing in the park is now remembered, historicized, and sanctioned. "We used to meet in the park every day" emotes Myrtle, Alma's sister. Through *Seats*, the Aboriginal appropriation of urban public space is rendered meaningful in multiple and complex ways. The messages that the installation sends are powerful in the context of white opinion that Parkies do not belong in such areas and are otherwise lazy, drunken, and unclean.

On "Who Aborigines Should Be"

Opposition to *Seats* was publicly voiced by the conservative columnist Andrew Bolt soon after its dedication. In an article in the *Herald Sun* (May 18, 2005), Bolt clamored for attention with the headline "Our Racism in Bronze."[10] It is important to quote this critical thought piece at length so that readers can understand the distinct context in which the *Seats* project was situated.

> Watch out for the compassion industry. It really does prefer you to stay pitiful. Take Port Phillip Council, which has spent more than $5000 on a new "statue" to make Aborigines feel good, and whites feel kind. Sounds worthy, until you realise the statue is in fact three bronze crates for Aborigines in O'Donnell Gardens to sit on as they drink and spend an aimless day. Until now, they had to sit on milk crates from nearby shops. Now they can sit on rate-payer funded bronze. . . . But do Aborigines really want to be celebrated as park dwellers? Is this the image, or aspiration, they deserve or need? Strange, how idleness shameful in anyone else is honored in Aborigines. How patronising. How destructive. And how racist.

How racist, indeed. It is obviously important to acknowledge Bolt's reputation as a well-known right-wing columnist and television pundit. Amid other controversies, his claims that Australian authorities' historic removal of Aboriginal children from their families is "just a theory" has led to accusations of historical denial against him. Yet Bolt's reaction to *Seats*, his view that the installation was a reconciliatory measure ("to make Aborigines feel good, and whites feel kind"), reveals his particular positioning. For Bolt, it is the image of the Aboriginal as a particular kind of person—the idle, aimless drunk—that is offensive, not only to him but to society in general. Of course, his critique of the memorial as "patronising" and "destructive" is made all the more ironic for its lack of historical and social depth. In his narrow approach there is no room for Aboriginal voices or agency or the lived experiences of the Stolen Generations.[11] Bolt's position is mired in the politics of appropriation: that is, who, from an archetypal white point of view, Aboriginal peoples should be, what they deserve to be, and who they should be celebrated as.

Instead of dismissing Bolt's verbiage out of hand, I recall it because it reminds us of the embedded nature of Indigeneity—of what it is to be Indigenous—within a structure of ever-changing power-infused relationships. In this relational sense, *Seats* is not a static art installation but an intervention in the intercultural space of the city (cf. Myers, this collection): a place, in other words, that gains meaning through the configuration of ties that "meet up there" (cf. Massey 1999). This understanding of the installation highlights the open-ended and ongoing process of Indigeneity in suburban Melbourne and the negotiation over meaning of which *Seats* is an integral part. For the moment at least, the installation's civic and subversive engagement with urban history, memory, and experiences finds overwhelming support in the local community. As Mayor Ray has declared, "We're not ashamed to remember the past in Port Philip and unlike other places, we demand that Koorie [*sic*] history be told" (City of Port Phillip 2005:2).[12]

Commemorating Continuity with the Past to Envision the Future: Ainu in Tokyo

As with *Seats*, the commemorative stone in Tokyo's Shiba Park is a small-scale and permanent marker of urban Indigenous history. It memorializes an agricultural school opened in Tokyo in 1872. The school served to educate thirty-eight Ainu brought down from Hokkaido. To clarify, Ainu are an Indigenous People native to what is now recognized as the northern Japanese archipelago. Ainu society survives today, albeit drastically transformed by history. The same year as the school's opening, for example, the Meiji government officially nationalized Ainu lands and embarked on a policy of assimilation that, by the end of the nineteenth century, had reduced Ainu to a "dying race" and historical footnote to Japan's modernization (Siddle 1996). The rationale for the school, established by Kuroda Kiyotaka, the then–vice minister of development within the Hokkaido Development Commission, sought to eradicate the hunter-gatherer ways of the Ainu by turning them into productive, farming citizens of the emerging Japanese nation-state. By extension, it also sought to assuage late nineteenth-century fears about the threat of Russian influence and encroachment from the north.

Out of the Ainu group who made the journey to Tokyo in 1872, four died of illness (Kanō 2003; see note 6). Due to truancy and requests for extended periods of leave, a mere five students returned for the second school year. At the end of the second year (1874), the educational experiment was terminated. Now, 140 years later, Ainu who live and work in Tokyo gather annually at the beginning of August and transform the grass area in front of the stone into a space for a *sinrit mosir koicarpa* (hereafter "icarpa"), meaning "memorial for the world of ancestors" (Hasegawa 2003:11). The ceremony is a cultural performance but it is also a significant social event. The purpose of the icarpa is to pray for the Ainu who died at the school but, in the words of Hasegawa Osamu, the ceremony's chief coordinator, it is also to memorialize all Ainu who have left the homeland and died without returning (Hasegawa 2003:11). This is an important position. In light of a landmark resolution passed by Japan's parliament in 2008, Ainu are now officially recognized as an Indigenous People (see Stevens 2008). Still, Ainu affairs, especially in the domain of Indigenous rights, are complicated by questions of who Ainu are and, more pertinently, where they belong.

The current-day situation of Ainu living in Tokyo has its roots in Japan's postwar era. From the 1950s on, an increasing number of Ainu from the historical homeland of Hokkaido started to move south to Tokyo and other major cities in search of employment, marriage, and new opportunities (see Watson 2010). Based on suggestions that more Ainu may now live outside of the traditional northern homeland of Hokkaido than within it (Umesao and Ishii 1999:219), non-Hokkaido Ainu groups openly question the conventional territorialization of Ainu history, society, and policy to the north.[13] In this context, the icarpa reaches back to the nineteenth-century school to provide a symbolically poignant anchor for a history of Ainu life in the capital city, steeped in metaphors of displacement, struggle, and emotional longing. At the same time, the formal ceremonial properties also generate an embodied awareness of the collective Tokyo Ainu experience; as we see below, the ritual of commemoration is a performance of memory through which Ainu are reminded of their relational attachment to a historical community and their traditional emplacement as Ainu in a physical (urban) world populated by *kamuy,* or "spirits."

The Icarpa

Preparations for the icarpa began in earnest in 1999, four years prior to its first performance, although Hasegawa had initially proposed the idea as early as 1995. Locating the site of the school was not an easy proposition. It took several years of extensive research by Ainu, supporters, and academics to uncover it, as very little information remained about the geography of the school in relation to the modern-day cityscape of Tokyo.

In order to understand its cultural and social significance, we need to address the ceremony's format. It revolves around the central use by Ainu of a *kamuynomi,* or "prayer to the spirits." Essentially, this requires two things: first, a functional hearth for *ape fuci kamuy,* the deity of fire, to whom Ainu offer prayers as the mediator between this world and the world of kamuy, or spirits; second, male participants must be able to offer sake to particular deities represented by *inaw* (shaved wooden fetishes) laid out in a *nusa* (altar) (Yamada 2000). Traditionally, these inaw represent the most important deities drawn from the local landscape, for Ainu believe that everything in the world is imbued with kamuy. Nusa in Hokkaido can hold upwards of twenty or thirty inaw. Indicative of a new urban Ainu landscape, however, at the first icarpa in Tokyo in 2003 only five deities were identified.

The Five Kamuy

A principal kamuy that Tokyo Ainu identified was *kotan kor kamuy.* Traditionally recognized as the protector of the Ainu *kotan,* or village, its incorporation in the Tokyo icarpa was critical. Its inclusion represents the entire capital region as a kotan in need of protection and therefore identifies the city as a physical location of communal Ainu life. The overt symbolism of this move contradicts the perceived "northern-ness" of the geographical boundary around Ainu society.

Another deity identified was *nupuri kamuy* (deity of mountains). Ainu regarded its referent to be Atagoyama (Mt. Atago), located to the west of Tokyo. Although today it is better known as the site of the Atago Shinto shrine, its environment is that of a coastal shrub forest and is rich in a variety of natural and agricultural resources. Jomon-era artifacts found there indicate the use and habitation of the area dating back five thousand years. The organizers considered that for the Ainu students at the nineteenth-century school it probably represented a symbol of home and a nostalgic haven in the middle of a burgeoning metropolis.

A third deity to whom prayers were offered was *rera cise kamuy* (the deity of the Rera Cise). The Rera Cise was, at the time of the first icarpa, an Ainu-run restaurant serving modern Ainu cuisine in the city. Identifying a physical restaurant as a deity makes sense in Ainu cosmology, where all things (from natural phenomena to a man-made structure to a toilet) have kamuy. The restaurant was critical for Ainu in Tokyo for it also represented an important location for Ainu to congregate and practice cultural activities; it is the nearest thing Ainu in Tokyo have had to a community center.[14]

The fourth and fifth deities were *wakka us kamuy* (deity of water) and *sir kor kamuy* (deity of the earth). Traditionally, both of these deities are present in Hokkaido icarpa and were identified in Tokyo as representing fundamental elements of life.[15]

Icarpa as "Moral Practice"

The icarpa is a complex, local ritual but in ways reminiscent of *Seats* it is one that speaks to the collective faculty of memory. Beyond the notion of forging or what some may regard as "inventing" meaningful ties with past events, what the icarpa is actually commemorating at different levels of its performance is an explicit sense of continuity with the past (cf. Connerton 1989:48). To think of the ritual in the context of Ainu remembering together is to talk of social memory. Following Maurice Halbwachs ([1950]1992), Paul Connerton (1989) and others, this is not to imply that anybody other than individuals remember. My point is that to remember is, in itself, as Michael Lambek (1996) puts it, a "moral practice," a particular way of relating to and situating oneself in the world that draws on "affect and deep-seated struggles for personal and collective meaning" (Sutton 2001:86). As an act of commemoration, the ritual performance of the icarpa is about the construction of collective belonging in the context of the city. It is about Ainu recognizing their lives and experiences as based in the capital region and, as such, reflected in something greater than their informal network of relations with other Ainu. In other words, it is about normalizing "Tokyo Ainu" as a collective experience that extends both back in time (and therefore onward into the future) and, through association with kamuy, outward, in the present, into the city's landscape and by association therefore also inward and into the bodily experience of Ainu in the city.

Thus, in brief, we can talk of the icarpa in two ways: as a symbolic event and as an embodied experience. First, the ceremony is symbolic of a new way of imagining or thinking about Ainu society. Extending the memorial's point of reference to include not only Ainu who died at the school but also all Ainu who have died outside of Hokkaido speaks to the assumption of a preexisting narrative of Ainu society on the Japanese mainland. It gives today's community a sense of temporal and ancestral depth that organizers of the icarpa are seen not to be inventing but rather to be responding to in a formal and respectful way. From a political point of view, the evocation of a shared collective experience is critical in the context of Indigenous rights. Alongside various TV camera crews and journalists, I was not surprised to see a representative from the Tokyo Human Rights Office attending the first Tokyo icarpa at the invitation of the Ainu Association of Rera (the organizing Ainu group), in an ongoing attempt to initiate discussion over recognition and the attribution of social support to urban Ainu. This position on rights is embedded in the historical and sociopolitical contexts of poverty, homelessness, and day labor that is well known (by Ainu) to define the urban Ainu experience. It also refers to the conditions of institutional discrimination and social marginalization that Ainu have historically faced in the city and, as reported in two surveys of Ainu in the capital (1975 and 1989), the broader social problems Ainu may face in terms of a lack of formal education, practical qualifications for stable employment, or financial security (see Watson 2014a). In this sense, any move promoting the idea of a coherent and historically legitimate Ainu community in Tokyo can only benefit the movement, as it provides them a basis from which to negotiate with the government and Hokkaido Ainu organizations over rights.[16]

Second, the icarpa focuses attention on the bodily experience of Ainu. Here, for this essay at least, I am not so much interested in the habituation of ritual practice—how men sit vis-à-vis women, how prayers or offerings are made, and so on—as I am concerned with the broader implications that the incorporation of kamuy into the urban landscape has for communal memory. For this is not a mere mental exercise in representing physical Ainu landmarks on a two-dimensional map of Tokyo. On the contrary, the relationship between Ainu and kamuy is lived, it is felt; it is an elemental, emotional experience that also suffuses the bonds traditionally linking Ainu and their natural environment. Indeed, as the Native linguist Chiri Mashiho ([1955]1973) points out, this mutual relationship between Ainu and kamuy is integral to the very idea of what it means to be Ainu, that is, to be a human being.

Therefore, what the integration of cultural knowledge into the cityscape actually identifies is the lived experience of Ainu as the locus of ethnic continuity. This emphasis on the body has particular relevance for social memory; as Connerton asserts, the body is fundamental to the successful reproduction of social systems and their capacity to remember: "Every group," he says, "will entrust to bodily automatisms the values and categories which they are most anxious to conserve. They will know how well the past can be kept in mind by a habitual memory sedimented in the body" (1989:102). The evocation through ritual practice of an embodied experience of kamuy (and the landscape where they reside) reaffirms that normal sense of continuity with the past noted above and, in doing so, naturalizes the initiative on the part of individuals to reestablish traditional cultural and social relations in an urban setting. In light of an argument I have made elsewhere that the continued articulation of Ainu identities and formation of a community in Tokyo is not a foregone conclusion (Watson 2014a, 2014b), this move to formally bring kamuy back into Ainu social life is an important step in consolidating a group identity and rethinking the history and geography of Tokyo and the surrounding region as a place of Ainu life.

Remembering the Lived Experiences of Urban Indigenous Peoples

I began this chapter by quoting the fears of Guy Debord over the transformation of urban landscapes and their potential to erase social histories. I now return full circle to draw some conclusions concerning the agency of Indigenous memorials and their capacity to intervene in their surroundings. The sorrow for the riverbanks of the Seine that Debord expresses—"Whoever sees the banks of the Seine sees our grief"—characterised his general consternation for public memory. For him, modern urban geography was a palimpsest of time where the past fades from view. New buildings and construction layer over and "paralyse" the past and disable memory. Such concern carried over into Debord's agitation with the utilitarian design of cities and their planners' inexorable need to rationally organize and, consequently, severely delimit human experience of the urban environment. One way Debord and other members of the Situationist collective proposed people could avoid the city's proclivity for amnesia is to intervene in public space. This entails the construction of "situations," or happenings in public space, which would encourage urbanites to reconsider, through reflection on habitual practice, how they understand and experience their environment and why they do so.[17]

Seats and icarpa clearly are not situationist acts in the way defined above. Nevertheless, both memorials draw on deep historical approaches to unsettle normative ideas of Indigenous Peoples as latecomers or strangers to the city. I am both disheartened and perplexed by critiques that claim that small-scale memorials such as these fail to make obvious or grand public statements to monumentalize urban Indigenous history. Such comments miss the broader point of memorialization in the context of cities, Indigeneity, and belonging. We have seen above how in very different cities two discreet monuments refigure in similar ways many of the essentialist assumptions that (continue to) exclude Indigenous people from city life, disallow their appropriations of public space, and ignore their histories of colonization and marginalization. Perhaps, above all else and for all talk of memory, what we learn from these examples is that they are actually more about what lies ahead rather than what occupies the past, about expectation rather than loss. At the same time, they also significantly rework the symbolic paralysis of Australian Aboriginal Peoples or Ainu as spatial outcasts—peoples "out there"—or historical figures "back then" as obvious fictions. In this sense, I believe they typify the Situationist attitude by re-enchanting city life and, in the process, point to the range of possibilities for social transformation. Of course, it is not enough to stop at this very generalized understanding. To draw this essay to a close, I want to develop some of the questions and issues further.

Agency

Can we talk of these memorials as agents? I believe so, if, that is, we really know what it means to dismiss such memorials as inherently "static" or "fixed" monuments. Although neither *Seats* nor the commemorative stone in Tokyo intentionally acts, each is undeniably part of an open-ended, ongoing story of individual and collective life and memory and its intersection with the city. Echoing Setha Low's astute insight that "the 'city' is not a reification but the focus of cultural and sociopolitical manifestations of urban lives and everyday practices" (1996:384), we understand that integral to both memorials is attention to the biographical unfolding of life. That is, each memorial helps narrate, to both public and private audiences, the broader and deeper histories and experiences of local people's urban lives. Each memorial is an "existential statement" (Graham 2005, this volume) evoking stories that are an integral if overlooked or forgotten part of the respective city's historical development. In many respects, the memorials are symbolic of the very struggle of Indigenous Peoples to self-determine their own lives and histories.

The Tokyo icarpa, for example, is about forging new relationships with the spirits of Ainu who died at the school. Simultaneously it forges relationships with all Ainu who have passed away outside of the traditional northern homeland. Although the experiences being memorialized are framed in terms of "death" and "separation" from Hokkaido, they nevertheless act as a motif of a collective Tokyo Ainu experience and related issues of diaspora, identity, and culture that tie into that. In this way, the stone commemorating the history of the school is far from static. It is an integral part of an ongoing urban Ainu struggle over belonging. This struggle is redefining the northern, racialized geography of Ainu life in the public Japanese imaginary to legitimate their place, issues, and historical presence as Ainu and, therefore, as Indigenous people in Tokyo.

Similarly, the iron rods that pin *Seats's* crates into the earth signify the permanency of the Parkie community in the city. They speak to a definitive sense of Indigenous emplacement and experience in the city. They physically mark the legacy of family, solidarity, and collective history that previously existed only in people's actions and memories. Far from static, *Seats* is a dynamic expression of the social interactions that community members have engaged in within this space for many years. In the same way that the artist's use of bronze puts value on what was once plastic, *Seats* symbolically anchors and gives social value in public space to that which was once itinerant and temporary. It also riles against the dismissive interpretations of urban Aboriginal peoples as being "out of place." As the artist Shiels puts it, "The parkies feel that people look at them and dismiss them as a bunch of Koories [*sic*] drinking in the park. They don't understand the strength of their community, how they share everything" (City of Port Phillip 2005:2).

Indigeneity as a "Force"

As a comparative exercise, these memorials also provide commentary on the nature of Indigeneity itself. It is clear that neither example is preoccupied with claims of authenticity—the politics of which are irrelevant here. In fact, what makes these memorials "Indigenous" has nothing to do with their performance of visual difference but rather, and more tellingly, their conjuring of deeply personalized and evocative expressions of lived experience: encounters in life that are otherwise overlooked, muted, or, within the context of cities, typically forgotten. In my presentation of these memorials as interventions into the dominance of urban civic life, Indigeneity is less about a fixed, stable self than, as Shiels references above, the "strength" of community. Of course, one could quite easily reference here well-worn arguments over relationalism and Indigenous identities to interpret this statement, but I would like to ask if there is not something more urgent and fundamental at work here. What if we were to think of Indigeneity otherwise, as Mary Louise Pratt (2007:403) does, "not as a configuration or a state but as a force that enables, that makes things happen." And what is this "force" that is able to act in spite of the ravages of history, that "enables" and is never fixed, if not the strength or compulsion to remember: the capacity that is to have and retain knowledge of the past, a framework that allows the present to exist at all. Furthermore, we can ask, is this "force" reducible to individual action or does it operate through people? Does it operate to be made visible, perhaps, in moments of commemorative reflection and ceremony that are performed, and performed only because of habits that themselves can only be understood with reference to the body (Connerton 1989:4–5)?

Isn't this, then, the heart of the matter? The capacity of these memorials to act and retain such significance lies in the power they derive from social memory and their role in its reproduction in people's lives. Indigeneity, then, whether it be in Melbourne or Tokyo, becomes quite naturally about enabling memory in the city, a negotiation of individual experience with that of others that necessarily transforms the landscape in particular ways. Such acts unsettle in a strong and forceful manner dominant ways of knowing the city's history and geography. Debord would surely have approved.

Acknowledgments

I would like to thank the Ainu community in Tokyo for their kindness and cooperation during the two years I spent undertaking research in the city. In particular, I extend my appreciation to Hasegawa Osamu and Hasegawa Yūki for teaching me about the icarpa. However, I take full responsibility for the interpretation of events featured in this chapter. In Australia, I am most grateful to Julie Shiels for providing comments on an earlier draft of this essay and for permission to reproduce her photograph of Seats. At various times, funding for this research was received from the Japan Foundation, the Killam Foundation, the Royal Anthropological Institute, and the Faculty of Graduate Studies, University of Alberta. I would also like to acknowledge the support given by the European Research Council to the London conference In the Balance: Indigeneity, Performance, Globalization, at which I presented a version of this chapter in 2013. Finally, I thank Laura Graham and Glenn Penny, the editors of this book, for their initial invitation to participate in the 2009 symposium at the University of Iowa and for their encouragement and feedback at all stages of the writing process.

Notes

1. The Situationist movement fostered revolutionary fervor around the neo-Marxist edict that people are passive consumers complicit in their own alienation from reality through the consumption of spectacular images, what Debord regarded as a historic shift in human society from being to having to appearing (Debord [1967]1983:thesis 17). Broad familiarity with this brief characterization has often led to depictions of Debord as a postmodern precursor of Jean Baudrillard et al., yet such positioning mistakes the latter's nihilism for Debord's anxiety for social change. Guy Debord's

Society of the Spectacle, first published in 1967, for example, a collated manifesto of 221 theses, sought to impart a positive (revolutionary) intervention into social life.

2. My response is based on reports generated by two meetings. The first meeting, Expert Workshop on Indigenous Peoples and Migration: Challenges and Opportunities, was organized by the International Organization for Migration in cooperation with the Secretariat of the United Nations Permanent Forum on Indigenous Issues and was held in Geneva, April 2006. The second meeting, organized by the United Nations Economic Commission for Latin America and the Caribbean and other international groups, was held in Santiago, Chile, in March 2007 and called the Expert Group Meeting on Urban Indigenous Peoples and Migration. The meeting's report was entitled, *Urban Indigenous Peoples and Migration: A Review of Policies, Programmes, and Practices* (2010).

3. Phar Lap was a thoroughbred racehorse and national Australian icon in the 1920s. His heart, almost twice the size of that of a normal horse, was donated to the Institute of Anatomy in Canberra, where it was preserved. It is now on public display at the National Museum of Australia.

4. The National Day of Healing is the day of national reflection for the "Stolen Generation" of Aboriginal children forcibly taken from their families.

5. "Parkies" is the colloquial name given to urban, park-dwelling Aboriginal peoples.

6. The number of Ainu who died at the school is sometimes given as four. However, while four Ainu died of illness (beriberi), the fifth death refers to the birth of a stillborn child, named Hashinomi, on March 29, 1873 (see Kanō 2003; Kanō and Hirose 2007:98–102). Furthermore, and following convention, all Japanese names cited in this chapter are of surname-first format.

7. On the question of Aboriginal forms of memorialization, see Batten and Batten (2008).

8. The crates continues to serve as a meeting place. As a local journalist noted just prior to the installation of *Seats*, "A group of St. Kilda Kooris known as the 'parkies' still perch each afternoon on plastic crates borrowed from nearby businesses. Boom Boom and Aunty Alma were the backbone of the group, which now also meets at a local health centre" (Lucas 2005).

9. Six kilometers north of St. Kilda, in Melbourne's Central Business District, one finds a plaque from 1881 dedicated to the entrepreneur John Batman. The inscription reads that he founded the original settlement "on the site of Melbourne then unoccupied." Only in 1992 did the city council add another plaque beneath the original, which concluded, "It is now clear that prior to the colonisation of Victoria, the land was inhabited and used by Aboriginal people." One can view this as a proud public moment of postcolonial history at work and perhaps even suggest that it sides more favorably with Batman's own instrumentalist understanding of events at the time—Batman being the only private citizen in Australian history to have drawn up treaties with Aboriginal groups. Still, in light of continued ambivalence toward the status of urban Aboriginal people, it is obvious that claims "to

remember" written into the plaque—"it is now clear [to us] . . ."—aim for explanation rather than radical understanding.

10. Besides Holt's column, there were other reactions to *Seats* in the local and regional print media. Alongside Kate Hagan's newsworthy piece in the *Port Phillip Leader* (July 7, 2005), there was Clay Lucas's in the *Melbourne Age* (May 15, 2005), which opened with, "Crate idea leaves sour taste as monument theme milked." In this brief article Lucas used the ruminations of a Mr. Colin Bell to question the usefulness of the sculpture and the "pack of weirdos on [the] council" who funded it.

11. As Philip J. Deloria (2004:225) puts it from a North American perspective, expectations of who Indians are "underpin the many ways non-Indian Americans blithely ignore the requests, opinions, and assertions of Native people."

12. "Koori" (sometimes seen as Kori or Koorie) is the term most commonly used by Indigenous Australians in Victoria, Tasmania, and parts of New South Wales to identify themselves. It derives from the word *gurri*, meaning "person" or "people."

13. Although Ainu are active in other mainland cities, such as Kyoto and Nagoya, it is their movement in and around the capital region of Tokyo (also known as Kantō) that has received most attention (see Ogasawara 1990; Watson 2010).

14. Unfortunately, after fifteen years in business, the restaurant closed in 2009.

15. Usually *wakka us kamuy* is divided into notable features of water, such as a river or lake. Since there was no obvious attachment to a specific body of water or water source for Ainu at the colonial school, given its location in the middle of the city, its signifier at the first icarpa was left unspecified.

16. The icarpa is part and parcel of a broader movement of Ainu in the capital region. Since the 1960s, Ainu self-organization in Tokyo has been based on a sustained campaign to equalize the rights of urban mainland Ainu with those living in the homeland (on this issue, see Watson 2010, 2014a). The movement has also sought—with varying degrees of success—to provide urban Ainu with an exclusive "safespace," such as a community center where people can meet, practice, or learn cultural activities and receive help in finding employment or accommodation (cf. lewallen 2006).

17. This act would unveil the normalcy of life as an effect of power instituted by a dominant (capitalist) order.

Bibliography

Appadurai, Arjun
1988 Putting Hierarchy in Its Place. Cultural Anthropology 3(1):36–49.
Attwood, Bain
1996 The Past as Future: Aborigines, Australia and the (Dis)course of History. *In* In the Age of Mabo: History, Aborigines and Australia. Bain Attwood, ed. Pp. viii–xxxviii. St. Leonards, Australia: Allen and Unwin.
Austin, J. L.
1962 How to Do Things with Words. Oxford: Clarendon Press.

Batten, Bronwyn, and Paul Batten

2008 Memorializing the Past: Is there an Aboriginal Way? Public History Review 15:92–116.

Bonnett, Alaistair

2006 The Nostalgias of Situationist Subversion. Theory, Culture & Society 23(5):23–48.

Chiri, Mashiho

[1955]1973 Ainu. *In* Chiri Mashiho chosaku shū, vol. 3. Pp. 231–44. Tokyo: Heibonsha.

City of Port Phillip

2005 News release, May 10.

Connerton, Paul

1989 How Societies Remember. Cambridge: Cambridge University Press.

Cronon, William

2007 Foreword: Present Haunts of an Unvanished Past. *In* Native Seattle: Histories from the Crossing-Over Place. Coll Thrush, ed. Pp. vii–xi. Seattle: University of Washington Press.

Debord, Guy

[1967]1983 Society of the Spectacle. Detroit: Black and Red.

de la Cadena, Marisol, and Orin Starn

2007 Introduction. *In* Indigenous Experience Today. Marisol de la Cadena and Orin Starn, eds. Pp. 1–30. Oxford: Berg Press.

Deloria, Philip J.

2004 Indians in Unexpected Places. Lawrence: University Press of Kansas.

Ehrkamp, Patricia

2005 Placing Identities: Transnational Practices and Local Attachments of Turkish Immigrants in Germany. Journal of Ethnic and Migration Studies 31(2):345–64.

Gell, Alfred

1998 Art and Agency. Oxford: Oxford University Press.

Graham, Laura R.

2005 Image and Instrumentality in a Xavante Politics of Existential Recognition: The Public Outreach Work of Eténhiritipa Pimentel Barbosa. American Ethnologist 32(4):622–41.

Hagan, Kate

2005 Crates Shrine to "Parkies." Port Phillip Leader, July 7.

Halbwachs, Maurice

[1950]1992 On Collective Memory. Chicago: University of Chicago Press.

Hart, L. K.

2006 Against Hauntology and Historicide: Urban Indigeneity in the White Imagining. http://www.julieshiels.com.au/public-space/Hauntology-and-Historicide.pdf, accessed June 19, 2012.

Hasegawa, Osamu

2003 Tokyo: Icarpa Hōkoku. Ureshipa Charanke 22:10–12.

Jacobs, Jane M.

1996 Edge of Empire: Postcolonialism and the City. London: Routledge.

Kanō, Yūichi

2003 Kaitakushi Karigakkō ni okeru Ainu kyōiku. *In* Fukyū keihatsu semina—
hōkokushū. Zaidan hōjin Ainu bunka shinkō/kenkyū suishin kikō, ed. Pp. 54–59.
Sapporo: Zaidan hōjin Ainu bunka shinkō/kenkyū suishin kikō.

Kanō, Yūichi, and Ken'ichirō Hirose

2007 Kaitakushi ni yoru Tōkyō de no Ainu kyōiku. *In* "Tōkyō Icarpa" e no michi:
Meiji shoki ni okeru kaitakushi no Ainu kyōiku o megutte. Tōkyō Ainu Shi
Kenkyūkai, ed. Pp. 39–142. Tokyo: Gendai Kikakushitsu.

Lambek, Michael

1996 The Past Imperfect: Remembering as Moral Practice. *In* Tense Past: Cultural
Essays in Trauma and Memory. Paul Antze and Michael Lambek, eds. Pp. 235–54.
London: Routledge.

lewallen, ann-elise

2006 "Hands That Never Rest": Ainu Women, Cultural Revival and Indigenous
Politics in Japan. PhD dissertation, Department of Anthropology, University of
Michigan.

Low, Setha M.

1996 The Anthropology of Cities: Imagining and Theorizing the City. Annual
Review of Anthropology 25:383–409.

Lucas, Clay

2005 Crate Idea Leaves Sour Taste as Monument Theme Milked. Melbourne Age,
May 15.

Massey, Doreen

1999 Spaces of Politics. *In* Human Geography Today. Doreen Massey, John Allen,
and Philip Sarre, eds. Pp. 279–94. Cambridge: Polity Press.

Morgan, George

2006 Unsettled Places: Aboriginal People and Urbanisation in New South Wales.
Kent Town, Australia: Wakefield Press.

Ogasawara, Nobuyuki

1990 Shoppai Kawa—Tokyo ni ikiru Ainutachi. Tokyo: Kabushikigaisha.

Pratt, Mary Louise

2007 Afterword: Indigeneity Today. *In* Indigenous Experience Today. Marisol de
la Cadena and Orin Starn, eds. Pp. 397–404. Oxford: Berg.

Pritchard, Evan T.

2002 Native New Yorkers: The Legacy of the Algonquin People of New York. San
Francisco: Council Oak Books.

Savage, Kirk

    2009 Monument Wars: Washington, D.C., the National Mall, and the Transformation of the Memorial Landscape. Berkeley: University of California Press.

Siddle, Richard

    1996 Race, Resistance and the Ainu of Japan. London: Routledge.

Stevens, Georgina

    2008 Subject, Object and Active Participant: The Ainu, Law, and Legal Mobilization. Indigenous Law Journal 7(1):127–67.

Sutton, David E.

    2001 Remembrance of Repasts: An Anthropology of Food and Memory. Oxford: Berg.

Thrush, Coll

    2007 Native Seattle: Histories from the Crossing-Over Place. Seattle: University of Washington Press.

Umesao, Tadao, and Yoneo Ishii

    1999 Taminzoku no kyōzon ni mukete shisō no ōkina tenkan o. *In* Nihonjin to Tabunkashugi. Yoneo Ishii and Masayuki Yamauchi, eds. Pp. 195–241. Tokyo: Yamagawa Shuppansha.

Watson, Mark K.

    2010 Diasporic Indigeneity: Place and the Articulation of Ainu Identity in Tokyo, Japan. Environment and Planning A 42(2):268–84.

    2014a Japan's Ainu Minority in Tokyo: Diasporic Indigeneity and Urban Politics. London: Routledge.

    2014b Tokyo Ainu and the Urban Indigenous Experience. *In* Beyond Ainu Studies: Changing Academic and Public Perspectives. Mark J. Hudson, ann-elise lewallen, and Mark K. Watson, eds. Pp. 96-117. Honolulu: University of Hawaii Press.

Yamada, Takado

    2000 The Revival of Rituals among the Sakha-Yakut and the Hokkaido Ainu. Acta Borealia 17(1):77–115.

Contributors

CATHRINE BAGLO received her PhD from the University of Tromsø, Norway, in 2011 with the thesis "På ville veger? Levende utstillinger av samer i Europa og Amerika" (Agents abroad? The living exhibitions of Sàmi in Europe and America). She is currently an independent scholar living in California.

MICHAEL L. CEPEK is an associate professor of anthropology at the University of Texas at San Antonio. His research explores the relationship between socioecological crisis, cultural difference, and directed change at the margins of global orders. His first book is *A Future for Amazonia: Randy Borman and Cofán Environmental Politics* (University of Texas Press, 2012).

LAURA R. GRAHAM's research focuses on Indigenous agency in national and international arenas. The author of *Performing Dreams: Discourses of Immortality among the Xavante of Central Brazil* (University of Texas Press, 1995) and the producer and codirector of the film *Owners of the Water: Conflict and Collaboration over Rivers* (Documentary Educational Resources, 2009), she is an associate professor of anthropology at the University of Iowa.

DOROTHY L. HODGSON is a professor of anthropology at Rutgers University. Drawing on thirty years of research with Maasai pastoralists, she has published on such topics as gender, ethnicity colonialism, development, missionization, Indigenous rights, and gender justice. Her books include *Being Maasai, Becoming Indigenous* (Indiana University Press, 2011), *The Church of Women* (Indiana University

Press, 2005), and *Once Intrepid Warriors* (Indiana University Press, 2001).

BRENDAN HOKOWHITU is of Ngāti Pukenga descent, an *iwi* (people) from Aotearoa/New Zealand. In 2012 Hokowhitu became dean and professor of the faculty of Native studies at the University of Alberta, Edmonton, Canada, following a decade of working in Māori, Pacific, and Indigenous studies in Aotearoa.

GREG JOHNSON (associate professor of religious studies, University of Colorado at Boulder) studies Native American and Native Hawaiian religious life in the context of legal disputes, exploring repatriation and burial protection struggles as a means to understand the ways religious claims are announced, enlivened, and contested in the contemporary moment.

FRED MYERS, Silver Professor of Anthropology at New York University, has been working with Indigenous people in central Australia since 1973. His books include *Pintupi Country, Pintupi Self: Sentiment, Place and Politics among Western Desert Aborigines* (Smithsonian Institution Press and Australian Institute of Aboriginal Studies, 1986) and *Painting Culture: The Making of an Aboriginal High Art* (Duke University Press, 2002).

H. GLENN PENNY, professor of history at the University of Iowa, has been working on the interactions between Europeans and non-Europeans since the 1990s. His books include *Kindred by Choice: Germans and American Indians since 1800* (University of North Carolina Press, 2013) and *Objects of Culture: Ethnology and Ethnographic Museums in Imperial Germany* (University of North Carolina Press, 2003).

BERNARD PERLEY is Wəlastəkwi from Tobique First Nation, New Brunswick, Canada, and an associate professor of anthropology at the University of Wisconsin–Milwaukee. His monograph *Defying Maliseet Language Death: Emergent Vitalities of Language, Culture, and Identity in Eastern Canada* (University of Nebraska Press, 2011) is a critical program for Indigenous self-determination.

BEATRIZ PERRONE-MOISÉS is a professor of Americanist ethnology in the Department of Anthropology at the University of São Paulo and a researcher at the Centro de Estudos Amerindios (CEstA-

USP). She has lived with Krahô and the Aparai-Wayana Indigenous Peoples. Her research interests include Amerindian political philosophy, Amerindian mythology, Indigenous rights, and European-Indian relations in the Americas.

TY P. KĀWIKA TENGAN is an associate professor in the Departments of Ethnic Studies and Anthropology at the University of Hawai‘i at Mānoa. He is the author of *Native Men Remade: Gender and Nation in Contemporary Hawai‘i* (Duke University Press, 2008) and teaches on Indigeneity, gender, and empire in Hawai‘i and Oceania.

MARK K. WATSON is an associate professor in the Department of Sociology and Anthropology at Concordia University, Montreal. Informed by ongoing interest in the comparative analysis of urban Indigenous collectivity and political rights, his most recent book is *Japan's Ainu Minority in Tokyo: Diasporic Indigeneity and Urban Politics* (Routledge, 2014).

Index

Chapin, Mark, 20n24
Charles IX, 116
Chernela, Janet, 7, 308, 334, 337n19, 339n42
Chomsky, Noam, 19n7
Churchill, Ward, 193
Circus Krone, 178, 180
Clark, Jeff, 217
Clifford, James, 18n2, 137, 153, 162n1, 267n3, 293, 308, 371, 380
Clinton, William Jefferson, 209
Cocama, 96, 97, 102, 124
Cody, William F. *See* Buffalo Bill's Wild West show
Cofán, 14, 83–104
Cohen, Matt, 18n5
Cohodas, Marvin, 382n2
Coimbra, Carlos E. A., Jr., 336nn12–13
Cold War, 1, 4, 188, 192
Collins, James, 250, 267n3
Collins, Jane L., 78n5
colonial: patriarchy, 218, 231–32, 234, 277, 283, 286–87; power regimes, 32–33, 35, 43, 47, 51–53, 55–56, 60, 62, 65, 103, 110, 119, 138, 182, 193, 211, 213, 215, 217, 220, 226, 277–98, 398; settlers, 36, 53, 83, 182, 207–15, 221, 231, 363, 377, 397; studies and programs, 10, 36, 221, 278, 297; subjects, 9, 32, 35–53, 55, 219, 220, 280–85. *See also* neocolonial; postcolonial
Columbia, 105n1
Comaroff, Jean, 7, 160, 335n6
Comaroff, John L., 7, 160, 335n6
Coney, Patrick Henry, 148
Conklin, Beth, 7, 9, 20n16, 55, 62–63, 76, 94, 312, 322, 324, 335n6, 335n11, 336n14, 338n37
Connell, R. W., 215, 223, 226
Connerton, Paul, 403, 405, 408, 412
Conquergood, Dwight, 19n11
Conrad, Rudolf, 178, 192

Conrow, Joan, 254, 268n8
Cook, James, 209, 267n1, 279, 396
Coombe, Rosemary, 7, 377, 380
Cooper, James Fennimore, 170, 189
Coronil, Fernando, 324, 338n30
Coulthard, Glen, 294
Crocker, Andrew, 368
Croft, Brenda, 384n11
Cronau, Rudolf, 183
Cronon, William, 395, 412
cultural imperialism, 195
cultural sovereignty. *See* sovereignty
Czechoslovakia (Czech Republic), 58, 194–95

Dagbladet, 136, 148, 162
Daher, Andréa, 119
Daniels, Barbara, 195–96
Danielsen, Elias, 155
Danielsen, Signe, 155
Danielsen, Waage, 163n4
Debord, Guy, 390–91, 395, 398, 405–6, 409, 409n1, 412
Debrunner, Hans Werner, 143
decolonization, 208, 211
Dega, Michael F., 254
Deloria, Philip J., 84, 139, 155, 172, 181, 327, 411n11, 412
Deloria, Vine, Jr., 10, 37, 138, 152, 153, 181, 185
Denis, Ferdinand, 113
Denmark, 142, 155
Desmond, Jane C., 220, 229
Diaz, Vicente M., 215
Dickason, Olive Patricia, 128
Diecke, Jörg, 171–72, 174, 176
dioramas, 139
Dirlik, Arif, 293
Dix, Otto, 170
Doyle, Laura, 286
Drago, Andre, 127
Dreesbach, Anne, 163n1

CPSIA information can be obtained
at www.ICGtesting.com
Printed in the USA
LVHW051703200723
752869LV00001B/24

9 780803 256866